To Louis Emmerij, Enrique Oteiza and the
late James Coleman in gratitude and appreciation
for their recognition

Contents

The IMF and the South

The Social Impact of Crisis and Adjustment

Edited by Dharam Ghai

Zed Books Ltd
London and New Jersey

on behalf of

UNRISD
Geneva

ISER/UWI
Kingston

The IMF and the South was first published by Zed Books Ltd.,
57 Caledonian Road, London N1 9BU, UK, and
165 First Avenue, Atlantic Higlands, New Jersey 07716, USA,
on behalf of the United Nations Research Institute for Social
Development (UNRISD), Geneva, and the Institute of
Social and Economic Research (ISER) of the University of the
West Indies, Kingston, Jamaica, in 1991.

Cover designed by Sophie Buchet.
Typeset by EMS Photosetters, Thorpe Bay, Essex.
Printed and bound in the United Kingdom
by Biddles Ltd., Guildford and King's Lynn.

British Library Cataloguing in Publication Data

The IMF and the South : the social impact of
  crisis and adjustment.
  1. Developing countries. Economic development. Financial assistance by International
  Monetary Fund.
  I. Ghai, Dharam *1936*–. II. United Nations,
  Research institute for social development.
  332.152

  ISBN 0-86232-950-7
  ISBN 0-86232-951-5 pbk

Library of Congress Cataloging-in-Publication Data
The IMF and the south : the social impact of
  crisis and adjustment/edited by Dharam Ghai.
       p.   cm.
  Includes bibliographical references and index.
  ISBN 0-86232-950-7.
  ISBN 0-86232-951-5 (pbk.)
  1. International Monetary fund. 2. Economic
  assistance. 3. Economic development – Social
  aspects. 4. Debt relief – Developing countries.
  5. Deficit financing – Developing countries. I.
  Ghai, Dharam P.
  HG3881.5.I58I395   1990
  332.1'52–dc20   90-39961
                                            CIP

Tables

Preface

This volume of essays addresses some of the most critical issues facing the Third World. Its value rests to a large extent on the case studies which focus on the experiences in Africa, the Caribbean and Latin America in a rapidly changing global economy. Hopefully, the lessons that emerge from these experiences will provide the necessary basis to formulate workable solutions to the contemporary economic crisis.

From the essays in this volume, it is evident that the countries of the South are at an important turning point in their history and prospects. Individually they represent countries of striking contrasts in size, resource endowments and physical and economic structure. Since the coming of political independence in the two decades after the Second World War, many of them have made significant strides in economic and social terms as well as in the management of their own affairs. The decade of the 1980s has however been very different. The large majority of developing countries have been experiencing serious setbacks in their economic growth and living standards, especially those which carry a heavy burden of external indebtedness.

Although there is general acceptance of the need for growth-oriented strategies of adjustment, substantial differences of view remain between indebted countries on the one hand and donor countries on the other. By discussing the scope and timing of adjustment measures in a cross–section of countries as well as the differential impact of the policy instruments employed, this volume has contributed greatly to an understanding of the impasse between debtor countries and donors, in particular the multilateral financial institutions.

What has also emerged from reading these essays is the range of social problems that are transcending national boundaries and thereby compounding the present economic crisis. These include environmental degradation, drug abuse and trafficking and a substantial flow of illegal aliens and refugees from many parts of the developing world. These issues are threatening the social fabric of developed and developing countries alike with alarming implications for the maintenance of law and order and even the democratic process itself.

In searching for solutions, I am pleased to note that the contributions by and large recognize the need to build upon the potential of the South. A major effort has to be made through education and training to upgrade the human resource capability to share equitably in world production and trade and in scientific and technological advance. In the next century, most of the world's remaining natural resources of minerals, metals, tropical timber and fisheries, to name a few, will be concentrated within the borders of the developing countries. Herein, I believe, lies the major challenge to development in this the last decade of the twentieth century.

I was pleased to have participated in the exciting conference which led to the publication of this volume. I greatly welcome this joint initiative of the University of the West Indies and the United Nations Research Institute for Social Development to contribute to the search for effective solutions to the economic and social crisis of the Third World.

Alister McIntyre
Vice-Chancellor
University of the West Indies

Acknowledgements

In preparing this book, I have accumulated a debt of gratitude to several institutions and individuals. First, my thanks go to the Institute of Social and Economic Research, University of the West Indies, and the United Nations Research Institute for Social Development which co-sponsored the conference in Kingston, Jamaica, where the papers contained in this volume were originally presented. I am especially grateful to Alister McIntyre, Vice-Chancellor of the University of the West Indies and Eddie Greene, Director of ISER, for ensuring strong participation of the Caribbean research community in the conference and for providing excellent facilities and a stimulating environment for discussions. I would like to extend my thanks to Stanley Lalta, Janet Liu Terry, Elizabeth Crawford and other supporting staff at ISER for all their work and effort to make the conference a success. In addition, I would like to express my gratitude to the Office of the Resident Representative of the United Nations Development Programme in Kingston for their assistance during the conference. I wish to express my warm appreciation to the Rockefeller Foundation and the Commonwealth Secretariat for providing partial financial support for the conference.

My thanks are due also to the paper writers and participants at the conference. Brian Van Arkadie worked with me in drawing up the initial framework for the papers. For their assistance in the editorial work, I thank Jessica Vivian and Ann Zammit. Cynthia Hewitt de Alcántara and Yusuf Bangura helped in the proofreading stage along with Jessica Vivian.

I am also grateful to Wendy Salvo and Rhonda Gibbes for their assistance in the preparation of the workshop. Françoise Jaffré helped with the documentation and the publication arrangements while Lawrence Boms provided research assistance.

Finally, my thanks go to Robert Molteno and his colleagues at Zed Books for the work they have put into preparing this book for publication in a relatively short period of time.

Dharam Ghai

1. Introduction

Dharam Ghai

The bulk of the sprawling literature on the economic crisis and the structural adjustment in the 1980s has been concerned primarily with technical analysis of the impact on macro-economic imbalances and efficiency in resource allocation. In recent years, some attempt has been made to analyse the consequences, for social welfare, poverty, employment and income distribution, of stabilization and adjustment policies. So far there has been very little systematic discussion of the wider impact of these measures on the social, economic and political forces and institutions of the affected countries. Yet the prolonged economic crisis and wide-ranging structural adjustment measures are changing the societies and politics of these countries in significant and distinctive ways. A clearer understanding of these changes is desirable, not only in its own right but also for a fuller appreciation of the viability and sustainability of the new economic strategies and policies.

The chapters in this volume attempt a new approach to the study of crisis and structural adjustment in seeking to place economic changes within the wider social and political context. More specifically, they attempt to deal with such issues as the impact of the crisis and adjustment on social structures and organizations, the struggles waged by different social groups to defend their economic interests, the effect of economic and social changes on the balance of political forces, on the nature and power of the state, as also on shifts in power between national and foreign economic and political interests. These issues are immensely complex, and clear and definitive conclusions are not to be expected. The chapters presented here should be regarded as a first step in the exploration of the changing configuration of the social and political landscape of countries convulsed by economic crisis and restructuring.

This chapter focuses on some of the leading themes treated in the contributions in the volume. It begins with a brief review of the global economic environment as necessary background for the understanding of economic crisis in developing countries. The stabilization and adjustment measures adopted by the developing countries to deal with the crisis represent a shift from what might be described as a national to an international project. There is thus first a discussion of the key features of the economic strategies pursued by most developing countries in the post-war period and the associated alliance of social forces underpinning the strategy. This is contrasted with the central features of the new policies. The discussion then reviews the main conclusions of the contributions relating to the political economy of the transition from the national to the international project.

The global economic environment

The crisis that struck Africa and Latin America in the late 1970s and the 1980s was intimately linked to changes in the world economy. A quarter of a century of rapid economic growth came to an abrupt end in the early 1970s. The subsequent years have been characterized by distinctly slower rates of economic expansion in the industrialized countries. The major contributory factors to sustained growth in the post-war years were accumulated pent-up demand of the preceding years, the reconstruction of the devastated European and Japanese economies, accelerated technological progress, high rates of profits, demand management to preserve full employment, increasing liberalization of trade and payments, and a stable international economic order assured by US political and economic hegemony. Likewise, a conjuncture of events has contributed to slower growth since 1973. These included declining profit rates caused in part by rising wage levels, increase in primary product prices led by the oil shock and attempts to control inflation and state expenditures.

These developments gave rise to significant changes in the economic policies pursued by most industrialized countries including reduction of aggregate demand through credit restrictions, increased real interest rates and restraints on public expenditure, deregulation of the economy, and a reduced role of the state in ownership and management of the economy. These policies contributed to reduced demand for primary products, sharp fall in commodity prices, rise in real interest rates worldwide, drastic falls in private investment and the virtual disappearance, after 1982, of the private bank loans to the Third World which had played such an important role in recycling petro-dollars thereby enabling many countries, especially in Latin America, to sustain high growth rates in the 1970s despite a deteriorating global economic environment.

These external events had a devastating impact on the economies of most developing countries. Particularly seriously affected regions were the Middle East, sub-Saharan Africa, the Caribbean and Latin America. On the other hand, most countries in Asia managed to achieve satisfactory rates of economic expansion and some, such as India, China and Thailand, even to improve upon their performance in the 1970s. Among key factors determining the differential impact of the changes in the world economy were the degree of dependence on trade, external investment and finance, the composition of exports and in particular the relative importance of primary products and manufactures, the level and terms of indebtedness and the flight of capital. The countries in sub-Saharan Africa, the Caribbean and Latin America which are the subjects of this study, were among the most adversely affected in large part because of the characteristics of their external economic relations.

The severity of the economic crisis and the principal mechanisms through which the external shocks were transmitted to African and Latin American economies are described in some detail in the following chapters. The crisis represented a sharp and unprecedented reversal of the experience in the post-war period of rising incomes, employment and social services. The exigencies of the crisis combined with pressure from external creditors and donors led to sweeping changes in economic and social policies in most of these countries. To appreciate fully the nature and characteristics of the new policies, it is necessary to review briefly the key feature of the development model as it had evolved in the post-war decades in the majority of the Third World countries.

The post-war development model

Despite a great deal of diversity in terms of economic and social structures and political systems, the majority of developing countries pursued a development strategy with some important common characteristics. The basic feature of this strategy was a strong role by the state in managing the process of economic growth. The state gave a high priority to industrialization, diversification and modernization of the economy. A variety of policies were pursued to attain these objectives including protection against industrial imports through tariffs and quantitative restrictions, input subsidies, provision of infrastructure, favourable tax regimes, and cheap food and raw materials. The policy instruments were eclectic, ranging from reliance on price mechanisms to direct allocation of scarce resources. The obverse of industrial protection was the relative taxation of the agricultural and mineral sectors. This was done through such mechanisms as export taxes, heavy taxation of surpluses generated in the mining sector, over-valued exchange rates, low prices for food and raw materials, and inadequate expenditure on agriculture and rural infrastructure.

The role of the state also extended in most countries to direct ownership and management of a wide range of industrial, agricultural, marketing and financial enterprises. The state further played an important role in the provision of social services such as health, education and housing to an increasing proportion of the population and in the improvement of infrastructure such as roads, water supply, irrigation and electrification.

This development strategy was underpinned by a certain configuration of social forces. In Latin America, it was sustained by an alliance between the industrialists, urban workers and the middle classes. This alliance proved strong enough to triumph over the interests of the agrarian and mining sectors in an increasing number of countries in the 1950s and 1960s. Both the middle classes and the urban workers benefited from expanding state and industrial sectors and from the extension of minimum wages and social security in the modern enterprises. The interests of certain social groups such as small peasants, rural workers, participants in the urban informal economy and, to a lesser extent, the landed oligarchy, received scant attention in development policies.

The process of industrialization was fuelled by foreign investment through multinational enterprises. In addition, foreign assistance and commercial loans sustained this model of development in the late 1960s and early 1970s when it came under pressure from internal weaknesses and adverse external factors. However, despite an important role played by foreign investors, the state determined for the most part the central thrust of the development strategy and policies.

Despite very different social and economic structures, the situation evolved along broadly similar lines in Africa. The state played an even more important role in guiding and managing the economy, priority was accorded to industrialization, diversification and modernization of the economy, and the mechanisms put in place during the colonial period to extract resources from agriculture and mining were further developed in the post-independence years. As in Latin America, the support for these policies derived from the industrialists, urban workers and state functionaries. Unlike Latin America, however, the proportion of the total population represented by these groups was relatively small. Although the rural population benefited from expanding social services and improved infrastructure, it is nevertheless surprising, given the weight of the rural population, that agrarian interests should have received so little attention in development programmes and policies.

At the political level too there were some similarities in the broad evolution of events in the majority of countries in the two regions. In a growing number of Latin American countries, the early years after the war were characterized by a national consensus represented by the emerging alliance of the political élite, the state officials, industrialists and the urban working class. In most of the countries, the government was based on civilian regimes elected through national elections. However, even as these groups gained ascendancy in one country after another in the post-war period and as the industrialization-based strategy consolidated itself, many countries were subjected to social strains created by sharp inequalities in the distribution of wealth and incomes, as also the persistence of mass poverty and widespread under- and unemployment. The failure of the development policies to resolve these problems was undoubtedly among the factors which contributed to the emergence or strengthening of movements and parties inspired by a more radical ideology.

The response to such development was the adoption of increasingly repressive methods and the replacement of civilian governments by military regimes in a growing number of countries so that, by the early 1970s, the majority of the Latin American countries found themselves in the grip of authoritarian and repressive regimes. In their early years, these regimes saw as their principal task the suppression of popular and radical trends in their societies. The central thrust of the development strategies inherited from the preceding administrations was intensified with increased emphasis on accumulation and industrialization achieved in part by the weakening or suppression of the trade union movement. However, with the onset of the crisis and the growing ascendancy of free market ideologies in the industrialized countries, some military regimes, as in Chile and Argentina, began the process of greater reliance on market forces and the opening up of the countries to the world economy.

The majority of African countries became independent in the late 1950s and early 1960s. The early post-independence years in most countries were characterized by national solidarity based on the alliance of all major social groups forged in the years of struggle for independence. This unity, however, came under increasing strain with the failure of most regimes to resolve the problems of corruption, mismanagement, accumulation of wealth by the élite and discriminatory treatment of certain regions, ethnic and social groups. It was not long before the old ethnic and regional animosities were revived and exploited and the embattled and increasingly unpopular regimes sought to stifle all opposition and consolidate power in the hands of the head of the state. This in turn paved the way for overthrow of civilian regimes or creation of one-party states in an increasing number of countries. Thus, by the early 1970s, plural political systems based on multi-party democracy were a rarity on the continent.

Adjustment under international auspices

It was against the background of heavy foreign debts and deteriorating economic performance that a large number of African, Latin American and Caribbean countries initiated the process of economic reform. Several factors contributed to efforts at reform. These included the severity of the crisis, the weaknesses of some of the previous economic policies, and, above all, strong international pressure exerted by multilateral financial organizations, commercial banks and donor countries. This pressure was the more effective as the countries were in dire need of foreign exchange to meet their debt obligations and maintain a minimum level of imports. In return for debt rescheduling and new credits, the foreign creditors insisted on a wide-ranging but a generally uniform package of economic reforms. Thus the initiative in formulating economic policies shifted from the national authorities to international sources.

The new policies represent a significant break with those associated with the post-war model. Economic planning has been all but abandoned by most countries. There is increasing reliance on market forces for regulating the economy. Price controls and subsidies are yielding place to price determination by supply and demand. Industrialization is no longer being promoted by deliberate policy measures; instead, greater incentives are being given to production of primary commodities. Likewise, the quest for a more integrated national economy has given way to efforts at export promotion. There is increasing liberalization of foreign trade and payments. Greater national ownership and control of the economy are no longer priority objectives of development policy. The emphasis is instead on incentives to foreign investment and privatization of state properties and their sale to foreign interests. There have been cut-backs in social services and the tax burden has become more regressive in many countries.

The new policies are likely to have far-reaching economic, social and political consequences. Some of these are already visible. In many countries, the relative importance of industry has declined with a corresponding rise in the share of agriculture, mining or services. The formal sector is losing in importance to small-scale and micro-enterprises. There have been significant changes in the level and share of income of different social groups. The urban working classes and sections of the middle classes have been impoverished. Certain groups of persons deriving their income from capital have prospered while others have suffered losses. These changes have given rise to a wide variety of individual and collective strategies of survival. Some of the established social organizations, such as the unions, co-operatives, and so on, have declined in power and influence in many countries while new ones, such as neighbourhood and self-help groups, have emerged to assist the basic-needs provisioning of the marginal sections of the population.

The above changes have resulted in important shifts in the balance of power among different social groups. The foreign investors and creditors have also increased their power and influence in national policy-making. Likewise, the influence of the domestic business groups, especially those with links or access to foreign capital and markets, has greatly increased. The working class and parts of the middle classes have seen a dwindling of their power to shape national policies. In brief, the post-war alliance between the state, the industrialists and the working class has been largely shattered but has not been replaced by a new stable configuration of social forces.

The power and the reach of the state have declined in practically all the countries affected by economic crisis and adjustment measures. There has been transfer of a vital part of economic decision-making from the state to foreign creditors. The squeeze on state finances has compelled the governments to reduce public services, infrastructural investment, employment and wage levels in the public sector. The growing privatization, marketization, informalization and internationalization of the economy mean that an increasing proportion of economic activity is slipping beyond the direct control of the state. The power of the state has been further weakened by the loss of qualified officials, decline in morale of the public servants and increase in ethnic and religious conflicts and in crime, violence and lawlessness.

The state, structural adjustment and social groups

The social dynamics of the crisis and of the transition from the national project to structural adjustments under international sponsorship constitute the principal themes of the chapters in this book. The chapter by Ghai and Hewitt de Alcántara explores the changes in incomes of different social groups brought about by the crisis and the associated policies of stabilization and structural adjustment. It argues that the cumulative impact of these policies has been to shift incomes in favour of capital to the detriment of labour. The urban working class and sections of the middle class have been particularly adversely affected by the new policies. The major beneficiaries have been the groups associated in one way or another with the international economy. The two major consequences of the new policies have been the internationalization and informalization of the economies in Africa, the Caribbean and Latin America.

The crisis and the new policies have led to a blurring of class distinctions and weakening of the established social organizations and institutions. Together with a massive decline in state power, the social and political situation has become fluid and uncertain, with at best ambiguous prospects for stability and democracy.

Sandbrook's chapter explores in greater detail the impact of the crisis and structural adjustment measures on the developmental role of the state in Africa. For historical, cultural and social reasons, there has been slow development of the "rational-legal state" in Africa. The African states have generally been characterized by patrimonial mechanisms of governance. The crisis and the new policies have further weakened the foundations of a "rational-legal state". The African states are faced simultaneously with fiscal, hegemonic and administrative capacity crises. Only liberal democracy holds the prospects of the emergence of political stability, competent administration and economic growth.

The role of the state and the impact of external economic forces figure prominently in the chapter by Mkandawire. He gives short shrift to doctrines that seek the roots of the African crisis in inappropriate economic policies, cultural traits, personal rule, urban bias and rent-seeking groups. It is the openness and the vulnerability of the African economies to external shocks which appear to be primarily responsible for the African crisis. Mkandawire interprets the adjustment policies as a derailment of the process of capitalist transformation of colonial economies into normal periphery capitalist economies. The structural adjustment process is looked upon as a defeat of the nationalist project by international capital and represents an attempt by external capital to seize control of the national economies.

Thomas offers a broader perspective of the crisis in the Caribbean region. The crisis can be viewed at many levels: the ideology and institutions of the post-colonial state, the East-West struggle, macro-economic imbalances and socio-economic tensions. While highlighting the centrality of the international economy for the Caribbean region, Thomas seeks the root causes of the crisis in internal production patterns, social structures and institutions. In contrast, Schvarzer traces the root and essence of the crisis in Argentina to the opening up of the economy to the outside world. The decision to open the financial sector of the economy exposed it at once to capital flight, the subsequent necessity of foreign borrowing and eventually to premature opening of the real economy with disastrous consequences for domestic industry.

Heredia explores the political and social dynamics of the process of transition in Mexico from an inward-looking, import-substitution industrialization strategy to one based on free markets and integration with the world economy. The earlier strategy pursued for nearly five decades rested on an alliance of the major social groups in Mexico represented in the single party which controlled the state. Through ownership of enterprises in the key sectors of the economy and extensive intervention, the state played a critical role in determining the pattern of growth and distribution of incomes and consumption. This model came under increasing stress with the exhaustion of import-substitution possibilities and the emergence of an inefficient industrial structure. Despite the sharp increase in petroleum prices, the viability of the system became increasingly dependent upon external funds. The administration of de la Madrid sought to resolve the contradictions by a total turnaround in economic policies – the keys to which were reduction of state expenditure, import liberalization, removal of subsidies, privatization and flexible exchange rate policies. This inevitably brought the administration into conflict with the social groups adversely affected by these changes, such as the working class, sections of the middle class and some entrepreneurs who bore the brunt of the stabilization and adjustment policies. Despite such strong opposition, the administration persisted, and largely succeeded, in its endeavour to radically alter the established economic policies.

The Uganda case illustrates the application of similar policies under vastly different economic, social and political conditions. Mamdani shows that the impact of liberalization and fiscal and monetary policies has been to shift incomes and resources away from the salaried and wage-earning groups in favour of traders and speculators. Thus there has been differentiation without productive accumulation. He also makes the important point that through a variety of agrarian institutions the surplus has been syphoned off from the peasantry to a parasitic and essentially unproductive group of persons. The stabilization and adjustment policies thus failed to address the critical obstacles to accumulation and production.

Mozambique and Nicaragua attempted structural change and basic-needs provisioning through central planning and allocation of resources. In both cases these attempts were made in conditions of civil war and economic dislocation provoked and abetted by external forces. The chapters by Wuyts and FitzGerald bring out the limits of such attempts in conditions of underdevelopment further aggravated by civil war and economic disruption. In both cases, the efforts to achieve structural change and basic-needs provisioning were undermined by mounting deficits, rampant inflation, chronic shortages and parallel markets. Both countries attempted to ameliorate the situation by decentralization, greater reliance on market forces and provision of incentives to the peasantry. While both countries relied substantially on foreign resources, in Mozambique this led to the creation of parallel structures controlled and administered by donor agencies whereas Nicaragua was more successful in integrating foreign assistance into the national strategy for defence and development. Nicaragua also appears to have been more successful in creating new forms of social organization such as co-operatives, local groups and militias to cope with the crisis.

The papers on Nigeria and Brazil deal with the response of the organized workers to economic crisis and stabilization and adjustment measures. In Brazil, the onset of the crisis coincided with political liberalization, which also created a space for trade union activities. After having been repressed for nearly two decades, the workers defended their interests through a central union allied with a political party. Amadeo and Camargo argue that the emergence of a strong union meant that the solution to the crisis could not be sought through the continuing decline in real wages – a process which financed the rapid accumulation and growth over the past two and a half decades. Bangura and Beckman describe in detail the struggle waged by the organized workers to defend employment and real wages, resist stabilization and adjustment measures and propose an alternative package of policies to surmount the crisis. The workers were also successful in mobilizing and channelling the opposition of other social groups to policies aimed at reducing the incomes and consumption of low-income groups. Despite these efforts, the unions were unable to reverse the general direction of policies pursued by the government.

Part 1:
Economic Crisis, Social Change and Political Implications: Regional Perspectives

2. The Crisis of the 1980s in Africa, Latin America and the Caribbean: An Overview

Dharam Ghai
and Cynthia Hewitt de Alcántara

Introduction

As they prepare to enter the last decade of the twentieth century, by far the majority of all countries in Africa, Latin America and the Caribbean are caught up in an economic crisis of unprecedented proportions, with far-reaching implications for the welfare of millions of people. Under the impact of recession and adjustment, patterns of survival are changing, and with them social structures and forms of political concertation.

While there is much in each national experience which is peculiar or distinctive, there is also much which is common across countries and even across continents. It is the purpose of this chapter to establish a certain minimum common ground for discussion of these experiences, of their similarities and their differences. To that end, the following pages will endeavour to provide macro-economic background on the crisis in Africa, Latin America and the Caribbean, before putting forward some hypotheses on the way changing life chances of various groups, and consequent adoption of particular kinds of survival strategies, seem to be affecting the broad contours of society in those regions. Finally, the possible political implications of the crisis, will be briefly considered.

Macro-economics of the crisis

Let us begin with some quantitative information on the economic crisis, looking first at the magnitude of, and contributing factors to, recession in sub-Saharan Africa and Latin America and the Caribbean (hereafter referred to as Africa and Latin America). This will be followed by a brief discussion of macro-economic adjustments and the manner in which the economic burden has been borne by different social groups. For ease of presentation, the situation in the two regions will be discussed separately, before providing a summary comparative picture of the macro-economics of crisis in Africa and Latin America.

An effort of this nature is beset with some serious difficulties. First, discussions at the regional level obscure important differences at the country level. The average regional data may conceal more than they reveal. This is especially so for two reasons. In Africa, the regional data are greatly influenced by the performance of the Nigerian economy, which accounts for nearly a quarter of the aggregate output. In Latin America, Brazil, and to a lesser extent Mexico and Argentina, have similar effects on regional aggregates. There are also considerable differences in the experiences of the oil-importing and exporting countries in view of the sharp fluctuations in oil prices over the past 15 years and the important role oil revenues play in several countries in the two regions.

The second set of difficulties arises from the weaknesses of official data on economic indicators. The situation has been made worse by the fact that the prolonged period of crisis has generated significant changes in the structure and pattern of economic activities which are unlikely to have been captured by official statistics. The reference here is not only, as we will show below, to the increasing importance of small-scale and informal sector activities but also to own production and consumption and a host of illegal and subterranean activities which by their very nature could not be reflected in official data. Indeed, the situation in some countries is so dramatic in this respect that the official statistics may bear little resemblance to the actual evolution of the economy.

While acutely aware of these difficulties, then, we have little option but to begin through reference to official economic data.

Economic crisis in Africa

Magnitude and contributory factors: The crisis has many dimensions and is manifested at several levels. A rough idea of its magnitude may be conveyed by a few macro-economic statistics. Real per capita GDP fell by about 25 per cent between 1980 and 1988. If account is taken of the deterioration in the terms of trade suffered by sub-Saharan Africa over the period 1980–88, per capita incomes have declined by about 30 per cent, or by slightly less than one third.[1] By any standards, this is indeed a staggering loss of income. In sub-Saharan Africa, with a per capita GNP in 1986 of US$370, or 35 times less than in industrial market economies, this represents a burden of overwhelming proportions.

Of course not all countries have experienced declines in income of this magnitude. Some such as Benin, Burkina Faso, Burundi, Malawi, Mali, have suffered declines in GNP per capita (1980–87) of less than one per cent per annum (explained probably by relatively high net resource flows) while at the other extreme, countries like Liberia, Madagascar, Mozambique, Niger, Nigeria, Rwanda, Sudan, Togo, Zambia, have experienced declines of more than 3 per cent per annum. However, the continental dimension of the crisis is brought out by the fact that out of 35 sub-Saharan countries for which data were available, only eight managed to prevent a decline in GNP per capita. Of these only three – Botswana, Cameroon and Gabon – achieved substantial growth in per capita GNP.

It is not the intention here to launch into a discussion of the origin and underlying forces behind the African crisis. This subject has been discussed extensively and has generated a veritable flood of publications. There is an increasing measure of agreement that the crisis is due to a deep-seated and complex set of forces, of both external and internal origin. It suffices here to make some general points on the crisis. Firstly, although the crisis assumed dramatic proportions in the 1980s, the process of declining growth set in much earlier. A broad indication of this is given by the trend in GDP per capita growth which declined from 3.7 per cent per annum over 1965–73 to 0.7 per cent in 1973–80 and about -3 per cent in the 1980s.

Secondly, while international economic forces have always played an important role in determining the level of economic activity in African countries, they assumed a decisive significance in the 1980s. Were this not the case, it would be difficult to account for a simultaneous deterioration in the performance of the great majority of sub-Saharan countries, as indeed of other regions such as the Caribbean and Latin America, North Africa and West Asia. A study covering an earlier period showed a very considerable diversity in the economic performance of African countries.[2]

As in other regions, the international economy adversely affected the situation in African countries in the 1980s primarily through four mechanisms: the deterioration in terms of trade, increase in real interest rates on external debt, reduced inflow of resources and massive (possibly accelerating) capital outflows. The first three mechanisms are reasonably well-documented but the fourth, taking many different forms, is largely unrecorded, though rough estimates made by some researchers point to the enormous proportions it assumed in some countries.[3] The relative importance of the first three factors has been neatly summarized in the following table taken from a United Nations report.

Table 2.1
Consolidated Change in External Financial Position of Sub-Saharan Africa between 1979–1981 and 1985–1987* (billions of US dollars per annum)

Terms of trade losses	2.9
Increased interest payments	2.1
Reduced credit flow	2.4
Reduced direct investment	0.2
Total deterioration	7.6
Increased official grants	1.1
Net deterioration	6.5

Source: United Nations. *Financing Africa's Recovery.* 1988.
* Excluding Nigeria

In Table 2.1, the figures, which exclude Nigeria, show that the deterioration in terms of trade caused the greatest losses, followed by a reduction in resource flows and an increase in interest payments. The total figure of $6.5 billion partly reflects the very substantial debt rescheduling that has taken place.

Without it, debt service would have been some $5 billion to $6 billion higher per annum than it actually was in recent years. Even so, these amounts are equivalent to roughly one-third of the total annual imports of goods and services of these countries in the 1980s and about 45 per cent of average annual export earnings.[4] Viewed in a different way, they amount to 10–11 per cent of their GDP and over 60 per cent of their gross capital formation. These figures, even without taking into account some elements of capital flight, thus serve to underline the decisive role played by the international economy in the African crisis in the 1980s.[5]

To highlight the external factors in the crisis is not to overlook either their interaction with domestic institutions or policies or to ignore the role played by other elements. As the latter have been discussed extensively in the literature on the African crisis, a brief mention should suffice. The prolonged droughts affecting the Sahelian, Eastern and Southern African countries for varying periods have been important in several countries. Likewise many countries have been wracked by political crises and disorder reflected in civil wars, conflicts with neighbouring states and, in the Southern African context, by struggles for national liberation and aggression by the regime in South Africa.

To these natural and man-made disasters must be added the long-run dynamics of accelerating population growth and deteriorating natural environment. Finally, there is a variety of factors which may be classified under economic mismanagement and inefficiency. These include inappropriate pricing, trade and foreign exchange policies, discrimination against the agricultural sector, poor investment decisions, corruption and misappropriation of resources. There has been a tendency, especially by economists, to single out inappropriate policies as the main culprit in the crisis. While they have played roles of varying importance in different countries at different times, it stretches credulity to attribute a dominant role to them in the intensification of the crisis in the 1980s. Indeed, as shown subsequently, African countries have undertaken significant economic reforms in the 1980s; but it is often not clear that these have had a positive effect. On the contrary, they have tended to be overwhelmed by a strong negative international environment.

Macro-economic adjustments: How have the African economies adjusted to a decline of nearly a quarter in GDP per capita and one-third in per capita incomes? This question may be approached from two angles: first in terms of adjustments in the main components of expenditure, that is, private and public consumption and investment; and secondly, in relation to incomes of major social groups such as wage and salary earners, peasants, informal sector participants, and business and professional groups.

Table 2.2 provides a summary of changes in some major economic aggregates in the two periods, 1965–80 and 1980–86.

Table 2.2
**Adjustment to Crisis: Some Macro-economic Indicators
in Sub-Saharan Africa***
(annual percentage changes)

	1965–1980	*1980–1986*
GDP	5.6	–0.0
Agriculture	1.6	–1.2
Industry	9.4	–1.5
(Manufacturing)	(8.5)	(0.3)
Services	7.5	0.1
Government consumption	8.1	–1.0
Private consumption	4.9	0.7
Gross domestic investment	8.8	–9.3
Exports	6.6	–2.1
Imports	19.5	–7.7

	Share in GDP: 1986
General government consumption	13
Private consumption	74
Gross domestic investment	14
Exports	19
Resource balance	-2

Source: World Bank, *World Development Report*, 1988.
* Inclusive of Nigeria

Between 1980 and 1986, GDP per capita declined by about 20 per cent. Assuming a population growth in the 1980s of about three per cent per annum, general government consumption per capita declined by 24 per cent over 1980–86, private consumption by 14 per cent and gross domestic investment by nearly 75 per cent. At the same time, while exports per head fell by about 30 per cent, imports declined by about 65 per cent. Hence, it is not too fanciful to talk of "import strangulation" of African economies.

We may conclude from the above that the burden of adjustment to the crisis fell disproportionately on gross domestic investment and on general government consumption. The latter includes expenditure on social and economic services. These developments have, on the one hand, impaired the increase in productive capacity and hence in the growth potential of African countries, and on the other hand, resulted in neglect and run-down of economic and social services such as roads, power, hospitals, clinics, schools, research, extension, credit and welfare programmes.

The period also witnessed some significant changes in the structure of the African economies. Agriculture increased its share of the economy while the relative importance of industry declined quite considerably. In per capita terms, agricultural output declined by about 11 per cent, industrial production by 22 per cent and services by about 18 per cent. In addition, because of a significant reduction in exports and especially of imports, the African economies became less trade- and export-oriented.

Adjustments in incomes of social groups: Stagnation in total output and changes in the pattern of economic activities have significantly affected the relative economic fortunes of different social groups. The latter are a reflection of a complex interplay of forces and pressures emanating from the world economy, as well as of struggles among different groups to preserve incomes and living standards in an era of shrinking opportunities and scarce resources.

Data limitations prevent a satisfactory treatment of this question. Not only are there no statistical categories reflecting the situation of a number of significant social groups, but, as argued earlier, the standard economic data are increasingly unreliable because of major shifts in the pattern of economic activities. Nevertheless, it is possible, through reliance on various indirect measures, to indicate in broad terms the pattern of income changes for some social groups.[6]

Shifts in the structure of income distribution have been induced by a number of increasingly serious and interrelated imbalances in various sectors of the economy, of which four may be highlighted here. First, there has been a worsening imbalance in labour markets resulting from an acceleration in the magnitude of the labour force and stagnation or decline in production. Second, the severe imbalance in the demand for and supply of foreign exchange has resulted in a sharp reduction in imports of intermediate, consumer and capital goods. Third, the fiscal crisis of the state has led to significant slow-down or reduction of expenditure on social services, infrastructure maintenance and net capital formation. Fourth, the modern private sector has also come under increasing pressure from shortages of materials and spare parts, declining markets, rising interest rates and scarce and expensive machinery.

These imbalances, in combination with the policy response to them (or lack thereof) have led to shifts in patterns of income distribution which are surprisingly similar in a large number of countries. In rural areas, the crisis has manifested itself in declines in real incomes, deterioration in the availability of public services and shortages of consumer goods. But the rural population has been shielded from the full impact of the crisis by the predominantly subsistence nature of production for the majority of cultivators and by their relative self-sufficiency in the means of production. Furthermore, in a number of countries, stabilization and structural adjustment programmes and policies have tended in recent years to improve the internal terms of trade in favour of agriculture. The bulk of the benefits from this have, however, accrued to large commercial farmers and "progressive" smallholders.

The brunt of the crisis had to be borne by the urban sector. Given the growing imbalance in urban labour markets, adjustment can take the following principal forms: reduction in rural-urban migration, rise in open unemployment, decline or stagnation in formal sector employment, fall in formal sector wages and expansion of informal sector employment accompanied by a decline in wages and earnings.[7] A review of the available evidence indicates a decline in migration flows to urban areas in some countries but overall the urban labour force is estimated to have expanded by over five per cent per annum in the period 1980–85 (Table 2.3). Urban unemployment rose sharply but still accounted for a relatively small proportion of the addition to the labour force. Employment in the formal sector grew by one per cent per annum. Thus the bulk of the increase in the labour force was "absorbed" by the informal sector, which is estimated to have expanded employment by slightly less than seven per cent per annum.

The major adjustment in the labour market took the form of a sharp decline in real wages, which fell by about 30 per cent between 1980 and 1985.[8] Real minimum wages declined by about 20 per cent over the period but by a considerably greater proportion since 1970. Thus in the 1980s at least the differentials in wages between the skilled and the unskilled have fallen quite sharply. As the informal sector served to absorb excess labour, it must also have been characterized by declining wages and earnings. Likewise rural-urban income differentials as measured by the ratio of minimum wage earnings to agricultural value added per person fell quite substantially in most countries.[9] There are no readily available data on the changes in the incomes of business and professional groups. No doubt some members of these groups, probably those associated with trading and financial sectors, have done well while others dependent upon manufacturing, construction and professional services may have suffered income declines comparable to those of wage and salary earners.

Table 2.3
Estimates of Urban Labour Force Utilization 1980–1985
(annual percentage change)

Labour force	5.3
Wage employment	1.0
Unemployment	10.0
Informal sector	6.7

Source: JASPA, ILO, *African Employment Report, 1980,*
Addis Ababa, 1988.

Economic crisis in Latin America and the Caribbean
Magnitude and contributory factors: The Latin American and the Caribbean region suffered deep economic crisis in the 1980s. Real per capita GDP in 1988 was about seven per cent below the level in 1980. The decline was widespread and affected practically all the countries in the region with the exception of Barbados, Colombia, Cuba and Brazil. Chile and the Dominican Republic managed a growth in real per capita GDP of less than two per cent between 1980 and 1988. At the other extreme, countries suffering declines of more than 20 per cent included Bolivia, Haiti, Panama, Nicaragua and Trinidad and Tobago; those between 10 and 20 per cent comprised Argentina, El Salvador,

Guatemala, Honduras, Mexico, Peru, Venezuela, with the remaining suffering
a decline of less than ten per cent. When account is taken of the net resource
flows out of the region and deterioration in the terms of trade, per capita
income probably declined by around 16 per cent between 1980 and 1988.
Overall the situation in the 1980s represents a major break with the experience
in the 1960s and 1970s when real per capital GDP rose by nearly three per cent
per annum.

The sharp deterioration in economic performance is due for the most part to
unfavourable developments in the world economy. The major factors have
been worsening terms of trade, increase in real interest rates, decline in external
resource flows and capital flight from the region. As shown in Table 2.4 the
terms of trade deteriorated by over 22 per cent between 1980 and 1988; real
rates of interest (LIBOR – consumer price index of industrial countries), which
were negative in the mid-1970s, rose from 1.8 in 1978–79 to about five per cent
in 1986–88; and net capital inflows declined from $27.7 billion in 1978–79 to
$9.2 billion in 1987–88. The result was that net external resources turned
around from an inflow of $15.8 billion in 1978–79 to an outflow of $22.8
billion, equivalent to 22.5 and 20.5 per cent of exports of goods and services in
the two periods.

Table 2.4
Macro-economics of crisis: Latin America and the Caribbean

	1980–1988 *(accumulated percentage)*
GDP per capita	–6.6
Income per capita	–16.0
(Loss due to terms of trade)	(–3.0)
(Loss due to resource transfers)	(–6.0)
Export volume	+56.0
Export per capita	+36.0
Import volume	–13.0
Import per capita	–33.0

	1978–1979	*1987–1988*
Ratio interest payments to exports of goods and services	16.7	–28.9
Transfer of resoures (½ billion)	15.8	–22.8
Resource transfers as percentage of exports of goods and services	22.5	–20.5
Rate of inflation (percentage)	46.0	336.0

Source: CEPAL, *Notas sobre la economía y el desarrollo*, December 1987 and December 1988.

As far as impact on per capita income is concerned, the deterioration in terms of trade added approximately three per cent, and the shift in net external resource inflows another six per cent to the seven per cent decline in GDP per capita between 1980 and 1988. In order to finance resource outflows, export volume grew by an impressive 56 per cent over 1980–88 or by 36 per cent per capita, while import volume declined by 13 per cent or by one-third on a per capita basis. Thus the regional economy became more export-oriented than before. Despite this huge effort, the ratio of interest payments to exports rose from 16.7 to 28.8 per cent between 1978–79 and 1987–88.

Finally unrecorded flight of capital constituted an additional contributory factor to the crisis. Table 2.5 shows the estimates of capital flight from seven Latin American countries over the period 1980–84. Note the especially high figures for Mexico, Argentina and Venezuela.

Table 2.5
Capital flight estimates[a]: 1980–1984
(billion dollars, cumulative)

Argentina	16.51
Brazil	1.33
Chile	−0.69[b]
Mexico	30.53
Peru	−0.11[b]
Uruguay	1.48
Venezuela	16.39
Total	65.24

Source: Donald Lessard and John Williamson, *Capital Flight and Third World Debt*, Institute for International Economics, Washington, D.C., 1987, p. 87.
Notes: [a]Defined as net errors and omissions plus "short term, other sectors" in balance of payments accounts.
[b]Negative sign denotes capital inflows.

Adjustment to economic crisis:[10] Table 2.6 shows how the burden of adjustment was shared among the major categories of expenditure over the period 1980-85. The main burden fell on gross investment, which declined by two-fifths on a per capita basis; fixed net investment fell even more sharply – by half in per capita terms. As the latter represents one measure of the addition to the productive capacity of the economy, it is clear that the crisis has seriously reduced the growth potential of the regional economy.

Total per capita consumption declined by less than seven per cent, shared fairly evenly between public and private consumption. However, what is striking is the difference in the behaviour of consumption between business (owners of capital) and labour. While consumption per capita of the former group rose by 16 per cent, that of the latter declined by 25 per cent. At an aggregate level, both groups suffered declines in per capita income – the owners of capital by 12 per cent and workers by 26 per cent. As will be discussed below, this general decline in business income is nevertheless likely to be more complex, masking advantage for big business in the midst of crisis for others within the sector.

Table 2.6
Macro-economic Adjustment to the Crisis: 1980–1985[a]
(cumulative percentage change per capita)[b]

GDP	−9.4
Gross National Income	−14.8
Total consumption	−6.6
– public	−5.5
– private	−6.8
– workers	−25.7
– business	+15.8
Total gross investment	−41.0
Fixed net investment	−51.0

Source: Derived from Table 4 in García, et al, 1988.
Notes: [a]Based on weighted data from 10 largest countries.
[b]Assumes a rate of population growth of 2.4 per cent per annum for all groups .

In terms of employment patterns, despite a considerable slowing down of total output, urban employment expanded by 2.8 per cent per annum, while unemployment grew by 6.3 per cent (Table 2.7). It is interesting to remark that the bulk of growth in modern sector employment came from public services and small enterprises. Thus, even in a situation of extreme crisis, the public sector continued to expand employment, at least until 1985. The crisis also generated a high rate of labour absorption in small enterprises and the informal sector.

Table 2.7
Changes in Employment Patterns of Urban Labour Force 1980–1985
(per cent per annum)

Unemployment	6.3
Employment	2.8
Modern sector	1.9
(Large and medium sized)	(0.3)
(Public services)	(4.0)
(Small enterprises)	(4.5)
Informal sector	4.9

Source: V. Tokman, "Adjustment and Employment in Latin America: The Current Challenge", *International Labour Review*, Vol. 125, No. 5, September–October 1986.

The above pattern of employment changes was accompanied by significant shifts in average incomes (Table 2.8). In general, the declines in the incomes of poorer groups – those in the informal sector and those earning minimum wages

– were greater than those of other categories of workers. The rural-urban income gap narrowed over the period. The rural sector, of course, comprises an extremely heterogeneous population of capitalist farmers, medium-sized commercial farmers, peasants, share-croppers and landless wage earners. It is likely that most of the gains have accrued to large and medium farmers, with agricultural workers and small peasants drawing few or no benefits. According to one estimate, the proportion of persons below poverty level remained unchanged in rural areas at around 54 per cent, while that in the urban areas went up from 21 to 29 per cent.

Table 2.8
Average Incomes and Wages in Urban Sector: 1980–1985
(cumulative per cent)

Informal sector	–27.0
Real wages:	
Manufacturing	– 8.4
Construction	–19.4
Minimum	–11.8

Source: V. Tokman, 1986

Some summary comparative remarks on the macro-economics of the crisis in Africa and Latin America

In sum, then, it would seem that the crisis in sub-Saharan Africa is far more severe, both in absolute and relative terms, than it is in Latin America, GDP per capita in Africa declined by three times as much as in Latin America (20 and seven per cent respectively) over 1980–85/86. In terms of per capita incomes, the decline in Africa was double that in Latin America (30 and 15 per cent). Given that the average per capita GDP in Latin America is six times the level in sub-Saharan Africa, the real burden of the crisis is even greater in Africa than suggested by the preceding figures. Inequalities in wealth and income distribution are, however, much greater in Latin America than in Africa. Combined with greater urbanization, proletarianization and landlessness than in Africa, the deprivation and impoverishment suffered by the working classes in Latin America are more serious than suggested by the data on average per capita incomes.

Coming now to the relative weight of different elements in the international economy, Africa suffered a deterioration in terms of trade of about 34 per cent compared with 22 per cent for Latin America over the period 1980–87. Given the greater export dependence of African countries (18 per cent of GDP compared with 11 to 12 per cent in Latin America in 1986), the adverse movements in terms of trade have inflicted greater loss in per capita incomes in African countries. On the other hand, the changes in external net resource flows, while deteriorating for both regions, were of much greater consequence for Latin America than for Africa. In the former, net resource flows changed by nearly six per cent of GDP between 1979–80 and 1986–87, so that in the latter period the region was sustaining an outflow equivalent to four per cent. In Africa, net resource inflows declined from about five per cent of GDP in 1980 to about two per cent in 1986. Thus, while interest payments as a proportion of exports of goods and services amounted to over 31 per cent for Latin America in 1986–88, the corresponding figure for Africa was in the region of 20 per cent.

Bearing in mind that the GDP per capita declined by three times more and per capita incomes two times more in Africa, it is not surprising that gross domestic investment per capita declined by 75 per cent in Africa, compared to 40 per cent in Latin America. Overall per capita consumption declined by about seven per cent in Latin America over the period 1980–85, divided roughly equally between government and private consumption; in Africa, government consumption declined by 24 per cent and private consumption by 14 per cent over the period 1980–86. Thus, the relative contraction in government current expenditure was greater in Africa.

A major contrast in the adjustment pattern emerges with respect to the trade sector. Whereas imports per capita declined in Africa by 65 per cent over 1980–86, they fell by 33 per cent in Latin America over 1980–88; and while exports per capita declined by 30 per cent in Africa, they rose by 36 per cent in Latin America. The vigorous expansion of exports is in part responsible for the relatively more favourable performance in Latin America with respect to output growth. But because of the massive burden imposed by debt servicing, it did not prevent a decline in per capita incomes.

Turning to patterns of adjustment in labour markets, it seems that in both regions formal sector employment has continued to expand (one per cent per annum in Africa, 1.8 per cent per annum in Latin America), despite stagnation or very low growth in output. This has been made possible in both cases by substantial declines in real wages. In other words, the choice between maintenance of wage levels and employment has been decided in favour of the latter. While real minimum wages fell by eleven per cent in Latin America (1980–85), they fell by 20 per cent in Africa (1980–86). At the same time, urban unemployment rose rapidly in both regions, by probably ten per cent per annum in Africa and six per cent in Latin America, and urban informal sectors expanded rapidly (4.9 per cent in Latin America and 6.7 per cent per annum in Africa).

Although very little is known about changes in income distribution in Africa, it is likely that the gap in rural–urban incomes has declined more sharply in Africa than in Latin America. Simultaneously, the share of GDP attributable to capital grew four per cent in Latin America, while that of labour declined by an equal amount. It would be interesting to know if there has been a counterpart to this in Africa. In most countries there are not enough data to make a judgement in this regard.

The reorientation of macro-economic policy

The specific policy measures that have been taken in each country as part of the effort to deal with the crisis have, of course, necessarily depended upon the local balance of political forces and the nature of particular economies. It is important to note, however, that in varying degrees and with varying success, most governments of Latin America and Africa have attempted to carry out structural adjustment programmes recommended by the international financial community and that the effects of these programmes have ultimately formed part of the dynamics of the crisis itself.

Structural adjustment "packages" were originally designed to deal with short-term balance of payments problems, not to correct problems of the magnitude confronted by most countries during a period of generalized stagnation in world trade and decline of commodity prices. Adjustment measures are in essence designed to reduce aggregate demand and improve trade balances within a context that strengthens market forces and widens the scope for private enterprise. Thus they comprise reduction of government expenditure, especially on social services and economic infrastructure, removal or reduction of subsidies, an increase in tax revenue, restriction of money supply and of bank credit, and an increase in real interest rates.

Liberalization of trade and encouragement of exports are important goals of structural adjustment "packages" and are brought about by such measures as devaluation, reduction or elimination of export taxes, removal of import licences, quotas and quantitative restrictions, and introduction of a uniform external tariff rate. Other elements of the package consist of an increase in producer prices and reduction in the wage bill, wage freezes, declines in real wages and salaries, and reduction or elimination of fringe benefits and labour welfare and protective measures. Finally, the insistence on privatization of economic activities has involved closure or sale of state enterprises in directly productive and financial sectors, reduction or elimination of state marketing agencies, and a series of incentives for foreign investment.

Rescheduling of debt and debt service, as well as the granting of new loans, foreign aid and trade credits, has been made contingent upon acceptance of this policy package, thereby paving the way for a degree of external intervention in national policy-making unprecedented in the post-war period. The strong insistence upon eliminating barriers to free trade, as well as upon reducing the role of the state in the economy, has in addition run directly counter to efforts by many Latin American and African governments to foster greater national economic integration within a framework of protection for local industry.

Changing structures of opportunity

The trends just outlined suggest profound modification of the structure of opportunity within which individuals and households must attempt to ensure their livelihood: the closure of numerous well-established routes of survival or upward mobility and the concomitant opening of others. Various groups within each country of Africa and Latin America thus experience the current recession differently, and as they do so, society changes. The structure and vital interests of the élite may be altered or reinforced, the size and composition of the working class may change, entirely new social forces may be created, which alter the balance of power and provide new bases of support for or opposition to the state. If one stops to consider how social structures in Latin America were altered by the opportunities and constraints thrown up by the Great Depression, the importance of examining what may be happening to contemporary societies in the crisis becomes obvious.

Patterns of differentiation within the upper class

Let us begin with a brief discussion of the changing structure of opportunity confronting the upper classes of Latin America and Africa as an outgrowth of almost a decade of recession and adjustment. Although it is common for students of the crisis to consider changing survival strategies of the poor, there is sometimes a tendency to overlook the fact that the crisis also has profound implications for the life chances of the rich. And there is also a tendency to talk of both rich and poor as if they were internally rather homogeneous groupings. In fact, of course, they are not; and one of the most important questions to be asked when attempting to understand macro-structural shifts is how life chances are changing for particular categories of people *within* various social classes, as the fortunes of some may rise while those of others may fall and the overall balance of power and interests may in consequence be significantly altered, even within the confines of a single, general class.

In the case of the upper class of most countries in Africa and Latin America, it would seem that recession and adjustment are promoting a considerable process of internal differentiation. Some factions of the élite are being presented with extraordinary opportunities, while others are being harshly treated by the crisis. In Latin America, this has a great deal to do with the dynamics of devaluation, inflation and capital flight. In Africa, such elements seem less important in determining the ability of some members of the élite to preserve or enhance their position (while others are unable to do so) than location in the political-administrative hierarchy, involvement in foreign trade, and/or association with transnational capital.

Turning first to the situation of countries which have experienced significant capital flight, there is no doubt that lines of differentiation within the upper class, and particularly within business groups, have been increasingly drawn in relation to access – or lack of access – to funds held outside the country. As devaluation of the local currency relentlessly increases the value of foreign-held wealth, the income of families with large foreign bank accounts increases spectacularly. New markets for luxury goods and services thus appear incongruously as the crisis advances, and there are startling manifestations (on the streets, in commercial districts) of advancing polarization.

The fact that significant segments of the upper class in some Latin American countries base their consumption not only on nationally held assets but also on their ability to finance expenditures from foreign accounts may explain in part the trend, captured in national accounts statistics and noted above, for the consumption of upper-income groups to have increased during the course of the crisis, while the registered (national) income of that group seems to have declined. *The parameters of livelihood for this segment of the élite are no longer national, but international*, and their situation is not captured by standard national accounting mechanisms.

At the same time, the dynamics of inflation and devaluation, which accompany the crisis and assume particular importance in Latin America, have a tendency to make the very rich richer, even in the absence of complications introduced by capital flight. It should be remembered that in the effort to protect local savings and to stem capital flight, governments are encouraged to raise internal interest rates – often to extremely high levels. Although this is harmful for those who borrow, it can produce windfall gains for large savers. Those who maintain high levels of bank deposits eventually receive such large returns that they are once again likely to engage in enormously conspicuous consumption.

This skewing of opportunity within the upper class toward groups that have access to foreign currency and/or live primarily from speculation or from the receipt of interest obviously has implications not only for individuals but also for businesses, and thus for the evolution of the structure of the economy. In a situation of local capital scarcity and high interest rates, transnational enterprise in principle enjoys an increasing advantage over domestic firms unable to obtain adequate financing and to overcome the problems posed by shrinking domestic and/or export markets.[11] The point to be made here is not that transnational enterprises are necessarily expanding in Africa or Latin America as a result of the crisis; in some cases they may be doing so, while in others they are clearly retrenching in reaction to unfavourable economic trends. What is important to note is rather the fact that international companies are often better able to withstand the crisis than are their national counterparts and this constitutes another likely internationalizing effect of the crisis.

In a paper prepared for a conference organized by the Economic Commission for Africa, Sawyerr (1988) in fact makes clear reference to the centrality of association with foreign interests for those within African élites best able to weather the crisis successfully. Among the factions which he feels have gained from adjustment are top executives in private business, linked with foreign capital, local agents of foreign concerns, and those among importers and exporters able to obtain special access to foreign exchange in a situation of scarcity. Thus, in a time of marked economic recession, areas of business linked with outside interests seem to have become more privileged, in relation to those without such links, even when overall levels of foreign investment are shrinking. And in a period of privatization, those able "to buy up or buy into state-owned enterprises, usually at concessional prices", are also to be counted among the privileged.[12]

Concomitantly, both in Africa and in Latin America, the dynamics of recession and adjustment present an increasingly serious challenge to formal-sector entrepreneurial groups not, at least partially, protected by association with international capital. The extreme uncertainty introduced by inflation, devaluation and irregular access to credit undermines the very bases of predictability on which productive investment must rest. When imported components are required for manufacturing or farming, which is most often the case, uncertainty increases. And the fact that economic activity must ultimately depend upon utilization of public infrastructure, which is often badly maintained as a result of restrictions on government spending, constitutes a further negative complication. Opportunity presents itself, under the circumstances, either to the strongest and most internationally linked among the capitalist class or to the most flexible and daring of entrepreneurs emerging within the informal sector. It does not favour the survival of relatively more dependent and import-vulnerable entrepreneurs doing business within a structure of fixed economic obligations.

If this picture of changing life chances within upper-income groups is relatively adequate, then we are witnessing the demise or serious weakening of a particular pattern of indigenous capitalist growth associated over the past half-century in Latin America – and more recently and incompletely in Africa – with import-substituting industrialization. At the same time, we observe a tendency toward increasing polarization within society, as some of the upper class becomes even wealthier, while others within that category are not able to maintain their positions, thus reducing the number and variety of people still forming a national élite.

Relative impoverishment and political engagement of the salaried middle class
A diagnosis of polarization is further indicated by consideration of the plight of the salaried middle class during the past decade of recession and adjustment. Although a part of the indigenous business élite may be falling into the middle class, a considerable segment of the latter is, in turn, being relatively impoverished. One can infer from figures on employment and services analysed above that, given the great dependence of middle-class families upon salaried employment and upon the public goods provided to urban dwellers over the past few decades of imitative development in the Third World, the level of living of that group has been extraordinarily undermined by the crisis.

There are, of course, many sectors and interests within the broad category called "middle class", some of which are likely to be favoured by such adjustment measures as opening the internal market to foreign products. This is particularly the case in Latin America, where domestically produced goods have represented an important part of all middle-class consumption and where there is a long-frustrated desire within middle-class circles to have access to foreign goods. The upper-middle class in Latin America may also have foreign bank accounts and thus be protected from or even advantaged by continuous devaluation.

For a great many middle-income families, however, it is probably not an exaggeration to say that, just as in the case of households within the popular sector, 'the crisis represents, in the last analysis, a total restructuring of everything one has learned', of everything one was taught to expect.[13] Specific paths to advancement, clearly laid out within the culture of modernizing African and Latin American states – the value of education, the importance of obtaining government employment – have been closed or severely restricted. The status associated with technical, professional or bureaucratic pursuits is challenged not only by falling real income, but also by declining ability to fulfil one's professional obligations. As the infrastructure of hospitals, schools and other public institutions is weakened by lack of funds, doctors, nurses, teachers and other public servants cannot adequately provide the services expected from them; and their frustration, expressed in work stoppages, strikes and other forms of protest, assumes increasing (and often novel) political significance.

While a minority within the middle class thus may have a stake in the kind of society being forged during years of recession and adjustment, most middle-income people clearly do not constitute a support group within any alliance favouring continuation of adjustment programmes. Like established formal-sector businessmen without international ties (by whom many in the Latin American middle class are in fact employed), they are hurt by the current conjuncture. And the way they interpret the roots of their misfortune and devise a remedial strategy is likely to be a crucial element in the political arrangements that will be characteristic of particular Latin American and African societies in the 1990s.

Informalization and the working class
When added to the downward movement of incomes among middle-class sectors, the inordinately steep drop in income suffered by formal-sector workers over the past decade would seem sharply to reinforce the long-existing tendency for differences between life chances of the very rich and the average-income family in African and Latin American countries to widen. In Africa, the bargaining power of a relatively small industrial working class has been fundamentally weakened by the shrinking job market and consequent threat of unemployment, as well as by repressive measures, which close off avenues of collective action in defence of wages. In Latin America, the underlying dynamics restricting formal-sector efforts to protect wage levels are similar, although the greater strength of the labour movement in a number of Latin American countries has permitted some of the more skilled workers, in larger industries, to defend themselves better. Thus, while statistics presented earlier show wage differentials within the African working class to be narrowing under the impact of the crisis, as the relatively more skilled are hit hardest by recession, this is less the case for Latin America, where minimum-wage earners seem to be harder hit than workers with incomes above the minimum.

Although commentary of this kind could be utilized to reinforce the old argument that there is indeed a 'labour aristocracy' in Latin America, it is important to stress the fact that the level of real wages now in effect, even for favoured strata, is hardly high enough to lend credence to the concept of an aristocracy within the working class of the late 1980s. There is in fact little evidence supporting the contention that skilled workers currently define their interests differently from the majority of the working class, although they may bargain in Latin America within industry-specific institutions, which gives them somewhat greater negotiating strength.

On the contrary, recession and adjustment would seem to be homogenizing working-class interests, precisely because the crisis further diversifies the survival strategies of all wage earners, whether skilled or unskilled, and whether in formal or informal sectors. It has of course always been the case that households containing industrial workers of various kinds are likely also to include members engaging in other kinds of work, often in the so-called 'informal sector', and therefore to have very diverse interests. In Africa, the picture is further complicated by the frequency with which urban families maintain ties with rural communities and retain rights to land. This lack of total dependence by most industrial working-class families on industrial employment, and at times lack of complete dependence upon wages, has often affected the nature of their bargaining behaviour and of their political participation, as many studies of Third World trade unions have noted.

At present, however, there is a massive tendency for the working class to be informalized (as in fact there is also for the lower-middle class to find sources of income in the informal sector). Lines between lower-middle and working classes are further blurred, just as the concept of the 'working class' itself becomes extraordinarily imprecise. One finds a mass of lower-income families engaged in a very wide range of activities, some of which may provide opportunities for reconstructing an adequate livelihood, but most of which do not.

As figures cited earlier make clear, the ill-defined 'informal sector' now constitutes the most significant locus of indigenous entrepreneurial activity in many crisis-ridden Third World cities. There is a certain apparent promise for urban lower-income strata in this situation, to the extent that declining incomes throughout most of the salaried and wage-earning population encourage less consumption of the products of modern industry and a reversion to dealing with tradesmen and artisans. Thus the same forces that eliminate jobs for the relatively more skilled within the formal industrial sector simultaneously create them, at a lower level of technological sophistication and productivity, in the informal sector. Small industries are growing faster than any others. Nevertheless, the latter frequently have some difficulty taking full advantage of demand for their goods and services, for they themselves may be dependent upon access to goods produced in the modern capitalist sector and thus be unable to isolate themselves successfully from the crisis.

The growing 'informal sector' of course represents far more than an exclusively low-income survival strategy. It provides opportunities for survival and/or profit to capitalist industry, whether national or international, also shifting out of the formal labour market into domestic piece-work arrangements, which eliminate the payment of fixed overhead and legal labour benefits. It shelters large, vertically integrated commercial operations, frequently employing an army of street vendors. It contains an important financial sector. In a process which is parallelled in the developed industrial world, the informal sector has become a kind of catch-all unregulated market, merging into a subterranean economy, through which workers are linked to many other segments of society without obligatory reference to the laws or norms which have been publicly established and legally sanctioned to regulate economic relations among parties.

Repeasantization?

As unemployment and declining real wages in urban areas make survival there more difficult, many governments (and donors) would like to encourage the return of considerable numbers of people to the countryside, on the assumption that it is impossible to continue generating sufficient sources of sustenance in the cities, or to continue subsidizing survival there, and that means of subsistence are easier to obtain in rural areas. There is some indication that this kind of return migration is in fact occurring. In Mexico, for example, the number of those employed in the construction industry (always a principal source of employment for migrants from peasant villages) has declined markedly during the past five years, while the number of people registered as economically active in agriculture has risen. In Ghana, many urban dwellers seem to be returning to their villages to take up rights to cultivate the land, or simply to live with extended families. Surely, other cases of such return migration could be mentioned.

One should ask, however, whether a significant reversion to rural life is really an answer to the urban dilemma of the late 1980s in many parts of Latin America and Africa. Individuals and groups of kin may be moving from city to countryside in many areas, but there is still a simultaneous tendency for others to be migrating in the opposite direction. In many cases, resources in the countryside are simply not sufficient to provide a livelihood for a significant return flow of population; and in many (particularly in Latin America), the structure of land tenure, resting on private title, leaves no opening for the urban poor to engage in agriculture, except as wage labourers.

The survival of communal land tenure and traditional structures of kinship in Africa of course provides an extraordinary mechanism through which urban dwellers can in principle be reabsorbed in the countryside. The experience of over one million Ghanaian migrants, expelled from neighbouring countries, who returned to their villages without need for any special programme of resettlement, is a dramatic case in point. But communal lands are not always as fertile or community structures as resilient as in the West African tropics. In many parts of the continent over-population, erosion, and the scourge of warfare constitute significant limitations on the repeasantization of low-income city dwellers in the 1980s.

Advantage and disadvantage in rural areas

It is the intention of international financial institutions and donors, involved in setting the agenda of policy reform for indebted Third World governments, to orient the adjustment process toward support of agriculture, and particularly of peasant agriculture (although in practice there is a good deal of determination to promote larger commercial farming as well). In country after country, pricing and marketing policies have been altered in favour of agricultural producers, on the assumption that the crisis of the 1980s can be attributed to a considerable extent to previous official insistence on extracting cheap products from the countryside. Declining food production and falling volumes of export crops are seen to be related to the inability of agricultural producers to make a living at farming and to their consequent abandonment of production or withdrawal from the market. Because such an explanation has been elaborated by observers of African rural life, there is a tendency to emphasize the exploitative role of state marketing agencies, which have been especially important in the African context, and to insist upon the utility of encouraging private enterprise in the field of rural marketing.

The adjustment process of the 1980s is therefore associated, in Africa, with the stimulation of new forms of rural entrepreneurship, particularly in the food marketing sector. In a number of cases this constitutes little more than formal recognition of private commercial activities which were carried out previously in what has been called the 'parallel market' – disallowed by official marketing policy but thriving in fact in many parts of the country or areas of commerce beyond the power of the state to control. In other cases, however, it represents a new departure and creates new economic opportunities. The same can hardly be said for Latin American rural areas, in which private trade has long been dominant and tends to operate through the association of petty commerce with highly oligopolistic centres of private merchant capital.

Is agricultural production and/or productivity responding to pricing and other policy incentives in a way which suggests a positive impact of adjustment on small farmers? Although the question can be answered in the affirmative for countries such as Zimbabwe and Ghana, a negative reply would seem more generally in order. Devaluation, foreign exchange crises and the deterioration of physical infrastructure have made it extraordinarily difficult for most small cultivators to grow or market more, despite the nominal incentive held out by higher producer prices. Fertilizer has been scarce and inordinately costly; tractors and trucks break down and roads or railroads become more difficult to utilize. In one illustrative case, the lack of foreign exchange with which to purchase jute sacks was instrumental in the loss of over one million tons of grain, which could not be collected after harvest and therefore became not a credit but a debit against the account of the small farmers who had invested to produce it. Under such circumstances, higher producer prices lose significance.[14]

In addition, within Latin America and some regions of Africa, rural money-lenders and merchants form a solid wedge between the higher prices encouraged by government policy, on the one hand, and prices actually paid to the small producer in the field. Peasant families who live on credit extended them by patrons do not have the opportunity to question the price they receive for crops ultimately delivered to the latter.

Agricultural producers who may benefit from the current crisis, as the latter alters the parameters of economic relations in Latin American and African societies, are most likely to be those among the large and medium-sized capitalist farmers who are well enough organized to ensure control over their supply of inputs and who can offset the rapidly rising cost of such inputs by taking advantage of sinking levels of wages for agricultural labour; or small peasant producers who need virtually no credit or manufactured inputs, as is the case of cocoa and coffee growers in Ghana or Côte d'Ivoire, and who also are likely to be able to produce most of the food they need locally. In certain countries, transnational corporations once again emerge as prime examples of the first kind of enterprise, and some governments are, not surprisingly, interested in encouraging the expansion of foreign investment in agriculture. National entrepreneurs must be very well organized and receive strong support from the government in order to protect themselves from the financial uncertainties of investment in agriculture under the present circumstances.

The kinds of peasant communities that fall within the second category – enjoying good land and requiring few inputs, while producing adequate basic staples for family consumption without much need to rely on purchased foods – do not feel the impact of rising food prices.[15] But most villages in Latin America and many in Africa do not fit this pattern. In the extensive areas of Latin America where most of the rural population is landless, and lives by offering wage labour, rising grain prices – an inevitable concomitant of inflation and input bottle-necks, even in the absence of specific attempts on the part of the state to push prices upward – cause great hardship.

In sum, then, while the crisis is clearly reducing the gap that formerly existed between the monetary income of poorer strata in urban and rural areas – narrowing the advantage of the urban poor and, when the non-monetary subsistence income of some kinds of rural people is added into the calculation, perhaps sometimes eliminating or reversing urban advantage altogether – it is important to remember that by far the greatest number of rural households is also being impoverished by recession and adjustment. And low-income rural families cannot as easily attempt to remedy their situation through engaging in petty services and trade, unless they migrate.

Individual and collective reactions to crisis

Macro-economic trends thus seem to be redefining the parameters of livelihood in Latin American and African societies in various ways: reinforcing a tendency for international interests to be favoured over national ones, and for financial speculation to take priority over productive investment; encouraging entrepreneurship within the informal, rather than the formal, sector; decreasing the importance of national capitalist and working-class groups; enormously increasing the pool of labour engaged in petty services, trade and domestic manufacturing; challenging the ability of small farmers and peasants to engage in commercial agriculture.

Within this context people react, both individually and collectively, to emerging opportunities and threats, to protect their standard of living as well as their way of life. They may also take measures to protest against existing situations and engage in organized efforts to bring about change. It is important to examine these individual and collective strategies, not simply as efforts to survive the recession, but as patterns of behaviour that contribute to changing the overall structure of society and which furthermore have important political implications.

One can begin by thinking about the fact that the macro-economic environment associated with recession and adjustment imposes upon various kinds of people, located at different points within the overall economy of any country, certain necessary and inevitable kinds of economic behaviour. And although the latter may seem highly personalistic and defensive (strategies restricted to the most individualistic kinds of calculations made within the confines of each household) they in fact come to have broad social and political significance.

Thus the attempt to obtain foreign income through migration or remittances is an individualistic strategy, but its effect on local economies and societies is profound. The migration of professionals should perhaps especially be mentioned here, since their loss to more developed countries deprives less developed ones of a particularly scarce form of human capital.[16] Similarly, the upper- and middle-class practice of holding large foreign accounts (particularly in Latin America) eventually alters the parameters of economic opportunity in a way which affects the longer-term evolution of structures of opportunity. Even the attempt by middle-class families in Latin America to stave off impoverishment in times of rising inflation through liquidating assets and placing the proceeds in interest-earning bank accounts has important socio-political, as well as economic, implications. The fate of a large number of savers comes to be tied to high interest rates, and lowering the latter then becomes a significant political problem.

There are, in other words, a number of defensive strategies, made virtually mandatory by the form of the crisis itself, which constantly reinforce the international links and speculative elements inherent in the crisis and which may also alter the bases of political support for existing regimes. Other attempts by households to cope with the crisis have, when viewed from the perspective of the nation as a whole, a similar tendency to act against resolution of the crisis within the boundaries of present policy. From the point of view of a family faced with falling real income, for example, it is essential to send more members, including women and the very young, into the labour force; but from the vantage point of working people as a whole, that may well be a disastrous development.

The same might be said of engaging in corrupt practices or turning to crime as ways in which individuals can react to falling income and attempt to recuperate some lost ground. The rising crime rate in African and Latin American cities testifies to the importance of this option, as does the particularly virulent growth of activities associated with narcotic drugs. These are the only avenues of advancement or survival available to many people, but they are provided within a context of violence and illegality which undermines the most basic principles of civil society. In so doing, they too reinforce, rather than counteract, the disintegrative dynamics of the crisis.[17]

Corrupt and/or criminal activities are of course likely to be carried on not only by single individuals, engaged in a personalistic survival strategy, but also to be woven into social networks which form increasingly important institutions within the broader society. Thus while public institutions, charged with carrying out the normal activities of state and private sectors, may be weakened, other particularistic ones are simultaneously being reinforced. These are often based upon kinship, ethnic ties or varied forms of religious brotherhood. Their growing importance may well have negative implications for national integration, particularly in situations of ethnic or religious conflict.

At the same time, there is of course a potential for the crisis to encourage changes in social organization and political practice which contribute to the creation of a more participatory society in nations where exclusion for many groups has long been the rule. For example, the strengthening of ethnic or regional solidarity may in some cases be extremely salutary, if this protects vulnerable families and permits them a voice in politics. Similarly, the challenges thrown up by recession and adjustment lend momentum to other kinds of family and neighbourhood co-operation which go beyond simple 'survival strategies' and create centres of dialogue and mutual assistance within an inchoate civil society. In some cases, like neighbourhood soup kitchens, families draw together in co-operative efforts to reduce the cost of subsistence; in others, the neighbourhood presents collective demands to local authorities and may be further integrated into a hierarchy of federations or confederations with the capacity to make itself heard at the national or international level.[18]

Three characteristics of this growing tendency for local level co-operation among inhabitants of African and Latin American cities should perhaps be underlined. Neighbourhood associations tend above all to be concerned with questions of consumption, whether collective or individual; members are drawn together to protest against unacceptable living conditions, the elimination of subsidies on such public goods as utilities or transport, the lack of credit for housing, the sudden rise in food prices. They may be concerned about the environment. Their demands are not generally framed, however, around issues of employment and remuneration, that is, around conditions of production. And since this is the case, these organizations (growing remarkably in numbers over the course of the 1980s) are fundamentally involved in a dialogue with the state, not with private enterprise. The political implications of this dialogue are significant.[19]

Simultaneously, the kinds of civic organizations springing up in many urban areas of Latin America and Africa as a result of the crisis tend to involve a disproportionately large number of women, for the obvious reason that women are most likely to be concerned with difficulties arising in the sphere of consumption. Neighbourhood organizations are drawing women out of the isolation of the home and into organizations which must deal with the state, not necessarily because women were originally directly concerned with politics but because they were concerned with guaranteeing the future of their families. As one collection of essays on Latin American women put it, 'if the market and the state create ever more intolerable conditions within the private sphere, the domain of women, women will rightly emerge in the public sphere to denounce the situation and demand a solution'; and this implies significant new forms of political practice.[20]

Finally, it is important to note that although some civic associations of this kind become affiliated with a particular political party, the majority seem to prefer political independence and to exhibit noteworthy scepticism toward the established political structure. Neighbourhood organizations thus tend to fall outside the framework of traditional state and party channels, and to present a challenge to political systems set up along corporate lines.

Unwillingness to continue to operate within the framework of earlier political pacts is also reflected in the activities of many working class and peasant or farmers' organizations attempting to deal with the uncertainties of the 1980s. In fact, trade union confederations in a number of countries have mobilized massively to protest against the imposition of austerity programmes by unpopular governments, and have won concessions ranging from retraction of policies to a change of regime. In such activities, trade unions have been joined by a broad array of popular groups, at times including middle- as well as low-income urban organizations and peasant unions.[21] On the question of protecting more specific interests of their members in the workplace, however, it would seem that trade unions in Africa and Latin America have generally not been very successful over the course of the past decade, in large part because the threat of unemployment hangs over the head of all workers. There have been sporadic outbreaks of strike activity among industrial and transport workers, and workers in the service of state bureaucracies, as well as among professionals, in most Latin American and African countries; and in some cases these strikes have threatened to cripple the adjustment effort. But on the whole, unionized workers have bargained with management and have been willing to accept serious cuts in welfare without taking measures that might place their employment at risk.[22]

For a farming family, the equivalent of a strike is a retreat into subsistence, or reduction in the amount of marketed output. This may come as a result of a conscious decision to leave the market or as a consequence of insufficient opportunity to continue producing and marketing crops. Since there has been a tendency over the past decade or more for the marketed agricultural surplus to decline in many rural areas of Africa and Latin America, one may assume that there is also growing disaffection among the peasantry for the programmes of ruling political parties or coalitions. This in turn would imply the further weakening of local co-operative unions in Africa[23] and the creation of new forms of representation and/or solidarity in the Latin American countryside.

In relation to the latter, a number of different patterns seem to be emerging in the 1980s. Deteriorating livelihood in some parts of the Latin American countryside has led to the growth of guerrilla movements as well as the definition of territories under the control of drug traffickers. In these areas, the state has lost virtually all control.[24] In others, in contrast, the activities of military contingents impose state authority with an equal loss of options for local participation. In still others, new forms of independent peasant organization are bargaining seriously with the state and private enterprise, while specifically opting against affiliation with any political party. Like the urban civic associations, there is here an embryonic structure of interest groups aware of the advantages of playing one political party against another, rather than falling under the complete control of any one of them.[25]

Political implications of the crisis

It is obvious that recession and adjustment are seriously affecting the capacity of the great majority of African, Latin American and Caribbean states to establish stable parameters for economic activity and to invest. Faced with sharply declining public revenue, frequent balance of payments crises and the enormous burden of servicing the debt, many governments have over the past decade or more been unable to fulfil either their international or their internal commitments. Public services have declined in quality or simply disappeared; public works and infrastructure have deteriorated; public regulatory and administrative functions have been abandoned or sharply curtailed.

The trends toward internationalization and informalization which have characterized patterns of social change over the past several decades form part of the dynamics of state retrenchment, both contributing to and growing out of the declining capacity of public institutions. Governments that can no longer ensure a stable currency see even their efforts to adjust and reform the national economy falter in the face of massive speculative activities and capital flight. In a similar vein, the flow of migrants across borders in search of a better livelihood implies the creation of remittance economies which (like flight capital) cannot be taxed or even adequately quantified. The decline or collapse of much formal sector economic activity, and the massive turn to informal arrangements among both wealthy and poor, further weakens the tax base and the structure of public regulation and services.

In addition, the urgent need to maintain an inflow of foreign capital (in the form of grants, loans or foreign investment) and to renegotiate the terms of debt repayment, makes most African, Latin American and Caribbean governments particularly open to influence from lending institutions or donors – so much so in fact that the study of economic policy-making was often framed in the decade of the 1980s in terms of the "politics of conditionality". The policy initiative, in this context, is likely to arise outside national boundaries, although the ramifications of policy (including the reactions of internal groups) are managed by and directed toward the state.

The bases of support for the state are in turn inevitably affected by these processes, first because the ability of governments to protect and promote the interests of major sectors of society is constantly challenged and second because those interests are themselves changing as people devise new livelihood strategies. In countries ruled by extremely narrow cliques or by networks of territorially based strongmen, where a predatory style of governance prevails, political practice may be little altered. But in nations where the governing coalition includes workers, public sector employees, elements of the urban poor, perhaps a national agricultural and/or industrial élite – as well as those engaged in internal and external trade and finance – the existing structure of interest aggregation and compromise may well be shaken.

As employers, both of civil servants and workers in state-owned industries, most Latin American, Caribbean and African states have attempted, as we have seen, to avoid laying off employees even at the cost of drastically lowering per capita remuneration. At the same time, although deep cuts have been made in subsidies on basic foodstuffs and transport, which provide a relatively diffuse form of remuneration to a large urban clientele, an effort has also been made not to eliminate such subsidies completely. Nevertheless the drop in revenue associated with recession and adjustment implies such a clear decline in the ability of the state to provide for its support groups among urban lower- and middle-income strata that disaffection and protest are virtually inevitable. Sporadic but violent riots in a number of countries over the past few years bear witness to this problem.

Strains may also appear in relations with industrialists oriented toward the national market. In the course of adjustment, the capacity of the state to protect local, formal sector entrepreneurs producing goods for internal consumption is threatened: to the extent that it must open the internal economy to foreign imports, devalue and greatly restrict credit, a state dependent upon alliances with those entrepreneurs faces serious internal struggles. In such cases, either the local industrial sector is strong enough to force the government to resist international pressure, or it becomes disaffected and the government loses an additional element of political support.

Strains of this kind, implying an erosion of support for many states and a threat to the continuation of post-colonial or post-war patterns of alliances, are being managed in some countries with relative success. It is precisely the precarious nature of the balance which must be struck between all interests which makes much of the adjustment effort in such circumstances seem so contradictory and internally inconsistent. In other cases, however, a broader pattern of alliances seems to have given way to far narrower arrangements, in which states increasingly return to prototypical "neo-colonial" patterns characterized by the clear dominance of a foreign-trade-oriented or financial élite. And in still others, we witness the virtual disintegration of some national societies, as regional and ethnic conflict is spurred by declining standards of living and the weakening of already very fragile political pacts.

A critical issue which arises at this point concerns what is increasingly referred to as the conundrum of "governability". How are the wide range of conflicting interests associated with crisis and adjustment to be channelled and expressed within a stable political environment at a time when the legitimacy and efficacy of many states are being so thoroughly undermined? How can sufficient sense of co-operation and purpose be developed to permit an adequate collective response to the crisis?

The question can be answered in part by referring to the encouraging tendency just noted, for new forms of co-operation to emerge among many groups affected by the crisis and for these groups to remain outside what often have been rather clientelistic and corporate channels of interest representation in Latin American, African and Caribbean states. This is a development which can in principle contribute to the formation of a more democratic political practice, in which the interests of various groups are expressed in an open political arena.

This arena must, however, exist; and it must function well enough to process demands, aggregate interests and convert decisions into policy. In other words, there must be a functioning state, with capacity for dialogue and sufficient control over the economy to be able to allocate resources. With some frequency, however, one now finds situations in which states are either too narrowly based and restrictive to accommodate grass-roots demands or too weak to process them. In such conjunctures, innovative local level response to the crisis is shortcircuited. It may be supported by international donors or non-governmental organizations, but it cannot serve to strengthen a national project.

Faced with urgent and conflicting demands for assistance during hard times, and with a fundamentally weakened state, governments attempting to avoid a total collapse of public authority can opt for an authoritarian and repressive solution.[26] This was a pattern characteristic of much of Latin America during the first decade of economic crisis (as it was among a number of states confronted with depression in Central Europe) and it may become so again.[27]

It would seem, however, that the extent of reorganization of society during the recession may in fact make the imposition of discipline by force – discipline of a kind required to maintain a functioning national economy – increasingly difficult. The informalization of many societies, the tendency for much economic activity to go on without reference to governmental controls, the appearance of new kinds of solidarity which lie outside the traditional corporate structure, imply blockage of major avenues of social control.

Alternatively, the demands of various groups can be put forward, and strategies for change developed, within a framework of democracy. The advance of informalization and internationalization of the economy and the society, in company with extensive hardship imposed on most people by the crisis, nevertheless also implies enormous difficulties for transitions to more democratic models of relations between state and society.[28] Excessive fragmentation of interests, made worse by the crisis, may create virtually unmanageable pressure on the government, while institutions capable of deciding upon the distribution of gains and losses in public fora accountable to the majority of the voters are yet to be developed. History suggests that increasingly polarized societies in which growing numbers are pauperized, are enormously handicapped in the search for democracy.

Notes and References

1. Unless otherwise stated, data presented here are taken from various World Bank publications, principally the annual Development Reports. The terms of trade declined by approximately 4 to 5 per cent per annum over 1980–88, which translates into a loss in income of roughly 1 per cent per annum, given that exports and imports amount to about 20 per cent each of GDP.

2. Over the period 1960–82, 11 countries achieved an annual growth in per capita GDP in excess of 2.5 per cent, while 10 experienced a decline in per capita GDP. See Ghai, 1987.

3. For example, estimates of capital flight from the Sudan have been put between $14 to $60 billion for the period, 1977–78 to 1984–85 (Umbadda, 1989).

4. United Nations, 1988.

5. Some of the capital flight, to the extent that it takes the forms of over-invoicing imports and under-invoicing exports, is presumably already reflected in the figures on deterioration of terms of trade. But capital flight also takes many other forms, which constitute an additional source of loss of foreign exchange and savings for the economy.

6. Ghai, 1988; Jamal and Weeks, 1988; Jaspa, ILO, 1988.

7. For a detailed analysis as well as additional empirical material, see Ghai, 1988, on which this section is based.

8. Jaspa, ILO, 1988.

9. Jamal and Weeks, 1988; Ghai, 1988.

10. This section is based largely on García, Infante and Tokman, 1988.

11. For discussion of this point in the context of Mexico, see L. Mertens, 1986.

12. Sawyerr, 1988, p.22.

13. Feijoo, 1988.

14. For a discussion of adjustment-related problems with collecting a bumper harvest in Zambia, see Good, 1986.

15. See Posnansky, 1980, for a good description of a village situation in which adjustment has implied rising incomes.

16. For a study of the brain-drain from Africa to the United States, see Logan, 1987.

17. See Bagley, 1988, on Colombia; and Morales, 1986, on Peru.

18. The growth of popular organizations in Chile is discussed in Leiva and Petras, 1986. For Mexico, see Carr, 1986.

19. See Calderón and Dos Santos, 1987.

20. See Arizpe, 1987. The Mothers of the Plaza de Mayo constitute an important example of such practice. See Feijoo and Gogna, 1987.

21. For a good discussion of 'co-ordinating committees' which have organized a series of massive general protests in Mexico, see Carr, 1986.

22. On anti-government protest by teachers in the Côte d'ivoire, leading to widespread industrial action in 1987, see *New African*, March 1989, p. 35. For Nigeria, militancy among professional unions is discussed in Isamah, 1986.

23. Holmquist (1980) analyses the process of demobilization of semi-autonomous peasant organizations in Africa.

24. For a discussion of the Sendero Luminoso movement in Peru, see Morales, 1986.

25. The experience of independent peasant organizations in Mexico is discussed in Gordillo, 1987.

26. See Stepnan, 1985; Kaufman, 1985; Anyang' Nyong'o, 1987.
27. Concern for such a development in Africa has recently been expressed by Timothy Shaw, who concludes that many countries on the continent are 'ripe for repression' (Shaw, 1988: 319).
28. See Cardoso, 1988; Hansen, 1987; Kaufman, 1985.

Bibliography

Anyang' Nyong'o, Peter, (ed.) (1987) *Popular Struggles for Democracy in Africa*, United Nations University, Zed Books Ltd., London and New Jersey.

Arizpe, Lourdes, (1987) 'Prólogo' in Elizabeth Jelin (ed.) *Ciudadanía e identidad: Las mujeres en los movimientos sociales latinoamericanos*, Geneva, UNRISD.

Bagley, Bruce, (1988) 'Colombia and the War on Drugs', *Foreign Affairs*, Vol. 67, No. 1, Fall.

Calderón, Fernando and Mario Dos Santos, (1987) *Latinoamérica: Lo político y lo social en la crisis*, Buenos Aires: Consejo Latinoamericano de Ciencias Sociales.

Cardoso, Fernando Henrique, (1988) 'Olas chocando contra los arrecifes. El estado ante la perplejidad social', *David & Goliath*, Revista del Consejo Latinoamericano de Ciencias Sociales, Vol. XVIII, No. 53, August-September.

Carr, Barry, (ed.) (1986) *The Mexican Left, the Popular Movements and the Politics of Austerity*, San Diego, Center for U.S.–Mexican Studies.

Chazan, Naomi and Timothy Shaw, (1988) *Coping with Africa's Food Crisis*, Boulder, Lynne Rienner Publishers.

Feijoo, María del Carmen, (1988) ¿*Y ahora que? La crisis como ruptura de la lógica cotidiana de los sectores populares*, Buenos Aires, INDEC, Documento de Trabajo No. 4, April.

—— and Mónica Gogna, (1987) 'Las mujeres en la transición a la democracia', in Elizabeth Jelin, *Ciudadanía e identidad: Las mujeres en los movimientos sociales latinoamericanos*, Geneva, UNRISD.

García, A., R. Infante and V. Tokman, (1988) 'Meeting the Social Debt', Roundtable on Human Development: Goals and Strategies for the Year 2000, Amman, Jordan, 3-5 September.

Ghai, Dharam, (1987) 'Successes and Failures in Economic Growth in Sub-Saharan Africa: 1960–82' in L. Emmerij (ed.), *Development Policies and the Crisis of the Eighties* OECD, Paris.

—— (1988) *Economic Growth, Structural Change and Labour Absorption in Africa: 1960–85*, Discussion paper series, UNRISD, Geneva.

Good, Kenneth, (1986) 'The Reproduction of Weakness in the State and Agriculture: The Zambian Experience', *African Affairs*, Vol. 85, No. 337.

Gordillo, Gustavo, (1987) *Campesinos al asalto del cielo*, Mexico City, Siglo XXI.

Hansen, Emmanuel, (1987) 'The State and Popular Struggles in Ghana' in Peter Anyang (ed.) *Popular Struggles for Democracy in Africa*, United Nations University, Zed Books Ltd., London and New Jersey.

Holmquist, Frank (1980) 'Defending Peasant Political Space in Independent Africa', *Canadian Journal of African Studies*, Vol. 14, No. 1.

Isamah, Austin, (1986) 'Professional Unionism in Nigeria', *Indian Journal of Industrial Relations*, Vol. 21, No. 4, April.

Jamal, V. and J. Weeks, (1988) 'The Vanishing Rural-Urban Gap in Sub-Saharan

Africa', *International Labour Review*, Vol. 127, No. 3.

Jaspa, ILO, (1988) *African Employment Report, 1980*, Addis Ababa.

Jelin, Elizabeth, (ed.) 1987 *Ciudadanía e identidad: Las mujeres en los movimientos sociales latinoamericanos*, Geneva, UNRISD.

Kaufman, Robert, (1985) 'Democratic and Authoritarian Responses to the Debt Issue: Argentina, Brazil, Mexico', *International Organization*, Vol. 39, No. 3, Summer.

Kowarick, Lúcio, (ed.) (1988) *As lutas sociais e a cidade*, São Paulo, Paz e Terra-UNRISD-CEDEC.

Leiva, Fernando Ignacio and James Petras, (1986) 'Chile's Poor in the Struggle for Democracy', *Latin American Perspectives*, Vol. 13, No. 4, Fall.

Logan, Bernard, (1987) 'The Reverse Transfer of Technology from Sub-Saharan Africa to the United States', *Journal of Modern African Studies*, Vol. 25, No. 4.

Mertens, L, (1987) *Employment and Stabilisation in Mexico*, Geneva, International Labour Organisation, WEP Working Paper No. 10.

Morales, Edmundo, (1986) 'Coca, Cocaine Economy and Social Change in the Andes of Peru', *Economic Development and Cultural Change*, Vol. 35, No. 1, October.

Posnansky, Merrick, (1980) 'How Ghana's Crisis Affects a Village', *West Africa*, 1 December.

Sandbrook, Richard, with Judith Baker, (1985) *The Politics of Africa's Economic Stagnation*, Cambridge University Press, Cambridge.

Sawyerr Akilagpa, (1988) 'The Politics of Adjustment Policies', Economic Commission for Africa, Addis Ababa, Document ECA/ICHD/88/29, Khartoum, Sudan, 5-8 March.

Shaw, Timothy, (1988) 'State of Crisis: International Constraints, Contradictions and Capitalism', in Donald Rothchild and Naomi Chazan, *The Precarious Balance*, Westview Press, Boulder.

Stepan, Alfred, (1985) 'State Power and the Strength of Civil Society in the Southern Cone of Latin America', in Peter Evans, et al, *Bringing the State Back In*, Cambridge, Cambridge University Press.

Tokman, V, (1986) 'Adjustment and Employment in Latin America: The Current Challenge', *International Labour Review*, Vol. 125, No. 5, September–October.

Umbadda, S, (1989) 'Economic Crisis in the Sudan: Impact and Response', paper presented to the ISER-UNRISD Conference on Economic Crisis and Third World Countries: Impact and Response, Kingston, Jamaica, 3-6 April.

United Nations, (1988) *Financing Africa's Recovery*, New York.

3. The Economic Crisis and the Commonwealth Caribbean: Impact and Response

Clive Thomas

Introduction

In this chapter's examination of the impact and response of the Commonwealth Caribbean (CC)[1] to the economic crisis, which since the late 1970s, and more especially the 1980s, has been affecting a number of Third World Countries, the CC is treated as a sub-set of the larger Caribbean. Justification for this is based on two considerations: manageability and relative cohesion. The Caribbean is the world's most balkanized region, and although the CC is only a fraction of its size, it nevertheless comprises 12 countries of different sizes and historical experiences, with a combined GNP in excess of US$13 billion and a total population of 5.7 million. As Table 3.1 shows, these countries range in size from classic mini-states with population, land area, and GNP sizes below 100,000 persons, 300 square kilometres, and US$100 million respectively, to countries with populations exceeding one million and market size exceeding US$2.5 billion for small countries (Jamaica and Trinidad and Tobago), and relatively large land areas, for example, Guyana, approximately 215,000 square kilometres. Similarly, the level of per capita GNP varies from a low of under US$400 to a high in excess of US$10,000. To compress these experiences in a meaningful way in the space available is difficult, and for the larger area impossible without resort to caricature and generalization. Additionally, while the larger region shares many historical similarities, which have encouraged notions of regional co-operation, at present only in the CC, by the formation of a common market structure (CARICOM), have concrete and substantial forms of co-operation emerged. Despite the clear focus of the paper, however, on certain important issues, reference will be made to the wider region.

The following pages first examine the application and meaning of the term crisis in the region, and propose a characterization, which is fleshed out in the next two sections. Regional responses are then examined, and a conclusion follows.

Crisis: meaning and application

The dislocations that followed the end of the long boom in the global economy in the mid-1970s have brought the term crisis into wide usage in the Caribbean. Unsurprisingly, a wide variety of meanings have become attached to this term, although they all capture the sense of an unstable period in which critical occurrences are symptomatic. One set of interpretations accepts the view current in many other Third World countries, that the crisis is principally located in the institutional, ideological and leadership structures of the region and is principally focused in the post-colonial state.[2] Because of their small size, limited resources and a difficult international environment, nowhere in the Caribbean are the local states capable of sustaining 'sovereignty'. They are, therefore, constantly 'beleaguered or besieged'. They are also 'overloaded' and unable to deliver basic goods to their constituencies, to provide the entrepreneurial drive required to survive in a fiercely competitive world, and to manage the economy and society efficiently. Finally, like their colonial predecessor they remain 'set apart' from the rest of the society, engaged at best in ritual imitation of Westminister-type parliamentary forms.

Another interpretation elevates the region's geo-strategic location to its most important aspect. The crisis is then portrayed as the consequence of the interplay of East–West struggles for global hegemony. On the right, radical nationalism and popular manifestation against worsening conditions are therefore reduced to leftist conspiracies; while on the left pragmatic policies, calls for non-alignment and mutual respect in an inter-American system, are dismissed as neo-colonial options.

A third set of views – the adjustment theorists – locates the crisis in the persistent macro-economic imbalances which have emerged since the late 1970s. Several countries of the Caribbean are witnessing their deepest and longest recession since the 1930s. In the CC as a whole real growth rates have been in decline and per capita real income is today no higher than in the mid-1970s, although the incidence of this is very uneven.

For example, in one territory, Guyana, the figure is estimated to be as much as 50 per cent lower, while in some of the OECS states (the Leeward and Windward Islands) marginal increases have occurred. Investment per worker has declined to levels far below 1970 (see Table 3.2). The combined balance-of-payments deficit of the area currently averages close to US$2 billion or about one-sixth of its GDP. Total external indebtedness currently stands at US$9 billion. The incidence of this is also uneven and in such places as Guyana, Antigua and Jamaica, the per capita debt (at about US$2,000) is among the highest in the world. Unemployment ranges between 12 and 30 per cent. In recent years macro-economic imbalances have been most acute in Guyana and in Trinidad and Tobago, where there have been several currency devaluations, double digit inflation exists, capital flight, monetary substitution and the emergence of strong black-markets for goods and foreign exchange prevail.

A fourth set of views is largely empiricist and details the growing list of adverse socio-economic manifestations in the region. In addition to macro-economic imbalances and several failed stabilization programmes the list would include:

- the 'scissors squeeze' on land, brought about by the disintegration of domestic food systems and difficulties with traditional export crops, on the one hand, and the rapid rise of transnationals' (TNCs) agro-processing industries based on imported inputs, on the other:

- a worsening distribution of income, wealth, and access to productive resources, especially in those countries where structural adjustment policies have been introduced; massive, persistent and increasing unemployment and growing under-employment;

- woefully inadequate social services, especially social security provisions for the unemployed, aged and infirm;

- high rates of emigration among skilled workers; the growth of huge underground/parallel/informal sectors, which divert entrepreneurial talent and allocate much of the available foreign exchange to their own priorities;

- increased corruption, nepotism and clientism, evident in the heavy penetration of drug dealers and traffickers into the highest political circles in the Bahamas, Jamaica, Turks and Caicos, the Cayman Islands, Barbados, St Kitts-Nevis and Trinidad-Tobago, to name a few, and in the critical roles they play in mobilizing productive factors;

- massive flight of capital and high turnover of assets in the region;

- a weakened trade union movement in the face of increasing unemployment, declining living standards and widespread poverty;

- the penetration of foreign media, values and culture into the region, symbolized by the 'satellite dish' culture found in every island, no matter how small;

- the systematization of repression and political murder as techniques of social control;

- the institutionalization of fraudulent and rigged elections in some countries; accelerated foreign control of domestic resources, despite the localization and nationalization programmes pursued by several governments;

- the impact of the war in Nicaragua and the invasion of Grenada, seen particularly in the increasing militarization of the region; the failure of the Caribbean 'right' and the much touted private sector to solve the problems of poverty and powerlessness; the equal failure of the 'left' to adjust to its past record of 'political failure';

- intensified environmental degradation, especially of the sea, inland waterways and the natural vegetation; and

- the massive depletion in several countries of the social infrastructure (especially internal transport and power supplies). These latter are reflected in the decline in investment per worker shown in Table 3.2 and reduced capital inflows as shown in Table 3.3

Each of these interpretations yields important insights; but they remain limited, as the analysis focuses on either selected areas (for example the state), remains at a pragmatic level (the adjustment theorists), or cites empirical manifestations, denying or ignoring any deeper meanings. The challenge therefore remains of creating some scientific order out of these myriad details. My own judgement is that in the CC there exist, with varying territorial incidences, four dimensions to the crisis, which operate at three distinct levels of intensity. The causes of the crisis and their related impact are identifiable in two general areas, acting in symbiosis. The four dimensions to the crisis are:

1. The persistence of acute macro-economic imbalances which cannot now be denied, and more importantly show, in their persistence, no automatic tendency to 'disappear' of their own accord, as it was initially argued.

2. A rupture of the inherited economic structures. This is of a more long-term and secular origin, as it involves in a fundamental way, all the major sectors of the economy.

3. A systemic disorder, that is, a wider crisis of society, involving not only its eocnomic structure, but all major social spheres.

4. A historic conjuncture in which crisis conditions are located not only in the regional economies but, simultaneously, in the world system.

These four dimensions operate at three distinct levels of intensity, all of which may not be present in all the economies at all times. First, in all the regional economies a permanent or on-going crisis condition exists, which is inherent to the socio-economic structures and their characteristic historical forms and motion. This is the familiar crisis of underdevelopment. Secondly, there are periodic crises, which occur when the process of accumulation is interrupted, declines in real profitability over several major sectors emerge, contraction of markets, especially overseas ones, takes place and when the disproportions endemic to the structures of production and internal demand (needs) become acute. The most dramatic manifestations of the periodic crisis are to be found in the acute monetary imbalances that develop among various spending units. These crises may be precipitated by either internal or external events, but more usually the latter.

From time to time, the convergence of internal and external processes creates the possibility (and only the possibility) of a qualitatively deeper entrenchment of the old order, on the one hand, or of a radical (even revolutionary) rupture with the past, on the other. These conjunctures form the most intense periods of crisis and should be classed as periods of general crisis. The best known examples of these in the region's history are the collapse of slavery in the 1830s, the collapse of the indenture system during World War I, and the widespread rebellions against the colonial order in the 1930s. In certain territories, the current crisis operates at all three levels of intensity. It should, however, be stressed that since social advance is not a unilinear process there should be no expectation that this general crisis would yield qualitative social advances as it has done in the past. It may result merely in the reaffirmation or worsening of the old order.

Generally, the more immediate causes of the crisis are located in the changes in the international economy. The root causes, however, are to be found internally, as these stem from the historical stage of the development of the economies. The latter is, in the main, responsible for the internal intensification of the difficulties precipitated by changes in the international economy, and it is here that the impact of the economic crisis is most dramatically revealed.

The foregoing typology shows that the crisis is not a simple transitory economic phenomenon. It is rooted in internal and external circumstances whose continuous interaction causes both its intensification at the economic level and a widening to other spheres of social life. The crisis therefore is as much social, political, cultural, institutional, and psychological, as it is economic. Clearly a systemic disorder of this nature rules out the possibility of a solution by way of a return to the previous models of social development. Restructuring of the economy, as well as a fundamental reconstitution of the bases of social life, are requirements for any enduring solutions.

The international aspect

The immediate causes of the acute form of crisis reside in three aspects of the international system: the changing character of the international division of labour; related changes in international trade, aid, and preferences directly applicable to the region; and, the specific geo-strategic location of the region.

The international division of labour
As a general rule, the region benefited greatly from the long upswing of global economic activity which lasted until the mid-1970s. The boom facilitated a significant expansion of public services; the rapid growth of state property in commercial productive sectors such as mining, tourism and agriculture; an enhanced public commitment to the provision of basic needs for the population at large; and sustained efforts to restructure the inherited colonial economy, mainly through the expansion of services (finance and tourism) and the promotion of import-substitution in manufacturing and agriculture. At the same time, foreign investment diversified into new mineral (alumina) and agricultural (bananas) exports. Since the 1980s, however, despite some exceptional occurrences, global growth has been lower than in the previous historical period, even for the OECD countries now boasting a seventh year of positive growth. The incidence of this slower growth has fallen particularly heavily on the majority of Third World countries and the majority of the population in the countries affected, as it has meant a virtual halt to public sector expansion and the provision of basic goods, along with the abandonment of the post-World War II state-led process of economic restructuring.

In analysing this development, most theorists concentrate on the slower growth of the world economy, ignoring the full implications of the seven year record of continuous growth in the OECD countries. They project the world system as being in a structurual crisis long in the making. Space precludes any extended discussion of this issue. Elsewhere I have argued that the slower growth is not the major feature of the present period, and that instead, greater emphasis should be laid on the fact that:

> the 1970s marked the emergence of a *fundamental disjuncture* in the development of the capitalist world economy. The process of restructuring which is taking place is in effect a *process of transition* to a qualitatively different world economy . . . epic changes [are occurring] no less significant or revolutionary in their implications than those [of the] First Industrial Revolution.[3]

Reduced to its barest essentials this thesis leads to the view that the crisis is being fuelled by fundamental changes in the global division of labour. For the present purposes the following aspects of this are highlighted:

1. Technical changes in the areas of robotics, information and transport are leading to losses in the region's wage cost-location-propinquity advantages in relation to the US-Canadian market.

2. The radical decrease in the raw material intensity of global economic activity, together with rapid advances in new materials technology, producing sustained adverse market pressures on the region's major raw material exports: oil, sugar and bauxite-alumina.

3. Advances in new processes, which produce traditional products from very different raw material bases, are affecting several sectors, in particular sugar, which is being rapidly replaced by high fructose syrups in North American markets.[4]

4. Unprecedented advances in the flexibility of production processes combined with rapidly shifting market preferences are reducing the region's propinquity advantages in textile exports (which is its leading manufacturing export) as North American firms are seeking to reduce lead times by re-locating their production at home where styles and fashions are changing at breakneck speed.

5. Specifically, the technical advances in agriculture threaten the environmentally specific advantages of the area, as increasingly tropical products are being produced in non-tropical areas. This has affected traditional exports and threatens also the non-traditional exports such as ornamentals and exotic fruits, which are emphasized at present.

6. The region's large off-shore finance industry faces a structural challenge from advances in information management, the marketing of financial instruments, the emergence of 23-hour financial markets stretching across the globe, and improved white-collar crime detection methods in the USA.

7. The impact of technical changes in the cost of travel has already reduced the region's propinquity advantages *vis-à-vis* the North American market.

8. Finally, the generalized impact of the items listed above and others too numerous to mention here has fundamentally altered global supply and demand balances, leading to sustained adverse price pressures on the region's exportables.

Changes in international economic relations

Three areas of changing international economic relations have been making inputs to the crisis in the region even though, as we shall see later, some of these changes have been designed as solutions. The areas referred to are: export preferences afforded to the region; the restructuring of global economic relations now underway; and changes in the tax, financing and "white collar" crime policies in the United States.

Export preferences: In a world of high-profile deregulation and free market initiatives, the CC enjoys, and has been recently afforded, more export preference than any other region of the world. In addition to the Generalized System of Preferences, the region enjoys preferences from the USA under the Caribbean Basin Initiative (CBI) which came into force in 1984, its 'super-807' status in US tariff regulations, and the related Puerto Rican 'twin-plant' scheme for the use of 'Section 936 funds'; the Lomé Convention with the European Community (EC); and the Canada-Caribbean Free Trade Arrangement (Caribcan).

Despite these, the region's dynamic growth of exports has been less than either that of the world as a whole or other developing countries as a group. The reasons are to be found in the nature of the preferences and the structures of the region's economy. As an example of the former, the CBI's duty-free entry to the US market is riddled with exceptions, which are important to the region's export manufacturing thrust (for example, textiles and footwear). Also, duty-free access for some commodities (1,300 products or seven per cent of existing regional exports) coexist with duty-free access for 60 per cent of the region's exports before the CBI, and reduced market access for traditional exports (for example, sugar). As an example of the latter, the region's lack of a basic materials sector or a vibrant entrepreneurial class makes it difficult to secure the domestic value component to enable the products to be afforded enhanced preferential status.

Restructuring of global economic relations: Two factors in the present crisis are: the proliferation of segmented trade circuits in external markets of importance to the region; and paradoxically, the global thrust in favour of freer markets. Of special significance in the former case are the recent USA–Canada free-trade agreement and the proposed unification of the European Community's market in 1992. These developments have justifiably created much uncertainty and concern, as both have the potential either for destroying the region's external trade or expanding it. Two examples of the former are the threats posed by experienced Asian and Latin American immigrant communities in Canada displacing the region's textile exports to the US, and other countries (for example, Spain and the Dominican Republic) promoting trade displacing activities. The potential for trade creation of course resides in the region's preferential access being widened to larger and, hopefully, more dynamic markets.

Proposed changes in international financial and trade regulations increasingly favour freer trade. This thrust, if it materializes, will eventually undermine all preferential systems. This has created reservations in the minds of investors hoping to build on the region's exceptional access to preferences. Additionally, in the case of GATT, preoccupation with services, intellectual property and agriculture poses particular hazards to the region.

Other policy changes in the USA: Several changes in US fiscal, financial, and crime regulatory policies underlie the external origins of the region's crisis. For example, the use of 936 funds is subject to finalization of tax information exchange agreements with the US. For a region whose off-shore financial industry has grown up under the dubious advantages of 'no-questions asked secrecy', this is a development of some concern. Similarly, the exemption from taxation of interest earnings on non-resident deposits held in the US has considerably reduced the financial advantages of locating off-shore deposits in the region's financial havens and has, in fact, encouraged capital flight by local residents. The frequent use of the region's ports as transit stops for drugs going to the US has already led to the imposition of large fines on aircraft and ship owners ferrying regional exports. This has disrupted external trade, and some companies have indicated they are considering withdrawing their services from the region.

The coming into force of these regulations in the US stems from two considerations. The need for the authorities to minimize tax evasion and tax avoidance, if only because of the large fiscal deficit, and the pressures on them from citizens' groups to curtail the drug trade and its related financial laundering. There are therefore almost inexorable political forces behind these regulations and when it is considered that the drug trade, although unrecorded, is probably the region's main foreign exchange earner, and that secrecy is the life-blood of the region's off-shore financial industry, the implications of this for the crisis are quite evident.

The geo-strategic context

Several important issues fall under this heading; space again permits only a very brief indication of some of these. The frequent designation of the region as the 'backyard' of the USA, or its 'third frontier', testifies to its geo-strategic importance in a divided world. There is little doubt that much of the global tension affects the region. This has been significantly aided by the propensity of political leaders of all sides, in defiance of the small size of their countries, to propel themselves to leading positions on the world stage of contesting ideologies and propaganda. Without gainsaying the internal mobilizing appeal of these stances, when a significant gap emerges between the real capacity of states to intervene on the world stage and the propaganda posture of its leadership, this invariably facilitates the transmission of conflicts at the international level to the local society.

There are other important considerations. One is the traditional links of the European and American powers to the region's traditional élites, and the almost reflex hostility these generate in response to populist, nationalist, reformist, and revolutionary social movements. This has made the search to develop an authentic inter-Caribbean system, and paradigms of development alternative to those of the North, especially difficult. While command of force is the ultimate sanction of the North's hegemony in the region, 'persuasion' is its most widely used instrument. This has been effective, as many élites in the area have 'internalized' their ideological constructs, resulting in a situation in which the articulation of the region's interest, its conception of the crisis, and solutions so far attempted derive their legitimacy, in the main, from the extent to which they are coincident with those of the North.

The internal roots of crisis

The root causes of the crisis, and therefore its major impact, are located in the internal structures of these societies. This section concentrates on four principal areas: changes in the structures of production; fundamental internal and external macro-economic disequilibria; changes in the social structure; and institutional tensions and conflict, especially as they pertain to the state.

Production changes

Despite rapid growth, by the mid-1970s certain features of the region's production structure stood out: a significant export commodity concentration in a few markets of unprocessed and semi-processed primary crops and minerals (sugar, cocoa, coffee, bananas, rice, bauxite-alumina, and petroleum), which in a few countries were vulnerable to cyclical swings and product cycle changes. The colonial legacy of foreign ownership in these sectors, however, was by then significantly reduced, mainly through localization policies in the three leading commodity exports; sugar, bauxite-alumina, and petroleum. These were also extended to the services sector, especially finance and tourism. At the same time, most of the wage-goods consumed (food, clothing and building materials) were imported.

By the mid-1970s too, a manufacturing sector geared towards import replacement, very much reliant on fiscal subsidies, and employing rudimentary technologies for the transformation of imported inputs had been created at considerable social cost. This sector was characterized by limited linkages with other sectors.

A significant services sector had by then been brought into existence: off-shore financial havens, 'convenience flag' shipping, and tourism. This sector was based on a package of fiscal incentives designed to encourage overseas capital and to exploit the advantages of the region's closeness to the US.

In sum, it might be said that a cross-sectional view of the region's production structure continued to display many of the heterogeneous and multi-structured production forms of the colonial period. At one end of the scale large state enterprises and branch firms of TNCs could be found, and at the other, a complex mixture of medium, small-scale, and micro-enterprises of a 'backyard-type'. The rural economy was no different in this regard. Dynamically, this production structure showed a form of motion in which the region continued to produce what it did not consume, and to consume what it did not produce.

Since then, under the impetus of external and internal considerations the region has witnessed the decline and rise of certain sectors; reflecting both the impact of the crisis as well as a source of its fuel. Leading the decline have been the traditional export agriculture and mineral exports, and domestic food supplies. Thus, the volume of the regional sugar exports in 1988 at about half-a-million tons was less than half the total of the early 1970s. The alumina plants in Guyana have been closed for the past several years, while the volume of its bauxite exports in 1988 was less than half that of earlier peak periods. Between 1980 and 1986, the value of Trinidad and Tobago's petroleum exports was halved. Meanwhile, the region has moved into food deficit, and currently imports about US$1.3 billion-worth of food, that is about one-tenth of its gross national expenditure. At the same time, manufacturing import-substitution based on local, and latterly regional markets, has more or less exhausted itself, while under budgetary pressures the social and economic infrastructure of many of the territories has declined.

Important elements in the above have been the decline in investment per worker (see Table 3.2) and the related fall in official capital inflows, from US$1.3 billion in 1981 to US$0.4 billion in 1986 (see Table 3.3). Indeed, by 1986 officially recorded outflows from the region in the form of debt repayments exceeded inflows by US$97 million. Traditionally, official aid donors have been the major source of finance for the region's infrastructural capital works. The rationale has been that the dis-economies of small-scale combined with the level of fiscal burden already attained do not make the local provision of this capital stock feasible. The result is that, uncharacteristically for a developing region, the bulk of its external debt (about two-thirds) is due to bilateral or multilateral official agencies and only one-third is due to private commercial lenders.

On the expansion side there has been a growth in services, especially tourism and finance. Tourism receipts in the CC, at over US$2.5 billion in 1987, were more than three times the value received in 1977, and the countries whose tourist sectors have grown the fastest, Antigua-Barbuda and Belize, have had the highest growth rates; this pattern is also true for the wider Caribbean area. Over the last few years too, there has been a significant growth in the region's export processing zones (EPZs) closely linked to the export preferences discussed above. The leading commodities in this sector are textiles, electronic equipment, and pharmaceuticals; but in very recent times much emphasis has been placed on the stimulation of 'non-traditional' agricultural products, mainly ornamentals, exotic fruit, and 'winter' vegetables for North American markets. Certain domestic service sectors have also expanded, the most notable of these being the provision of 'security' services, underscoring the salience of the many social problems thrown up by the crisis. Finally, mention must be made of the rapid expansion of the informal sector. If this sector is defined to include illegal activities then, in several countries, it would be either the principal source of foreign exchange earnings, the major outlet for 'entrepreneurial drive', the major locus of capital flight and monetary substitution as well as the final arbiter of the 'ruling' foreign exchange rate. Additionally, the informal sector has supported the spread of runaway commercialism, consumerism, and the 'get-rich-quick-at-any-cost' outlook which, many lament, now characterize economic life in the region.

Fundamental macro-economic disequilibria

As we have already indicated, high per capita external debt, double digit inflation, fiscal deficits, excess domestic liquidity, devaluation, capital flight, monetary substitution, black-markets for foreign currency and goods, unemployment, and persistent balance-of-payments disequilibria, all characterize several economies of the region. While these fundamental disequilibria have been precipitated by changes in the international division of labour, they have also been exacerbated by mismanagement of several economies, the evidence of which now abounds. The stablization-adjustment process has been protracted and riddled with false starts. The conflicts which they have generated have produced intense popular struggles over the choice of options in stabilization-adjustment programmes and how their social cost may best be minimized and the burdens equitably distributed. Because the region's traditional élites were strategically placed to appropriate for their use much of the earlier benefits of the capital inflows, the question has now arisen as to how legitimate it is for them to seek a 'socialization' of these costs and the placement of disproportionate burdens on the disadvantaged. The consequent struggle for economic shares has aided the intensification of the crisis.

Changes in the social structure

While of immense importance to the determination of the economic crisis the issues under this heading are very numerous. Space, however, permits only a serial listing of some of these issues accompanied by very brief annotations.

1. Development of the region's manufacturing sector was linked to the creation of a Ricardian class of dynamic capitalists, which was expected to lead not only the development of the sector and indeed the country at large, but provide the solution to the permanent or ongoing crisis conditions associated with underdevelopment. This has not occurred, and much of the crisis can be attributed to the failure of this enterprise. Very similar to the former absentee planter class that dominated these economies in the 18th century, the majority of members of the region's business class currently hold dual citizenship and

are imbued with a 'dual vision' based on dual loyalties and twin opportunities. Furthermore, as a class, it has displayed serious limitations in two areas, which have in fact been the traditional strong points of a vibrant capitalist class. Its leading members' attitude to economic affairs is not one that sees in economic crisis the virtue of the constant revolutionizing of their means of production, nor is there a great willingness to embrace socio-political reform as a response to economic crisis.

2. In the rural areas, landlordism continues to be strong and resistant to efforts at productive reorganization and, as a result, the traditional weakness of the region's small farming community has worsened, as is evidenced from the limited land distribution figures that are available, the collapse of the domestic food system alluded to earlier, as well as the decline of the more traditional export agriculture. Lacking redress, many have left the land to swell the ranks of the urban unemployed, or to seek migration overseas.[5]

3. Unemployment, which traditionally has been large, has been made more acute by the effects of various stabilization programmes.

4. The growth of the state property sector in agriculture, public services, and heavy export products has created new strata of state employees at all levels of the production process. In some instances economic crisis and the pressure on wages have consolidated sentiment against the state, which as the 'common employer' becomes the 'common enemy'. As a result the synergy between industrial conflict and political conflict, between workers and the state, is strengthened. This is very often pivotal in the generalization of the production crisis to the political affairs of the society.[6]

5. Rapid promotion of growth, and the social pressures created by this were greatly eased by the availability of mass migration outlets in the early 1950s and 1960s. For the 1980s, this 'relief' has not been available, and this has made the reduction in growth rates all the more severe.

6. Stabilization policies pursued in the region have led to the marginalization of new sectors of the working people; a good example being state employees and other fixed income recipients who, in previous historical periods, were the most 'secure' sections of the employed. This new development of the 1980s is a drastic reordering of social priorities and has added much to the social discontent. If we take into account also the decline in the availability of social programmes for the needy, we are faced with all the classic elements that exacerbate economic decline.

7. Finally, the stress of events in the 1980s has probably halted improvements in ethnic relations. This is evident in the apparent revival of Afro-Indian economic and political 'competition' in Guyana and in Trinidad and Tobago. In other instances, there has been some reconstitution of minority ethnic élites at the apex of the economic system. There has been on the whole some considerable reinforcement of the nexuses between colour, wealth, and power that have bedevilled the region for much of its history.

Institutions

Much of the instability of the 1980s is attributable to certain institutional dynamics, particularly in regard to the state. Starting as far back as World War II, CC states, some not yet independent, had become the leading force in economic development. Despite current policies of divestment and privatization, this is still the case. The 'retreat' of the state in the region, which is said to characterize numerous Third World societies, is limited and far more apparent than real. Nevertheless, there is a need at this juncture for a restructuring of the state–society relation. The more important aspects of this dilemma are represented in the following:

1. Coincident with the economic downturn there has been a decline in the fiscal capacity of several states. Internally, slow growth has led to falling revenues while social pressures to deliver basic goods have intensified. Externally, high debt payments, reduced capital inflows, and structures of productions which are highly import-intensive have created serious foreign exchange cash flow difficulties.

2. Recent stablization programmes, with their cuts in public services, removal of subsidies and price controls, devaluation, rising import prices, and so on, have generated acute social conflicts. This is linked to the 'retreat' of the state from its role as guarantor and provider of basic needs, reinforcing the 'besieged' and beleagured atmosphere in which these states operate.

3. The crisis is affected by the 'creeping privatization of the state', a phenomenon evident in many other Third World countries and declining real income has forced state employees into 'other economic activities' while remaining in state employment. While some activities are 'legal', trading on their own time, for example, a lot has been 'illegal', for example, selling 'favours', the 'use' of state facilities, and state property.

4. The factors above have combined with the abandonment, and in some instances even reversal, of efforts to make these states more participatory. There is a noticeable tendency towards authoritarianism, alienation, and cynicism in public life. This has intensified the adverse effects of economic decline, threatening the very foundations of civic relations in some territories.

In addition to the state, other institutional relations are important to the crisis. One of these is the declining effectiveness of trade unions brought about by increased unemployment, the increasing shift to informalization and self-employment, the decline of the traditional wage-paying sectors, and stabilization policies premised on the use of state power to secure declines in real wages, retrenchment of state employees, and the 'containment' of industrial unrest. The trade union movement is now disoriented, and its leadership all but paralysed. In the absence of the emergence of alternative worker organizations, workers have limited means of securing their livelihood and living standards in a period of crisis. Similar organizational disarray and institutional weaknesses are evident in the small farming community. Indeed, it might be argued that it is only business organizations in some countries that have shown vitality, much of this stemming from the encouragement given by regional governments, along with that of the USA and its private sector.

While in the social and cultural spheres there has been an increase in the number of some institutions, and in particular women's institutions (linked in several countries to the state and/or political parties), in general these have been weakened, allowing the social and cultural ambit of the crisis to widen progressively. Thus, while there have been highly publicized initiatives at the cultural level, particularly those tied to 'tourist promotion', indigenous cultural expressions have generally received limited support, the crisis having generated a marked shift in public attitudes away from autonomous cultural forms as part of a broader shift away from conceptions of autonomous economies and societies in the region. Noteworthy, in contrast, is the remarkable penetration of North American culture into the region, greatly facilitated by the wide availability of the electronic media.

Finally, Caricom, which is the institutional expression of economic co-operation in the Commonwealth Caribbean, is itself a factor in the crisis process. Originally conceived of and established during the period of long upswing of economic activity, freer trade and freer markets were seen as the main vehicle of economic co-operation and a platform for the growth of regional business classes. Under the impact of slower global growth, Caricom trade has been in absolute decline for five consecutive years (1982–88), see Table 3.4. While co-operation remains a priority, member countries have, during the 1980s, adopted other priorities in their external relations.

Responses

Because of their varied assessments of the causes and impact of the crisis, as well as different political orientations, CC governments' responses to the crisis have been varied. For the sake of convenience, these are categorized under four broad headings: stabilization programmes; the promotion of deregulation and privatization; the search for external aid and export preferences; and political responses that emphasize militarization, ideology and containment. Although listed separately, these policies have not been singled out and pursued in isolation from each other. From time to time various combinations have been tried.

Stabilization and adjustment

The premise on which this category of responses has been based is that the crisis is one of internal and external macro-economic imbalances, which when remedied would permit the resumption of rates of growth no less than those achieved in previous periods. Pursuit of this return to 'normal' growth has resulted in considerable reliance on IMF-World Bank support, 'favourable' responses by friendly governments to pleas for balance-of-payments assistance, and the restoration of capital inflows to the levels of previous historical periods. As the data introduced earlier have shown, more than two-thirds of the region's external indebtedness is to official multilateral and bilateral sources. The result of this approach has been that external agencies exercise a remarkable influence on both the interpretation of the crisis and those solutions followed. Their influence, in fact, stretches far beyond the funds they disburse, these having been reduced in a period when their influence has risen. Thus the World Bank chairs the Caribbean Group for Cooperation in Economic Development (CGCED), co-ordinates assistance of aid donors to the region, provides most of the technical analysis and proposals for consideration at the annual CGCED meetings. Three-quarters of the funds loaned by the regional development bank (CDB) comes from outside the region. Concurrently, the IMF's influence in shaping economic policy on a day to day basis is now legendary. In general, friendly governments have thrown their weight on the side of these institutions, thus further enhancing their role.

As regards the stabilization programmes, the three worst cases, Guyana, Jamaica, and Trinidad and Tobago have yet to come close to successfully overcoming the macro-economic disequilibrium. Frustration and disappointment over this has been increasing, leading to some recognition of the view which argues that growth and equity are inseparably linked to any successful stabilization. At the moment, however, adherents to this view are far from influential enough to secure its implementation, and growth remains narrowly focused on export-led growth pushed by local and foreign private investors made dynamic and invigorated by widespread deregulation. In support of this, those measures that inhibit the free and unrestricted inflow of capital (and by implication outflow) are being resolutely dismantled as opportunities present themselves.

Privatization
In the period leading up to political independence in the area, and indeed immediately thereafter, there was widespread acknowlegement of 'market failure' under the previous colonial system. This gave support to those views which saw development as impossible without the state becoming the leading force. Right up to the late 1970s this was probably still the dominant outlook among the leading classes, regardless of political orientation. Since then the crisis has engendered among these classes the view that 'political failure' of the state-led process is so complete that the only solution is the unconditional embrace of market-led forces. Development is possible only if there is a leading role for the private sector. Similar developments abroad, in the USA and Britain in particular – and recently reinforced by popular interpretations which present *perestroika* as proof of state political failure in the development process – have given this outlook unprecedented legitimacy.

Organizationally, this tendency has been strongly supported by the formation of the Caribbean-Central American Association (CCAA) and the Caribbean Association of Industry and Commerce (CAIC). The mission of these institutions is to promote private sector organizations in each country, and they have been doing so vigorously. In noting this development it is instructive to recall that in April 1980, when the CCAA was formed, it was promoted as one of President Carter's leading initiatives to overcome the economic elements of the Caribbean/Central American crisis, and the negative effect it was having on US relations in the region. In turn the CCAA's first achievement was a revival of the CAIC, which had been founded as long ago as 1963 but which by 1980 had become moribund, hamstrung by chronic underfunding and the lack of a permanent secretariat. Funding was provided by the CCAA and USAID and a secretariat was established in Barbados. Since then, in a relatively short period, both these institutions have become powerful arbiters of Caribbean development. As will be seen in the next section, this initiative was to pave the way for the creation of CBI. It is, therefore, instructive to note that one view that motivated the formation of CCAA as expressed by one of its leading officials is that: 'these places can't get along without outside investment, outside technology. Alone they are not viable; they will in the end have to become something like offshore states of the United States'[7].

Aid and export preferences

Stabilization and privatization have been complemented by vigorous efforts to encourage the inflow of foreign assistance and to maintain export preferences to assure market access for exports. While the data show the former has not been successful, the latter has been, as was noted when the region's preferences systems were outlined earlier. By far the most important of these arrangements are those which centre on the CBI. To accommodate space constraints this sub-section will focus on issues related to the CBI.

The CBI and related legislation (Section 807 of US tariff regulations and the Puerto Rico twin-plant scheme) are the most concrete economic manifestations of the importance of the Caribbean Basin to the USA – the so-called 'third frontier'. The logic of this preference system is to stimulate, through foreign and local private enterprise, a process of export-led growth directly linked to the large US market. It is immediately obvious that this model of development contrasts with at least two others practised in the wider Caribbean area: the Cuban socialist model linked to the CMEA, and the mixed economy model of autonomous development, which was experimented with earlier in Jamaica under Manley in the 1970s, Grenada under Bishop, and in Nicaragua after the revolution. The CBI system is designed to achieve a number of objectives: 1) to phase out protection for the region's traditional agricultural and mineral exports; 2) to encourage emphasis in two major export areas to the US, namely, non-traditional agriculture (exotic fruit, winter vegetables, and ornamentals) and certain categories of labour-intensive industrial products, (textiles, semi-conductors, switches, support equipment, and pharmaceuticals). It is further expected that the production arrangements for the latter would centre on the typical export processing zone model. And 3) to protect Puerto Rican interests which may be threatened by this approach, and if possible to consolidate that country's role as a leading force in regional affairs.

As Rivera has observed, although based on a preference system this model of export-led development conforms both to neo-classical market theories of comparative advantage and development (where emphasis is placed on relative wage costs as a trade stimulating factor), and theories of the globalization of production processes (in which comparative advantage, as measured from the overall profit position of the TNC, is located not in an entire product, but in a phase or phases of its production sequence). This can also be extended to those theories which centre on product and manufacturing cycles.[8] Such a model is clearly not preoccupied with short-run disequilibria. It focuses, correctly, on the long reconstitution of the region's export and production structures. What, however, have been the results so far?

Since its inception, trade between the US and the CBI beneficiaries has declined from US$9.2 billion in 1983 to US$6.2 billion in 1987. US imports from CBI beneficiaries which represented 3.4 per cent of its total imports in 1983 was more than halved – down to 1.5 per cent. At the same time, US direct investment in the CBI countries, which was 1.6 per cent of its total overseas investments in 1980, had been reduced to 1.1 per cent by 1983 and to 0.9 per cent by 1985. The Puerto Rican development agency, Fomento, had, through CBI-related schemes, generated investments totalling only US$62 million in eleven CBI countries, covering 53 projects, 49 of which were in operation by late 1988. The number of jobs which this had created is estimated at 5,000. Meanwhile, as of September 1988 it had endorsed US$134 million in investments out of Section 936 funds.

The World Bank data, which show US, EC and Canadian imports from CC countries, reveal that except in the case of Canada, whose share of imports in 1986 was only ten per cent, the total value of merchandise trade fell considerably in the 1980s. Much of this decline is concentrated in the traditional products. There has, however, been expansion in export manufactures and a growth in Canadian imports from the region. Between 1980 and 1986 the region's manufacturing exports, mainly textiles under the 'super-807' arrangements grew by nearly 90 per cent. In Trinidad and Tobago, resource intensive exports based on natural gas (ammonia, methanol, and urea) and steel production grew rapidly, amounting to two-thirds of its exports to the EC and four-fifths to the US and Canada by 1986. Canadian imports grew by about 60 per cent over the period, increasing its share from about two per cent in 1980 to approximately ten per cent in 1986. Overall, however, US imports of Caricom products fell from 1.8 per cent of total US imports in 1980 to 0.4 per cent in 1987. This was a worse performance than that of developing countries as a group, but was similar in pattern to the CBI region as a whole.

Manufacturing export growth is heavily focused on enclave platforms, where production is undertaken either as an intra-firm arrangement or under contract to US-based corporations. Little or no local taxes are paid, and these firms are guaranteed the repatriation of their profits, with the effective risk of expropriation being virtually zero. These platforms are heavily dependent on a foreign entrepreneurial class attracted to the region by its low wages, tax holidays, and 'cheap' infrastructure. There is a noticeable lack of strong linkages to the local entrepreneurial classes, making many of these firms 'footloose'. Surveys have also shown very minimal technology transfer, very limited upgrading of local skills, negative net foreign exchange contribution to the local economy, low domestic value added, extremely limited linkages with the local economy, and surprisingly low levels of employment, given the magnitude of investments behind these schemes.[9] Finally, experience has indicated that the management of these operations tends to be hostile to trade unions and other forms of organized labour.

If to these considerations we add concerns expressed about the bilateral nature of the CBI arrangements, and the 'unequal' strength of the two parties, we can appreciate why the view has been held that the CBI is more closely linked to the US's global security interests, its war on the narcotics trade, and efforts to control tax evasion than to regional development. The point at issue however, remains: which takes precedence, a development model for the region, or a security network for the US? Until this is unambiguously resolved there is every reason to cast doubt on a process of export reconstitution which promotes little or no internal linkages, produces minimal capital reinvestment in the local economies, locks the region's resources into export activities geared to specific countries and firms, discourages local entrepreneurship and product substitution of inputs, and is ultimately premised on the attraction of low living standards (the very antithesis of development) to give it a relative cost advantage. While acknowledging that forms of diversification are emerging under the CBI, the conclusion must be that the vulnerability of these economies still remains their central characteristic. This seems almost inevitable if the logic of outside capital with its own economic and geo-political designs prevails over the pursuit of local and regional interest. Bearing in mind the region's past history it is well therefore to keep to the forefront of consideration the description of this process given by Emmanuel Cellen, the US congressman to whom has been attributed the major role in piloting free-trade zone legislation in the US. He defines a free trade zone as: 'a natural stockaded area where a shipper can put down his load, catch his breath, and decide what to do next'.[10]

Militarization and ideology

In the Commonwealth Caribbean, ideology has always played an important role in shaping economic policies. The great regional debates which had begun even before independence, on such themes as the role of the state in economic development, public control of the commanding heights of the economy, the relationship of industrialization to development, and the search for paths of economic development which would enhance the region's sovereignty, show this admixture clearly. As societies struggling for independence this ideological admixture was, and remains, important as a means of mobilizing people for change and in raising their consciousness. These considerations still colour the current great debates on privatization, open versus inward-oriented economic policies, and the stabilization programmes. Because of the profile of the US in the region, however, the CBI model has also entered into these debates, and because of the preferences it offers it has undoubtedly given considerable leverage to the views of US allies within the region.

Since independence, militarization too has been an important feature of the region, at present laying claim to considerable resources. In Guyana in the mid-1970s it was estimated that as many as one in every 35 persons belonged to one of the state security services. The creation of official and semi-official militia has been accompanied by a rapid growth of private security firms as well as the 'security' arms of several major political parties in the region.

From the point of view of the present analysis two issues are critical. One is that adherents to the view that the crisis is the product of East–West conflicts for hegemony might well support a violent or 'physical' solution of the crisis, particularly if it is felt that the 'mischief-makers' on the other side of the political fence can be contained. The other issue relates to the geo-strategic context. If trade preferences are promoted as the carrot with which to draw the region into particular North–South axes, then it might be believed that a military stick should be developed as a complement. This is critical as, even before the Cuban revolution, or recent events in Grenada, Haiti, and Nicaragua, military action in the area has been frequently exercised as an option at times of crisis. Prior to 1980, only Jamaica among the CC countries received significant external military aid from the US. Currently this aid is estimated to be running at about US$80 million annually.

In recent times the international system has witnessed a considerable reduction in tension. If this process is sustained then the risk of 'physical' solutions being imposed as a way out of the crisis will recede. This will also be encouraged if the current 'ideological' successes of conservative positions can be maintained.

Conclusion

Certain requirements for a successful resolution of the crisis emerge from the foregoing analysis. Firstly, it is clear that correct diagnosis is critical to the correct choice of options. The dynamic interconnectedness between the economic aspects of the crisis and the wider social aspects at this particular conjuncture is the only correct starting point for effective solutions. To locate the crisis in an exclusively economic sphere, or to pursue its treatment separately from the wider issues of economic reactivation, reorientation, growth and development, will leave it unresolved.

Second, the analysis shows that many of the solutions offered, and indeed attempted so far, have been either imitative of perceived successes elsewhere, or non-existent, priority is given to the 'recovery' of the earlier drive towards more and more autonomy in the formulation and implementation of economic policies which characterized the struggles for independence. This assessment is neither a call for autarkic solutions nor a down-playing of the enhanced interdependence of the global economy which characterizes the present period. It is simply a reassertion of the principle that the region needs to pursue, as far as possible, the modification of its present engagement in the international economy, if the broader social goals of economic development and independence, economic and social justice, are to be realized. Such a perspective, for example, does not permit the pursuit of macro-economic balance as a distinct and separate goal from the reactivation and development of the economy. It also stands out against the present orientation in which policies are relentlessly geared to dismantling and diminishing the already extant autonomous bases of policy formulation, which were acquired at huge social cost in earlier periods.

Thirdly, the history of the industrialized market economies during crisis reveals two striking features of their leading classes. One is the resolute way in which they call upon the state for policies supporting capital restructuring, the recomposition of productive assets at the disposal of the community, and the introduction of new techniques, as economic responses to economic crisis. The other has been their ability to pursue political and social reform when the pressure from the masses becomes irresistible. The underdeveloped character of the leading classes in the region is revealed in their dependence on a process of externally initiated restructuring as described above. At home too, their efforts at political and social reform remain severely limited. In a few of the territories, elections are neither 'free and fair, nor free from fear'. When they are, however, little effort has been made since independence to deepen and entrench the forms of the Westminster model inherited from the colonial period. Indeed, the extent to which behind these forms, in the countries from which they originate, lie the substance of centuries of accumulated precedents, rule-of-the-game, characteristic behavioural patterns and forms of social consciousness, seem not to be widely appreciated. Thus, we find democracy is paid only lip-service. Community and local government today is weaker than it was a decade ago; in some countries (St Vincent, 1974) local government having been abolished! There has been, in other words, very little promotion of participatory systems of decision-making to counter the authoritarian traditions of previous colonial rule. Policies of income redistribution and institutional reform have all but disappeared with the arrival of the crisis.

Allied to this development is the central role given to the state by all classes (including those calling for privatization), in the resolution of the crisis, with little attention paid to the structure of the state and the emergence of important non-governmental organizations. Yet the period has witnessed major individual-family-household responses to the crisis, independent of the state and sometimes in direct opposition to it. Referred to here are such matters as the growing informalization of the economy, migration, the development of small-scale inter-island producing and trading, the proliferation of informal savings arrangements and even the increase in the numbers of 'economic' and 'political' refugees. While much of this reaction is 'survival' oriented and therefore very immediate, there is a potential here for the revitalization of civil society which needs to be harnessed before the crisis can be overcome.

Fifthly, dramatic as they may appear today, the choices facing the region are not altogether new, although the context in which they appear might differ. I refer here to the many choices running through this analysis: state versus private sector; inward versus outward development models; present versus future consumption; power-to-a-few versus power-to-the people; ownership versus control; security versus development; planning versus market; and authoritarianism versus democracy. There is a rich regional experience to draw from, especially among the older independent states of the Caribbean. Comparative study could, therefore, yield important lessons and help to avoid the repetition of past mistakes. Of particular significance is the way the state–society problematic is posed in regional debates. This is often reduced to a zero sum game, where one side of the equation advances at the expense of the other. Yet the region's history shows that there is no a priori determination of an ideal state-market relation. As in all contemporary societies, there is a necessary interdependence and complementarity between state and market. How this is regulated is a political matter, resolvable only out of the balance of political interests in any given society. There is no natural or divine law to fix this choice.

Finally, the smallness of the territories that comprise the region makes deeper forms of regional co-operation indispensable inputs towards solving the economic crisis. Everyone is for integration in the region, and, like democracy, much lip-service is paid to this idea too. In practice, however, little qualitative advance has been made in the system of economic co-operation since the crisis. Yet at this critical juncture a further deepening of the process seems imperative. In concluding this presentation, given below are a few indications of measures which are both desirable, and which with a small modicum of political will could be made feasible:

- Higher levels of political-legal co-operation are imperative. Here then is an urgent need for the creation of some form of regional assembly, even if initially of very limited powers. This would not only create a forum for debate and discussion but would give political expression to regional issues.

- The consolidation of the influence of non-governmental organizations in the framework of the co-operation institutions is long overdue. This is especially true as regards workers' and farmers' organizations, womens' groups, church bodies, professional and business associations as well as human rights groups.

- Restrictions on the freedom of movement need to be drastically reduced. As it has been publicly acknowledged these still require someone from, say, Martinique to take two days to travel to Jamaica, while requiring two visas for transit purposes!

- Joint-venture arrangements in areas customarily seen as requiring 'extra-regional' capital, for example gold-mining, beverage and alcohol products, the production and marketing of regional 'brand name' products in overseas markets, are some areas where economic co-operation can be fruitfully advanced.

Without the systematic reassertion of the goal of building a genuine inter-Caribbean system and concrete efforts in this direction, the many dimensions of the present crisis cannot be overcome. At this stage the region's redefinition as an appendage of some other system remains the most likely prospect. Importantly for the future, some are resisting this.

Notes and References

1. The Commonwealth Caribbean refers to the following 13 countries, all ex-colonies of Britain: Antigua, Bahamas, Barbados, Belize, Dominica, Grenada, Guyana, Jamaica, Montserrat, St Kitts-Nevis, St Lucia, St Vincent and Trinidad and Tobago. These countries comprise about one-sixth of the population of all the Caribbean islands, the two mainland territories listed above, and Suriname and Cayenne, traditionally included in the Caribbean. For a brief discussion of the definitional issue see C.Y. Thomas, 1988.
2. See for example W. Bgoya and G. Hyden, 1987.
3. C.Y. Thomas, 1989, pp. 331–2.
4. C.Y. Thomas, 1986.
5. For available data on land distribution see C.Y. Thomas, 1988, pp. 136–7.
6. This thesis is elaborated in C.Y. Thomas, 1984.
7. Cited in C.Y. Thomas, 1988, pp. 333–4.
8. P.J. Rivera, 1987.
9. F. Long, 1985.
10. Quoted in W. Diamond and D. Diamond, 1987, p. xviii (c).

Bibliography

Bgoya, W. and G. Hyden (1987) 'The State and the Crisis in Africa. In Search of a Second Liberation'. Report on an International Conference at the Dag Hammarskjold Centre, Uppsala, *Development Dialogue*.
Diamond, W.H. and D.B. Diamond (1987) *Tax Free Trade Zones of the World*.
Harker, T. (1989) 'Cooperation between Caricom and non-Caricom Countries'. Paper presented to the Working Group on Integration, Association of Caribbean Economists, mimeo, 1989; and 'Caribbean Economic Performance: An Overview', Second Conference of Caribbean Economists, Barbados, May.
Inter-American Development Bank, (1988) *Monthly News*, October.
Long, F. (1985) 'Employment Effects of Multinational Enterprises in Export Processing Zones in the Caribbean', mimeo.
Ramsarran, R. (1988), 'Saving, Investment and Growth: Trends and Determinants in Selected Caribbean Countries in Recent Years'. Paper presented to the 20th Annual Meeting of the Regional Programme of Monetary Studies, Trinidad.
Rivera, P.J. (1987) 'The CBI and the Twin-Plant Scheme: Are they Development Alternatives'. Paper presented to the First Conference of the Association of Caribbean Economists, Jamaica.
Thomas, C.Y. (1984) *The Rise of the Authoritarian State in Peripheral Societies*, New York.

———— (1986) *Sugar: Threat or Challenge (An analysis of the impact of technical changes in the High Fructose Syrup and Sucro Chemicals Industry)*, International Development Research Centre, Ottawa.

———— (1988) *The Poor and the Powerless: Economic Policy and Change in the Caribbean*, Latin America Bureau, London.

———— (1989) 'Restructuring of the World Economy: Political Implications for the Third World', in A. MacEwan and W. K. Tabb, (eds), *Instability and Change in the World Economy*, Monthly Review Press.

United Nations, *International Trade Statistics* (various issues).

World Bank (1988a) *The Caribbean, Export Preferences and Performance*, Country Study.

World Bank (1988b) *Caribbean Countries (Economic Situation, Regional Issues and Capital Flows)*, Country Study.

APPENDIX

Table 3.1
Caribbean: Selected Indicators 1987

Country/Region	Size Km	Population (000 1988)	GNP Per capita Current US$ 1988
Caricom			
Antigua	440	82	3399
Bahamas	13942	243	11447
Barbados	431	254	5747
Belize	22960	180	1250
Dominica	750	82	1550
Grenada	345	106	1346
Guyana	214970	756	455
Jamaica	11424	2374	1219
Montserrat	102	12	3997
St Kitts/Nevis	269	47	2119
St Lucia	616	145	1400
St Vincent	388	114	1210
Trinidad & Tobago	5128	1234	3782
Non-Caricom			
Anguilla[a]	91	7	2300
Aruba[b]	193	64	7500
British Virgin Islands	150	12	9492
Cayman Islands[a]	260	21	12930
Cuba[b]	110860	10199	3000
Dominican Republic	49000	6700	810
Haiti[b]	28000	6200	360
Neth. Antilles[a]	800	200	6110
Puerto Rico	8800	3300	5574
Suriname	163265	411	2510
Turks/Caicos[a]	417	10	4490
US Virgin Islands[a]	344	111	9280

[a] = 1986 data; [b] = 1987 data

Sources: Economic Commission for Latin America and the Caribbean, IBRD; and, as cited in Harker (1988) and World Bank (1988 b).

Table 3.2
Investment per Worker

Country	Investment Per Worker (1980 = 100)									
	1960	1970	1980	1981	1982	1983	1984	1985	1986	1987
Barbados	57.4	121.8	100.0	107.6	82.8	72.2	59.2	55.6	58.8	59.4
Guyana	181.1	155.5	100.0	89.5	68.6	58.6	54.5	55.1	60.7	59.8
Jamaica	203.1	363.9	100.0	121.2	124.0	125.1	111.1	109.2	87.4	96.0
Trinidad & Tobago	25.9	30.0	100.0	81.4	83.8	73.0	52.7	54.0	43.1	36.2

Source: Inter-American Development Bank, *Monthly News*, October 1988.

Table 3.3
Net External Capital Flows to CGCED Countries,[a] 1981–86
(in US$ million at current prices)

	1981	1982	1983	1984	1985	1986
Official Donors/Creditors	1,318	1,389	1,063	928	779	394
Bilaterals	764	807	462	628	441	334
Grants	228	229	138	242	325	298
Net Loans	536	578	324	386	116	36
Multilaterals	554	582	601	300	338	60
Grants	67	54	46	51	54	57
Net Loans	487	528	555	249	284	3
Private Creditors	172	171	155	16	220	162
Suppliers	36	6	3	13	67	–23
Banks and Other	136	165	152	3	153	185
TOTAL ALL SOURCES	1,490	1,560	1,218	944	999	556
Outflows (interest paid)	392	439	519	525	587	653

a Includes: Antigua and Barbuda, The Bahamas, Barbados, Belize, Dominican Republic, Grenada, Guyana, Haiti, Jamaica, St Kitts and Nevis, St Lucia, St Vincent and the Grenadines, Suriname, and Trinidad and Tobago.

Source: World Bank (1988b).

Table 3.4
Intra-Caricom Trade: 1970–1988 (EC\$ million)*

Period	Domestic Exports		Imports	
	Value	% change	Value	% change
1970	160		164	
1971	182	14	183	12
1972	218	20	242	32
1973	269	23	296	23
1974	460	71	508	71
1975	567	23	649	28
1976	718	27	739	14
1977	730	2	724	–2
1978	783	7	898	24
1979	971	24	1168	30
1980	1341	38	1412	21
1981	1420	6	1615	14
1982	1407	–1	1540	–5
1983	1207	–14	1377	–11
1984	1088	–10	1214	–12
1985	1078	–1	1169	–4
1986	747	–31	784	–33
1987	783	5	858	8
1988	951	21	983	15

*Figures given in Eastern Caribbean dollars. Current exchange rate: EC\$2.70 = US\$1.

Source: Caricom Secretariat.

4. Opening Up the Economy, Debt and Crisis: The Inescapable Relationship

Jorge Schvarzer

Introduction

The present crisis in Latin America can be viewed from widely differing angles.
In this chapter it is treated as part of (and, apparently, a condition of) a process
of structural change in the functioning of Latin American economies. These
countries have experienced a sudden contraction in their rates of economic
growth as compared with those in the 1970s, and the crisis has also engendered
socially negative conditions and ongoing changes whose nature calls for in-
depth evaluation. Among these changes must be listed the pressure for
curtailing public expenditure and the visible redistribution of income both
among social groups (from workers to businessmen) and sectors (from those
working for the domestic market to exporters and from those in production to
those in financial sectors).

The causes of these changes are new. Were it necessary to summarize their
root and essence in one phrase, the 'opening up of the economy' would serve to
describe the fundamental factor that modifies – and indeed drastically reduces
– the state's regulatory capacity. This opening, and its impact on the state, has
affected the distribution of income within Latin American societies, by
generally benefiting the privileged sectors. It has also, in one way or another,
altered the conditions determining the dynamics of production.

In drawing attention to those actions which open up the economy, emphasis
here is placed on the conditions under which such an opening takes place. A
process based on a gradual opening of consolidated productive structures to
the exterior (as in the case of the European countries or Japan) is not the same,
either in cause or effect, as a process based on linkages between the financial
sectors and the world market. In the first case, the opening is the consequence
of a productively mature economy, whereas in the second it is an effect that
profoundly influences the orientation and capacity for growth of an economic
system.

The external debt is closely linked to the present crisis in Latin America, as
well as to the opening of the economies of the region. This chapter, rather than
taking the debt as the cause of the crisis, incorporates it into the global
phenomenon of economic transformation. In this way it can be seen that, in the
first instance, the debt is the result of policies designed to instigate a financial

opening of the economy. In the second instance, subsequent to the difficulties of 1982, the debt has served to consolidate the opening up process.

This chapter aspires to be reflective rather than assertive, and attempts to put forward an overall view of the problem. To that end it has opted for a schematic presentation of the relevant economic aspects, while focusing on the political and social dimensions of the Latin American crisis. Economics is quite simply a social relationship between individuals: the society distributes wealth (and to some extent, prestige and power) by means of markets. The economic analysis here, therefore, is intended to serve as a basis for political and social reflection rather than as an accumulation of purely statistical economic information.

It should also be noted that the focus is almost entirely on Argentina, due to the author's specialization in this field. It is appropriate, however, because it can serve as a point of reference for the description of other cases. In certain aspects, for the purposes of understanding the crisis, Argentina can be regarded as a 'model'. Even though it may not be entirely representative, it can serve as a point of contrast and comparison when studying the evolution of other economies. Ultimately, although the crisis is global, it is nonetheless true that the different economic and social conditions in each country lead to different results.

The crisis in Argentina

The starting point of the crisis in Argentina can be traced to 1975. Since then the GNP of the country has not grown: the production of the economy has oscillated around virtually unchanging values. The stagnation of production is the clearest indicator of a crisis, but changes in social indicators give a better appreciation of its severity. The population of Argentina has increased by approximately 15 per cent over the 14 years since 1974; this implies that the per capita national product has decreased proportionately over that period. Moreover, real disposable income has deteriorated even further due to the fact that a large proportion of available resources are now earmarked for external debt servicing, while during the early 1970s net external incomes were positive. Lastly, the redistribution of income over this period has been to the detriment of the least favoured sectors of society, whose share of the already dwindling total income of the country has been reduced. For these sectors the crisis is more evident and more painful than the statistical averages suggest.

The structure of Argentina's economy has changed considerably over the last 14 years. Although the value of the total national product has remained fairly constant, its composition has not remained the same. During this period, appreciable growth was experienced in the agricultural sector of the Pampas, and a noticeable industrial restructuring took place, including an exponential growth of certain services – particularly those oriented towards higher income groups – and a marked hypertrophy of financial operations. In other words, the crisis did not occur against a background of stagnation in every branch of the economy. Rather, its intensity and duration accompanied and facilitated global transformations related, directly or indirectly, to the opening up of the economy.

Macro-economic trends recorded since 1974 suggest no watershed changes which would correspond to the emergence of the debt crisis in 1982. Global recession and changes in the composition of GNP started before and continued after this time; the same can be said of other indicators of the crisis. Annual inflation, for example, one of the most conspicuous phenomena of modern Argentina, has consistently been over 100 per cent since June of 1975, and has averaged 300 per cent annually in this 14-year period. The only major variable that has shifted since 1982 is the investment rate in relation to the national product, which has registered a rapid decline after the outbreak of the debt crisis. This trend originated in part, but not entirely, with the need to allocate part of national saving to debt service payments. The decline in investment suggests a dark future: the current recession will remain for a number of years with no possibility of any substantial increase in installed productive capacity until the trend is reversed. On the public side, spending has been significantly restricted and in consequence there has been a decrease in investment by the state. The private sector has also reduced investment because the crisis itself promotes non-growth strategies.

Argentina's crisis is persistent, profound and significant. Its social and political consequences are too well-known to be detailed here, but this does not make them any the less serious. The lack of funds for investment means that there are no immediate prospects of finding a way out of the problem of production stagnation, while the stabilization policies applied have served to consolidate the process of change within the stagnation initiated in the mid-1970s.

The economic opening and consequent debt

In June 1975, a 'shock' applied by those responsible for official economic policy triggered an escalation of inflation, which rapidly approached annual figures of 1,000 per cent. This intense and unexpected inflation in turn prepared conditions for changes in economic policy while fanning the flames of social chaos and political discontent. Many observers consider the effects of this shock to have had a great deal to do with the March 1976 *coup d'etat* which opened the way to eight years of military government.[1]

This inflationary shock eroded confidence in the national currency and destroyed the old financial system in a single blow. The demand for dollars increased at a vertiginous rate as society sought stable havens for its savings. At the same time, ingenious financial instruments, characterized by their liquidity, short-term nature and high benefits, recreated a new financial market. The economic strategy applied from March 1976 under the military government led to a consolidation of these trends. Instead of pushing down inflation to reasonable levels as soon as possible, the government actually preferred to give priority to the modification of the financial system's rules of operation together with a drive to a more rapid opening to the international market.

Gradually but systematically, the new economic team liberalized the foreign exchange market, offering economic agents the long-desired opportunity of obtaining foreign currency by legal means. With equal determination, the team organized the transformation of the financial system to bring it into line with conditions of high inflation; the new norms authorized short-term placements – up to one week – at free interest rates, and created devices that made it possible to adapt long-term credit to constantly varying conditions in the short-term interest market.

In 1978, two years after the *coup d'etat*, inflation remained high, at around 200 per cent annually, the financial market operated with an average placement period of 20 days, while the foreign exchange market was the freest in decades. The military government's Minister of Economy admitted then in a public speech that his financial measures prevented a more rapid reduction of inflation, thus implicitly recognizing his administration's priorities.

At the end of that year the team applied a new strategy, which consisted of a fast opening up of the economy with the idea that international prices would rein in domestic prices. Applying a policy based on the Chicago School theory – at that time already in application in Chile – the economic team established a timetable progression for evolution of the exchange rate for 1979–80, and took measures to greatly liberalize both financial and commercial transactions with other countries.

The commercial opening was very important although, in effect, it was actually only over a limited period of time. The entry of imported goods took over six months to gather impetus, due to operational lags, and lasted less than two years. Imports benefited from the delay in devaluation caused by the exchange progression, which made local prices for foreign goods much lower than the prices of equivalent domestic goods. But the external crisis, which broke in 1981, compelled the closing of the domestic market again, thereby rendering the import strategy transitory, although its effects on the later strategy of Argentinean entrepreneurs were by no means negligible.

The quick financial opening, on the other hand, enhanced by highly mobile capital under the prevailing conditions, had considerably more profound and long-lasting effects than the commercial opening. The difference between local and international interest rates ensured high benefits for those operating in both markets; we have estimated that a 50 per cent annual rate of return could be gained on dollars in the years 1979 and 1980 through the simple expedient of obtaining credit on the international market and placing the money locally.

Naturally, this possibility generated a strong inflow of foreign capital, and led to expanded offers of credit within the national financial system. This money was taken by local agents as credit on the international market. Facilities for obtaining foreign-currency financing in this period, together with active support in this from the Argentinian government, set the scene for the acceleration of external indebtedness for purely speculative purposes. According to official statistics, in 1979 the private sector was indebted externally for over five billion dollars for this reason alone.

In 1980, economic agents began to suspect that the exchange rate could not be maintained much longer; devaluation was therefore to be expected. They then chose to withdraw their financial instruments in national currency and change it for dollars and other external currencies. The government complied with this demand, selling foreign exchange they obtained from external loans. Thus, between January 1980 and March 1981, the public debt increased by some 14 billion dollars simply in order to satisfy the private sector's appetite for currency.[2]

The crisis in the external sector broke in March 1981 at the same time as an already planned change in the military government. The political transition helped disguise the fact that the crisis would have occurred sooner or later. The system was unsustainable – a conclusion that the failure of similar economic policies in Chile and Uruguay was to confirm. By this time the external debt had reached 28 billion dollars; the earlier development of the market suggests that this increase was the counterpart of a similar amount of foreign currency held by Argentineans who were reacting to economic policy.

It is maintained here that the strategy followed by Argentina in the late 1970s and early 1980s generated a close link between the local and the international financial markets which has become difficult to alter. Argentinians have continued to accumulate foreign currency through capitalized interest earned on previously held stock, as well as through increased capital flight. The present amount of flight capital, whose real size can only be estimated, represents a formidable amount of currency when compared with other macro-economic dimensions of the country. It is estimated that the foreign currency which remains as such in the local market amounts to more than the total financial assets in local currency; it is no coincidence therefore that the dollar is moving to replace the *austral* in domestic transactions. The Argentinian economy is in fact operating under a two currency system: the *austral* which must be used to pay wages and taxes, and the dollar, which is now almost impossible to avoid using in transactions among privileged social sectors.

This trend is of great significance. Once there has been a financial opening of this magnitude, it is very difficult to turn back the clock. The government loses control over monetary and financial regulation since it can no longer influence either the amount of money in circulation – which has come to include an appreciable number of dollars – or the interest rate which has come to be defined as a function of the international rate.

Furthermore, the government loses the capacity to collect taxes, while inflation tends to make the system more regressive. The so-called 'inflationary tax' basically affects those who have assets in *australes* and who are, by definition, the least favoured, while privileged groups are not subject to such pressure because they hold dollars. Ultimately, the government also loses capacity to keep any local market closed, since financial opening applies pressure to open up the rest of the economy.

The financial opening acts as a lever that reduces the government's role in the economy and simultaneously calls for broadening the economic opening to other areas. From that position arises intense pressure to link each local market with international markets.

The debt: a factor in opening up the economy

By March 1981, Argentina had piled up a foreign debt of some 28 billion dollars and had been met with restrictions for obtaining new loans. International creditors' lack of confidence in the economic team of that period was reflected in their negative attitude to any new operations. Creditors even refused to refinance the interest falling due on the previous debt, in spite of the fact that, at least in the short term, Argentina had no means to pay it. The amount at stake was quite large because of the sharp increase in international interest rates since late 1979. Throughout 1981, therefore, Argentina ceased payments; the same situation has occurred repeatedly since then in Latin America, although Argentina's was a special case because it preceded the international debt crisis.

International financial conditions were ripe for the debt crisis to occur, although for several reasons it did not break out until the end of 1982, and the beginning of the 'Mexican problem'. The prevention of an open crisis extending to the rest of the international financial system at that time did not, however, diminish the seriousness of the financial situation of Argentina. The country received no credits in 1981 or in 1982, and, with a few exceptions, succeeded only with difficulty in refinancing its immediate external obligations. The cumulative effect of interest falling due was sufficient to increase the debt to 39 billion dollars by late 1982. At that time, the debt problem began to gain the attention of international public opinion and negotiations on the matter were no longer an individual country's problem.

Refinancing efforts the following year were favoured by prospects of a local political transition. The goal of facilitating the transfer of power to a democratically elected civilian government after the military defeat imposed by Great Britain helped credit negotiation during 1983. Renegotiations took place but, because there were no new credits, when the new democratic government took power at the end of the year accrued interest had generated new obligations amounting to 44 billion dollars. From then on, arduous negotiations with creditors have been taking place, with courses of action and consequences which are well described in the literature on the debt crisis.

The current refinancing of part of Argentina's debt has been arranged subject to the condition that certain policies be implemented by the debtor. Among these policy commitments, as is well known, a privileged place has been awarded to the opening up of the economy to international competition. It is said that the aim here is to have the debtor countries export more in order to generate a surplus which will enable it to make debt commitments. But the logic of the system and certain international pressures have led to an opening of the economy in both senses (export and import), the pace of which is checked only by resistance from the local business class. Experience suggests that such resistance tends to be overcome with the appearance on the scene of other internal actors, including the financial sector, which supports opening up the economy in compliance with external pressure.

Consequently, the economy is opened up as a result of the debt, but the debt is neither the sole cause nor the sole effect of this opening. It is well known that the sacrifices demanded by debt servicing prevent payment of annual interest charges; consequently, nominal debt continually increases while the crisis persists as a way of life, and the adjustment conditions imposed by the international financial community persist as an absolute requirement. At the end of 1988, Argentina owed over 56 billion dollars, representing 75 per cent of its GNP, and it has been compelled to adopt a series of economic policies in order to obtain refinancing from its creditors.

The financial opening of the 1976–81 period played a decisive role in the formation of Argentina's external debt. Subsequently, from 1981, the debt itself has played an equally decisive role in enlarging and consolidating the external debt of the country; at the same time, as the size of commitments continued to increase, the capacity of creditors to influence local policy became increasingly greater.

The financial opening at the end of the 1970s had already, by its very presence, generated strong pressure for its continued extension to other areas of the economy. The convergence of the trend as an offshoot of the external debt made the opening up of the economy inevitable. A vicious circle was set up by which the opening generated the debt which, in turn, consolidated the opening. Tremendous economic, social and political costs are associated with this process, the description of which lies outside the scope of this chapter. Moreover, there is a single path common to debt and opening, the opening up of the economy having established close relations between the local and the international financial sectors.

Opening up the economy

The opening up of the economy is common to all post-war nations. It has become increasingly evident that it is not possible to confine the productive structure to what have become the narrow limits of a national state. The generalization of economic opening has thus made it possible to observe the development of certain correlated trends, such as reduction of the regulatory capacity of the state, a relative decline in national independence and the subjection of certain processes to the conditioning factors of the world market. There is also a less frequently mentioned aspect of economic opening that arises from differences in dynamism and ways of functioning brought about by different opening processes.

Western Europe and Japan opened up their economies on the basis of an outflow of production. The strengthening of businesses and productive sectors, technological renewal and the improved quality of labour, among other factors, made it possible for these countries to increase exports to a very high proportion of their output. Naturally, this outflow was accompanied by similar growth in imports, which progressively brought about a deeper monetary and financial interrelationship with foreign markets. The essential point about these economies lies in the fact that their opening was extended to new sectors when these countries were already mature enough to compete productively with their external counterparts and to adapt to new conditions.

The case of Japan is something of a paradigm in this sense because of its amazing export offensive which, until recent years, was brought about with a minimum opening of its financial markets. Recently, the government of Tokyo has started to prepare conditions for a regulated opening of its markets, carefully and closely linked to the competitive capacity of its productive activities and financial sector. Even so, this programme coincides with a prodigious accumulation of wealth in the form of foreign exchange from Japan's large positive commercial balance.

Argentina, on the other hand, in common with other countries of Latin America, has been forced to open up its economy under different circumstances. The very fact that it starts from a previous financial opening implies, for example, that Argentina has no possibility of regulating interest rates, only a minimal capacity to control exchange rates, and almost no opportunity to channel capital flows in the way desired. The productive opening in Latin America has come after the financial one, meaning that Latin American nations are not following the same path as countries of the North, which started the other way around. The opening up process, therefore, is likely to have different consequences for the South.

Some differences among the countries of Latin America might be mentioned to illustrate this case. Brazil is probably the country which, for a number of reasons, could best have opened up from the productive point of view since the late 1970s. Consequently, this country has margins of manoeuvre and future prospects different to those of the countries not having the same experience. At the other end of the spectrum, nations such as Uruguay, which emphasized the role accorded to financial services in their economies, have minimum opportunities to structure a stable and efficient productive sector, at least until any possibility of obtaining benefit through the system created in recent years is exhausted.

Whether in Argentina or Brazil, Japan or Germany, however, the opening up of the economy has created new conditions in every country. The consequence in developed nations has been to increase 'interdependence', whereas in developing nations uneven economic relations have transformed interdependence into plain dependence; these countries' relatively less advanced structure of production converts the opening up of the economy into a condition that restricts possibilities for progress.

It is evident that there is an interdependence of developed nations: they are all faced with difficulties in defining exchange rates, interest rates, wage levels and even the rate of production in conjunction with world market conditions or with the policies applied by the major world power. Developing nations' dependence on world market conditions took expresssion in the middle of the crisis and is so closely linked to the latter that it is difficult to separate the two phenomena even though they are different.

Economic opening is, however, a multifaceted phenomenon which is difficult to quantify. The percentage of exports or imports in relation to the gross national product reveals little about sectors which, for various reasons, have special privileges; implicit forms of protection exist in such ways as transport costs, customs duties, and even climate in each country, and cannot always be fully evaluated. Similarly, the degree of financial opening of any one country cannot be directly measured by any available criterion. Therefore, the very idea of one type of economic opening preceding another is qualitative rather than quantitative; at least until the idea is developed and criteria and instruments of measurement can be defined.

In Argentina, all aspects related to the opening up of the economy appear almost abruptly, and they are not easily visible to the society. Consequently, it is my opinion that discussions about how to overcome the problem appear confused and go hand in hand with assessments that need to be dismantled in order to arrive at an understanding of the problem. The main characteristics of current positions on this subject will now be considered.

Responses to the crisis

The initial spontaneous response to conditions resulting from the crisis affecting Argentina was a return to the past. If the government had previously been capable of regulating the economic cycle, defining the main economic variables and thus the direction of economic development and the distribution of income, why not return to these practices? This question and the answer are present in many diagnoses of and proposals for the situation and have become widespread through the positions adopted by representatives of the main popular political parties. The memory of a Keynesian past which, in retrospect, might be considered to have been successful, underlies the action and decisions of a number of today's economists. They would do well to recall Keynes's own statement that living economists were prisoners of the ideas of a dead economist. Keynesian strategies could be applied only, as he himself emphasized in his analysis, in a closed economy. A return to a Keynesian model would require a closed economy, an objective which would hardly be easy to obtain under present conditions.

It is not possible to close the real sector of the economy – imports in particular – when the financial sector remains open. The pressure of foreign currency available in the hands of individuals ensures that goods will continue to enter from abroad, if their prices are lower than local prices, by all possible means. The experience of the so-called 'centrally planned' economies shows the pressure to consume imported goods once the citizens of these countries have started to obtain the foreign currency necessary to purchase them.

Consequently, the economy could be closed only by starting with the financial sector, an undertaking that appears to be simply impossible. By definition, the foreign currency owned by Argentinean citizens lies outside the national economy – even though it may be physically in the country – and to control it is therefore difficult. Only a very rigid system, requiring at least, and among other conditions, a political dictatorship, could begin to regulate such a fundamental asset as foreign currency owned by citizens. Even then, such regulations would be of doubtful effectiveness. Moreover, this undertaking could not be tried without a default on the payment of the external debt and the conditions that create its service. The close relationship between these phenomena allow us to suppose that such action would isolate the country internationally. It is likely that the cost of isolation would be greater than the benefits to be achieved from closing the economy and applying a Keynesian model.[3]

The ruling class sees this situation clearly, and consequently some of its representatives are warning that a victory of populism would only bring economic chaos. Their statements convey not so much fear as the conviction that economic opening is irresistible, and that by itself it creates conditions limiting the application of different policies.

In defence of economic opening, the ruling class is also looking back to the past and recalls that until 1929 Argentina was an open and successful economy. This is not the place to discuss this aspect of local economic history except to indicate that the country had a tremendous comparative advantage in agricultural production, which enabled it to obtain what has been called a differential rent allowing the country to enjoy a very high per capita income. In common with the oil-producing countries after 1973, Argentina benefited from the exploitation of one of its natural resources – the fertility of the land – which gave the image of a rich society. Now, returning to an open economy without this differential rent – which exists no longer because it has been eliminated by the impact of technological progress in the agricultural production of developed nations – does not, as its supporters assume, imply recovery of a high per capita income. On the contrary, the difficulties of productive development which confronted the country at the time and, ultimately, prevented its transformation to a modern economy when the boom came to an end would reappear.

Those who refer back to the remote past – before 1929 – add to their ideas the objective fact of existing pressure in favour of economic opening. Consequently, these persons are advancing with the tide, supported both by theoretical and historical models that justify present policies. But their argument ought not to be made solely on the basis of the economically closed economy of the past – such as that which prevailed between 1929 and 1975 – but from a position which admits present restrictions, including the need to extend policy areas with a social meaning and in favour of growth.

Economic theory is lacking here. Numerous and successful experiments, which have been undertaken concerning the management of different aspects of social and economic policy in open economies, lead us to suppose that there are wider margins of flexibility than have been generally supposed in this sense. The problem is that these experiments have been undertaken or are being undertaken in countries which have already reached an appreciable degree of development, and which therefore have stronger and more flexible social and productive structures and greater ability to face the challenges of the world market. The Scandinavian countries, for example, offer various alternative models that have met with varying degrees of success.

By contrast, some experiments have been made in developed nations which have tried to revert to older models, but the results have been considerably frustrating. French efforts in this regard, following the 1981 Socialist victory, had negative effects and brought into question the economic policy that had been adopted; the rapid reversal of direction in subsequent years constituted an experiment which served as a basis for other governments of the same tendency in different European countries.

There are, therefore, available models which are difficult to apply because of differences in stages of development, as well as counter-examples which help to avoid erroneous policies. A strategy must be designed taking into account the two aspects of the situation that seem crucial. The first is how to ensure better social egalitarianism without having recourse to the old Keynesian tools; the second is how an open economy, which has established its linkage with the world market from the monetary and financial sector, should grow.

No answers to these questions are available, but this is the core of the matter in the present crisis. It remains necessary to reflect in detail on this matter on the basis of proper diagnoses and sufficient flexibility of methods. Subsequently the problem of implementation of the proposed solutions will arise, for which political power and the will to change will be necessary. In addition, everything points to the fact that this situation can be reached only over time. Although the crisis is already upon us, desirable and rational solutions are apparently not yet at hand for application.

Notes and References

1. For a detailed analysis of economic policy for this period see J. Schvarzer, (1987) *La política económica de Martínez de Hoz*, Hyspamérica, Bueno Aires.
2. See ibid. for statistics and details.
3. The German experience of the 1930s comes to mind as a possible example for some debtor countries. In 1933 Germany repudiated its debt (generated by demands for war reparations from the allies after 1918), isolated itself politically and economically from the international scene and started a process of economic reactivation, which was later reinforced by the development of military activities. The political and social costs of this solution are too well known for us to insist further on this example.

5. Crisis and Adjustment in Sub-Saharan Africa

Thandika Mkandawire

Introduction

The multiplicity of crises that Africa is facing has compelled some to ask whether indeed Africa will survive. The first part of this chapter presents some global and sectoral evidence of these crises, which will be limited to major economic indicators. The many political, social and cultural manifestations of the crises, such as urban and even rural pauperization, religious fundamentalism, sectarian violence, crime and so on, will thus, despite their importance, not be dealt with here. A critical review of some of the explanations of the crises follows and, finally, the process of adjustment and some of the results will be examined.

Manifestations of the crisis

Overall economic performance
Although it is currently fashionable to suggest that the economic crisis in Africa came with independence, the fact is that in most African countries, the immediate post-independence years witnessed substantial progress in production in a wide range of activities. For the period 1965–80 the weighted average growth rate of GDP was 5.6 per cent for the region. This performance compared favourably with that of other non-oil exporting developing countries. More significantly, this performance permitted positive growth rates in per capita incomes. For the 1980s the picture changed drastically. Between 1980 and 1986 the weighted average growth rate was zero, leading to declines in per capita incomes in virtually all African countries. It should be noted that performance was quite uneven among countries of the region – growth rates of GDP ranged from 0.3 per cent in Nigeria to 14.3 in Botswana during the 1965–80 period and from –3.2 per cent in Nigeria to 11.9 in Botswana in the period 1980–86. The unusually good performance of Botswana is accounted for by the exploration of relatively new diamond mines.

In addition to declining per capita incomes, the 1980s saw the undermining of the basis for future growth through the dramatic destruction of physical infrastructure, as maintenance as well as new investments came to a halt. The weighted average of 9.3 per cent decline of gross investment in 1980 has wiped out all the investment gains made during the 1970s. The dilapidated buildings, abandoned factories, pot-holed roads are all the visible outcomes of the working out of negative exponential on Africa's physical stock.

Other macro-indicators of the crisis were accelerating rates of inflation and a stifling debt burden. As in other regions, these factors have led to declines in the provision of social services in public and private investment, and in per capita levels of consumption. Available evidence suggests that urban wage earners and the urban poor have borne much of the brunt of the decline in the sub-Saharan African economies.[1]

Although the trends are well-documented elsewhere (see, for example, Chapter 2 of this book) the two elements of the crisis that have special relevance to the African context – de-industrialization and the agrarian crisis – will be discussed here briefly.

De-industrialization

As Africa entered the crisis phase it was the least industrialized continent both in terms of industrial output per capita and structure of industry. The low level of Africa's industrialization is one of the most conspicuous inheritances of colonialism. Elsewhere I have discussed how Africa 'missed' some of the rare opportunities that some, more sovereign Third World states were able to exploit to initiate the process of industrializaton.[2] Suffice it to state here that both implicit and explicit colonial policies blocked African countries from engaging in import substitution industrialization during both the Depression and World War II period. In addition, during the immediate post-war period, industrialization in much of the Third World was achieved through further import substitution, while most of Africa was still under colonial rule and could not therefore introduce the protective policies central to this strategy. Not surprisingly, at independence most African countries found that their levels of industrialization were far below the 'historical norms' for countries with their level of per capita incomes.[3]

In response to this colonial neglect or blockage, the 'right to industry' became a platform of the emergent nationalist movements. It was therefore with the attainment of independence that some concerted efforts at industrialization were to be observed. A few global figures will highlight this point.

Between 1960 and 1975 African industry grew at the annual rate of 7.5 per cent. This compared favourably with the 7.2 per cent for Latin America and 7.5 per cent for South-East Asia. Three factors should, however, be borne in mind: 1) Africa's starting point in terms of manufacturing value added (MVA) was extremely low; 2) within Africa itself there are great disparities in the levels and rates of industrialization. Nigeria, Zimbabwe, Kenya, Cameroon, Côte d'Ivoire together account for about 60 per cent of sub-Saharan Africa's manufacturing output, while the 30 least industrialized countries account for only 16 per cent of total output. Obviously, performance by these five relatively industrialized countries will tend to exaggerate Africa's overall performance; and 3) growth rates over the 15-year period were far from steady. Much of the growth took place in the first decade of independence as the most rudimentary type of industrial establishments were set up to produce such commodities as beverages, matches, and textiles.

It should also be added here that the qualitative aspects of this industrialization left much to be desired; criticisms of the pattern of industrialization followed in Africa are well-known, and will be only summarized here. Africa's industrialization is faulted for its lack of depth and its excessive concentration on consumer goods to the virtual exclusion of the production of capital goods. Its technological base is inflexible and dependent upon imports, and its rate of labour absorption has been relatively low when compared to the high levels of urbanization. The structure of the manufactured output in sub-Saharan Africa reflects the skewed patterns of income distribution and does not produce consumer or producer goods for the largest mass of producers: the peasantry. Nourished by protective policies of the state, the industry is characterized by inefficiency and low capacity utilization.

Even in quantitative terms, despite the not negligible rates of industrialization, the industrial sector remains small and enclaved, accounting for only 9.8 per cent of the region's GDP. Relative to world manufacturing output, Africa had a share of manufacturing value added of only 0.9 per cent in 1980 compared to a share of 2.7 per cent and 6 per cent for South and East Asia and Latin America respectively. Thus, by 1980 Africa was 'still the least industrialized region in the world'.[4]

Nevertheless, with all these caveats in mind, the 1960–73 period witnessed some important first steps in the process of industrialization in Africa. Most significantly, wage employment in industry increased at rates that surpassed population growth, although they were not high enough to keep up with accelerated rates of post-independence urbanization. The period also witnessed significant gains in skills through the creation of institutions of higher learning and 'learning-by-doing' within the new industrial structures.

The second decade saw Africa lagging behind the rest of the Third World, as most countries in the region registered much lower rates of industrialization than those achieved in the first decade of independence. But growth rates yielded increasing industrial output per capita.

The dramatic decline in rates of industrialization began to show after the first 'oil crisis'. Between 1973 and 1984, the rate of growth of low-income sub-Saharan Africa was a mere 1.8 per cent while that of middle-income sub-Saharan Africa was 0.5 per cent, resulting in rapid declines of industrial output per capita.

Agrarian crisis

The most conspicuous and most painful signs of the crisis have been transmitted through agriculture, and have shown up in the famines and starvation in large parts of Africa due to declining food availability. Unreliable though the data on food production are, most of them point to the fact that since the 1960s food production in Africa has lagged behind population growth. Indeed

Africa seems to be the only major region of the under-developed world which has suffered from declining food availability during the last three decades. This trend predates political independence in Africa. In the colonial era, decline in food production was reflective of the export bias of colonial governments. In the post-independence period declining food production is not unambiguously a result of export bias, there being evidence of positive correlation of food and export crop production in a significant number of cases. Rather it is a reflection not of a food crisis but a fundamental agrarian crisis in Africa – a crisis reflective of, on the one hand, the limits of a peasant-based agriculture reliant on extensive accumulation and saddled by a whole range of forms of surplus extraction and, on the other, the ambivalence of state policies towards capitalist agriculture.

Explaining the crisis

Explaining the African crisis has become a veritable industry and has spawned a considerable amount of literature.[5] Doubtless the dearth of statistical information and the possibilities that Africa offers for unrestrained imagination contribute to the wide range of explanations, which are all the more baffling since little effort is made to juxtapose the various explanations and subject them to theoretical and empirical tests.

Policy failures
The 'emerging consensus' is that African states have relied too much on state control and have stifled market forces.

More specifically, leading members of the international financial community hold the view that the ensemble of economic policies and measures followed by African states has led to trade regimes that have stifled agriculture and caused serious balance of payments disequilibria as a result of declining exports on the one hand and soaring food imports on the other, as well as inefficient industrialization and under-utilization of scarce resources. The peasantry, according to this view, as the single largest rural group, has borne the brunt of these policies. This argument is based on the neo-classical economic doctrine concerning the importance of the market, and its relation to the economy and the state. It was first advanced in the influential book by Little, Scitovsky and Scott,[6] and for African countries was restated more dogmatically by Elliot Berg on behalf of the World Bank.[7] Berg's study has had far-reaching consequences on policy formulation in Africa as its diagnosis not only underlies the policies of the World Bank and the IMF but informs much of the current practice of many other donors.

According to this orthodoxy, 'market distortions' are the major culprit in economic disequilibria. Consequently 'getting the prices right' should provide the necessary incentives to stimulate production in precisely those commodities in which African countries enjoy comparative advantage – and these need not necessarily be food crops.

Why, then, do African states persist with policies whose pursuit, according to the accepted wisdom, can lead only to ruination, while avoiding those that are obviously good for their countries? One set of explanations – the paternalistic ones – attribute policy failures either to ignorance due to inherited statist traditions of colonial rule, mistaken theories of development economics, or to the influence of the dominant Keynesian interventionist tradition informing much of aid planning. This kind of weakness, according to this view, can therefore be remedied through intellectual suasion rather than the heavy arm-twisting of aid conditionality.

More stubborn causes of policy failures, requiring tougher measures, are attributed to deep-seated 'biases' or interests. In sharp contrast to the 'externalist' formulations of the now beleaguered Dependency school, which dominated much of the discourse in 1970s, much of the current explanation is 'internalist'. Elements of the 'internalist' explanations include: 1) personalist rule; 2) cultural traits; 3) internal class interests; and 4) policy bias.

Personal rule

In the personalist rule literature it is argued that, for a host of reasons, African regimes are characterized by 'personal rule'. In some current political science literature, this personalization of the state is the *differentia specifica* of the state in Africa, and the main source of the continent's travails. The personal ruler's main interests are personal aggrandizement and the maintenance of power. With these as the principal objectives, developmental roles of the state are neglected. Indeed, according to some theorists, personal rule in Africa works inexorably towards decumulation and under-development. Exceptions may include cases in which the personal ruler is inclined towards some national developmental objective, but even under these circumstances any benefits from this type of regime are dependent upon the ruler's continued goodwill and sound mind.

According to personal rule theory, the political leaders in much of Africa work under no social restraints and are subject to no structural imperatives – internal or external. Jackson and Rosberg have pushed this argument furthest, stating that:

> It is apparent from historical evidence that African rulers and other leaders are not captives of their environments. They have intervened, sometimes decisively in the public life of African states, making some economically and socially unpromising countries orderly and some otherwise promising countries disorderly and insecure. In the provision or the destruction of such 'political goods' as peace, order, stability, and nonmaterial security, the actions of Africa's rulers and other leaders have been more important than anything else.[8]

The rule of the Amins, Nguemas and Bokassas have made this type of explanation plausible. Yet to generalize these tyrants' characteristics to the whole of Africa involves a gross distortion of the reality, no matter how venal, tyrannical and self-preoccupied African leaders may actually be. This theory's wide acceptance can be attributed only to the habit of suspending incredulity about any news from Africa.

'Culturist' argument

Another view is that the state in Africa is so steeped in instrumentalist preoccupation that it lacks the 'relative autonomy' essential to the pursuance of long-term developmental goals. One argument is that the states, faced with centrifugal forces, have substituted 'distributionist policies and support-oriented criteria for investment and productivity decision rules'.[9] The culturalist version of this perspective is that certain African cultural traits have atavistically reappeared to cause havoc in the state apparatus or have all along existed behind the veneer of modernity. This school offers a refurbished version of the 'modernization' thesis of under-development, which posited certain socio-cultural traits (those of the US in particular) as those toward which a modernizing society should move. Under-development could be measured by the extent of a society's divergence from these socio-cultural norms. The most cogently argued case within the culturist literature is that of Hyden, who argues that 'the economy of affection' characterizing much of Africa has insinuated itself into the modern economy and thereby lent incoherence to state policies.[10]

Hyden's critics have argued that his concepts are too vague. First the line of demarcation between the 'economy of affection' and the market economy is not as clear as he suggests. In addition, the concept is too static to provide meaningful analytical leverage and cannot explain the fundamental differences in the extent to which Africans have been affected by the advances of rural capitalism.[11] Furthermore, Hyden cites access to land as evidence of the peasantry being 'uncaptured' by capitalism, but he ignores many other forms of surplus extraction and extra-economic coercion under which the peasantry lives.[12]

The little evidence that exists on investment patterns does not support the 'culturist' thesis of the prevalence of profligate government expenditure on purely distributionist policies. Rates of gross investment in sub-Saharan Africa showed no particular divergence from trends in other low-income countries. The picture changes dramatically in the 1980s when investment declined sharply. There is no evidence, however, of heightened affective relations or the sudden reappearance of centrifugal forces that would have accounted for such massive declines in investment as those witnessed by sub-Saharan Africa in the 1980s.

Factions and rent-seeking interest groups

The increasingly dominant explanation for the persistence of 'policy failures' in Africa is a model that attributes 'market distortion' to 'directly unproductive profit-seeking' (DUP) activities pursued by interest groups that are mostly interested in redistribution rather than growth and development. The attraction of this 'new political economy' is that it can be reconciled to the underlying neo-classical economic analysis of the roots of the crisis while still maintaining that the seemingly 'irrational' DUP-activities are indeed outcomes of rational rent-seeking interest groups.[13] In the context of Africa, the work of Lipton and more directly Bates on agriculture policy is probably the most well-known.[14]

One version of this neo-classical political economy is the 'bias' model, which can be used either to explain the 'urban' or 'industry' bias of state policies.

The 'urban bias' thesis was originally advanced by Lipton,[15] largely on the basis of evidence from India. In his original formulation, the thesis was presented not only to explain 'why the poor remain poor' but also as a challenge to Marxian class analysis. Lipton argued that policies towards agriculture were shaped by policy-makers favouring a coalition of industrialists, bureaucrats and urban workers. This spatial rather than class bias accounted for poverty in the under-developed countries.

The 'urban bias' thesis is, of course, not new to Africa. It was always implicit in the work of Fanon and in the 'labour aristocracy' thesis of Arrighi and Saul.[16] Only in more recent years, however, has it been most explicitly and cogently applied to policy analysis in Africa, most insistently by Bates in a number of works.[17] Bates rhetorically poses and answers his own question in the following manner:

> What are the sources of government policy toward food crops? Put bluntly, food policy appears to represent a form of political settlement, one designed to bring peaceful relations between African governments and their urban constitutents. It is a settlement in which the costs tend to be borne by the farmers.[18]

Industry bias

Yet another important 'bias' theory – that of 'industry bias' – allocates top priority to industry as compared to agriculture. Here, the package of measures that are covered by the 'import substitution strategy' is blamed for various policy aspects that have been deleterious to agriculture. The high tariffs that protect industry have turned the terms of trade against agriculture by forcing the agricultural sector to buy the inefficiently manufactured products of a highly protected and highly subsidized industry. The over-valued exchange rates accompanying this strategy have discouraged production of agricultural products for export, as the returns to such exports in terms of domestic currency are very low.

A number of problems arise with this 'neo-classical political economy approach'. First is the vacuity of the populist and libertarian versions of this approach, in which it is supposed that unleashing of market forces on the parasitical distributional coalitions will erode or dissipate rents, and will benefit the peasant producers who have had no role in the coalitions behind state policies. The World Bank and the IMF are presented, in this literature, as veritable 'Friends of the People', since the measures proposed by these institutions are supposed to weaken the position of the rentier élites and strengthen the hand of the reformers. Despite its veneer of libertarianism and populist reforms, however, this is an essentially authoritarian model of conflict resolution, in which liberalization of the economy necessitates the shackling of the polity. Since it is assumed that the interests of the rent-seekers are strong, how are the new World Bank/IMF policies to be reconciled with the weakening of the state? The more candid advocates of these policies do not shy away from calling for fascist solutions or for external powers temporarily assuming control of African states. In any case, in Africa, the new policies have been accompanied by the banning of trade unions and the arrests of their leaders, the closure of universities, and the shooting of demonstrators. Furthermore, the fact that the 'élites' running the governments were either spawned or at least nourished by the same born-again international reformers is often conveniently ignored.

A second problem with the 'political economy' approach arises from its assumption of pluralistic politics in Africa in which different groups enter into 'distributional coalitions' that contend for rents generated by state policies. This model is diametrically opposed to the post-independence African experience of depoliticization and authoritarian rule and is as misplaced an abstraction of African politics as can be imagined. It gratuituously hypothesizes the existence of these coalitions following the *non sequitur* that, if a group has benefited from a certain set of policies, it must necessarily have fought for the outcome or entered into coalitions that fought for and defended the outcome. Yet we know that there are gains in Africa of a 'windfall' character and which evaporate as mysteriously as they arose.

In addition, when one examines the distribution of 'rents' in Africa, one notices that a major group in the coalition, the urban working class, has actually suffered dramatic losses in income in a manner that would be inexplicable if this class was indeed a member in the coalition responsible for the 'biases' in state policies.

Finally, the 'neo-classical political economy' has an excessively instrumentalist view of the state, and it fails to deal with the problems of legitimation and accumulation with which all states must come to grips. It also suffers from a reductionism that compels it to posit social groups that have a one-to-one relationship to certain state policies.

One problem with virtually all the 'internalist' arguments is that they can at best only account for developments since 1973. Prior to that time most African economies performed reasonably well. If one believes that Africa's economic problems arise from internal causes, therefore, it would be necessary to explain how a whole sub-continent could suddenly be afflicted by anti-developmental regimes, demented individual leaders, mistaken policies, and self-defeating proclivites or biases.

Assuming that no such sudden affliction occurred, and that country-specific factors such as internal policies were so determinant in economic performance, the ranking of countries in terms of growth of output would be expected to remain the same after the worldwide crisis as it was before. The performance of the 'success stories' in the post-crisis period may be lower than before 1973, but should generally be higher than that of the 'failures'. A simple test – the Spearman correlation – shows this not to be the case in Africa. A comparison of

African economies' performance for the periods 1965–73 and 1974–84 shows how insignificant domestic policies must have been (Table 5.1). We find that there was no relationship between performance in the first period and that in the second. This is in sharp contrast with the 'world' as whole, for which the test shows that there is a statistically significant relationship between the two populations.

Table 5.1
Spearman Rank correlation between pre-crisis and post-crisis performance in GDP

	Valid Cases	Spearman Rank	Significance
World	80	.34996	.00228
Africa	31	.00323	.93404

The point here is that a number of structural features underlined by the 'Dependency school' still afflict African economies, despite some efforts to decolonize them. African economies remain highly open and extremely vulnerable to external factors without always having the capacity to exploit opportunities afforded them by the external environment.

The economics of the diagnosis and prescriptions
Above and beyond the weaknesses of the political explanations for the crisis is the validity of the underlying economic analysis which underpins the current wave of policy changes and impositions. Most governments in Africa have entered into 'policy dialogues' with donors and have had to make 'structural adjustment' or 'standby arrangements' with the World Bank and IMF. They have had to accept the conditions that these organizations invariably and almost ritually impose. These conditions generally include devaluation of the local currency, import restrictions, export promotion, reduction in government expenditures, wage controls, removal of price controls, restriction on money supply, credit and interest rates, restraint on or privatization of state enterprises, relaxation of exchange controls and encouragement of foreign investment.[19] Consequently, the African continent is now witnessing an unprecedented wave of policy reforms. Over-valued currencies are being devalued, food subsidies removed, parastatal monopsonies dissolved and replaced by 'market forces', wages frozen, social expenditure curtailed and economies opened to foreign capital.[20]

The diagnosis is based on neo-classical nostrums about the working of the markets. Low producer prices have undermined agriculture, in which Africa's comparative advantage largely lies. More significant than the producer prices for the neo-classical economists are, however, the macro-pricing distortions in exchange rates and production factors.

But here too the evidence is not as persuasive as the usually tendentious reading of the effects of these policies would suggest. World Bank studies show that although poor price and exchange rate policies have had a generally negative impact on agricultural performance, such policies are not the most important factors explaining agricultural performance in Africa. Cleaver's study shows that the correlation coefficient of aggregate growth to nominal protection was only 0.13. Foreign exchange over-valuation could explain only a third of the variations in output. In other words, while currency over-valuation does agriculture no good, currency depreciation will have a significant but not very large impact on agricultural growth.[21]

To argue its case, the World Bank has constructed a 'distortion index' against which it has regressed output performance. Even with this composite index, however, only one-third of the variation in growth performance of 31 developing countries can be explained by the 'distortions'.[22] When the economy is disaggregated, the explanatory power of the index is reduced to only 17 per cent for agriculture.[23]

In the 1987 World Development Report, the Bank could categorically state that countries pursuing outward-oriented strategies performed better than those pursuing 'inward-looking strategies'. The Bank compared the performance of 41 countries for two separate periods, 1963–73 and 1975–85, and found a strong correlation between export orientation and various indicators of growth and development for these countries. The World Bank took no account of regional and income differences.

Two studies that are more disaggregated yield more nuanced results about the relationship between trade policy and economic performance. A study by Helleiner found that for low-income countries there is no evidence to support the view that the degree of export orientation accounts for high performance of GDP.[24] Import volume instability is a more significant determinant of slower growth than trade policy. Singer and Gray show that there was weak correlation between export orientation and growth in the first period, both for countries above and below average world demand for their exports.[25] In the last period, there was virtually no correlation between trade orientation and growth of GDP.

To sum up, there is increasing realization that the injunction to 'get the prices right' was an oversimplification. Although there have been some improvements in food availability and agricultural output in general, these have turned out to be not particularly impressive and have tended to be more readily explicable by recent favourable climatic conditions than by the structural adjustment programmes. The apparent culprit for this low supply response to price incentives is the rather low supply elasticities of peasant agriculture to price incentives.[26]

New solutions include 'getting technology right'. The argument is that African agriculture needs major technological breakthroughs, comparable to the 'Green Revolution' in Asia, if African producers are to respond significantly to price incentives. Eicher stresses the importance of scientific and technical advance to double African agriculture output within the next 15 to 20 years.[27] Bruce Johnson argues that sub-Saharan African countries will not be able to achieve their goals of economic and social development without a transition from a predominantly subsistence, resource-based agriculture to an increasingly commercialized, science-based agriculture and that, thus far, research has failed to produce appropriate innovations leading to widespread, cumulative increases in farm productivity.[28] There is, however, the distinct danger that this technicist perspective will suffer from the kind of one-sidedness that has vitiated the counsel of the pricists.

Conclusion

African countries, like all others had to adjust to the crisis. But the particular form of adjustment pursued in Africa under the aegis of international financial institutions is increasingly seen as fatally flawed. Despite the carefully orchestrated campaigns by these financial institutions to publicize the 'successful' adjustment programmes, the evidence in Africa shows the enormous suffering wrought by this particular form of adjustment. The growing feeling is that much of this suffering was unnecessary. Policies have been based on a gross mis-specification of the underlying economic structures and dynamics. Constraints on output growth have proved to be more than 'market distortions' created by the now emasculated state; trends in the world market have undermined export-oriented strategies; the foreign investment that was supposed to follow the IMF stamp of approval has become net outflows of capital from African countries; there has been no surge of private industry following privatization and the crowding out of the state; growth rates remain miserly.

A generous interpretation of these results is that the mis-specification of African political economies was not intended, and that the continued pursuance of wrong policies by international financial institutions is a reflection of ingrained habits and bureaucratic and intellectual inertia. Indeed, in some of the writing on the IMF and World Bank, there is the optimistic and, I believe, naive hope that the two institutions have learnt something from the debate and are now ready to admit their past errors, and are qualifying some of their former arrogant certainty about their prescriptions. The two institutions themselves have been making some backhanded admissions of mistakes. These admissions, however, have rarely been about fundamentals but rather are usually concerned with estimates of certain trends or economic magnitudes. Ignorance may, of course, play a role in all this. After all, the crisis and the extreme destitution resulting from it have opened the continent to all sorts of quackery. An incredible number of peripatetic 'experts' hop from one part of Africa to another, prescribing one standard drug against all ills, leaving behind them enormous suffering with absolutely no accountability to anyone in Africa.

The experience in Africa is one of an unrelenting insistence on a standard package of measures despite the demonstration of its disastrous social consequences and economic wrong-headedness. This can only lead one to surmise that there are other, deeper systemic objectives of structural adjustment policies, and to attribute the policies to causes other than mere ignorance or technical errors.

The current wave of adjustment and the increase in interference in the internal affairs of African countries by foreign governments and international financial institutions have cast into sharper relief a number of contradictory processes. On the one hand the crisis has revived interest in those features of African economies that were stressed by the Dependency school. These include the extreme openness of African economies, the vulnerability of the accumulation process to import squeezes among economies so highly dependent on imported capital goods; the weakness of the national bourgeoisie *vis-à-vis* foreign interests. On the other hand, it has highlighted processes which have been taking place in Africa since independence, and which the Dependency school's preoccupation with stagnation or 'under-development' tended to obscure. What was wrong with the Dependency view was not the snapshot stylization of the structures of the economies but rather its failure to spell out the dynamics of these economies.

The central process in the development of African socio-economic systems was the building up of a national bourgeoisie and national capitalist economies whose emergence had been previously blocked by colonial rule. This process necessitated a highly interventionist state, regardless of the ideological disposition of the individual leaders. The measures adopted included nationalization, indigenization, and protection. It also provided room for various forms of 'primitive accumulation' – import licences, illegal privatization of state assets, uncollected loans, and so on. Because of the political constitution of the nationalist coalition, state policies tended to include such populist measures as subsidized food, free medical services, and minimum wages.

The adjustment process constitutes a derailment of a process of capitalist transformation of colonial economies into 'normal' peripheral capitalist economies, with more or less national control. It is a defeat of the 'nationalist project' by international capital.[29] And so, if the main intention of international finance has been to torpedo the nationalist attempts to establish indigenous capitalist classes and thereby increase foreign control of African societies, then the current programmes are succeeding as sector after sector of African economies is recaptured by international capital through privatization, 'policy dialogues', re-expatriation of key state and parastatal managerial positions and net outflow of capital. If the intention is to change the internal balance of forces between labour and capital in favour of the latter and to thus cheapen the social reproduction of labour, then the policies are on track as real wages decline everywhere and retrenchment swells the reserve army of the urban unemployed.

Notes and References

1. See, for instance, Vali Jamal and John Weeks, 1988.

2. Thandika Mkandawire, 1988.

3. On the basis of regression analysis linking manufacturing's share of GDP with GNP per capita and population, Gulhati and Sekhar found the rates of industrialization of Zambia, Kenya, and Tanzania were below the expected "Chenery norms". For Kenya, the observed share of value-added in manufacturing to GDP was 45 per cent less than the expected one. Tanzania's shortfall was 80 per cent while Zambia's was 50 per cent. Gulhati and Sekhar, 1982.

4. UN Economic Commission for Africa, 1983.

5. The following titles are indicative of the writing on the 'Africa crisis'. John Ravenhill (ed.) 1986; N. Chazan and T. Shaw (eds) 1988; S.K. Commins, M. Lofchie and R. Payne (eds) 1986; Peter Lawrence (ed.) 1986; Richard Sandbrook, 1985; Phillip Ndegwa, 1985; Bade Onimode, 1988.

6. I. Little, T. Scitovsky, and M. Scott, 1970.

7. World Bank, 1981, 'Leftist' versions of this view are advanced by Sheila Smith in Peter Lawrence (ed.) 1986.

8. Robert H. Jackson, and Carl G. Rosberg, 1982, p.3.

9. Robert Rice, 1984.

10. Göran Hyden, 1983.

11. René Lemarchand, in Art Hansen and D. Macmillan (eds) 1986.

12. M. Mamdani, 1986; and in P. Anyang' Nyong'o (ed.) 1987.

13. For a succinct presentation of the 'Neo-classical Political Economy' in the context of development see T.N. Strinivasan, 1985.

14. Especially R. Bates, (1986) and in S.K. Commins, M. Lofchie and R. Payne (eds) 1986.

15. Michael Lipton, 1977.

16. G. Arrighi and J. Saul, 1973.

17. See Bates, op. cit.

18. Robert Bates, 'The Regulation of Rural Markets in Africa' in Commins, Lofchie and Payne, op. cit., p.49.

19. For some case studies since 'Crisis and adjustment' see special issue of *Africa Development* Vol. 10, No. 1/2, 1985.

20. For the extent of the reforms see Cheryl Christensen and Lawrence Witucki, in Commins, Lofchie and Payne op. cit.

21. Kevin Cleaver, 1985.

22. World Bank, 1983. For a sceptical note on the objectivity of the index see the appendix in David Evans and Parvin Alizadeh in R. Kaplinsky (ed.) 1984.

23. The explanatory power and the robustness of the index is further reduced for the African countries included in the study. We obtained the following linear regression estimates:

$Y = 9.376 - 2.09DI$

$(-1,5099)$

$R^2 = 0.20$.

where Y = Gross Domestic Product
DI = Composite distortion index
and the value in parenthesis below the co-efficients is the t-ratio.

24. Helleiner empirically tested a model of the form.

$$\frac{Y}{Y} = a\frac{I}{Y} + b\frac{L}{Y} + y_1\frac{M}{Y} + y_3 \text{ (IVI)}$$

where Y = Gross Domestic Product
I = Gross investment
L = Labour
M = Imports
IVI = Measure of instability of import volume. Helleiner, 1986.

25. Hans Singer and Patricia Gray, 1988, pp. 395–403.
26. In a study of the long-run aggregate price elasticities of agricultural supply in 9 sub-Saharan countries, Bond found that these were positive but very low, from 0.07 to 0.54 (averaging 0.21) with six below 0.17 (M. Bond, 1984). For a survey of the literature on prices policy and agriculture in Africa see M. Fone-Sundell, 1987. Fone-Sundell shows the misuse of empirical evidence by the World Bank in its 'get the price right' campaign. In a number of cases, the World Bank has ignored its own studies casting doubt on the faith placed in the price mechanism.
27. Eicher, in C. Eicher and M. Staatz (eds) 1984.
28. Bruce F. Johnston, in Bates and Lofchie, (eds) 1980.
29. See Bernard Founou-Tchuigoua, 1988.

Bibliography

Anyang' Nyong'o Peter (ed.) (1987) *Popular Struggles for Democracy in Africa*. London, Zed Books.

Arrighi, G., and J. Saul (1973) *Essays in the Political Economy of Africa*. New York, Monthly Review.

Bates, R. (1981) *Markets and States in Tropical Africa: The Political Basis of Agricultural Policies*, Berkeley, University of California Press.

―――― (1986a) 'The Regulation of Rural Markets in Africa' in S.K. Commins, M. Lofchie and R. Payne (eds) (1986).

―――― and M. Lofchie (eds) (1980) *Agricultural Development in Africa, Issues of Public Policy*. New York, Praeger.

Bond, M.L. (1984) 'Agricultural Responses to Price in sub-Saharan African Countries'. *IMF Staff Papers*, Vol. 30, 4, December.

Chazan, N. and T. Shaw (eds) (1988) *Coping with Africa's Food Crisis*, Boulder, Col., Lynne Reinner Publishers.

Christensen, Cheryl and Lawrence Witucki (1986) 'Food Policies in sub-Saharan Africa' in Commins, Lofchie and Payne (eds) (1986).

Cleaver, K. (1985) 'The Impact of Price and Exchange Rate Policies on Agriculture in sub-Saharan Africa'. Staff Working Paper, Washington, DC., World Bank.

Commins, S.K., and M. Lofchie (eds) (1986) *Africa's Agrarian Crisis: The Roots of Famine*. Boulder, Col., Lynne Rienner Publishers.

Commins, S.K., M. Lofchie and R. Payne (eds) (1986) 'Food Policy in Africa: Political Causes and Social Effects', *Food Policy*, Vol. 6, No. 3.

Eicher, C. (1984) 'Facing up to Africa's Food Crisis' in C. Eicher and M. Staatz (eds) 1984.

―――― and M. Staatz (eds) (1984) *Agricultural Development in the Third World*. Baltimore, Johns Hopkins University Press.

Evans, David and Parvin Alizadeh (1984) 'Trade, Industrialisation and the Visible Hand' in R. Kaplinsky (ed.) 1984.

Fone-Sundell, M. (1987) 'Role of Price Policy in Stimulating Agricultural Production in Africa'. Issue Paper No. 2. IRDC, Uppsala, Swedish University of Agricultural Sciences.

Founou-Tchuigoua, B. (1988) 'Crise et Recul du Nationalisme Economique d'Etat Collective en Afrique'. *Africa Development*, Vol. 13, No. 1.

Gulhati, Ravi and Uday Sekhar (1982) 'Industrial Strategy for Late Starters: The Experience of Kenya , Tanzania and Zambia', *World Development*, Vol. 10, No. 11.

Hansen, Art and D. Macmillan (eds) (1986) *Food in Sub-Saharan Africa*. Boulder, Col., Lynne Rienner Publishers.

Helleiner, G. K. (1986) 'Outward Orientation, Import Instability and African Economic Growth: An Empirical Investigation' in S. Lall and F. Stewart, 1986.

Hyden, Goran (1983) *No Shortcuts to Progress: African Development Management in Perspective*. Berkeley, University of California Press.

Jackson, Robert H., and Carl G. Rosberg (1982) *Personal Rule in Africa: Prince, Autocrat, Prophet, Tyrant*. Berkeley, University of California Press.

Jamal, Vali and John Weeks (1988) 'The Vanishing Rural–Urban Gap in Sub-Saharan Africa'. *International Labour Review*, Vol. 127, No. 3.

Johnston, Bruce F., (1980) 'Agricultural Production Potentials and Small Farm Strategies in Sub-Saharan Africa' in R. Bates and M. Loftchie (eds) 1980.

Kaplinsky, R. (ed.) (1984) *Third World Industrialization in the 1980s: Open Economies in a Closing World*. London, Frank Cass.

Lall, S. and F. Stewart (1986) *Theory and Reality in Development: Essays in Honour of Paul Streeten*. London, Macmillan.

Lawrence, Peter (ed.) (1986) *The World Recession and the Food Crisis in Africa*. London, James Currey.

Lemarchand, René (1986) 'The Political Economy of Food Issues' in Hansen, Art and D. Macmillan (eds) (1986).

Lipton, Michael (1977) *Why Poor People Stay Poor: Urban Bias in World Development*. Cambridge, Mass., Harvard University Press.

Little, I., T. Scitovsky and M. Scott (1970) *Industry and Trade in Some Developing Countries: A Comparative Study*. London, Oxford University Press.

Mamdani, M. (1986) 'Ebauche d'une analyse de la Question agraire en Ouganda', *Africa Development*, Vol. XI, No. 4.

——— (1987) 'Contradictory Class Perspectives on the Question of Democracy: The Case of Uganda' in Anyang Nyong'o, P. (ed.) (1987).

Mkandawire, Thandika (1988) 'The Road to Crisis, Adjustment and Deindustrialization: The African Case'. *African Development*, Vol. 12, No. 1.

Ndegwa, Phillip (1985) *Africa's Development Crisis*. Nairobi, Heinemann.

Onimode, Bade (1988) *A Political Economy of the African Crisis*. London, Zed Books.

Ravenhill, John (ed.) (1986) *Africa in Economic Crisis*. London, Macmillan.

Rice, Robert (1984) 'Neocolonialism and Ghana's Economic Decline: A Critical Assessment'. *Canadian Journal of African Studies*, Vol. 18, No. 1.

Sandbrook, Richard (1985) *The Politics of Africa's Economic Stagnation*, Cambridge, Cambridge University Press.

Singer, Hans and Patricia Gray (1988) 'Trade Policy and Growth of Developing Countries: Some New Data'. *World Development*, Vol. 16, No. 3.

Smith, Sheila (1986) 'What's Right with the Berg Report and What's Left of its Criticism' in Peter Lawrence (ed.) (1986).

Strinivasan, T. N. (1985) 'The Neoclassical Political Economy, the State and Economic Development'. *Asian Development Review*, Vol. 3, No. 2.

UN Economic Commission for Africa (1983) *ECA and Africa's Development 1983–2000: A Preliminary Perspective Study*. Addis Ababa, UN, ECA.

World Bank (1981) *Accelerated Development in Sub-Saharan Africa: An Agenda for Action*. Washington DC., IBRD.

——— (1983) *World Development Report*. Washington DC.

6. Economic Crisis, Structural Adjustment and the State in Sub-Saharan Africa[1]

Richard Sandbrook

Introduction

'Bleak' is the word usually employed to describe Africa's economic prospects. Not only has Tropical Africa had the world's lowest rate of economic growth, but solely this region has experienced a decline in per capita food production since 1965. Shocks emanating from the international economy, ecological degradation in the context of rapid population growth, domestic policy errors, and internal political-administrative weaknesses are the factors commonly adduced to explain this plight. Africa's record is far from uniformly cheerless, but people in many countries are poorer and hungrier today than at independence three decades ago.

By 1989, 35 sub-Saharan African countries had adopted structural adjustment programmes designed to relieve external and internal imbalances and facilitate the resumption of growth. These programmes, as is well known, are largely financed with loans from the World Bank and/or International Monetary Fund. 'Structural adjustment' is not a concept with a single or fixed meaning. In Africa, it generally involves a set of policy reforms to maximize reliance upon markets in domestic and external trade and capital flows, minimize the government's interventionist role by reducing public ownership, subsidies and regulation, and improve the state's efficiency in allocating and using resources.

But the economic benefits of adjustment in most African cases have been modest or lacking.[2] Few reform programmes have achieved the targeted growth rate or increase in per capita agricultural production, or improved the current accounts balance and external debt position.[3]

The reasons for the feebleness of Africa's recovery are several. International factors form a major set of impediments. The IMF/World Bank's policy of export promotion is misconceived in a world where commodity markets remain soft and many developing countries specialize in the same primary commodities. Africa's payments on its massive external debt also hobble recovery. The major trading partners, aid donors and creditors in the West have not supported the painful economic reforms with the requisite level of financing and improved trading conditions. Agricultural production requires, in addition to appropriate prices, credit availability, reliable infrastructure and research; but these non-price factors have often suffered as a result of austerity-induced declines in development expenditures.

There are also domestic political and administrative impediments which, I shall argue, structural adjustment programmes have unknowingly exacerbated. State incapacity and economic crisis are intimately interrelated. Institutional decay and political instability had already bedevilled development prospects in some countries in the 1960s and 1970s, most strikingly perhaps in Ghana, Guinea, Equatorial Guinea, Central African Empire/Republic, Uganda and Zaire. But governmental organizations in most countries continued to cope adequately in difficult circumstances. The decade-long depression of the 1980s has, however, revealed these organizations' fragility. Economic crisis retarded and in some countries eviscerated the process of forming functioning national states attuned (among other things) to the economic rationality of the market or the plan. And the technocratic orientation of structural adjustment unintentionally intensified the ungovernability of countries already reeling from declining living standards. This political-administrative decline has had a number of unfortunate consequences, not least for the viability of economic reform itself.

The role of the state

Paradoxically, the success of the orthodox market-oriented approach depends critically upon the state. True, the government's economic functions are to shrink, but within its more limited sphere an expert and effective bureaucratized state is required. This is obvious in so far as policy reforms are only as good as their implementation. Structural adjustment assumes an institutional capacity to design and implement complex policies concerning prices, trade, banking, finance and foreign investment, to reform parastatals, and to manage complicated negotiations with donors and the subsequent assistance programmes. The state, originally conceived as part of the problem of economic decline, is to contribute to the solution.

The state is also crucial in a more indirect way. Markets do not spontaneously come into being. They operate satisfactorily only within a particular political, economic and legal framework. If this framework does not obtain, it must be created, and this is the role of the state. One of Karl Polanyi's great accomplishments in *The Great Transformation* was to demonstrate the centrality of the state even in the case of Britain's *laissez-faire* capitalist experience of the eighteenth and nineteenth centuries.

> The road to the free market was opened and kept open by an enormous increase in continuous, centrally organized and controlled interventionism . . . [E]ven those who wished most ardently to free the state from all unnecessary duties, and whose whole philosophy demanded the restriction of state activities, could not but entrust the self-same state with the new powers, organs and instruments required for the establishment of *laissez-faire*.[4]

Max Weber (Collins 1980) perceptively observed that capitalism thrives only if a calculable environment exists. This requires national unification and the formation of a national market by the elimination of internal trade barriers, the creation of a recognized national currency, and the establishment of political order. It also requires the reliable functioning of a physical and social infrastructure; interruptions of electricity and water supplies, for instance, are very costly to manufacturing enterprises. Finally, and most importantly, a robust capitalism is possible only with a predictable system of law, taxation and administration that protects private property, sanctions contracts, fosters accumulation, and counteracts the anti-competitive tendency toward economic concentration (or at least regulates private monopolies).

The need for such a state, however, does not call it into being. In the 47 countries of sub-Saharan Africa, there is significant variation in the degree of state capability. Only a handful of well-articulated and effective states exists. Governments in Botswana, Cameroon, Côte d'Ivoire, Mauritius, Rwanda, Senegal and Zimbabwe are capable of maintaining social order and devising and implementing diverse policies. But 'effective' is a relative word. Attempted coups, localized insurrections and/or official incompetence and corruption are not strangers even in these countries. At the other extreme is a handful of states so ineffectual that they can barely be said to govern the territory over which they claim jurisdiction. Rulers in Zaire, Uganda, Sudan, Chad, Equatorial Guinea, Ghana and Mozambique can scarcely expect to see their writ obeyed in certain areas, let alone formulate and implement complex economic policies. The main goal of many public officials, except during periodic clean-up campaigns, is simply personal survival or aggrandizement; the common people and their concerns receive short shrift.

The majority of states fall somewhere between these two ends of the spectrum. That is, they possess at best a minimal capacity to create order, formulate and implement policy, and manage public boards and corporations. Periodic disorder and instability, the unreliability and inadequacy of the infrastructure, smuggling and black-market activity, and uneven or capricious public management and regulation are unconducive to productive entre-preneurial activities.[5]

Constraints on the formation of effective rational-legal states in Africa

Why are effective rational-legal states rare? The simple answer is that historical, social and material conditions obstruct their formation. This is true, indeed a truism; explanatory depth calls for the addition of three provisos. First, one must distinguish between the long-term historical processes that affect the governability of societies and short-term or contingent obstacles, such as a devastating economic depression. Secondly, historical, social and material conditions are far from uniform from one African country to another; any finely tuned comparative analysis of state capacity will explain the variance partly in terms of the *differences* in conditions. (Space unfortunately constrains the presentation of such a discerning and detailed analysis here.) Thirdly, the quality and goals of political leadership deeply influence the extent and form of state formation. For a dramatic illustration, consider the case of Uganda in the 1970s. The disastrous rule of Idi Amin was not inevitable, though the historical and structural conditions of Uganda made possible the emergence of such a ruler as Amin. Other leaders with less destructive tendencies would not have reduced the Ugandan state to the shambling and oppressive predator it became by 1975. Structural conditions shape possibilities; the actions and decisions of leaders and movements determine which possibilities are realized.

From a long-term historical viewpoint, the paucity of effective capitalist states is not surprising. Their formation is a long and conflictual process. In Europe, the formation of modern states began in the sixteenth or seventeenth century. State formation involved the gradual accumulation and centralization of power that enabled a government to exercise effective control within a territory and implement policies. This process was violent as well as long. On the one hand, the centralizing state-builders periodically increased their demands upon the dominated classes living within an expanding swathe of territory: demands for revenue, for recruits for the army, and for agricultural output. On the other hand, peasants resisted these exactions, and regionally powerful nobles mobilized against the incursions of the centralizing monarch. European state-formation was a story told against a background of class struggles, regionally based revolts, wars between rival state-builders, and factional palace intrigues.

The disorganization and disorder of most African states is clearly related to their recency and origins in foreign conquest. In all but a handful of cases – Swaziland, Lesotho, Rwanda, Burundi, Ethiopia – the history of statehood began only with the imposition of colonial or semi-colonial rule toward the end of the nineteenth century. During the ensuing 70 or 80 years, the imperial powers transplanted institutional models from the metropolis within the arbitrarily drawn boundaries of their colonies. Colonial governments, until the post-war period, were more or less adequate for their limited tasks, namely: the levying of taxes, the preservation of law and order, and the construction and maintenance of basic services. But the lack of any organic connections between recently installed governmental structures and the political traditions of their host societies, in addition to the often extreme cultural-linguistic diversity, would later impede state formation.

After independence, the new rulers tried to accumulate and centralize power on the basis of inherited institutions. They aimed to neutralize opponents, especially regionally/ethnically-based ones and push forward ambitious development programmes – 'socialism', rapid industrialization, pan-Africanism, and so on. But the limitations of state power soon became apparent.

Historical, social and material conditions hampered the consolidation of an effective, rational-legal state.[6] One constraint (discussed extensively later) was the states' weak fiscal basis owing to the relatively extreme poverty of most societies. Another was the lack of a long history of centralized rule and a homogeneous political tradition; this denied the new rulers a firm foundation in the habitual compliance of the population. Once the solidarity forged in the anti-colonial struggle dissipated, it was difficult to reconstruct. The traditional legitimacy of pre-colonial polities was largely irrelevant in the culturally heterogeneous contemporary state. Patriotism was unlikely to elicit consent in countries where the recency of territorial units and the saliency of ethnicity vitiated a strong sense of national unity. And class ideologies that elsewhere have facilitated compliance, especially liberalism and socialism, have few roots to sustain them.

This points to another constraint: the weakness of class as a source of political power. Ultimately, it is the political ascendancy of a bourgeoisie that channels and disciplines political power, ensuring that capitalist priorities and requirements are also those of the state. The bourgeoisie's ascendancy in Marxian analysis derives from its economic power, from its ownership of assets in an economic sphere that is autonomous from the state. But, in Africa, the capitalist class is weakened not only by its limited numbers, recent origins, foreign-local and ethnic divisions, but also by the limited scope of market relations outside the cities, and particularly the politicization of the economic sphere. The statist models of post-colonial development made economic success dependent upon political decisions. Hence, political power relations exercised through the state have conditioned property relations – in the formal sector at least – as much or more than the reverse. These factors constrain any hegemonic pretensions of indigenous bourgeoisies, except in thoroughly commercialized societies such as that in Zimbabwe.[7] The proletariat, whose struggles with capital and the state in Western societies have shaped the emergence of highly articulated social democracies, is in Africa small, only partially separated from the means of production, and subject to political control. If anything, the power of the working classes is in decline. By augmenting the insecurity of wage-earners and forcing them into supplementary self-employment in order to survive, the contemporary crisis weakens the cohesion of the labour movement. The vast majority of citizens are part-time or full-time peasants, pastoralists, traders, artisans and casual labourers – groups with an acknowledged incapacity for autonomous class organization. To reduce the state-society relationship to state-class relations in most African societies is to beg a central question and misunderstand the predicament of the post-colonial state.

A 'natural', though not inevitable, tendency of rulers in these circumstances is to have recourse to patrimonial mechanisms of governance. For Max Weber, patrimonialism was a form of authority that emerged in pre-industrial societies with large and politically inert peasantries and a nobility which competed for the favour of the monarch. The politics of patrimonial rule was not ideologically based but directed only at the distribution of material resources, power and prestige. It was a politics of factions, interrupted periodically by short-lived peasant rebellions and other disturbances. But history does not repeat itself; the conditions of sub-Saharan Africa are only analogous to those of traditional patrimonialism. Neither wholly pre-industrial societies nor hereditary monarchs and nobles are to be found here. And ideological themes and class conflicts do intrude into the political arenas. Nonetheless, in the context of many of Africa's peasant societies, one does find 'presidential-monarchs', a '*noblesse d'état*' (not yet a bourgeoisie-for-itself), and a political life characterized predominantly by factional manoeuvring and the exclusion of the peasantry. One can, therefore, in these cases, speak of *neo*-patrimonialism or personal rule – a form of governance based chiefly upon personal loyalties, patron-client networks and coercion.

Structural conditions, however, do not predetermine a neo-patrimonial outcome. The lack of a single political culture, the weakness of national integration, the widespread poverty, the predominance of the peasantry and the limited development of a class society – all these factors strain central institutions and encourage leaders to substitute personalistic authority, mercenary ties, and force for a weak institutional legitimacy. But these conditions vary in their severity from country to country. So, too, do the inclinations of leaders: while President Kenyatta relished the monarchical role, President Nyerere abjured it in favour of the stance of a *mwalimu*. Neo-patrimonialism is thus only a tendency, though an important one.

Personal rule is dangerous in that, while it provides a time-worn, albeit uncertain, formula for order under hostile conditions, it is potentially economically destructive. If unrestrained by an astute leadership, its short-term political rationality of personal and regime survival may generate a variety of economic irrationalities that smother capitalism's expansive dynamics. Clientelism and nepotism fill the ranks of the public sector with incompetent but politically loyal administrators. Maladministration contributes to a decline in essential services and the economic infrastructure. The privatization of public office breeds capricious as well as incompetent administration; corruption, embezzlement, bottlenecks, favour to political insiders and clients destroy the calculability that investors require. The consequent political instability has the same effect. Not risk-taking, market-oriented entrepreneurial activities but manipulation of state contracts and regulations, credit facilities, licensed monopolies, and foreign-exchange holdings – or even officially countenanced fraud and theft from the public sector – can become the easiest road to wealth. All of these activities vitiate economic efficiency and productivity.

By the early 1970s, these potentially destructive tendencies of personalistic rule had actually wrought extensive economic damage in a few countries, most notably Zaire, Uganda, Ghana and Guinea. Elsewhere, as in Botswana, Côte d'Ivoire, Kenya, Tanzania and Cameroon, shrewd political management kept these tendencies in check, and the public service continued to function competently. Then, the shocks of the late 1970s and early 1980s in the form of soaring oil prices, drought, rising interest rates and declining terms of trade precipitated or accelerated a downward spiral of economic and political decay. Only a few states could cope effectively as foreign debts became unmanageable, foreign exchange shortfalls eliminated essential imports, and poverty deepened. This debilitating politico-economic decline is now difficult to halt and reverse.

Political Obstcls.

Therefore, structural adjustment policies must today address a situation in which economic crisis has undermined already weakened state structures. Since the success of structural adjustment partly depends on the effectiveness and orientation of the state, policies should seek to buttress state capacity as well as correct economic shortcomings. Yet the conventional approach of the World Bank and the International Monetary Fund addresses only economic variables, regarding domestic political processes merely as obstacles to the adoption and implementation of 'rational' economic policies.[8] Political scientists are set to work to determine how the opposition of recalcitrant political élites, monopoly-rent collecting insiders, and urban workers can be assuaged or managed. But the problem is not simply to reassure reluctant governments that they can 'get prices right' and eliminate disequilibria without being overthrown. It is also to maintain or build the capacity of governments to govern. This requires policies to mitigate the deleterious social effects of structural adjustment ('adjustment with a human face'), but much more as well.

A rational-legal state capable of effectively carrying out its economic functions possesses three essential traits. It extracts adequate resources from society, rests upon the consent of most of its citizens, and utilizes a cohesive, differentiated, specialized and competent bureaucracy. These dimensions are interrelated. A state needs revenue to support its coercive and administrative apparatuses; and only the effective operation of an administration and a police force generates the needed resources. But an efficient coercive and administrative apparatus is not a sufficient basis for a stable, calculable political order. Governments reliant on coercion are wholly dependent upon the means of repression, and thus vulnerable to a *coup d'état*. As well, they will have to contend with the debilitating effects of popular hostility or indifference: widespread tax evasion, passive disobedience, military recruits who are unwilling to fight, and eventually bureaucratic malaise and corruption. The effectiveness and efficiency of a government, therefore, fundamentally depends upon the degree of willing compliance it commands – upon hegemony in the Gramscian sense. Legitimacy, a sense of obligation to obey, is the surest and cheapest basis of consent. In its absence, a pragmatically-based support will suffice. Such support derives not from moral considerations, but from a hard-headed calculation of material returns. Patronage and prebends often play an important role in building the assent that allows governments to govern, and minimally fulfil their crucial economic and political roles.

If capitalism is the most realistic economic system for satisfying basic needs in Africa's harsh circumstances, then states with these characteristics must gradually develop. It is difficult to know how to foster state formation; however, the prevailing economistic or technocratic approach is clearly inadequate. A more enlightened tack starts by recognizing that each of the three dimensions of state formation is impeded by economic crisis, and that current adjustment policies often aggravate the situation. To elucidate this statement, consider in turn the fiscal, hegemonic and administrative crises afflicting many African countries.

The effect of the fiscal crisis on African state-formation

A *fiscal crisis* severely limits African state-formation. This surfaced in the late 1970s as declining public revenues encountered a strong resistance to the reduction of public expenditures.

The principal source of public revenues is export–import taxes, especially levies on one or a handful of primary commodity exports. Income and profit taxes are rarely a major contributor to public coffers, owing to the limited number of enumerated income and profit earners and the opportunities for tax evasion where tax investigators are few and corruptible.[9] Levies on primary commodity exports typically generate, in one form or another, from one-quarter to one-half of public revenues.[10] In oil-exporting economies such as Nigeria's, or in copper-exporting economies such as Zambia's, the extractive sector accounts for well over half the government's income in the form of taxes on employees' incomes and corporate profits, royalties, and export duties.

Cyclical swings in commodity prices have had a disastrous effect on budgets (as well as on external accounts). During the era of price increases in the 1970s, most governments increased expenditures proportionately, or more so. The collapse of commodity prices at the end of the decade instigated fiscal crises for governments committed to ambitious projects with high recurrent costs. Of course, not all countries fell into a 'commodity cycle trap';[11] Cameroon and Botswana managed their boom revenues prudently. Cameroon used much of the extra revenues from the oil boom in 1979–81 to repay its external debt. Public spending in Botswana fell as a share of GDP during the diamond boom following 1983. Adjusting to the downswing in world prices was thus much easier in these two countries than in most of the rest.

Public expenditures rose sharply following independence, reflecting the statist approach to development of regimes whether professedly 'capitalist' or 'socialist'. The governments' expansive economic and social roles boosted growth of public employment. This commonly increased at a rate two or three times that of population; annual rates of growth of central government employment as high as 14 or 15 per cent were recorded in Zaire, Ghana and Tanzania for certain periods in the 1960s, 1970s or early 1980s.[12] Regionally, employment in regular-line agencies of central and local government grew by an estimated 240 per cent in the 20 years following 1960 – from 1.9 to 6.5 million. If non-financial parastatal organizations are included, public employment climbed by about 160 per cent in this period, to a total of about ten million. By 1980, the public sector accounted for half of those in non-agricultural wage employment.[13] Overstaffing sometimes reached major proportions. In one West African country, a consultant concluded that 6,000 of 6,800 headquarters staff in two ministries were redundant.[14] Censuses of their civil services carried out by the Central African Republic and Guinea in the mid-1980s discovered that 1,300 and 7,000 employees respectively were 'phantom workers' – bogus employees whose salaries were pocketed by those in on the scam.[15]

Recent adjustment programmes aim to equilibrate revenues and expenditures by squeezing the latter. If cuts have to be made, state managers are more likely to prune capital and maintenance costs than others.[16] External debt service has grown – usually to one-third or more of current public revenue – but this expenditure is unavoidable, barring a multilateral agreement on debt relief. Significant reductions in the defence budget are unlikely because, where governmental authority is shaky, political leaders are wary of alienating the armed forces. Governments also resist cutting public employment. The very identity of the state is bound up with the administrative apparatus. In the outlying districts, the only symbols of the state may be the local government offices, with the national flag flying out front, and an army detachment. Also, the public sector generally plays an important role in servicing the patron-client networks on which the political élite survival largely depends. As economic decline depresses middle-class living standards and exacerbates political discontent, the rulers resist reducing patronage to fickle supporters in the state apparatus. Administrative apparatuses do not serve only the end of economic efficiency; they are valuable as well as 'employers of last resort' when widespead unemployment and discontent threaten political order and national unity.

On the revenue side, adjustment policies create a perplexing dilemma. On the one hand, effective taxation rates of 50 per cent deter primary producers from increasing or even maintaining agricultural output. On the other hand, export taxes are the chief source of public revenue in most countries. How can governments reduce burgeoning budget deficits and massive external debts at the same time as they forego an important part of their revenues? The World Bank and other international agencies strongly press for a reduction in export taxes in order to channel more returns to producers. But there is no escaping the bind that reliance on the sale of a few commodities and faulty policy have created.

> Even for crops where the price elasticity of supply is very high, and where the revenues arising from increased sales would partly – or even fully – compensate the public sector for lower tax rates, the lag in supply response for most crops must imply that the short-term effects on public revenues would be strongly negative.[17]

Until world commodity prices rise, the prospect of solving the fiscal crisis is meagre.

Meanwhile, the budgetary cut-backs weaken the state and make production increasingly costly. Roads, railways, water, power and telephone systems deteriorate. Supplies to all public services diminish: classrooms lack textbooks and even chalk, health clinics and hospitals lack vaccines and medicines, agricultural extension workers and field officers lack means of transport or, if these are available, lack fuel or spare parts, and thus cannot do their job, and so on. The morale, honesty and efficiency of civil servants decline. Denied the tools to do their jobs satisfactorily, they give up. Denied adequate salaries and benefits, officials turn to moonlighting (often during office hours) or corruption to make ends meet. Once these patterns are established, they are difficult to reverse.

The effect of the hegemonic crisis on African state-formation

A *hegemonic crisis* is associated with this fiscal crisis. Willing compliance is the only sure basis for stable and effective domination of a leading class through the state. As consent declines so too does the governability of a society in which the coercive force at the centre is meagre or unreliable. This has been the story in many sub-Saharan countries.

One indicator of hegemonic crisis is the high incidence of political violence. These countries have suffered far more war and war-related deaths since 1960 (when many African colonies became independent) than other regions of the Third World with larger populations. 'War deaths' – those resulting from 'any armed conflict which includes one or more governments, and causes the deaths of 1,000 or more people per year'[18] – comprise deaths from both internal wars (national liberation struggles, revolts, insurrections, rebellions, revolutions and civil wars) and wars between states. An estimated 4.5 million people died from these political causes in sub-Saharan Africa (excluding South Africa and Namibia) in 1960–87. In the same period, war and war-related deaths claimed 330,000 in Latin America, 41,000 in India and 55,000 in China.[19]

Civil wars and insurrections have taken the major toll in lives and ruined economies. *Coups d'état* have been plentiful – one study is provocatively entitled 'Sixty Coups in Thirty Years'[20] – but most of these have been 'palace coups' with low human and (direct) economic costs. Benin holds the record with six successful coups, closely followed by Ghana, Uganda and Sudan. For each successful coup, there are generally three or four unsuccessful attempts and foiled plots. Interstate wars (for example those between Somalia and Ethiopia in 1977, and Tanzania and Uganda in 1978–79) have been rare and much less costly than wars of national liberation (in particular, those in the Portuguese territories before 1975, and Zimbabwe until 1979) and, above all, civil wars. Table 6.1 indicates that civil wars and insurrections accounted for almost four million of the 4.5 million African lives lost in large-scale political violence. Scattered riots and commmunal violence and flagrant official violations of human rights (as recorded in Amnesty International's annual reports) are further manifestations of hegemonic crisis in many countries.

What accounts for this disturbing record of violence and discord afflicting countries with well over half of Tropical Africa's population? Colonialism is implicated, directly in that many deaths resulted from national liberation struggles, and indirectly in that the colonies were conquered territories that arbitrarily grouped diverse cultural-linguistic groups within common boundaries. This, in conjunction with the uneven regional impress of development and the politicization of ethnic identities by ambitious politicians, fostered the regional/ethnic hostilities which, at their worst, can degenerate into civil wars. The other exogenous factor is the willingness of external powers

Table 6.1
Civil war deaths in sub-Saharan Africa (deaths in thousands)

Country	Opponents	Date	Deaths
Angola	UNITA	1975–87	213
Burundi	Hutu/Tutsi	1972	100
Chad	various	1980–87	7
Ethiopia	Eritrea	1974–87	546*
Mozambique	Renamo	1981–87	401*
Nigeria	Biafra	1967–70	2,000
Sudan	North/South	1963–72	500
Sudan	North/South	1984–87	10
Uganda	various	1981–87	102
Zaire	Katanga	1960–65	100
Zimbabwe	Ndebele	1983	2
Total			3,981

Source: Calculated from data in Sivard 1987, 31.

*Includes war-induced famine deaths.

to 'fish in troubled waters'. Foreign interventions, both overt and covert, have instigated or exacerbated local conflicts and regional wars – as recently in Ethiopia, Chad, Zaire, Mozambique, Angola, Lesotho and Zimbabwe.

But these foreign intrigues were feasible only because national governments did not command the loyalty of many of their citizens. Consent is firm when it has a normative basis in a legitimating ideology; but ideologies are unlikely to be persuasive in the absence of the appropriate material conditions. If the ruled are to consent to their subordinate position with a social order, they must believe that it satisfies their minimum material interests.[21] However, as suggested earlier (pp. 96–97) the ruling groups in post-colonial African countries have had difficulty in fashioning a legitimating formula for their domination. With its weak normative basis, the state is thus highly vulnerable to a prolonged economic depression. Disaffection grows with falling real wages and returns from cash crops, rising unemployment and under-employment, escalating prices, shortages of essential commodities and deterioration of public services. And the austerity introduced by structural adjustment programmes usually undermines further the government's popular support. The cities are the main site for public demonstrations of hostility to the state and the privileged classes. Disaffection also takes a regional-ethnic dimension where decline is regionally uneven and the rulers hail disproportionately from the prosperous regions. Moreover, the decline in public revenues and consequent deterioration of the transport and communications systems weaken the state's coercive arm, thereby encouraging the insurrectional tendencies of counter-élites.

But not only does economic decline heighten pressures toward state disintegration; political chaos in turn aggravates economic problems. Private investors flee. Agricultural production plummets. Financing the military machine and repairing war damage drain scarce resources from essential public services and capital investments. Whereas military expenditures accounted in 1984 for an average 3.0 per cent of GNP in sub-Saharan Africa as a whole, defence ate up a far higher proportion in countries engaged in internal wars: 14.2 per cent in Angola, 10.4 per cent in Chad, 9.3 per cent in Ethiopia, 4.8 per cent in Mozambique, and 6.2 per cent in Zimbabwe (which has committed 12,000 troops to securing a rail corridor through Mozambique to Beira).[22] The result of these factors is severe budget and balance of payments deficits.

In extreme cases, as in Mozambique, Ethiopia, Angola, Sudan, Chad and Uganda, civil wars eviscerate already faltering domestic economies. Mozambique's war has disrupted production and transport to the extent that 80 per cent of visible and invisible exports have been lost. The dislocation of almost half of the country's rural population – 4.5 million people – has decimated agricultural output. And defence absorbs 40 per cent of government spending.[23] Clearly, the macro-economic costs of war in Mozambique (and the other countries mentioned) outweigh even those of inappropriate policies, drought and shifts in the international terms of trade. When drought coincides with insurrection, starvation threatens even in countries with abundant land and no history of famine.

In less extreme cases of political disorder, insurgency shades off into banditry or isolated rebellions – as in Zaire or Nigeria in the past few years. The macro-economic and human costs are not as severe as in the former countries, though the general insecurity and incapacity of the state impede economic recovery.

Political disorder and economic decline are thus closely linked; a precondition for economic recovery where disorder prevails is social peace. Structural adjustment programmes cannot succeed in the context of a civil war, since they can only be implemented – and then merely partially – in 'secure' areas around cities and towns.[24] It is difficult to find the formulas for resolving these conflicts and generating consent, especially where outside powers are involved on opposing sides. But the World Bank and IMF could help by recognizing that policies must serve political as well as economic ends. Adjustment policies that ignore the political exigencies of weakly-integrated neo-patrimonial states place further strains on hard-pressed governments. Rulers must service patron-client networks and guarantee protection to rural dwellers in order to survive; and adjustment policies cannot be implemented if order disintegrates.

The effect of the crisis of administrative capacity on African state-formation

Economic depression is also reciprocally related to what some see as a *crisis of administrative capacity*. 'Crisis' is not too strong a word if it is true, as Robert S. McNamara declares, that 'a number of previously able and functioning institutions are now losing their effectiveness'. He sees:

> Entire central ministries that are no longer in adequate control of their budgets and personnel, public agencies that have lost their capacity to carry out their proper tasks, state universities, scientific facilities, and statistical offices that have seriously declined in the quality of their work, parastatal organizations and marketing boards that impede rather than promote productivity, and critically important agricultural research institutions that are becoming increasingly ineffective.[25]

Yet this picture is misleading in so far as administrative capacity varies widely. At one extreme are countries like Uganda, Zaire and Guinea which saw in the 1970s a virtual collapse of their civil services and professional standards. At the other are a few countries like Botswana, Zimbabwe and Côte d'Ivoire that have maintained effective bureaucracies. Most countries fall somewhere in between.

Two processes impinge on the capacity of the public service. One is the politicization of the bureaucracy attendant upon a growing resort to patrimonial mechanisms of rule. The other is the squeeze placed on the salaries, perquisites and facilities of civil servants as revenues shrink and external agencies press governments to reduce budget deficits. Both processes, unless carefully managed, vitiate administrative effectiveness.

Consider the impact on public administration of the emergence of neo-patrimonial rule. Bureaucracy at independence is vulnerable as office-holders have not had time to develop a distinctive *esprit de corps*. It will degenerate into patrimonial administration unless the supreme leader shields it from the corrosive impact of patron-client politics. Often, however, the presidential-monarch treats the administration as his personal property. He or his lieutenants select the top administrators on the basis of personal loyalties and assign their tasks as they see fit. The public officials, in turn, 'treat their administrative work for the ruler as a personal service based on their duty of obedience and respect'.[26] The ruler may even permit his officials to act arbitrarily and corruptly, provided this behaviour does not breed rebellion. Consequently, the bureaucratic virtues of hierarchical authority, expertise, neutrality, predictability and efficiency erode and may eventually vanish.

Yet this is not the invariable outcome. In Côte d'Ivoire, for example, bureaucratization has been relatively successful. This success is due to a consistent policy of President Houphouet-Boigny and his stable coterie of lieutenants: to Africanize the public service slowly and to ensure that key positions are filled, not with political clients, but with qualified applicants who have satisfied the high standards of a French-dominated secondary and post-secondary educational system. This, together with appropriate incentives and accountability, has permitted the socialization of public servants into bureaucratic norms and values:

> Given the natural tendency toward inertia, the longer a structure survives the more difficult it is to disrupt. In Côte d'Ivoire the deliberate policy of

maintaining [the bureaucracy's] continuity with the colonial past meant that the disintegration and weakening of bureaucratic values and procedures, caused elsewhere by rapid Africanization and political penetration, would have been avoided. The significance of the expatriate presence did not derive from the occupation of executive positions as such, but from the continuity of institutional procedures and "agency ideologies" which they ensured.[27]

When corruption, nepotism, inefficiency and arbitrariness reach the levels found in Uganda, Zaire, Guinea and Nigeria, unrestrained personalistic politics is usually a principal cause and must be reformed. Elsewhere, however, neo-patrimonialism has furnished a minimal basis for governance without bringing an economy to ruin. Patrimonialism originated in Asian and European countries in which élites lived by extracting a surplus from the peasant majority. It survived for a long time there, and thrives today in 'modern' guise in many countries (for example, Thailand, Philippines and Indonesia). In the unintegrated peasant societies of Tropical Africa, neo-patrimonialism is a form of governance which, though not inevitable, is compatible with social and material conditions. Should patronage flows be severely reduced, governance would rest more heavily on repression – heightening human suffering and undermining an already tenuous national integration and political stability.

The other damaging process is the recent shrinking of the salaries and amenities of public servants. Since it is politically suicidal for rulers to dismiss many civil servants in a context of massive unemployment and poverty, governments retain most of their employees while allowing their real incomes to fall. This is a way of reconciling political realities with the need to reduce budgetary deficits. But the decline of civil servants' salaries can be devastating. In Sudan, basic starting salaries fell by four-fifths between 1970 and 1983, while in Ghana and Uganda, real starting salaries had fallen below subsistence level by 1983.[28] In Guinea, the average salary in the civil service was only $18 per month by 1985.[29] Other countries in which middle-level officials cannot feed – let alone adequately house, clothe and educate – their families on their salaries include Somalia, Nigeria, Sierra Leone, and Tanzania.

Staff morale, honesty and efficiency usually decline along with real compensation. Without the facilities or tools to do their jobs efficiently, many civil servants simply become time-servers. Or they turn to bribes, embezzlement of public funds and/or moonlighting in order to supplement their meagre salaries and benefits. In Uganda, 'the system of official remuneration has the consequence of putting on sale public employees to the highest bidder'.[30] In Guinea, "[w]ith the devaluation of the syli and the low level of functionary salaries, there developed a system of "Ye Dogho" . . . or parallel side payments . . . for virtually all governmental services".[31] Some Guinean public servants earned ten times their salaries through bribes, kickbacks and embezzlement in 1985, according to a World Bank estimate.[32] The spectacular degree of administrative corruption in Zaire and Nigeria is widely documented.

It is also common for officials to be unavailable during working hours because they are attending to their private business affairs, often informal-sector activities. To survive in many countries, civil servants must use their ingenuity to generate supplementary incomes. Moonlighting that involves animal husbandry, poultry or foodstuff farming or urban transport can be productive and socially useful. But the costs include reduced administrative efficiency and possibly public disenchantment with unavailable or unresponsive civil servants.

Inadequate public salaries and other problems, especially urban lawlessness and physical insecurity, also spawn or exacerbate shortages of qualified professional and technical staff. Most African civil services cannot find qualified applicants to fill vacancies for engineers, managers, accountants, economists and doctors. In Nigeria, a survey in 1977 found that vacancy rates for scientists, secondary school teachers and other professionals all exceeded 40 per cent.[33] This situation arises because the more experienced staff quit or avoid the public service in order to seek employment abroad or in the private sector, Ghana, Ethiopia and Uganda have perhaps been the worst affected by a 'brain drain' of qualified professionals. A common decline in the quality of secondary and university education over the past decade or so aggravates the problem of finding qualified staff. Economic crisis and budgetary cut-backs have deprived educational institutions of the resources they require; hence, buildings and equipment have deteriorated, many distinguished faculties have departed, and curricula have become dated as instructors lose touch with thinking in their fields.

The lack of a cadre of well-trained indigenous economists and financial experts is particularly troubling for governments contemplating economic reform. Who is going to advise political leaders on the available economic options and strategies? The answer often is: expatriate economists under technical assistance programmes, or protégés of the World Bank trained in neo-classical economics at élite Western universities. But this is unsatisfactory, as many foreign and local technocrats lack an intimate knowledge of, or sensitivity to, local social, cultural and political conditions. Their advice, though pleasing to foreign agencies, is therefore unlikely to be attuned to political and social realities. These limitations of the techno-bureaucracy may further constrain economic recovery.

Conclusions

Capitalism, I have argued, requires that state and market develop in tandem. Structural adjustment programmes, though they imply more reliance upon markets and less upon state direction, nonetheless presuppose an effective rational-legal state operating within a limited sphere. A facsimile of a modern capitalist state was bequeathed by the departing colonial powers in countries where decolonization was relatively peaceful. But this prototype invariably underwent modifications in the 1960s and 1970s as political structures adapted

– or failed to adapt – to prevailing social and material conditions. Where personalistic dictatorships or breakdowns into political chaos occurred, economic decline soon followed. Most governmental organizations, however, maintained adequate levels of services and social order until the late 1970s. It was the current economic crisis, driven by climatic disasters, environmental deterioration, inimical global economic trends, as well as unsatisfactory policies, that overwhelmed the coping capacity of fragile states. Today, fiscal, hegemonic and administrative crises impede economic reform and recovery in many countries.

In extreme cases, the danger is 'Haitianization'. Haiti, an independent republic since 1804 and the poorest country in the Western hemisphere, exhibits many of the characteristics that are emerging in such counries as Guinea, Equatorial Guinea, Ghana, Liberia, Central African Republic, Zaire, and (until recently) Uganda. These include: a large, poor peasantry that produces a high proportion of the state's revenues through its production of export crops, yet whose organizational incapacity allows governments to ignore its interests; deforestation and soil erosion that intensify in the long-term the desperation and poverty of farmers; the emigration of trained professionals; and a corrupt, predatory and unstable state headed by a succession of autocrats – self-proclaimed 'presidents-for-life'.[34] A low-level equilibrium trap can develop in which personalistic dictators allow unproductive political insiders to prey on the surplus produced by oppressed smallholders, reinforcing disincentives to productivity and environmental protection, and perpetuating poverty and the instability of a detested regime. This is a pattern which has to be arrested.

But how? If capitalist development is so fraught with difficulties, why should vanguard groups not try to bypass the bourgeois phase by struggling for a socialist transition? The obvious problem with this strategy is that objective conditions, if unconducive to economic liberalism, are thoroughly hostile to socialism. The domestic obstacles are well-known, but are worth listing: mass poverty, underdeveloped productive forces, a tiny non-revolutionary working class, and ethnic/regional tensions. External impediments include the prospect that the United States (or France in the case of the former French colonies) will aid anti-socialist insurrections, as in Angola, Mozambique and Nicaragua, should revolutionary socialists seize power. And – if this were not enough – the economic crisis has magnified the dependence of vulnerable sub-Saharan economies on the advanced capitalist countries and the international financial and development agencies they control. A radical experiment may provoke the antagonism of these countries and agencies, thus risking its economic collapse.

Under these circumstances, socialism in Africa is unlikely to foster either prosperity or a relief from authoritarianism. Where are the state revenues, organized class-base and administrative cadres on which to build a state capable of the central planning which was a feature of actually-existing socialisms? How will the well-established tendency toward an authoritarian 'bureaucratic-collectivist' outcome of socialist transitions in underdeveloped countries be avoided?[35] There is a danger that the economic and political failure of a 'premature' socialism will discredit the project for many years to come.

Neither do 'developmental dictatorships' on the model of the East Asian Newly Industrializing Countries appear to be on Tropical Africa's agenda in the near future. Conditions such as a long history of centralized, bureaucratic rule, ethnic and cultural homogeneity, a major external threat, the weakness of hitherto dominant landlord classes, and the sponsorship of a generous superpower underpinned the strong state and revolution from above in South Korea and Taiwan.[36] But none of these conditions obtains in most of the African countries. Côte d' Ivoire and Malawi may be cited as instances of developmental dictatorships; but both reveal the shortcoming of such a model when a declining dictator refuses to cede power.

Is liberal democracy a practicable avenue for halting the downward spiral by means of political institutionalization and some measure of popular participation in political life? This seems unlikely at first glance, since liberal democracy is generally associated with advanced capitalism and consolidated states. Nonetheless, representative democracies, or proto-democracies, have survived for more than a decade in such countries as Gambia, Senegal, Botswana and Mauritius whose objective conditions seem no more facilitative of democratization than those in many neighbouring authoritarian regimes.[37] Moreover, the economic records of Botswana and Mauritius over the past two decades are among the best in sub-Saharan Africa, and Gambia and Senegal are not among the worst performers. Liberal democracy is at least not incompatible with rapid development in low-income countries. Democratization may, in a few countries, prove a feasible way of breaking or pre-empting the pattern of reciprocal political and economic decay, while protecting human rights.

In the short-term, however, factional loyalties and patronage will continue to be the 'glue' that holds many fissiparous states together and permits governments to govern. Enlightened structural adjustment policies, recognizing the importance of the state to economic recovery, will need to take account of these political exigencies. This will mean trading off some short-run efficiency to enhance governability. Public bureaucracies and public policies have legitimate, if unacknowledged, goals other than efficiency and distributional justice. What appears from an economistic viewpoint merely as 'waste' or 'mismanagement' may play a significant role in preserving order and some measure of unity. 'Reform' in sub-Saharan Africa is a far more complicated matter than many realize.

Notes

1. My thanks to Mahmood Mamdani, Cranford Pratt and John Saul for their tough-minded critiques. They are not responsible for errors of fact or interpretation.
2. This is the judgement in the 'Mid-Term Review of the United Nations Programme of Action for African Economic Recovery and Development', prepared by the UN Secretary-General and released in September 1988. See Harsch, 1988, p.57.

3. Ravenhill, 1988, p.204; Mosley and Smith, 1989.
4. Polanyi, 1944, pp.140–41.
5. See Sandbrook, 1985, chapters 5 and 6.
6. The next four paragraphs constitute a highly condensed version of the argument in Sandbrook 1985.
7. Ironically, the ZANU government professes Marxism-Leninism. However, in practice, the multiracial business class has blunted the government's radicalism, a process dramatically illustrated by the promulgation in May 1989 of a favourable new investment code.
8. Elliott, 1988; Leslie, 1987.
9. See, e.g., Ogbonna, 1975, pp. 53–61, and Nellis ,1972.
10. World Bank, *World Development Report 1988*, Table 24.
11. World Bank, 1988b, p.73.
12. See the statistics recorded in World Bank, 1983, p. 102, and World Bank, 1988b, p. 115. On Tanzania, see Mukandala, 1983, p. 254.
13. Abernethy, 1988, p.189.
14. World Bank, 1983, p.103.
15. World Bank, 1988b, p.116.
16. Hicks and Kubisch, 1984.
17. Colclough, 1985, p.42.
18. Sivard, 1987, p.28.
19. Computed from Sivard, 1987, Table on pp. 29–31.
20. McGowan and Johnson, 1986.
21. Przeworski, 1980.
22. Data drawn from Sivard, 1987, p. 45.
23. Green, 1987, p.7.
24. See, for example, Ottaway, 1988.
25. McNamara, 1985, p.9.
26. Bendix, 1962, p. 345.
27. Crook, 1988, p.23.
28. World Bank, 1988b, p.115.
29. Picard and Graybeal, 1988, p.11.
30. Mamdani, 1988, p.1166.
31. Picard and Graybeal, 1988, p.6.
32. Ibid., p.11.
33. World Bank, 1988b, p.103.
34. Lundahl, 1983.
35. For an elaboration of this familiar argument, see Kitching, 1985, Chapter 2; Harrington, 1972, Chapter 10; Sandbrook, 1981.
36. These conditions are fully explored in the contributions to Deyo, 1987.
37. Sandbrook, 1988.

Bibliography

Abernethy, D. (1988) 'Bureaucratic Growth and Economic Stagnation in Sub-Saharan Africa, in *Africa's Development Challenges and the World Bank*, S.K. Commins (ed.) pp. 179–214. Lynne Rienner, Boulder, Colorado, USA.
Bendix, R. (1962) *Max Weber: An Intellectual Portrait*. Doubleday, Garden City, USA.

Colclough, C. (1985) 'Competing Paradigms in the Debate about Agricultural Pricing Policy', *International Development Studies Bulletin*, Vol. 16, No. 3, pp.39–46.

Collins, R. (1980) 'Weber's Last Theory of Capitalism: A Systematization', *American Sociological Review*, No. 45, pp. 925–42.

Crook, R.E. (1988) 'State Capacity and Economic Development: The Case of Côte d'Ivoire', *International Development Studies Bulletin*, Vol. 19, No.4, pp. 19–25.

Deyo, F.C. (ed.) (1987) *The Political Economy of the New Asian Industrialism*. Cornell University Press, Ithaca, USA.

Elliott, C. (1988) 'Structural Adjustment in the Longer Run: Some Uncomfortable Questions' in *Africa's Development Challenges and the World Bank*, S.K. Commins (ed.) pp. 159–78. Lynne Rienner, USA.

Ghai, D. (1987) 'Economic Growth, Structural Change and Labour Absorption in Africa, 1960–85.' Discussion Paper, United Nations Research Institute for Social Development, Geneva.

Green, R.H. (1986) 'Sub-Saharan Africa: Poverty of Development, Development of Poverty'. Discussion Paper 218, Institute of Development Studies, Sussex.

——— (1987) 'Killing the Dream: The Political and Human Economy of War in Sub-Saharan Africa'. Discussion Paper 238, Institute of Development Studies, Sussex.

Harrington, M. (1972) *Socialism*. Bantam Books, New York.

Harsch, E. (1988) 'Recovery or Relapse?' *Africa Report*, Vol. 33, No. 6, pp. 56–9.

Hicks, N. and A. Kubisch (1984) 'Cutting Government Expenditures in Less Developed Countries', *Finance and Development*, No. 21, pp. 37–9.

Joseph, R. (1987) *Democracy and Prebendal Politics in Nigeria: The Rise and Fall of the Second Republic*. Cambridge University Press, Cambridge, UK.

Kitching, G. (1985) *Rethinking Socialism*. Methuen, London.

Leslie, W.J. (1987) *The World Bank and Structural Transformation in Developing Countries: The Case of Zaire*. Lynne Rienner, Boulder.

Lundahl, M. (1983) *The Haitian Economy: Man, Land and Markets*. Croom Helm, London.

Mamdani, M. (1988). 'Uganda in Transition: Two Years of the NRA/NRM', *Third World Quarterly*, No.10, pp.1151–81.

McGowan, P. and T. Johnson (1986) '60 Coups in 30 Years: Further Evidence Regarding African Coups', *Journal of Modern African Studies*, No. 24, pp.539–46.

McNamara, R.S. (1985) *The Challenges for Sub-Saharan Africa*. Sir John Crawford Memorial Lecture, Washington, DC.

Mosley, P. and L. Smith (1989) 'Structural Adjustment and Agricultural Performance in Sub-Saharan Africa, 1980–87', *Journal of International Development*, No. 1, pp.321–55.

Mukandala, R. (1983) 'Trends in Civil Service Size and Income in Tanzania', *Canadian Journal of African Studies*, No.17, pp. 253–63.

Nellis, J.R. (1972) *Who Pays Tax in Kenya*? Research Report No. 11, Scandanavian Institute of African Studies, Uppsala.

Ogbonna, M.N. (1975) 'Tax Evasion in Nigeria,' *Africa Today*, No.22, pp.53–61.

Ottaway, M. (1988) 'Mozambique: From Symbolic Socialism to Symbolic Reform,' *Journal of Modern African Studies*, No. 26, pp.211–26.

Picard, L.A. and N.L. Graybeal (1988) 'Structural Adjustment, Public Sector

Reform and the West African Political System,' Paper presented to the African Studies Association Conference, Chicago, 26–30 October.

Polanyi, K. (1944) *The Great Transformation: The Political and Economic Origins of Our Times.* Beacon Press, Boston, USA.

Przeworski, A (1980) 'Material Bases of Consent: Politics and Economics in a Hegemonic System,' *Political Power and Social Theory*, No.1, pp. 21–68.

Ravenhill, J. (1988) 'Adjustment with Growth: A Fragile Consensus,' *Journal of Modern African Studies*, No.26, pp. 179–210.

Rothchild, D. and N. Chazan (eds) (1988) *The Precarious Balance: State and Society in Africa.* Westview Press, Boulder, Colorado, USA.

Sandbrook, R. (1981). 'Is Socialism Possible in Africa?' *Journal of Commonwealth and Comparative Politics*, No. 19, pp.197–207.

———— (1988) 'Liberal Democracy in Africa: A Socialist-Revisionist Perspective', *Canadian Journal of African Studies*, No. 22, pp.240–67.

———— with Judith Barker (1985) *The Politics of Africa's Economic Stagnation.* Cambridge University Press, Cambridge, UK.

Singh, S. (1983) 'Sub-Saharan Agriculture: Synthesis and Trade Prospects,' Staff Working Paper 608, World Bank, Washington, DC.

Sivard, R.L. (1987) *World Military and Social Expenditures, 1987–88* (12th ed.), World Priorities Inc., Washington, DC.

Somerville, C.M. (1988) 'Economic Crisis, Economic Reform, and Political Democracy: The Case of Senegal,' Paper presented to the African Studies Association Meeting, Chicago, 28–31 October.

Wisner, B. (1988) *Power and Need in Africa: Basic Human Needs and Development Policies.* Earthscan Publications, London.

World Bank (1983) *World Development Report, 1983.* Oxford University Press, New York.

———— (1988a) *Beyond Adjustment: Toward Sustainable Growth with Equity in Sub-Saharan Africa*, Part II. Special Economic Office, Technical Department, Africa Region, World Bank, Washington, DC, November.

———— (1988b) *World Development Report, 1988.* Oxford University Press, New York.

Young, C. and T. Turner (1985) *The Rise and Decline of the Zairean State.* University of Wisconsin Press, Madison.

Part 2:
Structural Adjustment and Social Response

7. The Political Economy of the Mexican Crisis

Blanca Heredia

Introduction

The end of over 40 years of steady and rapid economic growth in Mexico triggered, in 1981, by plummeting oil prices and rising interest rates was much more than purely an economic affair. The roots of the crisis as well as its consequences also went far beyond the strictly national domain. The crisis was the complex and painful result of a combination of long-term structural trends and markedly adverse conjunctural circumstances, operating at both the political and the economic level and involving both domestic and international variables.

This chapter will explore the political dimensions of the worst economic crisis in Mexico since the end of the armed phase of the Mexican revolution (1910–17), focusing on the links between the economy and the polity and highlighting the critical importance of policy in explaining the impact of the crisis on Mexico's political landscape. Economic crises do not take place in a political vacuum. Large-scale economic downturns reveal and exacerbate accumulated tensions and contradictions between structural changes and institutional inertias. Crises act as solvents of deeply entrenched social, political and economic arrangements, some of which constitute powerful obstacles to further economic and political development. In theoretical terms, the study of crises is useful because it provides a window for analysing processes and structures that in 'normal' times remain hidden.[1] Crises are also significant because they provide a privileged vantage point for studying the deep and often extremely complex relationship between structural and action level transformation.

In 1982 the almost five decades of economic prosperity that had made Mexico so exceptional in the Latin American context came to an abrupt end. On 1 December 1982 Miguel de la Madrid assumed the Presidency of a country ridden by an almost 100 per cent rate of inflation, the highest public deficit in post-revolutionary history, the virtual paralysation of economic activity, an enormous public and private external debt, an unprecedented level of open unemployment and the sudden end of foreign capital flows.[2]

The enormous task of managing and eventually overcoming an economic crisis of such magnitude was made even more difficult by the political and social conditions that President de la Madrid inherited from his predecessor President José López Portillo (1976–82). The latter's decision to nationalize the private banking system led to open confrontation between business and government and created a climate of general uncertainty and mistrust that in the short-run deepened the crisis and severely constrained the policy options of the new administration in the long-run. The painful costs of managing the crisis were further increased by the heightened social expectations generated by the short period of oil- and debt-led abundance. In the electoral and partisan terrain the ruling party (PNR-PRM-PRI) also faced new challenges.[3] The increased visibility of elections and the strengthening of the opposition parties – particularly the Partido Acción Nacional (PAN)[4] – both of which phenomena were, at least partially, the result of the regime's political reformism of the 1970s – also reduced the regime's space for manoeuvre. Finally, a new administration in the US, firmly committed to the recuperation of US hegemony in world affairs, much less tolerant therefore than previous administrations towards Mexico's relatively independent foreign policy – particularly in Central America – and increasingly concerned about the Mexican political system's capacity to deal effectively with the economic crisis, further constrained the policy space open to the de la Madrid administration.[5]

The task for the new President was obviously not an easy one. Despite the limits and obstacles posed by the debt crisis, as well as by the general conditions under which the administration was inaugurated, conscious choices – not wholly dictated by external circumstances – were in fact made. These choices concerned the allocation of the costs of adjustment as well as the meaning and direction of structural economic transformation; they would eventually lead to the end of the era of import-substitution-industrialization (ISI), the demise of the social pact that had underlain the 'Mexican miracle' and the rapid erosion of some of the crucial mechanisms through which the ruling party's virtual monopoly over the political process had been traditionally reproduced and legitimated.

The background

From 1940 to 1970 the Mexican economy grew at an average annual rate of over 6 per cent.[6] During that period an essentially rural and agricultural country was transformed into an urban and industrial society. The speed of the process as well as its profound regional, sectorial and distributional imbalances, however, produced a social structure plagued by multiple forms of inequality.

As in other Latin American countries, import-substitution-industrialization (ISI) provided the basic framework within which the rapid transformation of the country took place.[7] Conceived as an ideological, political and social project, rather than simply as a set of economic policies, ISI became the axis around which a national economy and a national society were structured.[8]

In the Mexican context, ISI was particularly important because it was almost ideally suited to the pursuit of the three most important goals associated with the revolutionary heritage: economic nationalism; rapid socio-economic development and social justice. With time then, the inward-looking, state-led model of economic development became the concrete expression of the revolutionary heritage through which the PRI legitimated its monopoly of political power. The enormous weight of the social and economic groups born and strengthened under the auspices of ISI, as well as the tight organizational and ideological links between ISI and the political system, would eventually make its crisis one that would shake the very foundations of the country's social and political structure.

From 1940 to 1970 – and particularly from the early 1950s to the late 1960s – Mexico was able to avoid the recurrent balance of payments crises, high levels of inflation and cycles of political instability associated with ISI in other Latin American countries.[9] Mexico's relative success on this account had to do with three sets of factors:

The economic dimension: A dynamic agricultural sector – the conditions for which were created by President Lázaro Cárdenas' (1934–40) agrarian reform – a relatively diversified export structure, as well as a positive balance on the service account due to tourism and border trade.[10] Also important were the tremendous expansion of the world economy during the post-war period and the benefits – which overall, during that period, were greater than the costs – derived from the US border.

The economic policy-making institutions: A wide consensus around basic policy goals and a well-developed and coherent economic policy-making apparatus.[11] From the early 1950s up to the late 1960s the key policy-making institutions – Finance Ministry and Central Bank – were controlled by a tight group of fiscally conservative economic policy-makers who designed and implemented a policy package known as 'stabilizing development', whose central goal was rapid growth combined with financial stability. The groups' close ties with financial and industrial élites, along with its high level of insularity from the political cycle as well as from the demands of popular sectors – to a large extent made possible by the encapsulation of those sectors within the ruling party – consolidated the tacit alliance between big business and the state.[12] The leadership provided by this group of economic policy-makers – whose visible heads were Antonio Ortíz Mena, Finance Minister from 1958 to 1970, and Rodrigo Gómez, Director of the Central Bank from 1952 to 1970, resulted in a remarkable degree of policy continuity, and provided economic élites with their most important access point to the policy-making process.

The political system: A highly resilient set of political institutions that reflected the original balance of social and political forces produced by the revolution while at the same time providing the flexibility demanded by the ambitious modernization project central to the self-perceived mission of the winning revolutionary coalition. The centre of this set of institutional arrangements was the post-revolutionary state – more concretely, the executive branch – closely linked with the ruling party. The state and the party acted as the pivotal mediators among all social and political groups. Horizontal links among social actors were forcefully inhibited. Vertical forms of integration prevailed and the shifting balance between different groups and factions was, for a long period of time, ably managed by state and party élites. The essentially corporatist – or quasi-corporatist in the case of business – nature of the system favoured particularistic and highly fragmented forms of interest intermediation, and left the ruling party with the virtual monopoly over the political process. The social pact that underlay the whole arrangement included business – both the older and relatively more independent Northern factions born during the Porfirian era along with the new industrial entrepreneurs – as well as strategically placed groups of organized workers.[13]

Towards the mid and late 1960s the very conditions that had sustained the steady and rapid industrialization of the country in the context of remarkable social and political stability were either reversed – agricultural output declined, demand for foreign credit grew and the surpluses on the service account grew smaller – or transformed into sources of increasing socio-political strain. Thus for instance, the goals, practices and correlation of forces – favouring big industrial and financial conglomerates and a small, but strategic, group of labour élites loyal to the regime but enjoying a considerable degree of potential autonomy – generated during the period of 'stabilizing development', and which were already deeply entrenched by the later 1960s, severely constrained the government's capacity to deal with the mounting costs and obstacles associated with the continuation of ISI. In the political realm, the very success of economic policy in terms of fostering the creation of a modern – even if highly unequal – social structure led to the emergence of new social groups, particularly middle classes and marginal urban sectors, whose incorporation into the political system was severely hampered by the corporatist and quasi-monopolistic structure of the system.

Behind the formidable performance of macro-economic indicators, problems, tensions and contradictions grew.[14] The use of low levels of taxation, subsidies and high levels of protectionism as the preferred means to foster rapid capital accumulation led to the creation of an inefficient industrial plant and to the state's dependence on domestic – and increasingly foreign – savings in order to finance its fiscal deficit. Employment failed to keep up with economic and population growth and income distribution became increasingly skewed.[15]

During the Díaz Ordáz administration (1964–70) the limits of stabilizing development became evident and the rigidities of the political system were also starkly revealed. The regime's naked use of force in response to the demands of the 1968 student movement exhibited the repressive dimension of the political system, which until then had been considered a relatively benign form of authoritarian rule or even a peculiarly Mexican form of limited democracy.[16]

The inauguration of President Luis Echeverría in 1970 took place in a context marked by a slow-down in economic activity, a rise in domestic prices and a growing deficit on the current account. To these adverse circumstances, the new President had to add the enormous challenge of rebuilding confidence in a regime whose legitimacy had been severely eroded by the 1968 student massacre and which, despite its alleged revolutionary origins, had failed to fulfil the promise of social justice so central to the revolutionary heritage.

Taken as a whole, the 1970–82 period can be seen as the often contradictory and ultimately unsuccessful attempt to overcome the obstacles and, particularly during the Echeverría administration, correct the social conditions that had led to the model's virtual exhaustion simply prolonged the unwillingness and/or the incapacity to alter the structural and institutional conditions that had led to the model's virtual exhaustion simply prolonged its agony and in the end made its wholesale replacement almost an imperative.

In spite of their important differences, the two administrations that comprised the 1970–82 period (Luis Echeverría (1970–76) and José López Portillo (1976–82)) shared a number of critical traits and faced an overall similar set of conditions. The main characteristics of the period as a whole can be organized along three dimensions; all of them crucial for understanding the immediate context of the 1982 crisis.[17]

The economy: Mexico's economy was battered by internal contradictions and external shocks. In sharp contrast to the years of 'stabilizing development', these 12 years were marked by profound financial instability, recurrent balance of payments crises, spiralling inflation, a series of major devaluations and the accumulation of a massive foreign debt. The economy experienced a very unsteady, even if overall high, rate of growth. Internal contradictions were exacerbated by the impact of a failing international economy. Mounting fiscal and balance of payments deficits led in 1976 to a sharp devaluation, huge capital flight and the need to implement an IMF sponsored stabilization programme. From 1978 on dramatic increases in oil exports became the engine of high rates of economic growth. Since oil revenues were nevertheless unable to finance the formidable rise in imports and public expenditure, foreign borrowing experienced a steady and steep rise.

Economic policy-making: The two most important traits of economic policy during this period were the dramatic increase in public spending[18] and state participation in productive activities, and the progressive politicization of the economic decision-making process.[19] These years marked the end of the undisputed predominance of the fiscally orthodox group of policy-makers represented by Ortíz Mena, and witnessed the ascent of a group of structuralist and neo-Keynesian economic advisers and policy-makers. In spite of its control over key ministries, the new group – whose most visible leader was Horacio Flores de la Peña, Minister of Patrimony under Echeverría – was never able to achieve the supremacy of the previous group.[20] The resulting stalemate, as well as the private sector's loss of its most important ally within the policy-making apparatus, led to recurrent policy shifts and to mounting confrontation between business and government. Business's response to the breakdown of the informal mechanisms that had allowed it to shape economic policy was to openly reject the tacit arrangement that had made politics the exclusive terrain of the state and the ruling party while leaving the economy as a virtually private domain.[21] Even though important divisions within business, along with the brief period of oil- and debt-led abundance, made the consolidation of a solid business front difficult, this period was decisive, because it marked the beginning of the private sector's abandonment of its traditionally sectorial role and its transformation into an open and active political contender.[22]

The political realm: Between 1970 and 1982 the regime attempted to assimilate the social and political demands produced by a long period of economic growth, as well as to respond to the legacies of the 1968 crisis. In contrast to previous inclusion formulas, which centred around the hegemonic party–state system itself, the reformism of the 1970s was geared towards the expansion of electoral and partisan activities.[23] The main goal of the reform was to avert the risks of rigidity and to provide the regime with an expanded and firmer base of popular support. The ultimate objective of the project was to make a controlled version of political democracy the pillar of political stability. By promoting competition outside the hegemonic party, the reform was intended to revitalize and strengthen the PRI so as to allow it to gradually become a majority party in the context of open electoral competition. Overall, and despite its limits, the reformism of the 1970s produced a more open environment for legal opposition forces and a considerable strengthening of opposition parties. The most significant consequence of the reform, however, and one that would prove to be very costly to the regime, was the dramatic increase in the visibility and importance of elections in Mexican politics.[24]

During the last year of the López Portillo administration GNP experienced a negative growth rate of –0.5 per cent, inflation reached 98.9 per cent, the value of the peso was devalued by 466 per cent, and the government increased its foreign debt by almost six billion dollars. In August of that year, forced by the virtual depletion of public reserves, Mexico declared a temporary moratorium on interest payments. By the end of the 1982 the fiscal deficit stood at a record 17.6 per cent of GNP, the total foreign debt reached 84 billion dollars (89.9 per cent of GNP) and interest payments absorbed 43.6 per cent of the total value of exports.[25]

The nationalization of the private banking system and the establishment of exchange controls in September 1982 fuelled the already high levels of uncertainty and tension in business and government relations and led to momentous increases in capital flight.[26] A group of militant business groups responded to the bank nationalization by orchestrating a campaign of popular mobilization against the government. The 'Mexico in Liberty' campaign, although ultimately unsuccessful, was important because it signalled the incorporation of the demand for democratization as well as for a more effective balance of powers into their traditional anti-statist discourse.[27]

Crisis and policy

The social and political consequences of the 1982 crisis were profoundly shaped by the legacies of the 1970–82 period, as well as by the new correlation of forces, inside and outside the government, associated with the de la Madrid administration. The composition of the cabinet, the administration's new ideological discourse as well as its far-reaching social and economic project defined the political terrain within which the crisis was managed and dealt with. The new distribution of political and ideological forces represented by the de la Madrid administration was the critical hinge between the economic and the political dimensions of the crisis. Without due consideration to the crucial importance of economic policy, understood as the concrete expression of the new power structure, the most significant political consequences of the crisis, that is, the emergence of the Frente Democrático Nacional as the most formidable contender ever faced by the ruling party, cannot be adequately explained.[28]

De la Madrid's rise to power was marked by the ascent of a remarkably compact and ideologically coherent group of public officials. Most of the new ministers had longstanding personal and/or professional links with the President, and their political careers had taken place almost exclusively within the administrative apparatus. A large proportion of them had first entered government during the 1960s and had spent most of their active political life in the public financial sector. The group's ideological stance, as well as their views on economic policy, had been profoundly shaped by their training under the liberal developmentalist élite – the group headed by Ortíz Mena which presided over the period of stabilizing development – who dominated economic policy-making during the 1950s and 1960s. Their profound commitment to financial stability and fiscal orthodoxy was further strengthened by the goals and the ideological orientation of the financial institutions where they served lives throughout most of their active political lives.[29]

The most remarkable feature of the new cabinet was the virtual monopolization by the financial specialists of the whole executive branch. Almost half the new ministers came from the Ministry of Budget and Planning, headed by de la Madrid from 1979 and 1981; and the rest came mostly from the Finance Ministry or from the Central Bank. The composition of the cabinet left large sectors of the political élite unrepresented. The homogeneity of the new group and the marginalization of those who failed to fully coincide with the dominant policy orientation, particularly with those associated with economic policy-making during the Echeverría and López Portillo administrations led to decreasing pluralism within the ruling élite. All of these trends severely reduced the traditional bargaining space among rival groups and factions within the government and challenged some of the basic norms governing power-sharing and compromise-building that had guaranteed élite consensus for over 60 years.

Those directly in charge of economic policy traced the country's economic ills to the legacies of twelve years of 'economic populism', excessive state intervention, financial irresponsibility, and corruption, which had only magnified the adverse consequences of external shocks. In their very diagnosis of the roots of the crisis – remarkably similar to the private sector's views on the subject – they obviously revealed their own policy preferences. The new administration's stress on 'economic realism' was much more than simply a return to the years of financial stability. For President de la Madrid, as well as for his economic cabinet, the crisis provided the opportunity to overcome the obstacles to further growth through the destruction of the conditions that had made the 'excesses' of the two previous administrations possible.[30] The President argued repeatedly for the need to 'use' the crisis as the opportunity to radically transform the socio-economic structure of the country.

The administration's economic project had two basic dimensions:

1) A short-term stabilization programme whose central goals were: the control of inflation and public spending, the selective protection of employment and the industrial plant, and the recuperation of the state's control over the exchange market – particularly difficult in a country with a highly porous border with the US. The programme was negotiated with the IMF and constituted one of the most severe austerity packages launched in Latin America during that period. Specific policies included: a new devaluation, increases in public revenues – via increases in indirect taxes as well as in the prices of public services – and highly restrictive credit and wage policies. As a result, the public deficit was cut by half during 1983, private investment fell and most sectors of the population experienced a sharp decrease in their income.[31] The anti-inflationary programme was at first moderately successful – the rate of inflation fell from 98.8 per cent in 1982 to 80.8, 59.2 and 63.7 per cent in the next three years. But later, totally unable to deal with the pressures associated with the 1986 sharp drop in oil prices, in 1986 the rate of inflation rose again to 88 per cent and in 1987 to 105.7 per cent.[32] The lack of success of the programme from 1985 to 1987 had to do both with external shocks as well as with the adoption of a stabilization package – Programa de Aliento y Crecimiento – in 1986 that attempted to combine the reduction of inflation with the resumption of growth but, in fact, subordinated price stabilization to the promotion of growth via the relaxation of fiscal discipline.[33] After the severe crisis of October–December 1987, the government launched its third, and most successful, anti-inflationary package: Pacto de Solidaridad Económica. This last package constituted an important departure from the two previous ones and was made possible by big business' final willingness to support government policy.

2) A programme of 'structural adjustment' whose two basic pillars were: the rationalization and reduction of the role of the state in the economy and the redefinition of the relationship between the domestic and the international market. The project spelled the end of the era of inward-oriented, state-led industrialization; involved a radical restructuring of state–society and state–market relations; and saw the closer integration into the world economy and

the active promotion of exports, as the critical engine of economic growth. The formulation and implementation of the programme entailed a fundamental reshaping of the social coalition that had underlain Mexico's traditional developmental strategy, as well as the critical revision of the *legitimate* scope of state action.

The two dimensions of the project, though less coherent in practice than in discourse, together reflected the broad and fundamental changes in state–society relations taking place since the 1970s throughout the international political economy. Ever since recession replaced steady growth in the industrialized economies around the early 1970s, and particularly when inflation displaced full employment as the top priority in their economic policy agenda, the assault on state intervention, the adoption of restrictive monetarist policies and the stress on the need to 'liberate' market forces spread – in a truly epidemic fashion – across most of the planet. The liberalization, privatization and stabilization programmes that have been implemented in major Latin American countries since the mid-1970s in this new global context, have been much more than simply temporary deviations from traditional developmentalist strategies. Though superficially similar to those carried out in the 1950s and 1960s, the stabilization programmes of the mid-1970s in the Southern Cone, and of the early 1980s in Mexico, are profoundly different to their predecessors in terms of their ultimate objectives. Whereas in the heyday of ISI, stabilization programmes were conceived and used as short-term solutions for balance of payments crisis, today, stabilization policies are part of a package of structural transformation whose final goal is to reverse the historic role of the state as the engine of economic development, as well as to alter the traditional balance between the domestic and the international markets.

The neo-liberal discourse associated with orthodox monetarist policies, which came to dominate economic policy-making in most advanced industrial societies as well as economic thinking within the international financial community, found a highly receptive environment in the top echelons of the de la Madrid administration. The broad affinities between the IMF policy recommendations and the goals of the Mexican government, from 1983 on, were further strengthened by the administration's urgent need to regain the confidence of the private sector. The formal agreement with the IMF, upon which the renegotiation of the foreign debt depended, was crucial in this context because it provided business with an international guarantee that made the government's offer of security regarding economic policy more credible – at least partially.

A crucial objective of the project as a whole – in fact the *sine qua non* condition for its success – was the re-establishment of the alliance between business and the state. The legacy of distrust generated by the bank nationalization, the overall climate of uncertainty naturally associated with the economic crisis, along with the virtually irreversible effects produced by the private sector's politicization, made the reconstruction of the alliance a very difficult process. Though perhaps willing, the de la Madrid administration was often unable – due to political considerations as well as to international developments beyond its control – to meet the demands of the most militant factions of business. The high social and political costs of repeatedly and unsuccessfully attempting to do so, however, further eroded the regime's social bases of support.

Popular sectors, middle classes and small and private entrepreneurs bore the brunt of both stabilization and structural adjustment. The dramatic drop in real wages – estimated around 50 per cent during the 1982–88 period – rising levels of unemployment and radical cuts in popular consumption subsidies – over 70 per cent during the first three years of the de la Madrid administration – led to wide social discontent. The implementation of this costly and highly unpopular programme deprived the PRI's corporatist structures of the remnants of their representational function. During this period, corporatist mechanisms came to be used solely as instruments of exclusion and control. Even though labour élites continued to act as a critical pillar of the regime, their overall position, within the new correlation of forces represented by the de la Madrid administration, suffered a steady decline. The labour élite's dependence on the government, forced them to support the most anti-labour economic policy in Mexico's post-revolutionary history. Unable to extract any concessions for organized labour, except in a few isolated cases – most notably in PEMEX[34] – they were still able to keep that sector under control, especially after 1985, but were increasingly incapable of delivering the electoral support upon which the PRI had traditionally relied.

The other central objective of the administration's overall project was the strengthening of the state. Even though this goal might seem to contradict the government's frontal attack on state intervention, it was nevertheless crucially related to it. In the administration's view, rationalization of the public sector would allow the state to break the multiple constraints that entailed active participation in almost every area of the country's social and economic life. By retreating, the state would increase its effective capacity to act; by rejecting the legitimacy of some traditionally accepted demands it would recuperate its ability to decide. The achievement of these goals, however, required the destruction of very powerful groups and deeply entrenched structures of interest intermediation and social control; it demanded, in short, the disincorporation of the socio-economic actors who had been the pillars of the hegemonic party–state.[35]

From 1983 to 1985 the burden of managing the crisis, as well as the active opposition of the social forces associated with ISI and big business' unwillingness to fully support the government's new economic project, severely hampered the de la Madrid's capacity to act. The allocation of the costs of adjustment implicit in the stabilization programme, however, soon eroded the power of the groups most actively opposed to de la Madrid's far-reaching project of structural reform and provided the space for the re-establishment of the alliance between big business and the state. Forced by a new dramatic drop in oil prices in 1986 and aided by the severe weakening of labour and domestic industrial entrepreneurs dependent on state protection and on domestic demand, the government embarked, this time in earnest, upon an unprecedented programme of economic liberalization.

The pace of trade liberalization has been so dramatic that it has even exceeded the requirements imposed by the terms of Mexico's August 1986 accession to GATT. Import licence requirements have been virtually eliminated, and maximum tariffs have been slashed from 40 to 20 per cent.[36] Concerning the reduction of the role of the state in the economy the figures are equally impressive. Over 60 per cent of the public sector firms that existed in 1982 have been either privatized or liquidated.[37]

Popular consumption subsidies for basic foodstuffs as well as subsidies for public transportation were also severely cut – current transferences (which include subsidies) as a percentage of GNP fell from 6.5 in 1982 to 2.1 in 1987.[38] The prices for public goods and services grew considerably, without however producing the expected increases in revenue, due to the huge impact of plummeting oil prices in this areas. As a result of all these policies, the primary public balance – difference between total income and total expenditure in non-financial goods and services – as a percentage of GNP jumped from an 8 per cent deficit in 1982 to a 4.9 per cent surplus in 1987.[39]

The administration's success in reducing non-financial expenditures, as well as in dramatically increasing non-oil exports was, however, offset by a record six-year period of almost zero economic growth.[40] The most consistent goal of government policy has turned out to be servicing the foreign debt. Despite the allegedly favourable terms obtained by the administration through the 1983 and 1986 renegotiations, 1988 IDB figures indicate that Mexico, in spite of a smaller debt, has paid more interest in absolute terms than has Brazil.[41]

By directly attacking the social pact that underlay the PRI's hegemony in the political system, economic liberalization has dramatically altered the balance of power within the ruling party and throughout Mexican society. This abrupt shift in Mexico's developmental strategy eroded the regime's capacity to produce and reproduce consensus, as well as its capacity to disorganize and de-activate opposition and dissent and led, in 1988, to the worst legitimacy crisis in post-revolutionary history.

Historically, the legitimacy of the PRI's monopoly of political power has been primarily grounded in the pursuit of the goals associated with the revolutionary heritage rather than on the observance of formal procedures.[42] By directly challenging the close association between a relatively closed economy and the defence of national identity on the one hand, and state intervention and the promise of social justice on the other, the programme of economic liberalization has severely undermined the legitimacy of the hegemonic party–state. In so doing, economic liberalization has broken the delicate balance between conflict and consensus that guaranteed the cohesion of the ruling coalition for over 60 years. The assault on state intervention as well as the attempt to permanently exclude the left-wing of the ruling coalition has led to the emergence of horizontal solidarities among and between party officials and state bureaucrats, which threaten vertical and hierarchical controls. Finally, economic liberalization, understood as a new model of state–society relations, has meant the end of a social pact based on the promise of social justice. In a context where the state has effectively rejected the legitimacy of state intervention as the crucial instrument for protecting society against the most deleterious effects of market forces, important social groups rightfully perceive economic liberalization as a project within which their claims for state protection have, overnight, become illegitimate and where their very survival is thus at stake.

The impact of the crisis on civil and political society

The impact of the economic crisis on the organization of civil and political society was mediated by the peculiar structure of each of the two domains as well as by the economic project through which the administration handled the crisis.[43]

The contest over 'civil society'

In Mexico, civil society – an arena that comprises the activities of social movements and civic organizations – has been traditionally weak. In a context marked by vertical, hierarchical, and segmented forms of interest inter-mediation, all of which centred around the state, the creation of horizontal links across classes, and the constitution of social identities, at least relatively autonomous from the state, were severely constrained. Forty years of rapid socio-economic modernization, however, led to increasing pressures for the creation of new spaces for social and political action. The struggles fought by students, independent labour organizations and community associations forced the regime to open up new channels for political participation. The reformism of the 1970s responded to those challenges and created the conditions for their further – even if ultimately limited – expansion.

The 1982 crisis fell, then, upon an already activated terrain. Even though the social costs of austerity and structural reform led to more defensive forms of social action and tended to weaken the participation of the least well-off, 'civil society' continued to grow. The 1985 earthquake in Mexico City provided a formidable stimulus to the development of new social movements and popular organizations. The government's delayed response fuelled popular discontent and gave social groups a heightened awareness of their own capacity for collective action.[44]

The crisis also fell, however, on an extremely unequal terrain. The state's retreat from crucial areas of social and economic life obviously favoured those better endowed with material and organizational resources and thus tended to accentuate existing social, economic and political inequalities. The main beneficiaries of the state's retreat were private sector organizations. To put it succinctly: as the state moved out, business stepped in.

During the early 1980s the most active and vocal factions of business incorporated into their anti-statist discourse a militant defence of 'civil society', understood as the realm of 'private initiative'. The dichotomy between state and civil society became the axis of their new ideological project. Through this dichotomy they attempted to portray themselves as the representatives of an entire society placed in direct opposition to the state.[45] Business organizations became actively involved in the promotion of social movements and civic associations. Their superior material and organizational resources allowed them to fill the spaces opened up by struggles fought by others, as well as by de la Madrid's socio-economic project.

Political society

The realm of elections, parties and legislatures in Mexico has been marked by the ruling party's effective and longstanding electoral monopoly. Opposition parties have traditionally constituted the second tier of the country's party–state system.[46] Subordinated to the hegemonic party and often owing their existence to licences and concessions granted from above, opposition parties were, for a long time, simply unable to become real contenders for political power.[47]

The political reform of the late 1970s eased some of the constraints that had systematically inhibited the development of political society. As previously noted, however, the reform's most important consequence was to increase the importance and visibility of electoral processes.[48]

The Miguel de la Madrid (1982–88) administration's version of political reform was the 'democratization of society'. This programme constituted the political dimension of the administration's overall project of social and economic transformation. Its emphasis on 'society', rather than on the state, revealed the true nature of a project whose ultimate goal was to provide the institutional framework capable of managing a new form of state–society relations. Drawing on the basic orientation of the 1977 political reform, the programme was premised on the need to gradually make elections the most important legitimating structure of the state. The first results of relatively open elections, however, soon made clear that political liberalization in times of tremendous social and political stress was a very risky affair.

The 1983 municipal elections in the Northern states of Chihuahua and Durango produced some of the PRI's worst defeats since its creation in 1929. In the state of Chihuahua, PAN won municipal councils representing 70 per cent of that state's population, including the municipal councils of the city of Chihuahua – the state's capital – and Ciudad Juárez, the second-largest city in the state and fifth-largest of the country. In Durango the PRI also lost the state's capital to PAN.[49]

PAN's victories in the 1983 municipal elections led to serious and unusually publicized struggles within the governing coalition regarding the convenience of pursuing the project of political opening.[50] As a result of increasing conflicts among the various members of the regime, political liberalization experienced an abrupt halt. In December 1983 the army was called in to repress the leftist coalition, which claimed electoral victory in the municipality of Juchitán in the South-western state of Oaxaca. A year later, the army was again used to oust PAN supporters in the border city of Piedras Negras, Coahuila, who had taken over the municipal council alleging electoral victory.

The real test for the 'democratization of society', though, came in the congressional elections of July 1985 and in some critical local elections in 1986. Large-scale fraud, in a context where the regime itself had increased the visibility and significance of elections through its own project of political reform, back-fired.[51] Elections not only were not legitimating the PRI, they were doing precisely the opposite.[52] The meaning of fraud had changed; from being a tolerated mechanism in a country where elections did not carry the weight of legitimating political authority, it became a growing source of illegitimacy. The socio-economic project of de la Madrid, the worst economic crisis in post-revolutionary history and the abortion of a project of political reform took their toll.

The reversal of the project of political reform that had allowed the regime to channel anti-system opposition into the electoral arena was a concession to the groups within the ruling coalition most adamantly opposed to political opening. These groups were, however, the prime target of economic liberalization as a political project. The result of all this was a very odd and inherently tense alliance between political hardliners holding the key positions in the corporatist structures and neo-liberal economic reformers without an independent social base.

The rift within the 'revolutionary family'

The rise of de la Madrid's team to power and the adoption of the programme of economic liberalization broke the overarching consensus around goals and power-sharing that had traditionally kept intense competition among rival factions in the party–state network within manageable limits. The attempt to permanently marginalize all of those not directly associated with the faction that had taken over the state, led in 1986 to the emergence of vocal opposition within the ruling party itself. A small group of prominent party figures – Cuauhtémoc Cárdenas (President Lázaro Cárdenas's son), Porfirio Muñoz Ledo, and Ifigenia Martínez Navarrete – adopted the label of 'Corriente Democrática' and began to demand the internal democratization of the PRI. The group presented itself as the expression of the nationalist and progressive ideals that constituted the core of the revolutionary project for which the PRI stood.[53]

For Corriente Democrática, the selection of the architect of the programme of economic liberalization – Carlos Salinas de Gortari – as the ruling party's Presidential candidate in 1987 revealed the limits of internal opposition as well as the government's firm commitment to the pursuit of a project of socio-economic transformation within which the left-wing of the party simply had no place.

In 1987, Corriente Democrática's break with the PRI along with the success of PAN in mobilizing the electorate in the northern part of the country brought the issue of political reform back into the centre of the regime's political agenda. The team of the PRI's new presidential candidate attempted to regain the initiative. Convinced of the importance of clean elections for legitimizing an imposed candidate intimately associated with the social costs of the programme of economic modernization launched in 1983, they tried to recuperate control over the process of political change by presenting themselves as the vanguard of political reform. Their response, however, came far too late.

In the context of the process that culminated in the 1988 presidential and congressional elections, Corriente Democrática – at first only a minuscule group of PRI dissidents – became, in only a few months, the core of a broad left–centre coalition – Frente Democrático Nacional (FDN) – that was able to do what PAN, the country's traditional second electoral force, had never been able to achieve: break the PRI's electoral monopoly and challenge its exclusive claim over the heritage of the Mexican revolution. The FDN's capacity to do so, despite its meagre organizational resources, had a lot to do with the fact that the continuation of the programme of economic liberalization implicit in Mr Salinas' selection as the PRI presidential candidate was perceived by numerous party officials and state bureaucrats as a direct threat to their political survival. This removed the in-built divisiveness of a pyramidal structure where groups and factions permanently struggle with each other in their effort to reach the top, and generated horizontal solidarities (all felt threatened at the same time) as well as sympathies for the 'rebels'. By providing their quiet support and by failing to fully collaborate in the Salinas presidential campaign, middle-level party officials and state bureaucrats were critical in facilitating the FDN's electoral success. The Front's ability to become the rallying point of a large number of non-partisan opposition forces; its capacity to become the political expression of all of the groups excluded from the government's new 'national' project; along with the power of the ideals associated with Cárdenas's name, did the rest.

The 1988 presidential and congressional elections in Mexico inaugurated a new chapter in Mexican politics. For the first time since its creation in 1929, the ruling party lost its virtual monopoly over the political process. Thus, for the first time in post-revolutionary history, when the national Congress constituted itself in Electoral College for the Presidential election on 9 September 1988, not a single representative of the opposition certified the PRI's presidential candidate's electoral victory. Carlos Salinas was ratified as Constitutional President exclusively by the members of his own party, that is, with a margin of only twelve votes above the 51 per cent majority such certification requires. Even if one uses official results, highly contested by many participants and observers, Salinas's share of the presidential poll (50.4 per cent) was far smaller than that of any other PRI presidential candidate since 1917; Cuauhtémoc Cárdenas's – presidential candidate for the FDN – share (31.12 per cent) on the other hand, was the largest ever obtained by an opposition candidate against the PRI. Also, for the first time since its creation, the PRI, with only 263 seats out of the 500 total, lacks the necessary two-thirds majority in Congress to modify the Constitution.

The opposition's impressive victories in the 1988 elections, however, do not yet have a definitive meaning. The prospects for a democratic transition in a country with no liberal democratic tradition and where revolutionary legitimacy associated with the pursuit of goals remains a powerful contender to procedural legitimacy formulae; with a ruling party which still controls impressive resources; and with a society where parties have no firm grounding, remain uncertain.

All we know, as of yet, is that the de la Madrid administration's relatively successful attempt to radically transform the economy, along with his half-hearted and halting commitment to the project of political reform unleashed a process of social and political mobilization over which the regime has retained only precarious control.

The remarkably swift recuperation of the executive's capacity to undertake decisive action during the first few months of the new administration suggests, however, that the severe weakening of the PRI has not, as yet, undermined the other basic pillar of the Mexican political system: presidentialism. Nevertheless, the success of the new socio-economic project depends both on the capacity to decide and to act decisively against any form of resistance and opposition, as well as on the capacity to create a new alliance of social and political forces able to sustain and carry out the new project in the longer run. In the past few years, the Mexican political system has, overall, been more successful at removing constraints than at creating new bases of political and institutional support for the new national project.

Notes and References

1. Peter Gourevitch, 1986 p. 9.
2. Presidencia de la República 1985, p. 14.
3. The ruling party, Partido Nacional Revolucionario, was created in 1929 as a broad coalition of revolutionary factions, local political organizations and revolutionary caudillos. In 1938 President Cárdenas reformed and renamed the party, Partido de la Revolución Mexicana, and established its corporatist structure. In 1946 the party was again renamed with the label it retains until today: Partido Revolucionario Institucional.

On the PNR–PRM–PRI, see John Bailey, 1986; Garrido, 1986 and 1987; Meyer, 1978 and 1988.
4. Created in 1939 by a group of intellectuals, politicians, Catholic militants and private entrepreneurs in response to the progressive and nationalist policies of President Lázaro Cárdenas. See Carlos Arriola 1977; Soledad Loaeza 1974 and 1987; Donald Mabry 1973; Universidad Iberoamericana 1978.
5. On this issue see Adolfo Aguilar Zinser 1988 in Rolando Cordera et al.
6. Systematic overviews of the period can be found in Leopoldo Solís 1970; Roger D. Hansen 1971.
7. There is abundant literature on ISI, for the central arguments see Albert O. Hirschman 1971. For a more recent and comprehensive treatment of ISI-developmentalism see Katheryn Sikkink 1988.

8. The most well-known statement of Mexico's development strategy is René Villarreal 1977 in José Reyna and Richard S. Weinert (eds) 1977. For a partial critique of Villarreal that locates the beginning of ISI in the 1930s, see Enrique Cárdenas 1987.

9. For a profoundly influential analysis of the political dimensions of ISI in Argentina and Brazil, see: Guillermo O'Donnell 1973. For the debate generated by O'Donnell's work, see David Collier (ed.) 1979, especially the articles by Hirschman, Serra and Kaufman.

10. René Villarreal 1977.

11. A detailed account of the origins of Mexico's financial institutions during the 1920s, that highlights the collaboration between the financial groups and the revolutionary élite, can be found in Sylvia Maxfield 1988.

12. For the critical importance of bureaucratic independence from the political process and of the active support of business for policy success, see Sikkink 1988.

13. Major works on the Mexican political system include: Manuel Camacho 1977; Pablo González Casanova 1965; Robert Scott 1964; José Luis Reyna and Richard S. Weinert (eds) 1977; Nora Hamilton 1982; Susan K. and John F. H. Purcell 1980; Susan K. Purcell 1981.

14. José Blanco 1979; E. V. K. FitzGerald 1979 in Rosemary Thorp and Lawrence Whitehead (eds).

15. By 1970 26.8 per cent of the economically active population was either unemployed or underemployed. In 1950, 50 per cent of the country's households received 19.1 of the national income while the upper 10 per cent received 40 per cent of the total; 15 years later the upper 20 per cent received two-thirds of the national income while the lower 40 per cent received only one-tenth of the total. Villarreal 1977 pp. 75–6.

16. For the best account of the 1968 student movement, see Sergio Zermeño 1978.

17. There is abundant literature on this period; see, for instance, Gerardo Bueno 1983; Robert E. Looney 1985; Carlos Tello 1979; Lawrence Whitehead 1980.

18. This expansion was caused by the rise in government expenditures and the government's failure to increase its fiscal revenues due to the opposition of business to tax reform.

19. A revealing indicator of the politicization, stalemate and discontinuity of the economic policy-making process during this period is that, in sharp contrast to the two previous administrations, the head of the Finance Ministry was changed six times and the Central Bank had three different directors. Equally significant was the creation of the Ministry of Budget and Planning (Secretaría de Programación y Presupuesto (SPP) in 1977, which entailed the weakening of the Finance Ministry and made policy co-ordination increasingly difficult.

20. For the differences between the two groups and the conflict within the economic policy-making apparatus during this period, see: Miguel Bazañez 1981, pp. 67–70; Stephan Haggard 1986; Robert Kaufman 1988; Roberto Newell, G. and Luis Rubio, F. 1984, pp. 136–57, 207–9; Miguel Angel Rivera Ríos 1986, pp. 70–6.

21. This tacit 'division of labour' has often been labelled the 'alliance for profits', an expression popularized in Clark Reynolds 1970.

22. For the most important dimensions of business–government relations during the 1970–82 period, see Julio Labastida 1986; also: Carlos Arriola and Juan Gustavo Galindo, 1984; Edward Epstein 1980.

23. Soledad Loaeza 1984 p. 145.

24. On the different aspects of political reform during the 1970s, see: Silvia Gómez Tagle 1984; Cecilia Imaz 1981; John Foster Leich 1981; Kevin Middlebrook 1986 in Guillermo O'Donnell et al; Luis Villoro 1979 in Pablo González Casanova and Enrique Florescano (eds) 1979.

25. Presidencia de la República 1988 pp. 19, 25.

26. A wide consensus exists concerning the decisive importance of López Portillo's bank nationalization, but interpretations about its true goals vary considerably. For the President's views on this issue, see: José López Portillo 1988; For the analysis of one of López Portillo's key supporters, the Director of the Central Bank during those critical times, see Carlos Tello 1984. For a more balanced account, see Rogelio Hernández Rodríguez, 1988b; for an interpretation that reflects the private sector's views of the subject, see Newell and Rubio 1984.

27. For examples of this new discourse see some of speeches of business leaders published in *Decision* (1982), October–December.

28. On economic policy during 1982–88 period, see José Blanco, in González Casanova and Aguilar Camín (eds).

29. Rogelio Hernández Rodríguez 1988a.

30. A good example of this general orientation can be found in the constitutional reforms President de la Madrid initiated four days after he assumed power. Through these reforms, the roles and function of the public, social and private sectors were constitutionally defined. These measures failed to satisfy anyone – the left argued that the state was building its own straitjacket while the most radical factions of business argued that the reforms simply confirmed the trend towards greater and more obtrusive state intervention – their basic intent, i.e. to regulate state intervention explicitly so as to limit the margins for discretionary action was clear.

31. Wayne A. Cornelius 1984, pp. 91–4.

32. Presidencia de la República 1988, pp. 26–7.

33. For an excellent analysis of the relation between the Programa de Aliento y Crecimiento and the crisis that towards the end of 1987 led to the adoption of the Pacto de Solidaridad Económica, see Leo Zuchermann 1989.

34. Petróleos Mexicanos, Mexico's state-owned oil conglomerate.

35. For a similar argument, see Joseph Foweraker 1988 p. 26.

36. For trade liberalization, see Brian C. Brisson 1988.

37. Figures drawn from Economist Intelligence Unit. Country Report: Mexico, 1987–88. On the privatization process, see Wilson Peres Nuñez 1988.

38. Presidencia de la República 1988, p. 24.

39. Banco de México 1988 p. 439.

40. GNP: Annual Rate of Growth: 1982, –0.6; 1983, –4.2; 1984, 3.6; 1985, 2.6; 1986, –4.0; 1987, 1.4. Source: Banco de México 1988.

41. Banco Interamericano de Desarrollo 1988.

42. For the difference between goal–rational and legal–rational legitimacy formulae, see T. H. Rigby 1982 in Rigby and Feher (eds) 1982.

43. For the definitions of civil and political society I draw on Alfred Stepan 1985.

44. See El sismo: antecedentes y consecuencias (1985).

45. Matilde Luna, Ricardo Tirado, and Francisco Valdez 1987 in Sylvia Maxfield and Ricardo Anzaldua Montoya (eds), p. 38.

46. Giovanni Sartori 1976 p. 44.

47. Ibid., p. 231.

48. On elections during the de la Madrid government see Arturo Alvarado (ed.) 1987; Wayne A. Cornelius in Drake and Silva (eds) 1986.
49. Middlebrook 1986, p. 144.
50. Carlos Martínez Assad and Alvaro Arreola Ayala 1985; in Pablo González Casanova (ed.) 1985.
51. The most systematic evidence on the fraud in the 1986 Chihuahua elections is Juan Molinar Horcasitas 1987.
52. Soledad Loaeza 1985.
53. On Corriente Democrática, see Andrew Reding 1988.

Bibliography

Alvarado, Arturo (ed.) (1987) *Electoral Patterns and Perspectives in Mexico.* San Diego, Center for US.-Mexican Studies, Monograph Series 22.
Arriola, Carlos (1977) *Las Crisis en el Sistema Político Mexicano 1928–1977.* Mexico, El Colegio de México.
Arriola, Carlos and Juan Gustavo Galindo (1984) 'Los empresarios y el estado en México (1976–1982)', *Foro Internacional.* Vol. XXV, No. 2, October–December.
Bailey, John (1986) in Roderic A. Camp (ed.).
Banco de México (1988) 'La política económica y la evolucion de la economía en 1987'. *Comercio Exterior*, Vol. 38, No. 5.
Banco Interamericano de Desarrollo (1988) *Informe*, quoted in *La Jornada*, Mexico City, 15 January.
Bazañez, Miguel (1981) *La lucha por la hegemonía en México, 1968–1980.* Mexico City, Siglo XXI.
Blanco, José (1979) 'Génesis y desarrollo de la crisis en México, 1962–1979'. *Investigación Económica*, No. 150, October–December.
——— (1985) in González Casanova and Aguilar Camín (eds).
Brisson, Brian, C. (1988) 'Mexico Liberalizes Trade . . .'. *Business America*, 18 January.
Bueno, Gerardo (1983) 'El endeudamiento externo y estrategias de desarrollo en México: 1976–1982'. *Foro Internacional*, No. 93, July–September.
Camacho, Manuel (1977) 'Los nudos históricos del sistema político mexicano'. *Foro Internacional*, April/July.
Camp, Roderic A. (ed.) (1986) *Mexico's Political Stability: The Next Five Years.* Boulder/London, Westview Press.
Cárdenas, Enrique (1987) *La industrialización Mexicana durante la Gran Depresión.* Mexico City, El Colegio de México.
Collier, David (ed.) (1979) *The New Authoritarianism in Latin America.* Princeton, Princeton University Press.
Cordera, Rolando et al (1988) *México: El reclamo democrático.* Mexico City, Siglo XXI/ILET.
Cornelius, Wayne A. (1984) 'The Political Economy of Mexico under de la Madrid'. *Mexican Studies/Estudios Mexicanos*, Vol. 1, No. 1.
——— (1986) in Drake and Silva (eds).
Cosío Villegas, Daniel (1978) *El sistema politico mexicano*, Mexico City, Joaquin Mortíz.
Drake, Paul W., and Eduardo Silva (eds) (1986) *Elections and Democratization in*

Latin America 1980–1985. San Diego, Center for US–Mexican Studies/Institute of the Americas.

Eisenstadt, S. N. and René Lemarchand (eds) (1981) *Political Clientelism, Patronage and Development*. Beverley Hills, Sage.

El Colegio de México (1974) *La vida política en México, 1970–1973*, Mexico City.

El sismo: antecedentes y consecuencias (1985). *El Cotidiano*, No. 8.

Epstein, Edward (1980) 'Business–government relations in Mexico'. *Journal of International Law*, Vol. 12, No. 3, Summer.

FitzGerald, E. V. K. (1979) in Thorp and Whitehead (eds).

Foweraker, Joseph (1988) 'Popular Movements and the Transformation of the Mexican Political System'. Paper for Workshop on Mexico's Alternative Future, 23–25 March, Center for US–Mexican Studies, San Diego.

Garrido, Luis Javier (1986) *El partido de la Revolución Institucionalizada: La formación del nuevo estado en México (1928–1945)*, Mexico City, Secretaría de Educación Pública.

────── (1987) 'El Partido del Estado ante la Sucesión Presidencial en México (1929–1987)', *Revista Mexicana de Sociología*, Vol. XLIX, No. 3, July–September.

Gómez Tagle, Silvia (1984) 'Estado y reforma política en México', *Nueva Antropología*, Vol. 7, No. 25.

González Casanova, Pablo (1965) *La Democracía en México*, Mexico City, Era.

────── (ed.) (1985) *Las elecciones en México*, Mexico City, Siglo XXI.

────── and Hector Aguilar Camín (eds) (1985) *México ante la crisis*, Vol. 1, Mexico City, Siglo XXI.

────── and Enrique Florescano (eds) (1979) *México Hoy*, Mexico City, Siglo XXI.

────── and Jorge Cadena Roa (eds) (1988) *Primer informe sobre la democracía: México*, Mexico City, Siglo XXI.

Gourevitch, P. (1986) *Politics in Hard Times: Comparative Responses to International Economic Crises*. Ithaca/London, Cornell University Press.

Haggard, Stephen (1986) in Miles Kahler (ed.).

Hamilton, Nora (1982) *The Limits of State Autonomy: Post-Revolutionary Mexico*. Princeton, Princeton University Press.

Hansen, Roger D. (1971) *Mexican Economic Development: The Roots of Rapid Growth*. Washington National Planning Association.

Hernández Rodríguez, Rogelio (1988a) 'Los hombres del presidente de la Madrid'. *Foro Internacional*, Vol. XXVIII, No. 1, July–September.

────── (1988b) *Empresarios, banca y estado*. Mexico City, FLACSO/Miguel Angel Porrúa.

Hirschman, Albert O. (1971) *A Bias for Hope: Essays on Development and Latin America*, New Haven/London, Yale University Press.

Molinar Horcasitas, Juan (1987) 'Regreso a Chihuahua'. *Nexos*, March.

Imaz, Cecilia (1981) 'La izquierda y la reforma política en México'. *Revista Mexicana de Sociología*, Vol. XLII, No. 3.

Kahler, Miles (ed.) (1986) *The Politics of International Debt*. Ithaca/London, Cornell University Press.

Kaufman, Robert (1988) The Politics of Orthodoxy in Mexico. Unpublished ms.

Labastida, Julio (1986) *Grupos económicos y organizaciones empresariales en México*. Mexico City, Biblioteca Iberoamericana/Alianza Editorial/UNAM.

Leich, John Foster (1981) 'Political Reform in Mexico'. *Current History*, Vol. 80.

Loaeza, Soledad (1974) in El Colegio de México (1974).

────── (1984) 'Iglesia católica y reformismo autoritario', *Foro Internacional*, Vol. XXV, No. 2.

—— (1985) in *Nexos*, No. 90, June.

—— (1987) in Loaeza and Segovia (eds) 1987.

—— and R. Segovia (eds) (1987) *La vida política Mexicana en la crisis*, Mexico City, El Colegio de México.

Looney, Robert E. (1985) *Economic Policymaking in Mexico*. Durham, WC, Duke University Press.

López Portillo, José (1988) *Mis Tiempos: Biografía y Testimonio Político*, Vol. 2, Mexico City, Fernández Editores, pp. 1227–49.

Luna, Matilda, Ricardo Tirado and Francisco Valdez (1987) in Sylvia Maxfield and Ricardo Anzaldua Montoya (eds) 1987.

Mabry, Donald (1973) *Mexico's Acción Nacional: a Catholic Alternative to Revolution*. Syracuse, New York University Press.

Martínez Assad, Carlos and Alvaro Arreola Ayala (1985) in González Casanova 1985.

Maxfield, Sylvia (1988) International Finance, the State, and Capital Accumulation: Mexico in Comparative Perspective. PhD dissertation, Harvard University.

—— and Ricardo Anzaldua Montoya (eds) (1987) *Government and Private Sector in Contemporary Mexico*, San Diego, Center for US–Mexican Studies.

Meyer, Lorenzo (1978) 'Los inicios de la institucionalización: La política del Maximato'. *Historia de la Revolución Mexicana*, Vol. 12, Mexico City, El Colegio de México.

—— (1988) 'La democratización del PRI: Misión imposible?' Paper presented at the Workshop on Mexico's alternative political futures. San Diego, Center for US–Mexican Studies.

Middlebrook, Kevin (1986) in O'Donnell et al, 1986.

Minian, Isaac (ed.) (1988) *Cambio estructural y producción de ventajas comparativas*. Mexico, CIDE.

Newell G., Roberto and Luis Rubio F. (1984) *Mexico's Dilemma: The Political Origins of Economic Crisis*, Boulder/London, Westview Press.

O'Donnell, Guillermo (1973) *Modernization and Bureaucratic Authoritarianism: Studies in South American Politics*, Berkeley, Institute of International Studies, University of California Press.

—— et al, (eds) (1986) *Transitions from Authoritarian Rule: Latin America*, Baltimore/London, Johns Hopkins University Press.

Peres Nuñez, Wilson (1988) in Minian (ed.) 1988.

Presidencia de la República (1985) Unidad de la Crónica Presidencial, *Las razones y las obras: Crónica del sexenio 1982–88, Primer Año*, Mexico City, Presidencia de la República/Fondo de Cultura Económica.

—— (1988) Unidad de la Crónica Presidencial, *Las razones y las obras: Crónica del sexenio 1982–88, Sexto Año*.

Purcell, Susan K. (1981) in S. N. Eisenstadt and René Lemarchand (eds).

Purcell, Susan K. and John F. H. (1980) 'State and Society in Mexico'. *World Politics*, Vol. 32, No. 2, January.

Reding, Andrew (1988) 'The Democratic Current: A New Era in Mexican Politics'. *World Policy Journal*, Vol. 5, No. 2, Spring.

Reyna, José Luis and Richard S. Weinert (eds) (1977) *Authoritarianism in Mexico*. Philadelphia, ISHI Press.

Reynolds, Clark (1970) *The Mexican Economy: Twentieth Century Structure and Growth*. New Haven, Yale University Press.

Rigby, T. H. and Ferenc Feher (eds) (1982) *Political Legitimation in Communist States*. New York, St. Martin's Press.

Rivera Ríos, Miguel Angel (1986) *Crisis y reorganización del capitalismo mexicano.* Mexico, Era.

Sartori, Giovanni (1976) *Parties and Party Systems.* Cambridge, Cambridge University Press.

Scott, Robert (1964) *Mexican Government in Transition.* Urbana, University of Illinois Press.

Sikkink, K. (1988) Developmentalism: Ideas and Economic Policy Making in Brazil and Argentina. PhD dissertation, Columbia University.

Solís, Leopoldo (1970) *La realidad económica mexicana; retrovisión y perspectivas.* Mexico City, Siglo XXI.

Stepan, Alfred (1985) Military Politics and Three Polity Arenas. Unpublished paper.

Tello, Carlos (1979) *La política económica en México: 1970–76.* Mexico City, Siglo XXI.

────── (1984) *La nacionalización de la banca en México:* Mexico City, Siglo XXI.

Thorp, Rosemary and Lawrence Whitehead (eds) (1979) *Inflation and Stabilization in Latin America.* New York, Holmes and Meier.

Universidad Iberoamericana (1978) *El Partido Acción Nacional: Ensayos y Testimonios.* Mexico City, Editorial Jus.

Villarreal, René (1977) 'Import-Substitution Industrialization', in José Luis Reyna and Richard S. Weinert (eds).

Vílloro, Luis (1979) in Gonzàlez Casanova and Florescano (eds).

Whitehead, Lawrence (1980) 'La política económica del sexenio de Echeverría: qué salió mal y por qué?' *Foro Internacional*, No. 79, January–March.

Zermeño, Sergio (1978) *México: Una democracia utópica: el movimento estudiantil del 68.* Mexico City, Siglo XXI.

Aguiler Zinser, Adolfo (1988) in Rolando Cordera et al.

Zuchermann, Leo (1989) 'El proceso de toma de decisiones en la política económica en México'. Tesis de Licenciatura en Administración Pública, El Colegio de México.

8. African Workers and Structural Adjustment: The Nigerian Case

Yusuf Bangura and Björn Beckman

The case against the African workers

Workers as an obstacle to structural adjustment

In their attempts to pursue policies of 'structural adjustment' African governments meet resistance from African workers. Workers oppose wage freezes, privatization, public sector cuts, and increases in the prices of essential commodities and services. This opposition is seen by governments as obstructionist and irresponsible. Workers are accused of failing to take their due share of the sacrifices necessary for national economic recovery. Their demands are seen as unreasonable and unrealistic.

Workers' opposition is treated as particularly illegitimate as it is viewed as coming from a small, privileged minority, pursuing narrow self-interests at the expense of the mass of the people, the poor and under-privileged peasants. Workers are accused of taking undue advantage of being better placed, more organized, more articulate. What right do they have to speak for the common people, the silent majority? African governments, therefore, feel justified in applying repressive policies against workers and their organizations. They draw support not only from neo-liberal theories but also from populist positions, including those concerned with 'labour aristocracy' and 'urban bias'. The limited rights of unionization and bargaining, where these obtain at all, are often suppressed to facilitate the passage of IMF- and World Bank-sponsored structural adjustment programmes (SAPs).

These transnational institutions and the foreign aid agencies with whom they closely work show little concern for such anti-working class repression. On the contrary, there seem to be more worries that African governments are not firm enough with such irresponsible opposition. By making unwarranted concessions to workers' agitation, weak governments jeopardize the reform programme. The state is too 'soft'. It is held to ransom by an articulate and well-organized minority.

How justified is this view of workers as irresponsible and obstructionist? This chapter draws primarily on the Nigerian experience of the 1980s but also seeks to broaden the argument. We begin by sketching a Nigerian scenario as a backdrop to a presentation of the case against the workers. We distinguish an 'economic' and a 'political' case, the latter with a focus on the role of trade unions. We highlight and discuss some of the theoretical perspectives that inform such cases. The second part, looks more closely at the Nigerian experience; and the third and final part examines whether or not the case against the workers holds. Is there an alternative way of relating to workers' opposition? We conclude by arguing the need to address the political context of structural adjustment.

The battle of the 'oil subsidy': a Nigerian scenario

In Nigeria, in April 1988, an increase in the price of petrol precipitated a month of protest. What began as a peaceful students' demonstration in the city of Jos escalated into riots and a nation-wide strike by workers.[1] Why did a minor price increase cause such uproar and conflagration?

Central to the structural adjustment policies sponsored by the IMF and the World Bank, in Africa as elsewhere, is the demand that governments should remove 'subsidies' from prices of consumer goods. In most cases conflicts have concerned the prices of basic food items, for example, wheat in Egypt, maize in Zambia, and rice in Sierra Leone. When such goods are imported the subsidy is most apparent. But also, domestically produced items are said to be subsidized when they sell locally at prices fixed by the state below the world market price, if calculated on the basis of current exchange rates.

This has been the case with petrol in Nigeria. In the early 1980s, at a time when the naira was kept at par with the US dollar, one litre of petrol would sell at 20 kobo = 20 cents.

In 1986, as the crisis deepened, the government decided to almost double the price, removing what government then claimed to be 80 per cent of the 'subsidy'. In the context of a government-proclaimed wage freeze and fast declining real incomes, the price increase hit people hard. But this was only the beginning. As the naira was allowed to drop drastically to a six-to-one relation with the dollar, the 'subsidy' 'grew' correspondingly. The government came under pressure from the IMF and the World Bank to 'adjust' the price upwards in tune with the declining value of the naira.

Workers objected. In November 1987, government-sponsored advertisements sought to prepare the way for a 'removal of the oil subsidy'. The Nigeria Labour Congress (NLC), the central trade union body, responded with a counter-campaign. It published hard hitting anti-removal posters and organized protest rallies.[2] The state responded with repression. Leading union officials were detained and threatened with sedition charges. The Director of Public Prosecution declared that the position of the NLC was 'unreasonable in extreme', designed to meet the 'selfish interests of a few leaders' and to cause general dissatisfaction with the government.[3]

The state backed down. The unionists were released and workers were jubilant as the expected increase in petrol prices was not included in the January 1988.[4] But the truce was temporary. The standby agreement with the IMF expired at the end of 1987 and the Fund refused to endorse the performance of SAP. The World Bank withheld a US$500 million structural adjustment loan. Debt rescheduling and commercial credits were also held up.[5]

In February 1988, the government hit out again, taking advantage of the division between 'moderates' and 'radicals' within the unions. The NLC leaders were suspended and a Sole Administrator was appointed to 'bring about unity'. The suppression of union leadership came in the wake of a national conference where the government was condemned for trying to cripple the organization so as to prepare the way for an increase in the petroleum price.[6]

While the government succeeded, for the time being, in silencing the union leaders, it failed to contain workers' opposition. Although the April 1988 price increase was marginal, it was believed to be the first step in a gradual removal of the oil 'subsidy'. In the absence of the official leadership, unionists formed local 'Action Committees' to sustain the strikes. Local leaders were arrested and workers threatened with summary dismissals and long prison sentences as 'saboteurs', under government emergency laws. According to a spokesman for the President the disturbances were caused by the 'urban elites', not the peaceful rural majority.[7]

Again, the government was obliged to back down; confronted with this unprecedented spate of popular unrest and strikes it was forced to the negotiation table. Union leaders, worried about their capacity to sustain action and feeling that their point had been made, agreed to call off the strikes. Their opposition to the fuel price increase, however, was reiterated; also the 'moderates' who had co-operated with the state in engineering the break-up of the NLC were obliged to join a unity platform rejecting the price increase.[8] The stalemate persisted.

The 'economic' case: Workers are too many and too costly

How 'legitimate' is the opposition of African workers to structural adjustment? How 'irresponsible' and 'selfish' is it? Is it true that it primarily reflects the politicking of a disgruntled urban-based labour élite, representing neither the interests of rank and file workers, nor the silent majority of the rural areas? How far does such workers' opposition offer an alternative road out of the crisis? Or does it merely obstruct the government's efforts.

Let us look closer at the case against the workers, beginning with the 'economic' one. It is an old case but it has been greatly boosted by the economic crisis. The basic point of the structural adjusters is that workers are too many and too costly.[9] This is due to misconceived policies, including the development of an over-protected and therefore over-sized industrial sector. Another problem is the growth of over-staffed state enterprises and public services, with wage bills out of proportion to their carrying capacity and deficits paid for by state subsidies. There is a combination of budgetary laxity and the influence of corrupt, nepotistic, and/or clientelistic modes of labour recruitment.

The inflation of over-paid wage employment is reinforced by the policy bias against the private sector. The public sector is more insulated from market pressures and can therefore resort to administrative and monopolistic methods to prop up employment and high wages. The result has been to inflate the demand for public sector employment. Over-protection, subsidies, and monopolistic practices have led to wage levels which do not reflect the productivity of labour. Measured against workers' pay in 'comparable' Asian countries, African workers, it is argued, have been over-paid.[10] Uneconomic public sector wages have been imposed on the private sector directly or indirectly by means of minimum-wage legislation and the generalization of public wage awards. An excessive (artificial) demand for waged jobs has been further encouraged by policies that discriminate against non-wage employment. This takes two basic forms. One is the suppression of non-wage income, especially farmers', through taxation and price controls (marketing boards and so on). The other is the allocation of public resources in favour of the urban areas. The struggle for waged employment is therefore also a struggle to secure access to better education, health care, water supply, electricity, and suchlike.

The 'political' case: Workers are powerful and selfish

The 'political' case focuses on the place of the workers in the structure of power relations in African society.[11] The policy bias in favour of excessive wage employment, inflated wages, and a pro-urban, pro-worker allocation of public services and economic opportunities is, from this point of view, a result of the political entrenchment of an urban-based coalition in which workers play an important role. Despite their small numbers, they are seen as wielding excessive power in giving direction to government policies. In part, this is supposedly due to their physical closeness to power, including an ability to destabilize and bring down governments by taking to the streets. The senior partners of such political coalitions and their primary beneficiaries are politicians, senior bureaucrats, military officers, and other members of the élite proper. But the workers also benefit and provide support for pro-élitist and pro-urban policies.

It is in the context of such economic distortions and urban policy bias that worker's opposition to structural adjustment is seen as illegitimate, selfish, and unrepresentative of wider popular interests. Workers take undue advantage of their closeness to political power. They fail to take their due share of the sacrifices necessitated by the economic crisis. They look neither to the national interest, nor to the interests of the vast, mainly rural, mainly silent population whose mouthpiece they claim, wrongly, to be. The interests of the workers, it is argued, are opposed to those of other popular classes, particularly the peasants. The workers participate in the exploitation of the latter, sharing responsibility for the neglect of agriculture, premature or stunted industrialization, and a swollen, inefficient, and predatory public sector. Workers use their strategic location to extort preferential treatment, subsidies, high wages, and special access to commodities and services that are denied the rest of the (rural) population. They use their power to distort and obstruct national development.

African governments are either too weak to impose the programmes in the face of workers' opposition or too permeated by élitist self-interests to act resolutely in the interest of the nation and the rural majority.

Problems of the economic case against the workers

On the economic side, much of the case against the workers may seem to be validated by the sheer inability of employers, state or private, to pay wages and engage workers in productive activity. Factories close down or operate at a fraction of their installed capacity because of lack of foreign exchange to pay for basic inputs. School teachers and railway workers absent themselves en masse in search of alternative means of survival after months of non-payment of wages. Public institutions, including hospitals, become empty shells without necessary equipment. Wages collapse, not just as a result of a conscious policy but because of the shortage of basic wage goods in the markets.

In much of Africa, strong forces are thus at work causing contraction in employment and a reduction in wages. Cutting costs, reducing budgetary deficits, withdrawing subsidies, shedding 'unviable' activities, trimming wage bills, laying-off workers, are the imperatives everywhere. The case for cuts is often overwhelming as in Nigeria where, within the span of a few years, export earnings were reduced to one-quarter by the combined fall in the price and volume of petroleum sales.

Much of the public case against the workers is argued on such *prima facie* grounds. How can workers and their friends fail to recognize the imperatives of the situation? The perceived strength of the economic case makes opposition to structural adjustment appear not just unrealistic but irresponsible, selfish, and unpatriotic.

Looked at closer, however, the validity of the case against the workers is less than self-evident; it dissolves into a range of controversies. At one level it is a problem of facts and evidence, at another of policy and options. At a third level, the controversies concern the theoretical premises that underlie the selection and evaluation of both evidence and options.[12] What are acceptable levels of protection for infant industries? How sensitive are particular industries to variations in production costs? What price 'distortions' are acceptable in the interest of the national economy? What 'subsidies' are 'distortions' and what is an acceptable way of financing public services? What is a 'correct' exchange rate?

Problems of theory and policy are compounded by difficulties at the level of methodology when constructing the data base for any such argument. For example, how can wage levels be compared? How relevant are conversions on the basis of official exchange rates? What do relative wages mean in actual consumption baskets? How should such baskets be constructed in societies where both the structure of market-derived consumption and household organization differ so much? The problem is further exacerbated when turning to comparisons between urban and rural income, between wages and household production for own consumption. What is a meaningful comparison between the provision of public services in fragmented, only partially commercialized rural economies, on the one hand, and in cities, on the other?

Crucial to the case against the African worker are notions of low productivity, giving the impression that workers fail to work hard enough and that wage demands are therefore unreasonable. How much of this must be attributed to organizational problems, for instance in the access to inputs and maintenance that have little to do with labour performance? The policy implications differ. Is it a question of shedding labour or using it more efficiently? Moreover, the impact of high wage bills on the economy is also contested. To some, high wages lead to a contraction of overall employment either because labour-saving methods are introduced or because entrepreneurs abstain from investing. To others, high wages fuel demand and contribute to the expansion of employment and income in other sectors, including in peasant food production.

The controversies are further complicated by the specific dislocations caused by crises and crises policies. What balance is to be struck between abandoning and protecting existing assets? What are the relevant 'economic' criteria for assessing 'viability' in the volatile context of collapsing money markets? Pointing to the resource constraints and the need for drastic adjustment is merely stating the obvious. There is very little that is obvious, however, when it comes to the content of the adjustment programmes. The controversy over the allocation of the scarce resources is intense. It is not simply a question of policy preferences but deep divisions over facts and theory. Moreover, the issues must be addressed in the context of specific social formations and historical conjunctures.

Theoretical aspects of the political case
At the core of the political case against the workers is the notion of irresponsible and unrepresentative trade unions. It draws on different political and theoretical perspectives. For some neo-liberals, trade unions are cases of entrenched 'special interests' and 'social rigidities' that stand in the way of the market forces and economic growth. Unions, according to Mancur Olson,[13] use their power to obtain wages for their members above competitive levels. In doing so, they cause economic stagnation, inflation and unemployment. Neo-liberals seek to use the economic crisis to roll back union power. Other liberal positions are less extreme. Unions may serve useful purposes, but they should not be too strong, otherwise they pose a threat to national economic policies and economic growth.[14]

In the African context, liberal objections to strong unions are reinforced by statist and developmentalist positions. While acknowledging the distinct contribution of radical unionism during the independence struggle, in the post-independence period the imperative of national development was that unions should be firmly subordinated to the state.[15] The statist view covers a wide range of positions, including those of 'radicals' such as Nkrumah and Nyerere and of 'conservatives' as Senghor and Houphouet Boigny. Unions that refuse to toe the line have been repressed, whether in Sankara's Burkina Faso, Rawlings' Ghana or Babangida's Nigeria. There is a confluence of liberal, managerial, and statist/developmentalist positions, of both left and right colouration, in opposition to strong and autonomous unions. Both liberals and statists draw additional support from populist and 'peasantist' positions that pit selfish, privileged, and vociferous workers against silent, suffering peasants.

The radical, populist position has borrowed arguments from a Marxist tradition concerned with the problem of 'labour aristocracy'.[16] A section of the working class is seen as being bought-off and co-opted and thereby turned into an ally of the bourgeoisie. The transfer of surplus from the oppressed nations made this policy of co-optation possible in the advanced capitalist countries. On similar lines, it has been suggested that a section of the African working class has been co-opted as a labour aristocracy and bought-off with surpluses extracted from the peasants.

African trade unions, from this point of view, represent a small and relatively privileged section of the working people. They often draw their membership from a limited number of establishments, mostly in the state and transnational sectors. The bulk of the workers in transport, construction, trade, and commercial agriculture, for instance, are non-unionized. Moreover, the assumed lack of democracy within the unions has resulted in the entrenchment of labour élites, whose interests are similar to the parasitic, exploitative state bureaucracies into which they have been co-opted. The aristocracy argument is therefore applied either to the unionized working class as a whole or more specifically to the 'labour leaders'.

In the Marxist tradition, the working class and its organizations are credited with a leading political role in social transformation. The labour aristocracy argument aims to explain why it does not always turn out that way. Another Marxist-type argument has similarly been used to reinforce the anti-unionist case. It focuses on the question of class formation and class consciousness. Working-class political leadership is expected to emerge out of a process of class consolidation, including awareness of common identity and interests.

In the populist anti-union argument, such class cohesion and consciousness are assumed to be absent among African workers. From this perspective, the African working class is not 'real', either because so much of it is clerical (non-productive, non-industrial) and/or because it is structurally unsettled, migrant, with one foot in petty commodity production, and with a consciousness that is dominated by non-class identities of community, ethnicity, and religion.[17]

The class argument has been incorporated in the populist, anti-union argument. It can be used in rejecting labour leaders' claims to speak on behalf of a 'working class' when opposing state and structural adjustment. It is also helpful in denouncing working-class claims to offer leadership to wider popular forces.

The political case against the workers, in common with the economic case, needs to be evaluated in the context of concrete historical experiences. In the following pages we look more closely at one such context: first outlining the Nigerian crisis and how it has affected the workers, then examining the development of the working class and its organizations. Workers' strategies of fighting the crisis at the workplace and at the level of national policies are discussed and the empirical case is concluded by considering the role of workers in wider alliances for surviving economic crisis and state repression.

Nigerian workers and structural adjustment

Crisis and adjustment hit the workers

Oil replaced agriculture as the backbone of the Nigerian economy in the 1970s, accounting for more than 90 per cent of export earnings and 95 per cent of public expenditure by 1974. The large oil revenue of 65 billion naira that was received between 1973 and 1981 shielded the economy from the early phase of the world recession.[18] State expenditure rose sharply from 8.3 billion naira in 1975 to 23.7 billion in 1980. Investment expenditure, estimated at about 70 billion naira in current prices over the period 1973 to 1981, exceeded the value of oil revenues received. Import-substitution industries expanded and foreign exchange-based agricultural projects proliferated. The naira was allowed to appreciate in value.

The failure of industrial accumulation to generate its own autonomous sources of foreign exchange strained the external account. The importation of consumer goods rose from 440 million naira in 1974 to 3.9 billion in 1981; that of capital goods increased from 760 million naira in 1974 to 4.7 billion in 1979; and raw material imports jumped from 519.3 million naira in 1974 to three billion in 1981.[19] The dramatic increase in revenue that followed the oil price rises of 1979 and 1980 facilitated the relaxation of import controls. Federal and state governments resorted to heavy borrowing from the international capital market as a result of improved credit-worthiness and the availability of cheap credits from suppliers and bankers anxious to overcome the glut in demand for new investments in Western countries. Short-term trade credits accumulated rapidly. The cumulative external loans commitment, estimated at 18.5 billion naira at the end of 1983, was in sharp contrast to the total outstanding debt US$2.35 billion in 1978. The public debt service ratio jumped from 8.9 per cent in 1982 to 17.4 per cent in 1983.[20]

The sudden drop in oil revenues from US$22.4 billion in 1980 to US$16.7 billion in 1981 and 12.8 billion in 1982, following the decline in world oil prices, accentuated the structural problems of the economy. There was a serious fiscal crisis affecting both the federal and the state governments. The economy experienced a resource gap of about three billion naira in 1981 (6 per cent of GDP) compared to a resource surplus of 2.6 billion naira in 1980;[21] the balance of payments was in persistent deficit; capacity utilization in industry dropped to below 40 per cent in 1983, leading to massive retrenchment; and basic commodity prices escalated.

The imbalances at the domestic and external accounts called for major structural reforms. The stabilization programmes of the Shagari (1979–83) and Buhari (1984–85) administrations emphasized state controls, even though both regimes agreed with the IMF and the World Bank on the need to eliminate distortions, prune the public sector and introduce 'realistic' domestic price systems. Buhari's regime had problems with the IMF on devaluation, the withdrawal of the subsidy on petroleum products and trade liberalization. Alternative strategies of counter-trade, raising debt-servicing to 44 per cent and cultivating new sources of foreign finance, proved unsuccessful. Foreign credit lines were blocked and external debt rescheduling stalled. This affected the supply of essential commodities and industrial inputs. Massive cuts in public expenditure led to retrenchment and cuts in social benefits in the public sector.

Difficulties in the negotiations with the IMF were accompanied by repressive policies at home. Several decrees were introduced curtailing civil liberties and workers' rights. Decrees 17 and 19, for instance, prevented workers from appealing against retrenchment and the automatic receipt of retrenchment benefits. Babangida's administration (1985–) reopened the negotiations with the IMF. The regime substituted the World Bank for the IMF when the public rejected the IMF loan, but continued to work with the IMF to obtain its necessary support for the debt-talks with the creditors. Most of the IMF's demands on structural reforms were accepted without the standard stand-by facility. Currency over-valuations were to be removed through a second-tier foreign exchange market (SFEM); price distortions were to be eliminated through privatization, the rationalization of tariffs, and the removal of subsidies; and general imbalances were to be corrected through a policy of tight money supply and the regulation of public expenditure.

Workers have been hit by the shift in policy. Further cuts in public expenditure have led to new rounds of retrenchment. Rates of retrenchment have tended to correspond with the declines in turnover. Several industries have slashed their work force by more than 60 per cent between 1982 and 1988. Worst hit have been the construction, automobile, pharmaceutical and electrical equipment industries. Capacity utilization in the automobile firms, for instance, was only about 10 per cent in 1988. Most companies maintain a skeletal work-force.

Many social benefits have been either cut or suspended. Workers have had to pay high prices for drugs and declining health services; school fees have been reintroduced in most parts of the country; and levies of various kinds have been imposed by state governments to compensate for the fiscal crisis. In Niger state, for instance, a compulsory levy of five per cent of gross monthly salary and wages was introduced for public sector workers in 1984. This was buttressed by a five per cent purchase tax and an education levy of 20 naira; repressive methods have been used to enforce compliance. Wages and salaries were cut at the federal level in 1985 as part of contributions to an economic emergency fund; new employment and wage increases have been tightly controlled. The rate of inflation has increased sharply. Between 1981 and 1987 prices of such food items as gari, yams, beans, maize, plantains and rice rose by an average of about 150 to 330 per cent; those of sugar, milk and fish rose by more than 350 per cent. Real wages have indeed fallen sharply. Nigeria Labour Congress estimates show that the minimum wage of 125 naira was worth about only 25 per cent of its 1987 value.[22]

The naira has deteriorated sharply from N1=US$1.83 in 1980 to N1=US$1 in January 1986; N3.3=US$1 in January 1987; to about N10=US$1 in February 1989. Prices of essential food items have rocketed and production costs have increased. Many companies cannot cope with the current rate of exchange.[23] Some industries, such as breweries and textiles, able to find local substitutes, are doing slightly better. Most industries have, however, experienced reduced turn overs and low capacity utilization. The Manufacturers Association of Nigeria's half-yearly report puts the capacity utilization at 25 per cent in 1987, compared with 30 per cent in 1986. The rationalization of costs in industry has led to generalized retrenchment, more compulsory time off and an increase in the work load. Workers' living standards have fallen sharply. The withdrawal of petroleum subsidies has further worsened the situation. Workers are bound to react.

The Nigerian working class and its organizations
The development of the Nigerian working class dates back to the colonial period when labour was required to establish and run the colonial infrastructure and to extract mineral resources for export. From just a few thousands in the colonial period, the working class has grown in strength to several millions, covering a wide range of industrial activities and located in all the major towns of the federation. Industrialization has attracted a substantial number of workers into the manufacturing and service sectors. The commercialization of agriculture has also seen the rise of a small, but growing, working class in the rural areas. Small-scale industrial activities have flourished. The boom of the 1970s was significant in creating a large force of construction workers.

Workers have formed their own organizations to defend specific interests at the work place and in the wider society. Apart from the early civil service union of 1912, trade union organization started in earnest in the 1930s, with the formation of the National Union of Teachers and the National Union of Railwaymen. The issues of material living conditions, the right of unions to participate in politics and to be independent, and the establishment of a central organization, have dominated the history of the trade union movement since colonial times. The trade unions provided a platform for nationalists to challenge colonial rule. But labour unity has been affected by state interference and ideological differences that partly mirror the divisions among the international trade union organizations.[24] The state has consistently sided with the moderate factions to blunt the militant interventions of the unions in national affairs. No government has succeeded in either co-opting or completely subordinating the general movement; but neither have trade unions been able to float their own political parties. Attempts to do this in 1964, following the successful national strikes, ended in failure.[25]

The trade unions came to play a prominent role in national affairs in the 1970s, articulating a broad range of demands, which affected several other social groups. Workers' protests were instrumental in bringing about the package of wage/salary increases and social benefits announced in the Adebo report of 1971. The short-comings of the awards led to new rounds of agitation and culminated in the more comprehensive Udoji awards of 1974. Workers led the way in forcing policy-makers to channel some of the new oil revenues to the lower sections of the society. They also supported the business groups and the professionals in agitating for the indigenization of the economy; and were part of the social forces that protested against Gowon's decision, in 1974, to postpone the return to civilian rule.

The limitations of worker's struggles in the early 1970s, in the face of intensified state repression, led to renewed attempts by leading labour activists to reconcile the differences among the four competing labour centres. This culminated in the formation of a central labour organization in 1975, with the radical Nigerian Trade Union Congress dominating the leadership. But the state was anxious to impose its own version of labour unity on the workers. The petition of a faction, the United Labour Congress, against the new executive offered the new military government an excuse to intervene. The government dissolved the newly formed Nigeria Labour Congress, arrested several unionists and appointed an administrator to look after the affairs of the unions, pending the outcome of a probe into the activities of the unions. The unions were later restructured from over 1,000 to 42, and given a new central labour organization: the Nigeria Labour Congress (NLC). A ban was placed on affiliations with foreign trade union organizations; a system for deducting worker's contributions from their wages to support the new trade unions was introduced; and a labour bureaucracy with remunerations similar to those of the civil service was created. The victory of the radical unionists in the elections of 1978, however, underscored the concern of the majority of workers to keep the trade union movement independent of state interference.

The new labour constitution, though state imposed, gave the NLC considerable national significance. The trade unions now had a strong financial basis to employ the services of trained union officials to monitor industrial and national developments and improve upon their techniques of collective bargaining. Branches of the NLC were established in every state of the federation; federal spread meant federal power and influence. It allowed for co-ordination of union affairs, linking-up with non-workers' organizations and access to a variety of data on a national scale. No other organization could rival the labour movement in this regard.

Workers' strategies at the work place

Workers responses to adjustment have been varied and complex, ranging from those that are planned, militant, collectivist, and political, to those that are spontaneous, conciliatory, individualistic, and economistic. Variations reflect differences in levels of organization and consciousness, and the differential effects of adjustment on the public sector and on industry. We make a distinction between individual workers' strategies and union strategies. Non-unionized workers, especially those in the construction industry, have had a particularly raw deal. Options have been very limited; those who are lucky tend to fall back on the informal sector.

Some unionized workers have pressed for the payment of their gratuity to enable them go into petty trading, farming or small-scale transport services. Such entrepreneurial responses have been prominent among workers in the older industries such as textiles and the railways. Those with technical skills either establish repair shops or join already existing ones. Some of the workers dismissed in the aftermath of the demonstration in the automobile industry, Steyr-Nigeria, in 1985, for instance, were able to set up a small-scale enterprise to service the vehicles of the company in down-town Bauchi. It is not uncommon to find workers combining farming with full-time waged employment. In places where salaries have not been paid, especially in the public sector, workers pay less attention to their jobs, report late for work or attend to private matters during office hours. Authorities find it difficult to enforce the rules.

Unions are concerned about minimizing the impact of rationalization on the workers, defending activists and the union against harassment and repression, and reconciling conflicting workers' interests in the various departments of the work place. Individual workers' initiatives strengthen as well as weaken unionist strategies. In Kaduna Textiles Limited workers opted for resignation in 1983 and 1984 in order to collect their gratuity and look for alternative means of livelihood. Such a strategy was prompted by the company's deep financial problems and the fears expressed that workers' benefits might be frozen in the event of the company's collapse. Several anti-workers' strategies had been pursued by the management to keep the company afloat. These varied from the frequent resort to compulsory time off, pay cuts, the suspension of a wide range of social benefits, and periodic retrenchment. The National Union of Textile Workers leaned on the option of the workers to leave the company and collect their gratuity as a strategy to force the employers to halt retrenchment and accommodate some of the workers' demands. The company's inability to pay off the workers in one fell swoop led to a stalemate.[26]

But individualist responses also undermine collective union initiatives and militancy. Public sector workers in Ondo state were unable to take firm decisions on whether to embark on an industrial strike to protest against the non-payment of salaries for more than four months during the early stages of the crisis in 1984 and 1985. Large sections of the work-force had looked for alternative ways of survival, mainly farming, and paid less attention to their formal jobs. Unionists in the state believed that it would have been difficult to mobilize workers for a strike at that stage.[27]

Unions have relied on three broad strategies to influence the adjustment programme at the work place. The first is to operate within the logic of the programme, and to insist that the employers be held responsible for the problem. Managers and top bureaucrats are exposed as corrupt, inefficient and undisciplined. When such arguments are made workers see themselves as the embodiment of the national interest and the custodians of the factory systems on which their livelihood depends. The objective is to undermine the legitimacy of the employers and to win broad popular support for their more specific fights. Such a strategy also allows the unions to argue for the sharing of the burdens of adjustment. Even when employers do not moderate or reverse the contentious policies, the exposure of top officials as financially wasteful strengthens the morale of the rank and file workers and helps to prepare them for militant actions.

The union at the Glaxo pharmaceutical company in Lagos relied on the strategy of discrediting the management credentials of the official in charge of the raw material sector of the company to mobilize the workers against the industrial rationalization programme in 1986–87. The company had resorted to large-scale retrenchment, the withholding of end-of-year bonuses and delays in the payment of salaries in order to contain the crisis. Workers contested these measures and called for prudent ways of handling the resources of the company. They demanded the resignation of the farm manager whose alleged mismanagement of the resources of the farm exacerbated the raw material crisis. A bitter struggle ensued. Workers were locked out of the factory for a few weeks and stringent conditions were laid down for re-engagement. But the union remained adamant and continued to insist on the farm manager's resignation. Large numbers of workers were subsequently laid off; industrial relations have remained tense. Workers have little confidence in the crisis management policies of the company.[28]

A second strategy of the unions is to fight for the institutionalization of collective bargaining. This is intended to hold employers accountable for their policies, open up channels of communication, and advance alternative policies. The contract of employment, often exploited by the employers to lay off workers and curtail other benefits, usually comes up for attack. The union in Steyr-Nigeria used the disadvantages in the 'Workers Handbook', on issues pertaining to terminations, as the basis for challenging the rationalization programme in 1985.

Collective bargaining allows unions to wrest concession from the employers. Workers struggle over the yearly bonus; some compensation for time spent on compulsory time off; sharing the burdens of rationalization; spacing out retrenchment if it is inevitable; ensuring that non-discriminatory procedures are followed when staff are laid off; and insisting on retrenchment benefits to be paid on time. Despite the wage freeze and the suspension of collective bargaining between 1982 and 1987 several unions succeeded in getting employers to pay end-of-year bonuses, to offset some of the losses generated by the wage freeze.[29] Manufacturers were worried about the effect of the liquidity squeeze on sales.

A third strategy of the unions is to use strikes and demonstrations to obstruct production. Such actions are embarked upon when management refuses to negotiate with the unions; or when employers insist upon forging ahead with the contentious policies, following a breakdown in negotiations; or when management refuses to honour its own part of agreements already reached by both sides. Workers react militantly when they are side-tracked or ignored. Unionists come under considerable pressures from the work force for militant actions.

In Steyr-Nigeria, it was the arrogance of the managing director and his refusal to discuss the plight of the company with union officials that provoked the workers to a militant demonstration in 1985. Apart from the problems of contending with the periodic closures of the company following the drop in the supply of completely-knocked-down parts, workers were enraged to find out in one of the regional newspapers that the managing director had given an interview to the press hinting on a possible closure of the company. Unionists' attempts to book an appointment with the managing director to discuss the issue were rebuffed. The union declared a work-to-rule while further attempts were made to see the managers; but no one was prepared to talk to them. The workers lost their patience and decided to force-march the managing director from his office to the factory gates. A crisis ensued as management dismissed the entire work force and laid down fresh requirements for re-engagement. The workers successfully resisted the conditions even though they failed to get their union leaders reinstated.[30] Struggles continued to be waged in the courts and in the community to reverse the policy and compensate the sacked unionists.

The unions in Niger state were faced with a similar problem in 1984–85. They declared an industrial strike following the breakdown of negotiations with the state government and the latter's decision to press ahead with the contentious public sector cuts and levies. The military government had retrenched more the 5,000 workers in the public sector, imposed a variety of levies and suspended several allowances. Previous negotiations between the government and the unions had ended in deadlock. In January 1985, however, the unions succeeded in getting the government to agree to restore the allowances after six months, but in June 1985, the governor announced that the allowances would not be restored. Workers, he said, would spend the money to 'drink and marry more wives'. The unionists were insulted and aggrieved. Fresh rounds of negotiations produced no results and workers were mobilized for an industrial strike. But the government used a section of the unions to break the strike and threatened to terminate the services of those workers that refused to report for work on the day of the strike. Although the strike collapsed it dented the government's image and strained industrial relations in the state.[31]

Workers' experience in Niger state contrasted sharply with that of workers in Ondo, Benue and Cross River states, where they were able to wage successful strikes against their respective state governments. Negotiations between management and the unions in Ondo state, for instance, were protracted. The state government owed the workers about four months' salary and reneged on every timetable set for the payment of the salaries. Workers were more easily mobilized and the government's moral and political grounds were too weak for successfully wielding the 'big stick'.[32] The government had to raise money from federal sources and the banks to pay the arrears of salaries.

The Nigeria Labour Congress and the reform programme

Workers' strategies at the work place are reinforced by those of the NLC at the national level. The NLC monitors the industrial relations scene, identifies with the strategies of the industrial unions and defends aggrieved unionists and workers. The Bauchi state NLC was instrumental in sustaining the opposition of the work force to the harsh conditions laid down by the management of Steyr for readmitting the workers into the factory. The NLC acted on behalf of the national industrial union and collaborated with the in-plant union executive to negotiate the terms of re-entry.[33]

The NLC's co-ordinating roles have had a more serious impact at the state levels where public sector unions need the support of the private sector workers to strengthen their strategies. The fact that all unions in a state are represented in the state council executive of the NLC facilitates the harmonization of policies. In Niger state, for instance, private sector unions contributed to the discussions leading to the industrial relations crisis of 1985.[34] The NLC was also used as a platform by public sector workers' in Ondo state to obtain the private sector workers' support in the successful strike of August 1986.

But it is at the wider national level that the impact of the NLC has been decisive. The Congress has intervened in the debate on the IMF loan, the question of oil subsidy and other vital aspects of the reform programme. It is not surprising that Nigerian governments have used different methods in trying to neutralize the NLC's power to obstruct the stabilization programmes. Shagari's government, acting through the moderate unionists, attempted to amend the Trade Union Act of 1978 to allow for the establishment of more than one central labour organization. Buhari's approach was to keep the NLC at arms' length and rely on the repressive instrument of the state to quell any protests. Babangida initially attempted to co-opt the leadership of the unions into a tripartite committee, but finally suspended the NLC when co-optation failed to modify the militancy of the leadership.

Retrenchment, the defence of incomes, and struggles against certain aspects of price adjustments have generally occupied the NLC's attention. The capacity of the NLC to redress these basic issues is constrained by the objective decline of the national resource base and the inability to check the downward adjustment of the exchange rate. This general weakness is more telling in the area of retrenchment. But the NLC is not completely powerless. Several aspects of the reform programme are still contestable and are being contested. The NLC's strategy is to defend nominal gains in incomes and prices within a framework of mobilizing workers and other groups to discredit the general direction of the reforms. The strategy is premised on the fact that the government relies on a combination of market and administrative instruments to depress workers' living standards. Even though workers' incomes have already been eroded by the devaluation of the naira, and inflation, the government attempted to repeal the minimum wage, imposed cuts on wages and salaries and outlawed collective bargaining in the early phase of the crisis. By waging militant struggles on these issues, the NLC seeks to expose the insensitivity of the adjustment programme to the basic survival needs of workers.

Central to the logic of the programme is the depression of wages to control inflation, attract foreign capital and facilitate the competitiveness of local industries in the export market. The government introduced wage/salary cuts in October 1985, at the peak of the debate to decide Nigeria's relations with the IMF, and announced a state of economic emergency, which was to last for 15 months. A general pay cut both for the military and civilian employees was introduced, ranging from two to 20 per cent. The NLC opposed the cuts; its leaders contended that the government was implementing the contentious IMF conditions before the conclusion of the debate; that workers were not consulted before the cuts were announced; and that, unlike the business groups which appropriate profit and rent, workers have no alternative sources of income. The NLC gave an ultimatum to embark on a strike if the government pressed ahead with the deductions.

With barely two months in office, many groups were still prepared to give the government the benefit of the doubt. Journalists were still grateful to the regime for abrogating 'Decree Four', which under Buhari had limited press freedom. There was a virulent press campaign against the NLC's position. A compromise solution had to be worked out which would allow the NLC to call off the ultimatum and enter into negotiations with the government. Negotiations led to the formation of a tripartite committee, comprising of representatives of the state, labour and the business sector. The NLC later put forward a plan that recommended additional taxes on dividends, profit and rents; and demanded that the pay cuts should be converted into savings. Government's representatives on the committee were concerned about how to extend the cuts to other sectors. They held on to the terms of reference, which stated that there would be no trade-offs and that the pay cuts would not be rescinded.[35]

The failure of the NLC representatives to wrest concessions from the committee led to renewed calls among sections of the unions for industrial action. The NLC mounted a massive campaign to convert the pay cuts into savings. The announcement of the Structural Adjustment Programme (SAP) in 1986, which drastically devalued the naira and withdrew 80 per cent of subsidies from petroleum products, strengthened the NLC's case. In the 1987 budget the government announced the refund of the salary/wage cuts to lower categories of employees.

But the government was determined to keep wages down. An amendment to the National Minimum Wage Act in December 1986 exempted persons or companies employing fewer than 500 workers, and companies in agriculture, from paying the minimum wage. The NLC launched a mobilization campaign against the amendment and declared a state of emergency within the labour movement. Rallies were held in several big cities denouncing the amendment and preparing workers to resist the policy. The government was worried about the extent of the mobilization and the enthusiasm with which rank and file workers responded to the campaign. The amendment order was revoked in April 1987.[36]

As the liberalization measures further eroded workers' incomes, the NLC intensified its struggle for the ban on collective bargaining to be lifted. A wage freeze had been imposed since 1982. The NLC called on the government to allow wages to find their 'market' value, arguing that a policy of wage freeze was inconsistent with liberalization.[37] Manufacturers were also dissatisfied with the government's deflationary policies. A poll conducted by the Manufacturers Association of Nigeria revealed that 31 companies alone had approximately 70 million naira-worth of unsold stocks in their warehouses in the first half of 1987.[38] Manufacturers were, therefore, not opposed to an upward review of wages and a relaxation of the liquidity squeeze, but new conditions were imposed on collective bargaining. By insisting, for instance, that unions should not resort to the threat or use of strikes and other forms of industrial pressures the government attempted to blunt the effectiveness of collective bargaining and limit the upward adjustment of wages. How would recalcitrant employers be called to order? Negotiations turned out to be a muddle. The unrealistic conditions were ignored. Many unions had to embark on strikes before some agreements could be reached.

The politics of alliances

The reform measures have challenged some of the vested interests associated with the expansion of the post-colonial state and eroded general living standards. Those that stand to benefit from the reforms, such as the transnationals, exporters and sections of the agriculture lobby, have tried to build the necessary political alliances to defend the programme. Ruling-class groups that thrive on profits derived from bureaucratic influence and state protection are also organizing to moderate the full impact of the reforms. Subordinate groups are demanding alternative solutions, building popular fronts and contesting some aspects of the programme. The state is constructing its own political and social base to push through the hard-hitting economic measures.

The working-class movement has unavoidably been drawn into the dynamics of alliance politics. Workers provide leadership for a broad range of social groups that have been hit by the reforms. Workers are drawn into these alliances because of the experiences they share with other groups on general questions of falling living standards, the assault on the existence and autonomy of unions, the harassment of activists and the need to relate union alternatives with the specific demands of groups in other sectors of the economy. The struggles of academics and students for a just and democratic educational system, those of doctors for an improved health care system, and of journalists and lawyers for a free press and civil liberties have implications for workers' ability to challenge the reforms at the work place and at the level of the state. Workers play leading roles in the popular struggles because of their centrality in the production process; their long history of democratic struggles; and the national networks that unions have established since 1978.

Current attempts to construct alliances have focused primarily on urban employers of workers, journalists, academics, doctors, lawyers, traders and students, but the package of demands accommodates some of the interests of peasants and artisans. The urban popular opposition to the withdrawal of the petroleum subsidy drew attention to the problems farmers would face in transporting their wares to the market. Concern was also expressed, during the debate on the IMF loan, about the effects of devaluation on farm inputs.

The formation of alliances has been mainly an informal process. The only exception has been the alliance between academics and workers, resulting in the affiliation of the Academic Staff Union of Universities (ASUU) to the NLC in 1984. Groups are pulled together on a solidarity basis rather than on the basis of common structures. The strongest alliance to date is that between the

NLC, ASUU and NANS, the students' body. The NANS received the support of the ASUU and the NLC in 1986 during the general student uprising that followed the police brutalization of students in one of the universities. The three organizations boycotted the panel established by the government to investigate the crisis, on the grounds that the principal characters, the police chief who ordered the use of fire-arms and the vice-chancellor who precipitated the crisis, had not been suspended from office. The groups insisted that this was a minimum requirement for the panel to function without witnesses being compromised and crucial evidence suppressed. The composition of the panel was also challenged on democratic grounds. The NLC even planned a nation-wide demonstration to underline its concern for civil liberties and democratic rights. But the state descended heavily on the leadership, took over the secretariat of the NLC, disaffiliated ASUU from the NLC and suspended students' unionism on the campuses. Joint struggles continue to be waged to redress the abridged rights and protect the existence and autonomy of the unions.

The workers provide the backbone to popular struggles. Even when they had not initiated popular protests, workers' interventions had often changed their character. Students and the urban unemployed, for instance, acted as a catalyst to the nation-wide protests that greeted the withdrawal of oil subsidies in April 1988. But it was the workers' intervention that forced the government to enter into negotiations with the protesters. Workers' representatives negotiated on behalf of the groups that participated in the demonstrations. The April protests underscored the power of the workers to mobilize large sections of the population against the reform programme.

The case against the workers reconsidered

The legitimacy of workers' opposition
The crisis hits the workers hard. Unlike independent producers and traders, who constitute the bulk of Africa's population, workers have little direct access to commodities from which to bargain for survival. The anti-worker logic of structural adjustment is formidable. African economies are reconstructed on the ruins of the wage sector. Whatever 'privileges' workers may have had have been swept away. How legitimate is their self-defence? How futile? Must structural adjustment mean the destruction of the African working class?

In conclusion elements of an alternative case, that takes its point of departure from the aspirations of the workers and the leadership they may offer for more broadly based strategies of national reconstruction, is outlined. It is a critique of the repressive political programme that informs the crisis policies of most African governments. The capacity of the state to undertake social and economic reforms, we argue, depends on its ability to come to terms with the forces in the field. Attempts by governments to override, sidetrack, or ignore workers' opposition, as illustrated in the Nigerian case, is therefore self-defeating; the stalemate is merely cemented. Moreover, governments and their backers underestimate the capacity of workers' organizations to offer both leadership and backbone to wider alliances of popular social forces. It is because of their ability in this respect, not because they defend the interests of an entrenched and privileged minority, that workers are in a position to 'obstruct' structural adjustment.

Workers are no doubt 'self-seeking', but in defending their interests as wage earners they are obliged, as demonstrated by the Nigerian experience, to enter into wider alliances in order to fend off attempts by the state to isolate, control and repress them. It is true that the African working class is small and that its numbers have further dwindled as a result of the crisis. Politically, however, the workers are important as the popular stratum with the most advanced organizational experience. While the Nigerian working class is, for obvious reasons, bigger than working classes in other African countries, experiences elsewhere, for instance in Burkina Faso, suggest that working-class political capacity is not simply a matter of the size of the wage economy.

While in pursuit of their own interests, working-class organizations articulate wider popular grievances, urban and rural. This was clearly demonstrated by the popular support that rallied behind the Nigerian workers in their fight against the removal of the oil subsidy. Their defence of wage income forms part of complex household strategies, reaching deep into the peasant economy. Similarly, efforts to protect basic union rights bring workers, as we have seen, into wider coalitions of social forces, including the organizations of students, teachers, lawyers, journalists, and other professionals with a common interest in organizational survival and autonomy in the face of state impositions. It is as part of such broader alliances that workers offer an alternative to the politically repressive, transnational restructuring project that currently dominates the African scene.

Governments apply different tactics. Outright repression is only one. The Nigerian experience also points to efforts to co-opt and to marginalize. In many cases workers take 'unreasonable' positions simply because the state refuses to reason with them. 'Obstruction' is also a strategy of forcing governments and employers to the negotiating table. But the conflict of interest is profound and finding 'solutions' is not, therefore, simply a question of reasoning but of recognizing the strength of the opposite side and the constraints set by the balance of forces.

The failure of the state to recognize the limits of its own power is a major reason for the stalemate that characterizes so much 'crisis management' in Africa (and elsewhere!). Foreign intervention tends to reinforce this stalemate, by propping up and shielding regimes from popular political pressures. While succeeding temporarily in shifting the balance of forces in favour of ruling coalitions, such interventions simultaneously undermine the process of accommodation that is necessary to break the stalemate.

Is there a working-class alternative?

Workers are under no obligation to offer an 'alternative' structural adjustment programme. They are in their right to defend what they see as their interests, until they are convinced that what they are offered is the best they can obtain under difficult circumstances. They have as much interest as any other class in the speedy recovery and rapid development of the economy, but they are as concerned as all others that the road to such recovery should not go through the destruction of their own means of existence. It is the obligation of the state and its transnational partners to convince workers that their interests have been fully considered, otherwise it is the state, not the workers, which is responsible for any stalemate arising from the workers wielding whatever powers they can muster in self-defence. The state, not the workers, has the resources to explore the alternatives; it has the ministries, the central banks, the statistics, the professionals, the foreign advisers, the money, the arms. For workers to dig their heels in is neither selfish nor irresponsible. They are asserting their bargaining power, in the face of the state's overwhelming intellectual and repressive resources. 'Obstruction' signals two things: 'We are not convinced' and 'We are not defeated'.

Attempts to challenge the legitimacy of popular resistance to structural adjustment, with reference to the 'failure to offer an alternative', must be exposed for what they are: attempts to enforce submission by way of psychological warfare. This goes also for the accusation of selfishness and irresponsibility. This being said, however, the Nigerian experience suggests that workers have not been insensitive to the need to offer alternatives to government crisis policies, not the least as part of an attempt to create alliances.

In 1985, the NLC prepared an alternative crisis programme, 'Towards National Recovery'. This is an expansionist programme. Employment should be protected and expanded in order to avoid wasting human resources, and to stimulate demand and overall growth. Finance should come from cutting costs of inflated contracts, reducing defence spending and corruption, taxing the rich, and preventing tax evasion. Industrial investment should be accelerated, especially in the capital goods sector. Foreign exchange resources should be allocated in such a way as to ensure that existing industrial capacity is efficiently utilized. Raw materials and other industrial inputs should be given priority over luxury consumption. Foreign investors would have to wait to remit profits until the industrial recovery was well on its way. Retrenched workers should be reabsorbed and the wage freeze lifted. A ceiling of 20 per cent of export earnings should be placed on foreign debt payments. The state, rather than privatizing, should take a lead in the expansion of productive activity. In agriculture, big state development schemes should be abandoned in favour of a focus on small, peasant farmers and co-operatives.

Was this a realistic alternative to official structural adjustment? Realism in this context is of course as much a question of politics as of economics. We may argue that the NLC at this point was in no position to challenge politically the alliance of class forces, local and transnational, that saw as its primary task to 're-establish the international credit worthiness of Nigeria',[39] and to whom most of the NLC positions were objectionable. The economic realism of some of the proposals may also be questioned. In terms of its long-term strategic orientation, however, the NLC programme could not be dismissed lightly, either on political or economic grounds, representing views with strong support not only from labour leaders, but also from a wide range of intellectuals, professionals, and technocrats, while simultaneously expressing the aspirations of wage earners, unemployed, school-leavers, and, very likely, a good number of their peasant parents and relatives as well.

We are not, at this point, entering into any substantive discussion of such alternative, working class-based crisis programmes in Africa, but merely stressing the fact that they exist, that they represent significant social forces, and that, therefore, they need to be taken seriously.

Who speaks for whom?

But what about labour leaders exploiting, deceiving and misrepresenting workers? What about workers exploiting peasants? What about 'labour aristocracies' and 'urban bias'? Has not a case been made for rejecting such alternatives as selfish and irresponsible? Are not the allies of the workers mentioned above the very urbanites and élites that benefit from the continued distortions of African economies, at the expense of the poor peasants?

Let us first affirm that such distortions and contradictions exist. Many labour leaders are privileged and élitist and hold offices with a dubious democratic mandate. There are also real conflicts of interest between peasants and workers over prices and over the allocation of public resources. Workers cannot in this respect be expected to speak for peasants and vice versa.

Peasants in Africa have suffered a raw deal; they are oppressed and their interests are neglected. But so are the workers'; the overwhelming numbers of Africa's workers eke out a miserable existence in unhealthy and impoverished urban environments. Most are unable to survive on the basis of their wages, many are unemployed and insecure. Only few have been able to enjoy a sustained increase in real earnings; only few succeed in climbing into the middle classes or into business; as, also, do some peasants.

Notions of workers exploiting peasants and urban areas exploiting rural areas fundamentally obscure the differences in social existence within the two poles. They misrepresent the modes of exploitation and accumulation that have characterized the post-colonial economies. Workers and peasants are no fools; they can easily identify the beneficiaries of post-colonial development. The monuments of wealth and property belonging to the rich and their foreign friends are there for all to see.

Some labour leaders may have profited excessively from their union jobs. But little can be gauged from their personal affluence when seeking to assess their ability to voice the case of the workers. As workers' leaders they are subject to contradictory forces, including co-optation by state and management. But the pressures also come from below, and in the African situation of today they are stronger than ever. In Nigeria, labour leaders operate in a competitive context that widens the scope for such popular pressures.

The African working class may not conform to ideal-type notions of a 'proper', industrial working class. Its mode of integration into a wider petty commodity economy, however, rather than detracting from, may enhance its ability to voice wider, popular grievances and interests. A long history of trade union struggles as well as involvement in wider popular and national struggles have simultaneously generated collective experience and identity at the level of class organization.

Nigerian labour leaders have offered a working-class programme for national recovery. Have they a right to speak for the nation? Who has? The politicians who ruined it? The generals who usurped power? When the generals/presidents of today reject the rights of labour leaders to speak for the 'peaceful rural majority' we are reminded of the pronouncements of the colonial governor-generals of yesterday. In the 1920s, Governor Clifford ridiculed the educated nationalist 'gentlemen' that claimed to represent Nigerian interests: Who were they, he said, to dare to speak on behalf of the mass of the Nigerian peasant farmers? But who was he? Who did he represent?

As we think is evidenced in the Nigerian case, African workers may well have a stronger case than most other actors on the political scene to claim to represent broad popular interests.

Workers, state and democracy

Global and local ruling classes have plunged post-colonial Africa into a national crisis of an unprecedented scale. Embryonic transnational state institutions dabble in experiments of 'crisis management' and 'liberalization' with little knowledge of how they will work out in poorly understood economic, social, and political environments. Some interventions may be economically sound and reasonable; others play havoc with meagre resources and cause further destabilization, as in the case of the current disastrous auctioning of foreign exchange in Nigeria. It should come as no surprise that African people have little confidence in such crisis management or in the class agents that promote it.

Workers' opposition to structural adjustment deserves to be taken seriously. To the extent that African states do that they choose to respond with repression. This has become the political programme of 'liberal' structural adjustment.[40] We have argued that this is counter-productive even within the narrow parameters of the economic programme as it stands. The forces in the field have to be recognized. Even if they are too weak to enforce their own programme, they may be strong enough to obstruct that of the state.

We conclude by arguing for an alternative political programme that rejects state repression and manipulation. The case may first be argued in terms of the process of state formation. It is often suggested that the state in Africa is repressive because it is too 'weak' to handle opposition more gently. Peter Lloyd[41] warns that governments are fragile and 'strikes and mob violence may well lead directly to their collapse – a consequence perhaps unintended by the poor'. The implied warning is: Don't rock the boat or you are yourselves to blame. The repression or co-optation of trade unions have been explained with reference to the fragility of the state. The state can hardly afford opposition from such quarter, especially as the unions have proved themselves to be powerful political vehicles in the past.[42]

Let us turn this argument upside-down. Precisely because of its weakness the state should develop more advanced forms for relating to alternative sources of power in society. In our own understanding of historical experiences elsewhere, popular forces' pressures on the state from below are critical to the process of state formation, including the development of the capacity to manage social contradictions. The state is formed and disciplined from below.[43]

The challenge of structural adjustment at the present time is not simply to try out more new bright formulae for foreign exchange allocation, once the first set of experiments has failed. There is the need to address, politically, the social contradictions that have been aggravated by the economic crisis and exacerbated by politically repressive crisis management. Simply promoting one policy or the other will lead nowhere if the political context is not simultaneously addressed. State crisis management confronts a formidable credibility gap. If that gap is to be bridged at all, governments must learn to listen and argue more and to repress less.

What about co-optation? Is it not an 'alternative' to repression as a strategy for political crisis management? It is; African governments have tried it. The Nigerian government, as we have shown, has turned from one to the other, trying out various blends. On the whole, it seems, at least for the time being, that co-optation has failed. But contradictions have not been resolved; the stalemate is as precarious and potentially explosive as ever.

The state has failed to effectively co-opt Nigerian labour leaders. But even had it been successful, such a strategy is likely to have been counter-productive. Co-optation weakens the capacity of the labour leaders to offer leadership. It drains it of whatever popular credibility it can claim and renders it useless for the purpose of any genuine political crisis management. From this perspective, it could be argued that the preservation of union autonomy may even be in the interest of the state. There are signs that at least some members of the Nigerian ruling class have come to appreciate this, even if the repressive reflexes still dominate.

Is there a democratic option to the prevailing repressive political programme of structural adjustment? In Nigeria, the present military rulers claim that they are busy steering the ship of state towards civilian rule and democracy in 1992. They claim that structural adjustment and the return to civilian rule are two faces of the same transition programme. Both faces have ugly repressive and manipulative traits. Nigerian workers have unsuccessfully sought to impress themselves on that process of political transition by, for instance, defending their right to form a workers' party, in the face of the state's commitment to impose a two-party system of its own liking.

Whatever hopes and doubts may be pinned on 1992, the democratic challenge is not of the future; it is here and now. As long as labour leaders are whisked off into detention, unions proscribed, and demonstrating workers brutalized, in the name of structural adjustment, and with the backing of a formidable array of repressive labour laws, the democratic agenda of the workers is clear.[44] Workers are fighting for the rights to have their own organizations, to express their views, and to be protected against state brutalization. Workers' opposition to the crisis policies of the African states and their foreign backers is part of the struggle for such democratic rights.

It is important to see this direct link between workers' economic and political demands. We began by asking why a minor increase in the price of petrol in Nigeria in April 1988 resulted in popular riots and a nation-wide strike movement. Was it not proof enough of irresponsible workers' opposition? We have explained why the petrol price issue had become a symbol of resistance, going beyond the few kobo that were added to the price at that particular time. The immediate issue at stake was the petrol price, but to understand the full meaning of the protest we need to recall the proscription of the NLC leadership that preceded it. Workers were asserting the democratic aspirations of the people.

Notes and References

1. *Analyst* 3:1, 1988; *Newswatch* 2 May 1988; *West Africa*, 25 April and 2 May 1988.

2. *West Africa*, 28 December 1987.

3. Ibid.

4. *West Africa*, 11 January 1988.

5. Ibid., 7 March and 25 April 1988.

6. Ibid., 7 March 1988; *Newswatch* 14 March 1988; NLC 1988.

7. *West Africa*, 2 May 1988.

8. Ejiofoh, 1988.

9. The 'economic' case against the African workers is here primarily constructed from World Bank documents and reports, including the 'Berg Report' (World Bank 1981) and World Bank 1983a, 1984, and 1986. Many (but not all) of the points can be deduced from the section on 'adjustment programs' in the 1986 report.

10. World Bank 1986, p. 21.

11. The political dimensions of the 'urban bias' case are forcefully argued in Bates 1981. The World Bank documents are less explicit in this respect, although Bates' work is seen as providing support for the World Bank position (cf. Bienefeld 1986). The political case against the workers as outlined here, however, draws primarily on the responses of Nigerian governments to workers' demands.

12. For references on the controversies over structural adjustment policies and their theoretical and factual basis, see Cornia, Jolly and Stewart 1988, Havnevik 1987, Lawrence 1986, IDS Bulletin 1983. Mkandawire 1989 and Godfrey 1986 address specifically the labour and employment issues.

13. Olson, 1982.

14. Ubeka, 1983, pp. 192–3.

15. Hashim, 1987; Damachi, Seibel and Trachtman, 1979.

16. Waterman, 1975 and 1983.

17. See Lloyd, 1982.

18. World Bank, 1983a.

19. NEC, 1983.

20. CBN, 1983.

21. World Bank, 1983a, p. 4.

22. NLC, 1987.
23. MAN, 1987.
24. Otobo, 1986.
25. Cohen, 1974.
26. Andrae and Beckman, 1991; Bangura, 1987c.
27. Bangura, 1987a.
28. Aremu, 1987.
29. Andrae and Beckman, 1991.
30. Bangura, 1987b.
31. Bangura, 1987a.
32. Bangura, 1989a.
33. Bangura, 1987b.
34. Bangura, 1987a.
35. Interview with A. Oshiomhole, 7 February 1986.
36. Bangura, 1989a.
37. NLC, 1987.
38. MAN, 1987.
39. Buhari, 1984.
40. Ibrahim, 1986; Mustapha, 1988.
41. Lloyd, 1982, p. 22.
42. Hashim, 1987, p. 2.
43. Beckman, 1988a, 1988b.
44. Bangura, 1989b.

Bibliography

Andrae, G. and B. Beckman, (1991) 'Workers, unions, and the crisis of the Nigerian textile industry.' In I. Brandell, *Practice and Strategy: Workers in Contemporary Third World Industrialisation* (forthcoming) Macmillan.

Aremu, I. (1987) 'Glaxo Workers: A Report.' Lagos, NLC.

Bangura, Y. (1987a) 'Crisis management and union struggles in Niger state.' Zaria, Department of Political Science. Mimeo.

—— (1987b) 'The recession and workers struggles in the vehicle assembly plants: Steyr-Nigeria.' *Review of African Political Economy*, 39.

—— (1987c) 'Industrial crisis and the struggle for national democracy: Lessons from Kaduna Textile Ltd. and the workers demonstration of January 1984.' Zaria, mimeo.

—— (1989a) 'Crisis and adjustment: The experience of Nigerian workers.' In B. Onimode (ed.), *The IMF, the World Bank and the African Debt*. London, Zed Books.

—— (1989b) 'Authoritarianism and democracy in Africa: A theoretical discourse'. Uppsala, AKUT. Seminar paper.

Bates, R. (1981) *Markets and States in Tropical Africa. The Political Basis of Agricultural Policies*. Berkeley, UCP.

Beckman, B. (1988a), 'The post-colonial state: Crisis and reconstruction'. *IDS Bulletin* Vol. 19, No. 4.

—— (1988b) 'When does democracy make sense?' Uppsala, AKUT. Seminar paper.

Bienefeld, M. (1986) 'Analysing the politics of African state policy. Some thoughts on Robert Bates' work'. *IDS Bulletin*, Vol. 17, No. 1.

Buhari, M. (1984) Statement on the assumption of power by the military government of General M. Buhari, Lagos, January.

CBN (1983), *Annual Report and Statement of Account*. Lagos, Central Bank of Nigeria.

Cohen, R. (1974), *Labour and Politics in Nigeria, 1945–1974*. London, Heinemann.

Cornia, G. A., R. Jolly, F. Stewart, (1988) *Adjustment with a Human Face*. Oxford, UNICEF.

Damachi, U., H. D. Seibel, L. Trachtman (eds) (1979) *Industrial Relations in Africa*. London, Macmillan.

Ejiofoh, S. O. Z. (1988) 'Communique issued on behalf of 42 industrial unions by 14-man negotiating team on the impending negotiations with the government on the issue of increases in the prices of petroleum and petroleum products and general high cost of living etc., etc.' Signed by S. O. Z. Ejiofoh, G. O. Ulucha, E. D. Fidelis, M. *I*. Kazeem, F. E. Nwachukwu, A. Ogbonna, 10 June.

Godfrey, M. (1986) *Global Unemployment. The New Challenge to Economic Theory*. Brighton, Wheatsheaf.

Hashim, Y. (1987) State Intervention in Trade Unions. A Nigerian Case Study. The Hague, Institute of Social Studies, MA dissertation.

Havnevik, K. J. (ed.) (1987) *The IMF and the World Bank in Africa. Conditionality, Impact and Alternatives*. Uppsala, Scandinavian Institute of African Studies.

Ibrahim, J. (1986) 'The political debate and the struggle for democracy in Nigeria'. *Review of African Political Economy* No. 37.

IDS Bulletin (1983) 'Accelerated development in sub-Saharan Africa', Vol. 14. No. 1.

Lawrence, P. (ed.) (1986) *World Recession and the Food Crisis in Africa*. London, Currey/ROAPE.

Lloyd, P. (1982) *A Third World Proletariat?* London, Allen & Unwin.

MAN (1987) 'Half Yearly Economic Review. January – June'. Lagos, Manufacturers Association of Nigeria.

Mkandawire, T. (1989) 'Labour and policy making in Africa'. Dakar, CODESRIA (Draft).

Mustapha, A. R. (1988) 'Ever decreasing circles: Democratic rights in Nigeria 1978–1988'. Oxford, St Peter's College.

NEC (1983) 'The State of the Nigerian Economy.' Lagos, National Economic Council.

NLC (1985) Towards National Recovery: Nigeria Labour Congress' Alternatives. Lagos.

———— (1987) 'A case for wage adjustment for workers: A memo presented to the federal military government.' 29 July, Lagos.

———— (1988) 'Resolutions of 3rd Congress of the Nigerian Labour Congress Holding at Saidi Centre in Benin, 24–26 February 1988'.

Olson, M. (1982) *The Rise and Decline of Nations. Economic Growth, Stagflation, and Social Rigidities*. New Haven, Yale University Press.

Otobo, D. (1986) *Foreign Interests & Nigerian Trade Unions*. Oxford, Malthouse.

Sandbrook, R. and R. Cohen (eds) (1975) *The Development of An African Working Class*. London, Longman.

Ubeku, A. K. (1983) *Industrial Relations in Developing Countries: The Case of Nigeria*. London, Macmillan.

Waterman, P. (1975) 'The labour aristocracy in Africa. Introduction to a debate.' *Development and Change*, Vol 6, No. 3.

———— (1983), *Aristocrats and Plebians in African Trade Unions? Lagos Port and Dock Worker Organization and Struggle*. The Hague, Author.

World Bank (1981) *Accelerated Development in Sub-Saharan Africa: An Agenda for Action*. Washington.

———— (1983a) 'Nigeria: Macro-Economic Policies for Structural Change.' Report 4506, UNI, 15 August, Washington.

———— (1983b) *Sub-Saharan Africa: Progress Report on Development Prospects and Programs*. Washington.

———— (1984) *Toward Sustained Development in Sub-Saharan Africa. A Joint Program of Action*. Washington.

———— (1986) *Financing Adjustment with Growth in Sub-Saharan Africa, 1986–90*. Washington.

Newspapers and journals
Analyst. Monthly news magazine, Jos, Nigeria.
Newswatch. Weekly news magazine, Lagos, Nigeria.
West Africa. Weekly news magazine, London.

9. Brazil: Economic Crisis, Organized Labour and the Transition to Democracy

Edward J. Amadeo and José Márcio Camargo

Introduction

Brazilian history has been marked by an alternation between democratic and authoritarian political regimes. In the 1950s, and until 1964, democratic and populist governments dominated the political scene. Then came the *coup d'état*, installing an authoritarian military regime which remained in power until 1984. Even under the military, however, marked changes in the political climate made themselves felt. By 1974 a gradual movement of political openness had started, and in 1978–79 strong strike activity gave rise to a vigorous labour movement. Today, the leaders of the two main union confederations (CUT and CGT) are important social actors in the gradual transition to democracy currently taking place in Brazil.

The role of organized labour at the national level had been growing prior to 1964, but due to the anti-labour bias of the military regime, labour's role became insignificant for the next 15 years. During this period, attempts were made to weaken the labour movement: unions were repressed, and labour union leaders arrested. Many different arguments were used to justify the government's anti-labour attitude, from the technocratic argument that unions were responsible for the absence of flexibility in the labour market, to the ideological contention that the labour movement was dominated by communists, and should be seen as a threat to the national security and, ironically, to democracy.

In the 1980s, the labour movement was re-emerging after this period of repression, and beginning to recover from the destruction of union structure and organization, and the restriction of the role of organized labour in society and politics. Democratization plays a crucial role in this process, as unions and workers' parties re-establish their position at different levels of the social and political spheres. These changes in capital–labour relations will, in turn, affect the future of Brazilian macro-economic performance.

The transition to democracy is taking place during a period of economic crisis whose effects are well documented: between 1981 and 1984 there was a significant contraction in the rates of growth of output, employment, and real wages; an increase in the share of the informal segment in the labour market; and a fiscal crisis, which translated into a reduction in the state's capacity to foster growth and provide social goods. The attempt to create commercial surpluses through devaluations of the domestic currency and the resistance of the unions to a reduction in their share of wages have been important causes of the inflationary process in Brazil.

The importance of labour's actions to the success of any economic strategy must not be underestimated. In the last three years, repeated attempts to reduce the rate of inflation through such 'heterodox' strategies as price and wage freezes have failed. In the first two plans (1986 and 1987) the labour union confederations did not participate. But recently, for the first time in 25 years, the government seems to be considering labour confederations' participation in the discussions over the formulation of economic policies. The results have, however, been poor, due to the government's lack of credibility and the absence of a tradition of negotiations between the political and economic élites and the other groups in Brazilian society; in 1988 an attempt to establish a 'social pact' between workers, capitalists, and the government failed, and in January 1989 the unions were called upon to negotiate a new wage policy, with dismal results.

This chapter examines three aspects of the current process of transition to democracy and the current economic and social crisis in Brazil. In the following pages an overview of the Brazilian economic performance since the first oil shock is first presented, followed by a discussion of the deterioration of income distribution in the last two decades which characterizes the Brazilian 'exclusive' model. The re-emergence of the labour movement in the 1980s is then examined, the fiscal crisis and the reduction in the state's capacity to save and invest follow, and finally the conclusions are presented.

External constraint, distributive conflict and adjustment

Knowledge of the relation between external constraints and internal distributive conflict is quite important to an understanding of the performance of the Brazilian economy since 1975. During the period from 1966 to 1973, favourable international conditions, combined with the authoritarian regime's suppression of the distributive conflict, led to rapid expansion of the Brazilian economy. After 1974 conditions changed drastically with the oil price shocks of 1973 and 1979, the interest rate shock, and the transition to democracy, which established the conditions for the re-emergence of labour mobilization, and hence of the distributive conflict.

The so-called 'Brazilian miracle' depended not only upon policy designed to stimulate export production, but also upon an increased ability to import, access to the international financial markets, and a continuing strong economic performance of the OECD countries, which provided the markets for Brazil's products. The military regime's wage policies also contributed to the competitiveness of Brazil's products: the repression of labour unions reduced their power to affect nominal wage adjustment, and the government was able to impose a compulsory wage restraint, which reduced the product wage measured in dollars.

With the first oil price shock, the external situation changed dramatically. Between 1973 and 1974 the expenditure on oil imports increased by almost 300 per cent, increasing from 12 to 23 per cent of total imports. In 1974 the commercial deficit was US$4,673 million; in that year Brazil had to borrow US$6,254 million to meet balance of payments requirements.

Countries faced with this supply shock had two alternatives. The 'hard option' strategy, that many countries followed, was to reduce internal aggregate demand and the product wage measured in dollars in an effort to stimulate exports. This strategy necessarily implied, at least in the short run, the reduction of investment – which had deleterious structural effects – and an increase in the rates of unemployment and idle capacity – with obvious social costs.

The second alternative, and the one followed by Brazil, was to develop an investment programme directed towards the intermediate and capital goods sectors. The idea behind this strategy was to promote the final phase of the process of import substitution, and reduce the dependence on imports.[1] These investments needed to be financed from funds borrowed abroad.

To a certain extent, the Brazilian alternative was the result of the domestic political situation. In 1974, the official party lost the elections, and consequently the legitimacy of the military government was damaged. The effort to maintain the path of high growth rates was an attempt to regain credibility and preserve the military's control over the democratization process. The social costs associated with the 'hard option' strategy would have made the process of re-democratization, which began under the Geisel administration in 1974, much harder.

Hence 1974 can be seen as the starting point of two simultaneous processes, which together would constitute the central elements of the crisis of the 1980s, namely the growth of the external debt and the political opening, which gave rise to the labour movements of 1978–79. The attempt to adjust the Brazilian economy to the debt crisis through a shift in the functional distribution of income in favour of profits in the tradeable sectors, in the context of increasingly centralized and active labour unions and resistance of workers to reductions in their wages, led to recurrent periods of acceleration of inflation.

By 1979, after the second oil price shock and the increase in Brazil's debt – due to the growth strategy that it followed – from US$7,546 million in 1973 to US$38,247 million, the hard option strategy seemed inevitable. Attempts were made to stabilize the economy: the domestic currency was devalued by 30 per cent, and in 1981 the government opted for a contractionary monetary and fiscal policy, the acceleration of devaluation, the introduction of incentives to stimulate exports, and quantitative restrictions on imports. The GDP fell 3.1 per cent in 1981, but there was a substantial improvement in the balance of payments position.

At the same time, the government was not able to achieve its desired reduction in the cost of labour. As a response to the strike movement of 1978–79 wages were adjusted more rapidly to price changes, and the rate of inflation accelerated in 1980–81. In 1982, when the Mexican moratorium stopped the flow of new funds to the country, the cost of labour measured in dollars rose 22 per cent, exports fell 13 per cent, while, as a result of the domestic recession, imports fell 12 per cent.

The year 1983 was marked by a new wave of recession and a 30 per cent devaluation of the *cruzeiro* in relation to the dollar. This time wages could not keep up with the inflation rate: the high level of unemployment had checked the growth of the union movement. The cost of labour fell considerably until mid-1984.[2] The growth of exports, together with the 21 per cent reduction in imports resulting from recession and devaluation, led to a commercial surplus of US$6,500 million.

In 1984, with the recovery of the US economy, exports rose 23 per cent, imports fell ten per cent, the commercial surplus exceeded US$13,000 million, and the GDP increased by 5.7 per cent. In 1985 the GDP grew by 8.4 per cent and imports fell by 5.5 per cent.

Hence the growth-cum-debt strategy and the deepening of the import substitution process resulted in a significant reduction of the import coefficient and an increase in the rate of growth of GDP consistent with a commercial balance. The import coefficient fell from 11.96 in 1974 to 7.14 in 1982, and 4.63 in 1987.

But the accumulation pattern adopted during the military regime, and the need to adjust to the external debt problem, especially after 1979, gave rise to three important features of the current economic and social crisis. First was the extremely unequal distribution of income, which characterizes the Brazilian 'excludent' pattern of accumulation. Second was the high degree of distributive conflict and labour dissatisfaction, which gave rise to a wave of labour mobilization during the transition to democracy. Third was the fiscal crisis, which precluded the state from fostering growth and recovering the high rates of public and private investment of the 1970s. In the following pages these issues are discussed in turn.

The 'exclusive' model

Here, it will be argued that between 1964 and 1986 the Brazilian model was 'exclusive', in the sense that it excluded workers – in both the formal and informal segments of the economy – from the benefits of the process of accumulation. It will be suggested that in the face of changes currently taking place in capital–labour relations in Brazil – in particular the increasing political participation of labour – the system may change in the next decade, and become more inclusive, at least in terms of the urban workers of the formal sector. In a sense, therefore, the suggestion is that the Brazilian model may be in a transition to a model in which internal markets will become more important in the economy, and the growth of wages will become an important element in the determination of the level of aggregate demand.

The growth of labour militancy and union activism in the second half of the 1970s resulted in increasing real wages and growth in labour's share of output, along with declining income inequality. The crisis of the 1980s, however, with accelerating rates of inflation and increasing unemployment has generated a stalemate in the distributive conflict. Although the permanent increase in the social and political importance of the labour movement suggests that labour may become an important social actor in the political arena in the next decade, real wages, as well as the share of wages in output, declined during most of the 1980s. Many doubts, therefore, still persist about the future role of labour in Brazil.

As already noted, the military regime was essentially anti-labour. The political participation of labour as a group was minimal, and workers did not share the economic gains of the period. It is worth recalling that between 1967 and 1974 the Brazilian economy grew at an average rate of 11 per cent, and in the following period (1975–81) increased by seven per cent, while the figures on the distribution of income to the poorest worsened considerably. The Gini coefficient went from 0.499 in 1960 to 0.562 in 1970 and 0.581 in 1980. In the 1960s the Gini coefficient rose 12.63 per cent, and the share in the country's income of all groups, except the top ten per cent, fell. The share of the latter group increased by 20.5 per cent. The degree of concentration of income reached its highest point in 1972, when the Gini coefficient was 0.622.

Between 1966 and 1985 the level of output in the industrial sector and the productivity of labour grew continuously, the former 260 per cent and the latter 140 per cent over this period. The share of wages in the value of output in the industrial sector remained approximately constant between 1966 and 1975, and then grew by 12 per cent between 1976 and 1979. The debt crisis and the acceleration of inflation resulted in a 30 per cent decline of this share between 1980 and 1985, with the result that in 1983 approximately 30 per cent of urban workers earned less than one minimum wage, while the minimum wage itself had fallen by approximately 15 per cent between 1966 and 1985. Conditions were somewhat better in the formal than in the informal sector, which comprised about 35 per cent of the labour force and where, it has been estimated, close to 75 per cent of the workers earned less than one minimum wage.

In sum, the Brazilian model in the period 1964 to 1974 was essentially exclusive in the sense that it did not improve the standard of life of the working class as a whole. After a period of increase in the share of wages after 1974, the debt crisis, inflation and unemployment resulted in reduction in real wages. During this period, however, the ability of workers to fight against real wage reduction generated a very unstable economic situation and high rates of inflation (around 1,000 per cent a year in 1988).

Labour mobilization in the democratic transition

After 1974 the reduction of repression, together with the dissatisfaction of workers with their economic and working conditions, led to an explosion of union activism, culminating in 1978 in the first great strike since 1967, in São

Paulo. This was the first important aspect of the process of acceleration of inflation in the 1980s. The second was the government's response to the debt crisis, that is, the attempt to change relative prices, and in particular, reduce the cost of labour measured in dollars. The conflict between the objectives of the government and those of the unions seems to be at the root of the current economic crisis.

The response of the unions to the government's attempt to reduce labour costs was first to demand a change in the wage adjustment formula in order to make it depend only on past inflation, rather than the systematically underestimated future inflation rate. Second, as inflation increased, workers increasingly demanded the shortening of the wage adjustment period. Both objectives were successful. In November 1979 the adjustment period was reduced from one year to six months, as inflation accelerated in the first half of 1979 to an annualized rate of 100 per cent, and the future rate of inflation was abandoned as a parameter for wage adjustments.

Not until 1983, when unemployment due to recession had checked the rise of workers' mobilization, did a devaluation of the *cruzeiro* lead to a reduction in real wages. By June 1984 the economy, along with levels of employment, had begun to recover, and the average real income of wage-earners in the industrial sector started growing steadily. Wages in the formal sector as a whole grew by 4.5 per cent in 1984 and by 14.8 per cent in 1985. Due to labour mobilization, the government's policy of wage restraint had become ineffective in the determination of real wages in Brazil.

In February 1986 the government opted for a price freeze and a monetary reform – the 'Cruzado Plan'.[3] The plan can be seen as a non-negotiated incomes policy, secretly designed, which counted upon a great deal of social acquiescence. The latter was bought with the promise of the end of inflation, and an eight per cent increase in wages, which reduced workers' dissatisfaction, the creation of unemployment insurance for the first time in Brazil, liberal aggregate demand policy, and a price freeze for an indefinite time period. The plan failed to stop inflation, and in 1987 another plan with the same characteristics was adopted and again failed. On the other hand, despite the impetus of the labour movement, the average real wage has increased very little since 1986.

What is new in terms of the role of labour *qua* social actor in Brazil is the active participation of union leaders in discussions over the design of economic policies. The so-called 'social pact', in which union leaders, employers and the government negotiate not only wage policy but also other aspects of economic policy, has gradually become a practice. So far, the results have been quite frustrating, but the fact that there are signs of negotiations going on implies that an important change in the institutional setting is taking place.

In what follows, the recent changes in union organizational structure and capital–labour relations in Brazil will be explored in detail, as well as the rise of labour mobilization in the decade of the 1980s.

The transition to democracy in Brazil was marked by an increase in popular mobilization. This seems to be a result of many years of repression and of an economic model based on the economic and political exclusion of labour. Hirschman, commenting on the political opening process of Argentina and Brazil, refers to the social tensions that generally show up during the transition:

> When a civilian, democratic government first comes into power after a long period of repressive military rule, it is normal for various, newly active groups of the reborn civil society – particularly the long-repressed trade unions – to stake substantial claims for higher incomes . . . New inflationary and balance-of-payments pressures are of course likely to result from the granting of such demands . . . [I]nflation can nevertheless be a useful mechanism in this situation: it permits newly emerging or reemerging social groups to flex their muscles, with inflation acting as a providential safety value for accumulated social pressures.[4]

The percentage of the active labour force that is unionized in Brazil has never been very high – it was estimated to have been around 22 per cent in the period before 1978. After 1978, however, this percentage grew considerably: by 32 per cent among urban workers, and 50 per cent among rural workers. The degree of dissatisfaction of workers and the degree of distributive conflict can be measured by the strike activity between 1978 and 1986. Table 9.1 shows that since 1978 the number of strikes grew continuously, with the exception of 1980 and 1982. It grew significantly in 1979, 1983, and 1986. It is also clear that the most important groups are the industrial workers and the middle class wage earners. In the first group, the workers of the most organized segment – that of the metallurgy industry – were responsible for 34.8 per cent of the strikes. Also, 74 per cent of the strikes between 1978 and 1986 took place in the southeast of Brazil, that is, where most of the organized unions are based.

Table 9.1
Brazil: Strikes 1978–86
(Percentage given in brackets)

	1978	1979	1980	1981	1982	1983	1984	1985	1986
Industrial workers	84	77	43	41	73	189	317	246	534
	(72)	(31)	(29)	(27)	(50)	(54)	(64)	(39)	(53)
Middle-class workers	8	55	43	48	31	85	84	211	237
	(7)	(22)	(29)	(32)	(21)	(24)	(17)	(34)	(23)
Housing industry	8	20	19	7	4	10	18	23	45
	(7)	(8)	(13)	(5)	(3)	(4)	(4)	(5)	(5)
Others	18	94	39	54	36	63	73	139	188
	(14)	(39)	(29)	(36)	(26)	(18)	(15)	(22)	(19)
Total	118	246	144	150	144	347	492	619	1004
	(100)	(100)	(100)	(100)	(100)	(100)	(100)	(100)	(100)

Source: NEPP/Unicamp reproduced from Tavares de Almeida (1988)

As noted by Tavares de Almeida,[5] who reports these figures, the 'workers, and their unions, responded with more strikes to the frequent demand for moderation and a social pact on the part of the [new civilian government] . . . and increased the number of strikes during the Cruzado Plan'.

In the decade of the 1980s the organization of union structure changed dramatically, and both the activity and strength of the labour movement have increased considerably. In a sense, the 'new unionism' fills the gap opened by the inefficacy of the corporatist labour laws introduced in 1943 during the Vargas dictatorship, and the wage policies of the military governments. These laws are incompatible with a democratic regime with an independent and strong labour movement. In recent years, the unions have forced employers to negotiate not only wages but also working conditions; union leaders have influenced the preparation of the new Constitution, and recently have been able to affect decisions over wage policy and, to a certain extent, over macro-economic policy in general.

The wave of labour mobilization led to the formation of a centralized union movement, which has its pivotal institutions in a national confederation (the Central Unica dos Trabalhadores, CUT) and a political party (the Partido dos Trabalhadores, PT). In terms of Brazilian labour history, these two institutions are unique for their degree of centralization of representation of organized labour interests, their complete independence from the state, and the tight relationship they attempt to establish between the union movement and parliamentary activity. Until 1988, when the new Constitution was promulgated, CUT was illegal but was nevertheless recognized by the government. Today it represents a significant proportion of workers at the national level, including workers from the public sector, despite the fact that labour laws discourage the centralization of the labour movement.

The growth of the PT as a representative workers' party and its importance in parliamentary debates (especially during the preparation of the new Constitution) has put the discussion over wage policy and labour rights at centre stage. The attitude of the population towards the labour movement and union leaders, especially in the urban centres, has changed favourably in the last decade as a consequence of the popularity of the Workers' Party.

It is not clear why the Brazilian labour movement grew in this direction. Many hypotheses have been suggested, most of them related to the very poor working conditions of the mid-1970s, coupled with a very high rate of growth. As working conditions deteriorated during the 'miracle' period, workers felt that their work was not being adequately compensated. The feeling of injustice was very high. The prevailing doctrine at the time was to 'first increase the pie to distribute it later'. As the economic crisis made it impossible to distribute the pie, workers felt that they had been deceived. On the other hand, as the strike movement increased at the end of the 1970s, and the government used authoritarian labour laws to repress the movement, labour leaders discovered that to increase their power in collective bargaining an important change in the law was necessary. Thus came the decision to enter into political party activities.

The centralization of the labour movement and the relation between the unions and parliamentary activities are important features of labour organization in European countries and most especially in neo-corporatist societies (such as in Sweden and Austria). These features differ completely from those that characterized the labour movement in Brazil before 1978. As a consequence of the centralization of the movement, this new structure favours the capacity of unions to mobilize workers. The connection with the parliament, on the other hand, implies that the gains obtained by the major unions are frequently put to the Congress by the workers' representatives, and may be extended to the less powerful unions if they are eventually voted into national law. In short, it seems unquestionable that a transformation is taking place in capital–labour relations in Brazil as a result of the growth of the CUT and the PT.

External debt and fiscal crisis

The third element of the current economic crisis refers to the relation between the external debt problem, the fiscal crisis, and the significant reduction in the rate of investment, which has had deleterious short-run effects on levels of employment and capacity utilization, and long-run effects on the formation of fixed capital.

Since the late 1970s the rate of investment has been falling. In 1972, it was around 25 per cent, and in 1975 reached its peak level of 29.6 per cent. It then started falling, and in 1984 it reached its lowest level (16.5 per cent). Since the Second World War the Brazilian economy has had the highest rates of investment in Latin America.

The question is to what extent the lack of dynamism of the Brazilian economy is associated with the recent process of adjustment to the external debt crisis; and to what extent it is associated with structural changes related to the role of the state in the economy and in the capital–labour relations of the country?

In face of the huge external transfer of resources, and the intimate relation between the external debt and the public debt (to be examined presently), the solution for the lack of investment and growth prospects depends on some kind of negotiated policy between the main social actors, that is, the state, the representatives of the employers, and the leaders of the organized segment of the labour force. So far, the absence of negotiations has led to a process of chaotic 'solutions' to the distributive conflict in which inflation plays the part of the adjustment variable *par excellence*, and the prospects of a relatively stable growth path are close to zero.

The primary causes of the external debt in each Latin American country are different. In some cases they are associated with capital flight (Venezuela and Argentina), in others with the expansion of the import of consumption goods (Mexico) and in others with the finance of investment projects (Brazil). There is, however, a common cause for the tremendous jump of the debts at the end of the 1970s, namely, the interest rate shock.

According to the World Development Report (1987), interest rates (including spreads) in 1970 varied between 6.8 per cent (Chile and Brazil) and 7.5 per cent (Argentina, Mexico and Venezuela). In 1985, the rates were around 9.5 per cent, and in 1981–83 they were close to 20 per cent. As a result, as shown in Table 9.2, there was a considerable increase in interest payments as a proportion of GDP, and the debt service as a proportion of the GDP and of exports.

Table 9.2
Debt and Debt Service: 1970–85

	Total Interest payment on long-term debt (millions of $)		Long-term debt as percentage of GNP		Long-term debt service as percentage of of exports	
	1970	1985	1970	1985	1970	1985
Peru	162	278	38.0	74.9	40.0	16.0
Costa Rica	14	353	25.3	113.6	19.9	39.8
Colombia	59	861	22.5	33.3	19.3	33.4
Chile	104	1646	32.2	123.9	24.4	44.1
Brazil	224	7950	12.2	43.8	21.8	34.8
Uruguay	17	291	12.5	58.4	—	36.5
Argentina	—	—	23.3	56.4	—	—
Venezuela	—	—	8.7	46.1	—	—

Source: World Development Report, 1987.

After the Mexican moratorium in 1982, there was a considerable reduction in the flow of resources to Latin American countries. As a result, many countries had to implement restrictive policies to reduce domestic absorption. The social costs of the adjustment process are well known. As a result of the lack of external resources, there was an inversion in the sign of the net financial transfer (NFT) – the difference between the growth of the debt and the debt service in a given period. In Argentina, Brazil and Venezuela, the NFT was positive in 1980–81 and became negative in 1983–85, as shown in Table 9.3. A negative NFT implies that the country should generate a commercial surplus in order to equilibrate the balance of payments which in turn requires a reduction in domestic absorption and a reduction in the product–wage measured in dollars. If there is wage resistance, which is generally the case in countries where the union movement is organized, the adjustment variables tend to be the level of employment and the rate of inflation.

Another common phenomenon in highly indebted Latin American countries after 1982 is the growth of government debt. This phenomenon, and its effects in terms of the limitations it imposes on monetary and fiscal policies, has been the subject of many recent studies, including those prepared by

Table 9.3
Net Financial Transfer as percentage of GNP

	Average 1980–81	Average 1983–5
Argentina	1.9	–6.3
Brazil	1.2	–3.9
Mexico	4.4	–5.0
Venezuela	5.2	–4.7

Source: Reisen & Trotsenburg, (1987).

international agencies such as the World Bank and the OECD. Reisen and Trotsenburg[6] note that an important cause of the growth of the public debt has been the conversion of the private sector's debt into public debt.

In many countries – Brazil included – the government took responsibility for a significant proportion of the external debt in order to reduce the impact on private agents of major changes in the exchange rate or interest rate. Hence, depending on the volume of the private debt absorbed by the public sector, the external debt may become an important element of the government's expenditures. To the extent that the fiscal deficit increases or that the government has to cut other expenditures, the private debt becomes a social debt. The service of the public debt as a proportion of the GDP increased around 70 per cent in Mexico and more than 100 per cent in Argentina between 1981 and 1984. In Brazil it was already very high in 1981, and reached 41.1 per cent in 1984.

Table 9.4
Public and Publicly Guaranteed Debt Service as percentage of GNP

	1981	1984
Argentina	10.2	22.1
Brazil	39.1	41.1
Mexico	23.4	39.9
Venezuela	11.5	17.1

Source: Reisen & Trotsenburg, (1987).

In Brazil, the fiscal debt started to grow in the 1970s due to the massive subsidies to the private sector (especially to the agricultural and export sectors) and the payments of interest on the debt. As a consequence, the government's capacity to save (measured by the difference between taxes, on the one hand, and transfers plus subsidies, on the other), which accounted for 32.5 per cent of the GDP in 1970, fell to 12.8 per cent in 1980.[7]

After the first oil price shock, public enterprises played an important part in the process of structural adjustment through import substitution. Indeed, in the intermediate goods sector, public enterprises were the main investors. The relation between public investment and GDP increased from 2.8 per cent in 1970 to 8.2 per cent in 1980, whereas the share of public enterprises in the total formation of fixed capital rose from 15 per cent to 37.3 per cent in the same period.

The structural adjustment process in the second half of the 1970s was highly dependent on imports, and was essentially financed through external borrowing. This implies that the external debt of the public enterprises grew considerably during this period. Thus, the public sector as a whole became quite vulnerable to external shocks, and was seriously hit by the interest rate shock in the early 1980s.

The effects of the increase of the interest rate on the public debt were not restricted to the short-run. They affected the public sector's capacity to save (and hence invest) which, in turn, maintained a high degree of complementarity with the level of investment of the private sector. Thus, the restrictions imposed on the government's capacity to save tended to affect the aggregate level of investment, and the rate of growth of the economy. This is true particularly in the case of Brazil where the proportion of public investment in the overall level of capital formation is not at all insignificant. Before these effects are examined, the other causes of the public sector's external debt in Brazil, and the precise relation between the service of the external debt and the fiscal deficit, will be considered.

The public enterprises' debt was not the only factor in the growth of external debt under the responsibility of the public sector. In 1983, the Central Bank started to absorb the dollar-denominated external debts of private agents, who then became debtors in *cruzeiros* to the Bank. This was a way to reduce the vulnerability of the private debtors to changes in the exchange rate policy and the international rate of interest. Hence, since 1983, the share of the external debt of the public sector over the total net debt began to grow.[8] This undoubtedly represents a process of socialization of the debt and of the costs associated with the adjustment to the debt crisis. In 1988, close to 80 per cent of the external debt was under the public sector's responsibility.

The greater the proportion of the debt under the government's responsibility, the greater the relation between the service of the external debt and fiscal deficits. This is so because the proportion of exports of public enterprises to the overall volume of exports is quite small in comparison with the share of the government's external debt. Thus, to each dollar generated by net exports there corresponds an increase of almost one dollar in the fiscal deficit or the supply of money.[9] Not only that, but any devaluation of the domestic currency automatically increases the value in *cruzados* of the internal transfer between the private and the public sectors.

The relation between servicing the debt and the internal transfer between the private and public sectors imposes a serious constraint on the government's capacity to save, and hence reduces its capacity to invest and foster growth and provide public goods. The causality chain relating the external debt and the formation of fixed capital in Brazil starts with the growth of the public sector's debt, which reduces the government's capacity to save and invest, and increases the fiscal debt. The reduction of public saving leads to a smaller rate of investment by the public sector, which in turn affects the inducement for investment by private agents. The growth of the fiscal debt has a positive effect on the interest rate, which also tends to reduce the level of private investments. The government's investment in fixed capital fell by 25 per cent between 1980 and 1984; in the same period, the public enterprises' investment – a leading sector in the 1970s – fell by 33 per cent. As noted already, the rate of investment fell from an average level of 25 per cent in the 1970s to 16 per cent in 1984.

Table 9.5
Brazil: Government Fixed Capital Formation
(1980 = 100)

	1980	*1981*	*1982*	*1983*	*1984*
Government	100.0	103.6	99.03	70.16	74.84
Public Enterprises	100.0	105.68	104.10	73.1	67.42

Source: Werneck (1987).

In many Latin American countries the process of the socialization of the debt implied a substantial reduction in the share of education and health expenditures in the government's total expenditures. In Argentina and Brazil education's share fell more than 50 per cent between 1970 and 1985. In the same period, health expenditures fell by 70 per cent in Mexico and more than 35 per cent in Chile and Venezuela.

Table 9.6
Central Government Expenditures as percentage of Total Expenditures

	Education		Health	
	1970	*1985*	*1970*	*1985*
Chile	20.0	13.2	10.0	6.1
Brazil	8.3	3.2	6.7	7.6
Uruguay	9.5	6.4	1.6	4.1
Mexico	16.4	12.4	5.1	1.5
Argentina	20.0	9.5	—	14.7
Venezuela	18.6	17.7	11.7	7.6

Source: World Development Report, 1987.

Conclusion

Part of the responsibility for the current economic and social crisis may be attributed to the external debt crisis. The growth of the volume of resources transferred abroad imposes serious restrictions on the state's capacity to save, which in turn limits the overall process of accumulation. But the crisis also has domestic causes; these relate to the decisions concerning public expenditures and the relations between capital, labour and the state.

What was new in terms of the Brazilian social structure in the 1980s was the rise of a strong and centrally organized labour movement. Any successful attempt to stabilize the Brazilian economy and recover its capacity to grow depends on the co-operation of the organized labour movement. Hence, only a concerted solution seems able to re-establish the conditions for a systemic balance in Brazilian society.

The institutions on which capital–labour relations are based, as well as the attitude of the élites towards the labour movement are, however, not congenial for a negotiated solution. There are certain institutional and political requirements for the establishment of concerted policies. The main social actors must be centrally organized and representative; there must be a certain degree of agreement in terms of the necessity to negotiate and the objectives, and the government must have a certain degree of legitimacy.

None of these requirements is really met in Brazilian society today. As for the political aspects, there is a strong resistance on the part of employers to negotiate the demands of the union confederations. There are signs of change in the Brazilian social and political structure, but there are conservative forces threatening the process of modernization. In this sense, the country is living a stalemate and, at this moment, how this stalemate will be resolved is not really clear. The rapid growth of the labour movement at the electoral level seems to suggest that it is acquiring legitimacy not only at the collective bargaining table but also in society as a whole. How the élite will face this if the process continues is difficult to predict. In any case, political conditions are quite different from the past and to conclude that the changes going on in Brazil represent an important turn towards a more democratic and open society in the future is unavoidable.

Notes and References

1. See Castro and Pires 1985 for an analysis of the Brazilian strategy.
2. On pp. 170–4 we study the process of labour mobilization in the democratic transition.
3. See Amadeo and Camargo (1989a, 1989b, and 1989c) for an analysis of the Cruzado Plan in Brazil.
4. Hirschman, 1986, p. 39.
5. Tavares de Almeida, 1988, p. 329.
6. Reisen and Trotsenburg, 1987, p. 26.
7. See Werneck (1986, 1987) for a detailed analysis of the reduction in the capacity to save of the government, and its consequences.
8. See Bontempo (1988) for an analysis of this process.
9. In 1982 the share of the domestic public debt in GDP was around 13 per cent and in 1985 it had reached 20 per cent.

Bibliography

Amadeo, E. J. and J. M. Camargo, (1988) 'Política salarial e negociações: perspectivas para o futuro'. Mimeo, OIT/Ministério do Trabalho.

—— (1989a) 'A structuralist model of inflation and stabilization'. Mimeo, Helsinki, WIDER/UNU.

—— (1989b) 'Market structure, relative prices and income distribution: an analysis of heterodox shock experiments'. Mimeo, Helsinki WIDER/UNU.

—— (1989c) 'Choque e concerto', forthcoming in *Dados*.

Bontempo, H. C. (1988) 'Transferências externas e financiamento do governo'. *Pesquisa e Planejamento Econômico* Vol. 18, April.

Cardoso, E. and E. Reis (1986) 'Deficits, dívidas e inflação no Brasil'. *Pesquisa e Planejamento Econômico*.

Castro, A. B. and F. E. Pires, (1985) *A Economia brasileira em marcha forçada*. Rio de Janeiro, Paz e Terra.

Hirschman, A. (1986) 'The political economy of Latin American development: seven exercises in retrospect'. Paper for the XIII International Congress of the Latin American Studies Association, Boston, October.

Reisen, H. and A. Trotsenburg, (1988) 'Developing countries debt: the budgetary and transfer problem', OECD.

Tavares de Almeida (1988).

Werneck, R. (1986) 'Poupança estatal, divida externa e crise financeira do estado'. *Pesquisa e Planejamento Econômico*.

—— (1987) 'Public sector adjustment to external shocks and domestic pressures in Brazil'. Discussion Paper, Pontificia Universidade Católica de Rio de Janeiro.

Part 3: Crisis and Structural Transformation

10.   Uganda: Contradictions in the IMF Programme and Perspective*

Mahmood Mamdani

Introduction

To grasp the concrete significance of the IMF's programme for stabilization and structural adjustment, it is necessary to move away from the debate on capitalism vs. socialism. For the real significance of the IMF programme lies not in its defence of capitalism, but in the specific path of capitalist development for which its 'conditionalities' are supposed to clear the ground in the countries of 'sub-Saharan Africa'.

The concrete character of that path will be underlined in the course of the analysis of the IMF programme in Uganda. Here, it is sufficient to point out that the programme takes as its starting point the central weakness of the nationalist project of industrialization that unfolded in the 1960s. That project of import substitution industrialization (ISI) in fact created an entire complex of highly import-dependent industries whose very existence became predicated on continuous transfer of resources from agriculture. The critique of ISI has become the lynchpin in the IMF's call for a development strategy that amounts to a turning back on local markets and a renewed integration in external markets, a turning away from industry and a renewed focus on export agriculture. Such a development strategy is bound to recast the structure of African economies into a mould that will resemble the classical colonial export–import economy more than anything else. The IMF's brief is for the recomparadorization of African countries.

The very history of capitalism shows that paths to its development are various and different. Each path has its own implications, political and social. Even within the parameters of capitalism, the path of development embarked upon is not simply a technical issue to be settled by pundits reciting dogma, whether neo-classical or any other; rather, it is a question to be settled through a democratic dialogue, because it will decisively shape the nature of our politics and the type of society we shall create. To settle the question democratically, even within the parameters of a capitalist perspective, we must devise a

* My thanks to Professor Marc Wuyts, Institute of Social Studies, The Hague and Dr Kenneth Hermelle, AKUT group Stockholm, for their valuable comments on an earlier draft of this chapter.

development programme that is in principle compatible with a democratic polity because, in reality, it responds to the interests of a democratically constituted majority in society.

To devise such a programme, we must begin with a critical appraisal of the current IMF programme in the country. This appraisal needs to be combined with an initiative that both underlines the key lessons of our own economic and political history, highlighting our present capacities and limitations, and learns from the experience of others.

The objective of this chapter is to contribute towards the beginning of such a democratic dialogue, and in the process to cut through the suffocating climate of celebration that surrounds most discussion of the current IMF programme in the country. In the course of what follows, I shall try to show:

a) that the sources of the crisis in contemporary Uganda – of both the short-run fiscal (or budgetary) crisis of the state and the longer-run crisis of productivity in the economy – flatly contradict the assumptions regarding the genesis of the crisis in African countries that informs the IMF's standard Structural Adjustment Programme;

b) that the concessions made by the IMF to the National Resistance Movement (NRM) government in Uganda are peripheral and marginal, and do not significantly alter the character of the programme. The real significance of the programme, on the other hand, lies in the policy orientation specified in IMF 'conditionalities';

c) that the major achievement of the programme, a sharp reduction in the rate of inflation as a ceiling is put on government borrowing, is likely to be temporary as continued devaluation turns into a disguised form of deficit financing with side effects likely to be far more injurious to the people of Uganda;

d) that the real and main outcome of the IMF's set of 'conditionalities' – particularly its programme to free the market through liberal trade and credit policies, as part of a larger attempt to switch resource use from government to private sources, from popular classes to the narrow stratum of property owners, and therefore presumably from consumption to investment – will amount to a comprehensive injury to Ugandan society. Economically, it will tend to undermine any attempt to build an 'independent, self-sustained and integrated economy'. Politically, it will tend to undercut the momentum towards democratization in Ugandan society. And socially, the programme is likely to consolidate the very forces unleashed by the Amin and Obote II dictatorships. But because of the phrasing of the implementation part of the programme, these trends will come to surface only over time; and finally

e) that, in the present situation where we already find ourselves mid-stream in a second Structural Adjustment Programme, it is vital that we begin to think of an alternative development strategy for Uganda, and that we begin to do so in a public and democratic way.

Before discussing these points, however, it is first important to revisit the main assumptions of the IMF regarding the economic crisis in 'sub-Saharan African countries'.

The IMF point of view

The IMF's perspective can be summarized simply, in five related statements.

1) that it is the internal and not the external source of the problem that is significant from a programmatic perspective. In other words, the IMF does not argue that the international situation has been consistently favourable for the African countries, rather, it considers the international situation as a constant, and not a variable, for all practical purposes; as a part of nature and geography, and not of society and history. From the IMF's point of view, only demagogues will continue to harp on the international situation; practical analysis, on the other hand, must focus exclusively on the internal situation.

2) the problem – in the short-run – is a budgetary failure to practise good house-keeping, and to keep expenditure within limits of revenue; this is reflected in the fact that the demand for foreign exchange has far outstripped its supply. The emphasis on demand management in the short-run is also a recognition of the real fact that the demand side is much more responsive to policy shifts than in the supply side. The short-run solution, the 'shock' as the IMF likes to call it, is to drastically curtail demand.

3) the problem – in the medium- or longer run – is that of increasing supply. This, contends the IMF, must be done by establishing competitive market conditions that will ensure the most rational possible allocation of resources to activities which are internationally competitive and which can thus become the basis for sustained export-led growth for the economy.

4) the agent of this change must be the propertied classes in the African countries, an embryonic entrepreneurial class, which has long been stifled by anti-capitalist populism that has built up large, inefficient state structures subsidizing the consumption of better organized urban lobbies at the expense of economic growth for the whole country.

5) the way to liberate this group so that it may play its historic role of developing the productive forces is through two key measures: i) a transfer of resources to the entrepreneurial class through a triple combination: cutting the state budget, and especially unproductive service subsidies that will shift purchasing power from the popular classes to this entrepreneurial minority; privatizing state enterprises so as to increase the value of assets under control of this entrepreneurial group; and reforms in banking policy that will redirect the flow of savings from the public to the private sector; and ii) ending state restrictions on market transactions, both internal and external – in other words, freeing the market – thereby establishing the sovereignty of the entrepreneur who will now be free to respond to price signals in a competitive market.

Source of the problem: other views *(structuralist)*

The IMF position has been countered by a number of critics, both in-house and state radicals.

The in-house criticism comes from the World Bank, often echoed by several African governments. This point of view most often takes a 'structuralist' position in contrast to the 'monetarist' framework of the IMF. The World Bank's response has most often been to stress the breakdown in the infrastructure, or the unavailability of production inputs (seed, implements, and so on) or of technical expertise, that inhibit the elasticity of supply in response to appropriate price signals.[1]

The radical criticism, usually echoed by African states in their collective and public forums, stresses the 'external' origins of the crisis and implies that African states are more often than not helpless victims of forces beyond their control. While it has been a source of invaluable information on adverse changes in the international economy, state radicalism often sets up a false opposition between 'internal' and 'external' factors, so as to downplay the former and highlight only the latter.

The point of view contrasts adverse conditions in the world market in recent years with the relatively favourable climate after the Second World War. The period after the Korean War, 1953–73, is thus seen as quite unique in world trade, when world trade grew at eight per cent per annum and trade in manufactures at 11 per cent per annum, compared with growth in trade of 3.5 to four per cent from 1813–1900 and one per cent per annum from 1910 to 1940.[2]

The African countries' own Submission of 1986 highlighted the fact that real prices of primary commodities other than oil stood at their lowest since the Great Depression,[3] causing African foreign exchange losses of some US$13.8 billion over 1980–83.[4] Even the *Economist* recently estimated that commodity prices fell by 30 per cent in the 1980s.[5]

This point of view stresses two factors in emphasizing the external source of the crisis. First, structural (systemic) tendencies that underline such adverse developments as the fall in export prices for primary goods. And second, deliberate policies adopted by OECD countries to safeguard their own interests, such as the rise in interest rates on foreign debt.[6] While the first amounts to a drastic reduction in the financial resources at the disposal of African states, the second makes access to alternate resources even more expensive.

Source of the problem: the Ugandan case

Customarily, official sources stress political interference undermining sound technical management practices – a combination of the 'economic mismanagement' of the Amin period and the disruption caused by the civil wars of the following decade – as being responsible for the Ugandan state's fiscal crisis and the Ugandan economy's productivity crisis. This, in varying degrees, is the thrust of the argument in a series of sympathetic foreign studies of the Ugandan economy, ranging from the Commonwealth Report, after the fall of the Amin regime, to the IDRC Report after the fall of the Obote II and the Lutwa dictatorships.

The radical fringe of the official and quasi-official circles tends to lay stress on structural tendencies – adverse international terms of trade combined with a growing import dependence – as explaining this crisis. Internal debate in these circles revolves around the question of whether it is the internal or the external factors that are really responsible for the crisis.

While the 'external' causes of the crisis have undoubtedly had a telling effect, these should not be seen as an alternative explanation to an analysis of internal causes, but as a complement to it. Neither should technical explanations of the crisis be allowed to hide its essentially social character; nor should focus on short-run developments obscure an understanding of longer-run tendencies.

In the case of Uganda, external and internal, technical and social developments have combined to create a crisis of dramatic proportions. In this section, those factors that more directly explain the immediate fiscal crisis of the state will be addressed. Only towards the end of this chapter shall I be in a position to highlight longer-run tendencies that underline the Ugandan economy's crisis of productivity, a related but nonetheless distinct phenomenon.

A sharp deterioration in the international position marked the fortunes of Uganda's external trade during the last phase of the Amin regime up to the beginning of the first IMF programme in 1981. One look at Uganda's overall trade indices makes this clear. The terms of trade dropped sharply from 158 in 1977 to 45 in 1981. Similarly, the purchasing power of exports dropped markedly from 184 in 1977 to 42 in 1981.[7]

These trends continued right through the first IMF programme to the beginning of the second programme in 1987. Thus, the commodity price index for coffee, the source of over 95 per cent of foreign exchange, fell from 100 in 1981 to 61 in 1987.[8]

Internally, the 'economic war' of 1972 – the expulsion of the Asian minority, citizen and non-citizen, trading and non-trading – is usually taken as the starting point of a period of sharp economic destabilization and 'mis-management'. In its economic dislocation, the 'economic war' was akin to the sudden departure of the settler bourgeoisie and the rest of the settler population from the Portuguese colonies of Mozambique and Angola following liberation. As in Mozambique and Angola, in Uganda too the managerial vacuum could be filled only by a sudden and erratic expansion of the state sector.

But here is where the parallel between the 'economic war' of Amin and the 'liberation wars' in Mozambique and Angola ends. For, while the two had fairly similar disruptive effects, the social effects in both cases were quite the opposite: the 'economic war' of Amin lacked any of the socially liberating effects of the national liberation wars in the settler colonies.

What was previously one of the most efficient state sectors in Africa (with its fulcrum being the Uganda Development Corporation), was overnight turned into a prime example of unwieldy and corrupt state management. Why? Because the very function of the state structure changed following the 'economic war' of 1972. The *raison d'être* of the pre-1972 state structure was to service existing private enterprise in a number of ways, including initiating new economic ventures that would bring into partnership private and foreign capital. The post-1972 state enterprises, on the other hand, became the very springboard from which sprang many of the post-1972 private enterprises. Far from state enterprises 'crowding out' private initiative, as IMF mythology would have it, the assets of the former were stripped precisely to form the foundation for the latter. The obverse of state deficits was none other than private accumulation.

The 'economic war' gave rise to a rapacious state-created and state-protected stratum of big proprietors, popularly known as the *mafutamingi*. This trend did not come to a halt with the close of the Amin regime; all that event influenced was the regional composition of this stratum. While the beneficiaries of the Amin regime were principally 'southern' propertied interests, those of the Obote II regime were principally 'western' and 'northern'. Only in this sense may it be permissible to baptise the Amin regime as 'southern' and the Obote II regime as 'north-western'. Together, the two regimes fathered the many wings of the contemporary *mafutamingi*. In spite of sharp internal differences, it is this stratum that must be held primarily responsible for the fiscal crisis of the Ugandan state that the NRM government inherited in 1986.

Following the 'economic war' of 1972–73, there was a dramatic collapse in those sources of state revenue that were derived from the taxation of big proprietors. As a result, government revenue was derived almost exclusively from the taxation of peasants' and workers' incomes. Neither was this a temporary phenomenon. For while a new stratum of big proprietors (the *mafutamingi*) was constituted over the years, it did not figure as a significant source of government revenue.

The figures in Table 10.1 show clearly a dramatic collapse in tax on large proprietors (profits or income tax, for example) as sources of state revenue during the Amin period, with the trend continuing right through the Obote II period. This trend is that state revenue is derived directly from the incomes of the peasants, workers and earners of fixed salaried incomes. As the 1980s progressed, the principal sources of state revenue were two: export taxes (from the peasant crop, coffee) and sales taxes (from consumer goods mainly for mass consumption). The real divide was thus not urban vs. rural, but working people vs. big property owners.

My point is that the explanation of the fiscal crisis of the state lies on the side of revenue, not on the side of expenditures.[9] And that while it is true that total production (as measured by GDP figures) has been going down and this is undoubtedly connected with the decline in absolute state revenue, this does not explain why state revenue has been shrinking as a percentage of actual production.

Table 10.1
Uganda: Major sources of government revenue
(as % of total revenue for the year)

	Export	Income	Excise	Import	Sales
1966/67	16.78	16.41	16.93	23.89	—
1967/68	18.07	20.76	17.27	26.21	—
1968/69[a]	12.67	15.83	13.93	26.18	—
1969/70[a] (est.)	13.00	16.50	14.61	26.85	—

				Customs	
1982/83[b]	30.7	4.8	5.4	12.2	20.2
1983/84[b]	44.4	6.7	3.7	10.0	19.0
1984/85	58.8	6.1	3.5	8.9	19.9
1985/86	67.3	5.5	3.4	6.2	14.9
1986/87	39.9	11.4	6.8	11.9	25.3
1987/88	33.0	9.3	8.5	10.2	33.9

Notes: [a]For both 1968–69 and 1969–70, there is a tax category called "other" which comprises substantial amounts, that is, 15.7 per cent and 17.0 per cent respectively.
[b]For 1982–83 and 1983–84, foreign exchange profits comprise 22 per cent and 8.5 per cent of total revenue for the year.

Sources: Data derived from 1970 Statistical Abstract (Table UM.2, p. 69) and Background to the Budget, 1988–89 (Table 8, page A–12).

Table 10.2
Uganda: State Revenue and Expenditure as % of GDP, 1966–68, 1982–87

	1966/67	1967/68	1982/83	1983/84
Rev as % of GDP	13.34	16.74	10.9	8.9
Exp as % of GDP	14.32	18.00	14.3	10.9

	1984/85	1985/86	1986/87
Rev as % of GDP	8.7	7.7	4.95
Exp as % of GDP	11.9	11.6	9.6

Sources: Statistical Abstract, 1970, for the years 1966 to 1968 (Table UM.2, p. 69 for revenues; Table UN.1, p. 89 for GDP; and Table UN.1, p. 89 for expenditures); Background to the Budget, 1988–89, for the years 1982 to 1987 (Table 1.2, p. A6 for GDP; Table 13, p. A17 for revenues and expenditures).

Notes: 1. Revenue and expenditure figures are collected for the fiscal year, July to June. GDP calculations, on the other hand, are the calendar year, January to December. Following customary practice, I have compared fiscal year rev/exp figures with base GDP figures for the following calendar year (thus, 1982/83 revenue as calculated as a % of 1983 GDP).
2. Revenue figures combine recurrent plus development figures.
3. Expenditure figures combine those for recurrent plus development plus unallocated expenditures.

The state budget in Uganda, including military expenditures and debt servicing, was only 9.6 per cent of GDP in 1986–87. This is one of the lowest in Africa. World Bank and UNDP calculations for sub-Saharan African countries show the average figure to be at least three times as much: 31.4 per cent (1980–83), 31.6 per cent (1984), 31.9 per cent (1985), 32.1 per cent (1986), 31.2 per cent (1987).[10] The problem is not the size of the state budget, but of state revenue, which in turn is a direct result of limited revenue sources. The problem is, that while the Ugandan *mafutamingi* account for the highest share of import demand, they have been paying a dramatically declining share of state revenues. For, while as a percentage of GDP state expenditure is one of the lowest in the world, state revenue as a percentage of GDP is even lower! For example, in 1986–87, when expenditure was 9.6 per cent of GDP, revenue was only 4.9 per cent.[11]

How has the shortfall been made up over the years? Mainly through deficit financing. Two sets of figures are quite telling in this regard. The first (Table 10.3) computed by the Commonwealth team in 1979 for the Amin period, for selected years, compares the growth in money supply in the three East African countries.

Table 10.3
Growth in monetary supply in East Africa, 1971–78 (selected years)
(1971 = 100)

	1971	1975	1978
Uganda	100	280	611
Kenya	100	175	356
Tanzania	100	207	341

Source: Commonwealth Team of Experts, *The Rehabilitation of the Economy of Uganda*, Vol. 2, Table 1.3, p. 28.

The second (Table 10.4) shows the growing deficit over the 1980s, and its sources of financing, principally domestic.

Table 10.4
Uganda: The budget deficit and its financing, 1982–87 (figs. in shs. million)

	1982–83	1983–84	1984–85	1985–86	1986–87
Total Deficit	16,538	22,148	63,081	163,826	555,700
Financing:					
External (net)	3,634	3,010	13,473	47,430	136,200
Domestic	12,904	19,138	49,608	116,396	419,500
–Bank	11,365	(6,933)	53,887	77,521	218,200
–Nonbank	1,539	26,071	(4,279)	38,875	201,300

Source: Background to the Budget, 1988–89, Table 13, page A17.

Contradiction I: the IMF programme reinforces the above tendency

The short-run thrust of the IMF programme (what it likes to call 'demand management') is to reduce current demand – principally of the poorest sectors of society. This is because both the freeze the IMF advocates on wages and the reduction it demands on social expenditures put the burden of 'adjustment' primarily on the working and poor majority in society. This, and the processes it sets into motion that redistribute income further in favour of the rich, can serve only to exacerbate the problems of the downtrodden in contemporary Uganda.

On the other hand, the IMF's own assumption that the state's budgetary crisis is the result of swollen demand by popular sectors, particularly urban workers, is flatly contradicted by Ugandan developments. The ILO's own figures on the index of real wages in Uganda show an altogether different picture: following a sharp improvement in the period of nationalist agitation just before and after independence, from 29 in 1957 to 108 in 1967, and then levelling off to 100 in 1972, there was a fall to nine in 1984.

The point could not be more dramatic in formulation. A worker who could, with half his/her minimum wage purchase the family's food requirements (in 1967, 49 per cent, and 60 per cent in 1972) by 1984 needed 450 per cent the minimum wage to purchase simply the minimum food for the family. And this is before any money has been spent for such items as housing, clothing, transport, medicine or school fees! Of course, most workers survived physically (and thus had access to sources of income other than the minimum wage) but not as workers, rather in the process becoming either part-time hawkers or lumpens. But this was hardly the making of a parasitic and pampered urban working class to which the IMF constantly refers. And yet, in both the first (1981–84) and the second (1987–90) IMF programmes in Uganda, the brunt of the belt-tightening had to be borne by this class.

In the first of the two IMF programmes, from 1980 to 1983, the real minimum wage in Uganda declined by 26.4 per cent annually. And though in 1986 the ILO registered an annual decline of real minimum wages – dubbed 'sharpest average annual decline in ILO registered rates in 1986'[12] – this in no way altered the thrust of the second programme. The policy framework agreed upon by the government pledged to 'limit the wage bill' by the end of 1987.[13] As we shall see, implementation was delayed, but the plan remained unchanged.

In August 1988, the Minister of Finance decreed by circular[14] that each Ministry cut its wage bill for group employees by 30 per cent, 'whether by laying off some of the group employees or [by] redistributing their wages so that they get lower salaries'.[15] It is well known that the ranks of Ministry employees are swollen with non-existent employees on whose behalf a few officials continue to collect monthly wage packets. The irony was that the same Ministry hierarchy were now asked to decide whether to save 30 per cent of the wage bill by cutting wages across the board or by sacking any staff they dared or cared to! No wonder they decided on the latter, and that the National Organisation of Trade Unions decried these 'shocks and dictatorship' and demanded that before any on-the-scene employees were sacked the payment of non-existing employees should stop.[16]

Table 10.5
Minimum wage in nominal and real terms in Uganda, 1957–84, selected years

	Minimum Wage (shs.)	Price Index 1972=100	Real Wage Index 1972=100	% minimum wage needed to buy family food needs
1957	33	61.4	29	164
1967	150	75.2	108	49
1972	185	100	100	60
1984	6000	35000	9	450

Source: Vali Jamal and John Weeks, "The Vanishing Urban-Rural Gap in sub-Saharan Africa" *International Labour Review*, Vol. 127, 1988, No. 3, p. 288.

Simultaneously, another Ministry of Finance circular decreed that henceforth taxes would be levied not only on basic salaries, but also on leave pay, overtime pay, cost of living, or any other type of 'allowance'.[17] While it continued to exempt civil servants from personal taxation, the Ministry was literally waging a war on the class of wage earners.

Ironically, the IMF had recommended to the government this same strategy of cost-cutting by pruning the establishment of wage workers in its first programme (1981–84) and it had back-fired. Perhaps the best known case was the IMF/World Bank's ill-advised recommendation to the Uganda Posts and Telecommunications Corporation that it sack 50 per cent of its staff. This was justified as a cost-cutting measure, but was advanced without any consideration of the manpower needs of the Corporation. As a result, the Corporation was thrown into a critical staff shortage; only five years later, by the time of the second IMF programme, it was compelled to institute a crash recruitment and training programme.[18] Yet, the second IMF programme also began with an equally summary and large-scale dismissal of wage-earners from government establishments, whether from ministries, research stations, parastatals or co-operative unions.

In spite of the difference in the political context of the first IMF programme, it should not be forgotten that even a government as unresponsive to popular opinion as the Obote II regime felt compelled to increase wages and salaries of those on fixed incomes. But it lacked the political courage to do this by taking from the wealthy minority of the *mafutamingi*; instead, the government simply printed more money and sent the IMF programme into confusion by feeding inflation. Nevertheless, the second IMF programme seems to be emulating the 'successful' phase of the first: balancing the budget, not by increasing revenues, but by reducing expenditures; and not the expenditure for and by the propertied stratum, but of and for the working people.[19]

Contradiction II: differentiation without productive accumulation

The cutting edge of social differentiation in the IMF programme is two-fold: a sharp devaluation and an equally sharp credit squeeze.

Devaluation has two faces, external and internal. Though controversial, in the face of the tendency of political power to finance short-falls in recurrent state revenue through deficit financing, the external face of devaluation – especially at the outset of the programme – is necessary to restore real relations in foreign trade. What is far more contentious, however, is the continued and protracted use of devaluation as a policy instrument. The experience of the first IMF programme under Obote II showed that there was a tendency for an unholy alliance to develop between the IMF and government of the day behind the use of devaluation as a way to finance short-falls in the recurrent government budget. Around early 1984, the Obote II regime realized that the only condition under which the IMF would permit it to print more money was that of devaluation: devaluation thus turned into a disguised form of deficit financing. And the fact of continuous and protracted devaluation led to a loss of confidence in the value of local currency, which in turn led both to an all-round increase in prices, as traders exchanged liquid money for physical assets for speculative purposes, and to a decrease in the black market price of the shilling as these same traders also tried to transfer their savings into hard currencies to immunize themselves against the effects of the expected round of devaluation. The decrease in the black market price of the shilling was then presented as justification for the next round of devaluation! The result was what development economists often describe as a 'vicious cricle.'

The other face of devaluation, especially when combined with liberalization, is its internal effect. The overall impact of liberalization is discussed in the next section; here it is necessary to point out that, internally, every devaluation has turned into a contest between different classes in society, each trying to neutralize – and, if possible, go beyond that to turn into an advantage – the effect of devaluation by an increase in the price of whatever commodity it commands on the market. And every class, except for those who sell the commodity labour-power or its products in agriculture, has been able to do that.

Every devaluation has reduced the gains from production, and increased those from trade. The overall internal effect of devaluation has been double: first, to transfer savings from working people to the propertied stratum; but second, also to redistribute income inside these classes, shaping the very nature of class formation in society. The tendency has been for those on fixed incomes – particularly workers and civil servants, and much less export-producing peasants, because of low opportunity – to supplement their regular activities by moving into the sphere of distribution. This has resulted in the further disintegration of the wage-earning class by its gradual movement into petty trade. Similarly, inside the class of proprietors, there is a parallel movement of capital away from productive investments with a longer gestation period to commercial and even high-risk speculative investments with a much shorter period of gestation; in other words, from captains of industry to the *mafutamingi*. This is why the term *mafutamingi*, even in popular usage, does not mean anyone with property or investments, but only those with ill-gotten property and quick-yielding speculative investments. The term, in other words, refers not to a class but to a stratum.

The effect of devaluation on the peasantry often depends on the stratum of peasantry under consideration. For example, the agricultural prices paid to the export-producing peasantry are state-determined; though they tend to go up with every devaluation, the rate usually falls far short of the rate of devaluation. The result is a nominal increase in prices, which disguises a real fall.

A far more complex issue that requires detailed research is the effect of devaluation on that sector of the peasantry producing commodities for the internal market. Nonetheless, the general direction of developments is fairly clear and contradicts the naive and self-serving optimism of the World Bank, which concludes from an analysis of the movement of agricultural export prices (both nominal and real) that the position of the peasantry is improving. This is for two reasons. One, the increase in the nominal price of agricultural commodities can represent a monetary illusion since it may reflect an increase in the monetary income of the peasantry while its social income (subsidized transport, education, medicine, and so on) is declining. Secondly, the increase in the peasantry's real income (monetary plus social) needs to be analysed relative to the increase in the real cost of agricultural inputs.

The flow of social savings to the *mafutamingi* is further increased by the shift in bank lending policy which has accompanied the sharp credit squeeze. For the point of squeezing the flow of credits to the state sector is to increase its flow to the private sector.[20]

The logic of this ever deepening differentiation, in the eyes of the IMF, is that more money in the hand of entrepreneurs, with proper incentives, must lead to more investments, and therefore greater employment and output; and finally, greater returns to labour. What appears to be an unjust redistribution in the short-run, is the only way – so contends the IMF – of increasing social productivity in the long-run. This logic, however, ignores the concrete Ugandan context. For in a context where market incentives give no preference to productive over speculative investments, the net result of more money in the hands of proprietors is to further skew both investment and consumption activity in favour of luxury activities.[21]

The fact is that, throughout the two IMF programmes, commercial banking policy has failed to reflect and thus to reinforce any investment priorities. Lending rates have either made none or only nominal distinction between whether the loan is to be used for productive or for non-productive purposes. True, the interest rates became of significance only with the lowering of the rate of inflation; the point, though, is that – nominal as they are – these rates do signify the policy orientation of the programme, an orientation whose real importance has increased to the extent that the programme has succeeded in lowering the inflation rate.

Table 10.6
Uganda: Commercial bank lending rates to different sectors, 1982–88

	1982	1983	1984	1985	1986	1987	1988
Agriculture	14	18	24	24	38	22–25[a]	32–35[a]
Export & manuf	15	19	24	24	38		
Commerce	16–22	19–22	24	24	40	30[b]	40[b]
Unsecured	20	22	26	26	42		

Notes: The rates are in %ages, for December from 1982 to 1986, and for July for 1987 and 1988.

[a]for loans of a "short-term, commercial nature."
[b]for loans "exceeding one year".

Source: Bank of Uganda; *Annual Report*, 1985, p. 112. *Background to the Budget, 1988–89*, Table 16, p. 20.

The differences in lending rates between different activities only nominally favour productive over unproductive activities; given the structure of incentives institutionalized in the market as it exists, the discrimination is in fact reversed. This is clearly underlined by figures of actual loans made by commercial banks over the years (see Table 10.6).

Table 10.7
Uganda: Bank system credit to private sector by activity, 1982–87

	1982	1983	1984	1985	1986	1987[b]
TOTAL	36.4	112.6	137.0	408.4		
Bank of Uganda	0.5	18.0	33.5	59.8		
Crop finance	—	12.6	31.0	41.5		
Other credits	0.5	15.4	3.1	18.3		
Commercial banks	38.9	94.6	143.5	348.6		
Agriculture, of which	9.3[a]	32.6	44.6	165.6	526.9	214.3
Production	1.1	5.0	6.8	11.2		
Crop finance	8.2	27.6	38.5	154.7	486.2	912.0
Manufacture	6.2	16.9	21.6	61.8	97.1	44.3
Trade & commerce	10.6	31.2	43.9	69.9	129.8	51.4
Transport	2.2	10.6	12.4	19.1	31.4	11.8
Building & construction					20.9	7.8
Others	1.0	4.0	11.0	31.9	15.7	1.0

Notes: All figures are rounded off to one decimal point.

[a]While the total loan to agriculture for 1982 is 15.9, the only breakdown available between loans for production and crop finance is for December, for which the aggregate is 9.3.
[b]1987 figures are up to March only.

Source: For 1982–85 figures, Bank of Uganda, *Annual Report, 1985*, p. 53; For 1986 and 1987, *Background to the Budget, 1988–89*, Table 15, p. A19.

The figures in Table 10.7 show three things: 1) the highest loans, nearly half the total advanced by both the Bank of Uganda and the commercial banks, are for the extremely short-run and lucrative activity called 'crop finance'. This, strictly, should be regarded as a commercial loan; 2) of the remaining advances, the largest single category is 'Trade & Commerce'; 3) this category of advances show no sign of being eclipsed by production loans with the passage of time.

In Uganda today, there are two major areas of investment: luxury real estate; and infrastructure. Real estate in the urban areas is rented either for dollars or for shillings. Dollar rents are directly banked abroad, representing an outflow of local savings. But even that portion of local savings that is turned into local investments is directly influenced by the above trends. For the most lucrative market attracting the investment of local savings is private luxury housing and the entertainment 'industry'!

The other major arena for investments is infrastructure. Funds for this, however, are either highly concessionary loans (such as the IDA credits), or a state-determined priority (such as the 'bean road' from Kampala to Fort Portal, the result of a barter deal with the Yugoslavs). Neither would have been possible if one went by short-run market criteria. The concessionary funds flowing into the country for infrastructural development, it may be said, are the major positive side-effect of the IMF–World Bank programme; and a side-effect it must be termed, for it has nothing to do with the liberalizing thrust of the Fund's programme.[22]

But while social differentiation is putting more and more social savings at the disposal of the local propertied *mafutamingi*, these savings are becoming more the source of unproductive investments combined with increased consumption revenue rather than capital accumulation. And this is our major point. Never in history has the transfer of money led automatically and directly to the accumulation of capital. The cherished wisdom of 'underdevelopment' theory notwithstanding, even British industrialization cannot be understood as simply the result of the transfer of surplus from the colonies to Britain. The contrast between Britain and Portugal – where the transfer of fabulous riches from overseas possessions was simply turned into luxury investments and consumption revenue by unproductive dominant classes – should help underline the decisive significance of internal social relations in explaining the process of capital accumulation in a country.

The issue that needs investigation, if the focal point of interest is the possibility of capital accumulation in the Ugandan economy, is the nature of the dominant classes and the social position of the productive classes. This point will be dealt with when discussing the question of social transformation in Uganda. It will suffice here to underline the immediate economic effect of the IMF programme; a bonanza for luxury and speculative investments, and for the banks, which are the intermediaries in the transfer of social savings into the hands of the *mafutamingi*.[23]

Contradiction III: the consequences of liberalization

An ever-sharper differentiation and strengthening of the *mafutamingi* stratum is going hand in hand with a broader policy framework that is 'liberating' this group from political (state) constraints. Not only is a greater portion of social savings being put into the *mafutamingis*' pockets but they are also being given the freedom to determine how to utilize these savings. This policy orientation is summed up in a single policy objective: liberalization. And the trend to liberalization is summed up in a single policy instrument: Open General Licence (OGL).

The experience of OGL policies in the first IMF programme is worth recapitulating. The first IMF programme abolished import rationing to key sectors of the economy, contrary to the advice of the 1970 Commonwealth Team of Experts. The result was that 40–60 per cent of imports under the auction system were consumer goods.[24] Even more, one-quarter of all imports – in 1983–84, for example – were accounted for by three items: fabrics (17.1 per cent), soap (6 per cent) and cigarettes (2 per cent). And yet, that same year capacity utilization in industry was recorded at 22 per cent. Furthermore, the import bill also included a large category of luxuries, their real nature concealed by vague and general categories. Thus, items like motor vehicles (mostly fleets of luxury vehicles, such as Mercedes Benz for the *mafutamingi*: 7.6 per cent), household equipment (usually videos and domestic luxuries: 3.1 per cent) combined with expenditures on travel (5.6 per cent) and education (3.7 per cent) notoriously known to be the most abused categories whereby monies were simply purchased for export to foreign accounts. If one puts together the expenditure on these luxury imports (20 per cent) and on necessaries for which there was idle local production capacity (23 per cent), we get an astounding figure of nearly half of the foreign exchange auctioned at weekly markets.[25]

One difference between the second IMF programme and its predecessor is that this time the timetable for liberalization is phased. But the concession made by the IMF to the sensibilities of the government of the day is only tactical; the strategic orientation of the programme remains unaltered. That strategic objective is to put the power of defining social priorities into the hands of the dominant agents in the market, the *mafutamingi*.

The tactical nature of the concession is clearly spelt out in a number of official documents. These begin by talking of a 'gradual relaxation of import controls', specifying that 'at the outset . . . the coverage will be limited to imports of raw materials, spare parts and equipment, because of current scarcity of foreign exchange'. 'The coverage of OGL,' they add, 'will be reviewed and expanded on a quarterly basis, so that by end-1988 it would extend to all capital and intermediate goods, basic necessities and incentive goods.' But then follows the strategic orientation, what the IMF calls 'the bottom line': 'with the objective of encouraging economic efficiency and ultimately extending the OGL system to all imports, the Government will continue to review the tax and tariff schedule periodically.'[26]

With each phase in the expansion of OGL the limits within which the Ugandan state will be able to influence the priorities of economic and social development will contract further. Even the first phase – OGL for industries – which has been understood in official circles as a major concession to industry over trade, is at the same time a major step backwards: for an OGL for all industries is at the same time the absence of any industrial priorities.

To be sure, the government's Policy Paper does outline 'priority industries', being 'those producing basic consumer goods and construction materials'. Ironically, this very statement reflects a failure to come to grips with the concrete character of the industry built up over the past three decades. For the real distinction between priority and non-priority industries cannot be grasped simply by highlighting the end-product (mass consumer as opposed to luxury products, for there are hardly any 'luxury' industries); to grasp that real distinction requires looking at the production technology and the import requirement of each industry. Let us take but a few examples concerning industries that would otherwise be classified as 'priority' industries producing 'basic consumer goods and construction materials'. Three categories of industries: producer goods, basic consumer goods, and construction materials, will enable my point to be made.[27]

Let us begin with an example of an industry producing a basic producer good: fishnets. Uganda Fishnet Manufacturers, for example, imports all its raw materials (mainly hemp) from Japan. One of the best known industries producing a basic consumer item is TUMPECO. The enamelling section of Uganda Metal Products and Enamelling Co., Ltd (TUMPEC) imports all articles in shapes (for example, mugs, buckets, basins, trays), dips them in imported chemical solutions, only to dry them locally. Neither is Vita-Form in Jinja very different: it simply mixes various imported chemicals and water to form foam block which is then cut into various sizes of mattresses. Dairy Corporation, an industry in a country with a higher cattle–human ratio than can be found in most of Europe, takes this import dependence to the most absurd levels. Here, imported powder milk is mixed with local water, poured into imported packing materials, and is carried in imported plastic crates for sale in local markets. The packing machines are from Sweden and France, the former rented and the latter purchased; so 'patriotic' are these machines that the Swedish ones will only accept Swedish 'tetrapack', and the French ones only French cellophane sachets!

While industries producing construction materials are likely to be much less import-dependent in raw materials, it is nonetheless surprising to find instances to the contrary in this group. Take the example of Uganda Baati Ltd. which cuts imported coils of metal sheets, coats them with imported zinc, and brands them 'Made in Uganda' with an imported stamp to sell locally! All this, in spite of the fact that local asbestos from Tororo, instead of imported steel coils, would have made for a more durable product; sulphur could also have been procured from Tororo.

There is no better illustration of the unnecessarily high and unjustifiable import-dependence of much of Uganda's 'priority' industry than Uganda

Clays and Dairy Corporation. Uganda Clays is actually two plants, one established in the colonial period, the other in 1969. The contrast is illuminating, although both produce construction material. Whereas the first and older plant uses local clay from Kajansi or Mukono or Gomba, the later and more modern plant is highly dependent on imported glazes from Italy and borax oxide from the UK.

In conclusion, let us look at one of the most recently 'restored' industries in Uganda, the beneficiary of UNDP funds and UNIDO technical advice: Mukisa Biscuits. Previously established in the 1950s and integrated into using local raw materials, Mukisa Biscuits, as restructured by the UN agencies in 1982, used only local water to boil imported ingredients, cut them into precast shapes and pack them in French paper and cartons. Mukisa is simply a mixing plant for an industry all of whose linkages are in France or Germany.

There are many more examples. As with construction materials (clay), in textiles too one can contrast the high import dependence of UGIL with the local integration of NYTIL; and similarly, the increased import dependence in the more modern of the sections of NYTIL compared with the older ones that produce coarser cloth. All of these would be classified as priority industries, under the Policy Paper, as producing 'basic consumer goods', and under the Rehabilitation and Development Plan under the general category 'textiles'. My point is simply that although the phased OGL gives preference to industrial over other imports in the present period, official documents show no indication of a well worked-out industrial stategy that actually comes to terms with the heavy import dependence of the industries created over the past three decades.[28] Furthermore, the next section will show that the anti-inflation strategy of the programme is based on cutting domestic consumer demand, both rural and urban. Given that Uganda's industrial output is oriented to the domestic market, this is bound to lead to an industrial crisis. As a result, while the breathing space granted by the current phase in the introduction of OGL will come to naught, the IMF programme will soon take us into the world of 'market-determined priorities'.

Market determination of priorities – that is, a complete OGL – means that emphasis will be on the importation of those commodities for which trading profits will be the highest. It means, in short, accepting the priorities of the *mafutamingi* stratum as those of the society as a whole.[29] In a setting where short-term trading profits directly contradict medium-term growth needs, this is equivalent to losing control over the very direction of the process of development.

Contradiction IV: curbing inflation by increasing reliance on foreign markets and foreign capital

The IMF programme boasts of two successes in today's Uganda: rehabilitation of the infrastructure, and curbing inflation. Whereas the first is a development that has little to do with the policy imperatives of the programme, the second is indeed centrally connected to it.

There are two ways of combating inflation: one is to cut demand, the other is to increase supply. The consequence, in each, is dramatically different. The IMF fight against inflation has proceeded by way of cutting demand, partly because such an objective can relatively easily and directly be achieved through a policy reorientation, and partly because it is ideologically preferable to the IMF. The IMF sees the slashing of consumer demand of the popular classes as the necessary condition for increasing social savings in the hands of the class of large proprietors.

The major instrument that has led to a dramatic decrease in inflation is a sharp squeeze in bank credits available to the state. This policy instrument has created its own negative consequence: a shrinking domestic market, which in turn implies a greater reliance on foreign capital and foreign markets, as well as a crisis for industries producing for the local market. One thus need not be surprised that the industrial power sold by Uganda Electricity Board in 1987 was hardly 45 per cent of the 1980 figure.[30]

The shrinking home market illustrates the contradictory consequence of every policy instrument: one short-run, the other long-run; one static, the other dynamic. Thus a policy instrument that may cut expenditures and appeal to the short-run instincts of an accountant, may at the same time pose a sharp dilemma to a development economist with his/her eye set on the more dynamic and long-run theme of capital accumulation.

In spite of the public rhetoric of African countries learning how to 'live within their means', the real attraction of the IMF programme to the rulers of Africa is the promise of more funds from overseas if the programme is implemented. Thus, the implementation of the programme, in every instance, has seen an aggravation of the foreign debt of the country concerned, rather than a movement towards solvency.

The figures for Uganda clearly illustrate this tendency. Uganda's debt service ratio, 18.9 per cent in the year before the first IMF programme began (1980), leapt to 55 per cent in the year after it ended (1985). Latest figures record the debt/service ratio for 1987 at 59.6 per cent.[31] While the overall debt in absolute terms may have remained a little over one billion dollars over the past few years, the fact is that the financial gap (export revenue, that is import expenditure + debt servicing) for Uganda continues to grow. Are we not approaching a point where the mark of our 'achievement' is that we are simply – as a consultant for the Swedish SIDA remarked with reference to the effects of the IMF programme in Mozambique – 'managing to avoid impending bankruptcy by postponing it rather than by resolving the underlying imbalances'.[32]

In this, of course, Uganda's experience parallels that of most African countries, which by 1986 were said to be paying back more to the Fund than they were receiving in new loans![33] On the other hand, the standard solution of this state of affairs has been to reschedule debts; and yet, according to Sudan's experience, the rates applied to rescheduled debt (18 per cent) are considerably higher.[34] With this sort of a record, it would be no exaggeration to say that

Uganda seems to be following the lead of such countries as Sudan, Zambia, Mozambique and the Comoros, which are now in the unenviable position of having reached a debt service ratio exceeding 100 percent.[35] To what extent can such countries be regarded as independent in the realm of economic policy?

Need for an alternative strategy

The fact that policies usually have contradictory consequences makes choice of policy a controversial and difficult exercise. With economic policy, for example, it is not unusual for the short-run (that is, revenue) effect of a policy to run counter to its long-run (development) effect. To take an example most popular with the monetarists: to increase tax revenue in the long-run may well be by reducing taxes in the short-run so as to increase investment, output and incomes and therefore gross taxes. Whatever the merits of this example, the point is that it is important to take the long-run view over the shorter-run, the perspective of development over the view of an accountant.

Immediately one goes beyond the question of trade and markets, to pose the question of production and accumulation, three inescapable questions arise: 1) the agent of change, in agriculture and industry; 2) the nature of markets for expanded production, whether principally local or foreign; and 3) the source of finances for industrialization, also whether mainly local or foreign.

To begin answering these questions it is necessary to turn to historical experience, the very ground from which economic theory is formulated. To arrive at a theoretical formulation relevant to the Ugandan reality, the discussion must be grounded in the historical experience of this country.

Uganda's modern economic history can be divided into four periods: from the 1890s to the 1920s; from the 1920s to the 1940s; from the 1940s to 1972; and from 1972 to the present. My point is that the IMF period in Uganda's economic history is substantially a continuation of the economic history of the Amin regime; conversely, that the origins of the present economic crisis in the country lie in the changes that followed the launching of the 'economic war' by the Amin regime in 1972. But first, a brief look at the first three periods.

Following the establishment of colonial rule (1896–1928) was a period of sharp contention between peasants and European planters and local chiefs as to who was to be the engine of economic growth in the coming period. The experience of the post-World War I crash in commodity markets taught the colonial state that whereas planters could survive adversity only if granted lavish subsidies, such was not the case with peasants: thus, despite arguments from kith and kin, the colonial state refused to subsidize plantations, turning to peasant growers as a far more reliable and cheaper source of raw materials for export. This policy was inscribed into law during the next decade when, following a combination of rent increases and evictions, the tenants in Buganda began to reduce the acreage of cotton and simultaneously organized a mass political movement. To reverse these developments, the colonial state passed a land reform legislation (the 1928 Busulu and Euvujjo Law) that gave peasant growers security of tenure and thus freedom from eviction by landlords. These two decisions – marginalizing both planters and landlords in favour of peasant agricultural producers – established petty production by peasants as the backbone of Uganda's agrarian economy.[36]

In the second period (1928–49), Uganda's political economy was marked by a classic colonial division of labour. An immigrant trading and processing minority (from India) controlled the processing of export agriculture and the marketing of major agricultural exports and consumer imports, while agricultural production was the preserve of peasant producers with a reorganized, internally-oriented (sugar) plantation section complementary to it. Granting security of tenure to a previously landlord-oppressed peasantry acted as the institutional framework for expanding agricultural production, particularly reflected in the growth of coffee cultivation in Buganda in the 1930s. The period came to a halt with a political crisis: an emerging indigenous middle class organized peasant export producers against both the immigrant traders and processors, and against state-appointed local chiefs.

The political crisis that was marked by the 1945 and 1949 peasant uprising and workers' strikes forced concessions from the colonial state, and altered the existing division of labour. The hallmark of the third period (1949–72) was two-fold: on the one hand, the development of a co-operative movement that took over the marketing and processing of export crops from the immigrant bourgeoisie, but on the other the movement of this immigrant bourgeoisie from trade and processing to import-substituting industries. Neither movement was the product of the natural operation of market forces; both required direct political action by the state.

This period continued until 1972. The dynamism unloosed by reforms that simultaneously gave associations of peasant growers a degree of control over export marketing and processing, and facilitated the movement of hitherto trading and processing capital into industry, accounted for the relatively outstanding economic growth in this period. On the negative side, there was a counter-movement, evident after independence, whereby sectors of the newly liberated middle class utilized their newly gained political (state) power to seize control over former peasant co-operatives, and then proceeded to fortify this control by a series of legislative acts that did away with any democratic procedures in the running of the co-operatives and instead made them accountable to state officials and state organs.

A wholesale reversal of the period of the 'paramountcy of peasant agriculture', considered more or less a settled issue in the economic history of modern Uganda since 1928, began with Amin's 'economic war' of 1972. The drama of the 'economic war' – the expulsion of the immigrant bourgeoisie and the take-over of their assets by a combination of middle-class aspirants and military or civilian bureaucrats – hid from view yet another decisive shift in state economic policy. This was a shift of emphasis in state support away from peasant agriculture to the combination of landlords and big bureaucrats. The main feature of this shift, its legal embodiment, was the repeal of the 1928 Busulu and Envujjo Law, and the passage of the 1975 Land Reform Decree, which meant that every peasant who had formerly been a customary tenant became a tenant-at-will who could be summarily evicted from his land in the name of 'development'. The direct result was insecurity of tenure in so far as the peasantry was concerned. Combined with the top-down control of co-operatives that was the Obote I period's legacy to Amin – and that no regime since has tried to change – this established an institutional context most adverse to expanded agricultural production.

Against this background, it should be possible to return to the three questions posed above and draw some historical material for purposes of reflection.

Agent of change: Agriculture is the decisive sector in so far as Uganda's economy is concerned; this is where the bulk of the country's producers and the bulk of its annual product is located. The history of agriculture in this century has been a tug-of-war, with one side pulling in the direction of landlords, plantation owners and big bureaucrats, and calling for state policies that will transfer to them agricultural surpluses siphoned from peasant producers; and the other side, the peasants themselves and their middle-class allies, seeking to forestall or reverse such a development.

There have been two key periods in this struggle; both have been periods of crisis for large-scale agriculture – the first immediately following the First World War, and the second during the Amin regime – and both have demonstrated the resilience of small-peasant production in the face of great adversity. Both have shown the small peasantry to be the real dynamic force in Ugandan agriculture unlike, for example, Kenya, with its agriculture organized mainly along capitalist lines.

In industry, the major period of development was the two decades following the close of World War II. This was not because of any special dynamism inherent in the immigrant Indian bourgeoisie, but on the contrary, Indian trading and processing capital was literally forced into manufacturing investments. The major lesson of this period is that there is no pre-existing entrepreneurial class simply waiting to be discovered and 'freed'; rather, this period illustrates the critical importance of state policy in devising an appropriate structure of rewards and penalties that made it rational for owners of large-scale property to move into industrial investments. Without the stick that transferred both the marketing and processing of export crops to co-operatives and the carrot offered by the UDC in joint manufacturing investments, it would be difficult to imagine Indian trading capital moving into productive investments in industry so swiftly and in such a short time. Surely, it is an historical experience pregnant with lessons for the contemporary period with a state power keen on economic development and a newly-born *mafutamingi* stratum still tied to its embryonic activities in the realm of speculation and trade.

Markets for expanded production: In those same two decades following World War II, it was expanded local markets – and not any new suddenly discovered or captured external market – that sustained these industrial investments. In Uganda, these expanded markets – particularly in such wage goods as matches, batteries, cloth, paraffin, soap, radios, and so on – were the direct result of the increase in wages that followed the general strikes of 1945 and 1949. One result of working-class militancy was a fourfold increase in the minimum wage from 1957; as a result, a minimum wage that could have bought only three-fifths of the food requirements of an average urban family in 1957 had, by 1967, increased to the point where only half was sufficient to meet that requirement.[37] Far from acting as a constraint on local capital formation, the wage increases had a stimulating effect on local manufactures since they expanded the market for these. The case of Kenya was similar where recent research has shown that the major source of market expansion for manufacturing investments in the post-independence era was not the growth of export markets (accounting for 5.01 per cent of the relevant demand), nor even the substitution of existing imports (26.27 per cent), but increased domestic demand, whose growth accounted for 68.772 per cent of the market for manufacturing output.[38]

The lesson of agriculture too is no different. Though it is commonplace to say that agriculture in Uganda reverted to a subsistence trend in the Amin period, this conceals a far more complex picture: there was no single and simple trend in that period. On the one hand, there was the decline in export production as export prices declined and smuggling grew to rival official transactions; but on the other, there was a phenomenal expansion in food production, not for subsistence but for sale, because domestic markets for domestic food supplies expanded equally spectacularly in that period. The expulsion of the Indian community in 1972 dramatically changed the composition of the urban population and the structure of their demand for food items from those imported to those locally produced.

Source of finances for industrialization: To begin with, there are two alternatives, either local or foreign. In an expansionary era like that preceding the series of 'oil price shocks', it could conceivably be argued that foreign funds borrowed on low interest rates could finance large-scale developmental projects. But not any more. The international climate today – with high interest rates – is less favourable.

If, then, accumulation has to be based primarily on local savings, do these savings not necessarily have to come out of agriculture and does this not necessarily imply development policies that call for terms of trade against agriculture and in favour of industry? That, after all, was how the nationalists of the 1960s reasoned, not because they were anti-peasant, but because they were pro-industry.

But the nationalist strategy had its own pitfalls. For contrary to all appearances and even rhetoric, the nationalist strategy involved ripping-off the peasant without introducing any institutional changes. It involved transferring peasant surpluses in the context of relatively stagnant production levels; and it transferred these surpluses to an industry so highly import-dependent and inefficient that it could not exist without continued subsidies, once again at the expense of agriculture. In such a situation, as in large sections of the colonial period, it required the employment of force as central to economic policy. And, not surprisingly, it evoked frequent peasant resistance in the form of declining production. Even in Kenya, where a relatively strong agrarian bourgeoisie was much better placed to defend the interests of agriculture, the terms of trade were against agriculture except during the coffee boom of 1976–77.

The alternative to this nationalist paradigm can be found in the experience of certain South-East Asian countries, often on both sides of the ideological divide. For in both the Chinas, Taiwan and mainland, and in both North and South Korea, vital institutional changes took place that set the context for productive accumulation in the period that followed, whether by an industrial bourgeoisie (as in South Korea) or state agencies (North Korea). Equally true is that these very institutional changes acted as levers to liberate the productive energy of the peasantry, and therefore the surplus produced in agriculture. In a situation where increased surpluses were drawn from rising production levels, it was possible for increased agricultural incomes and increased savings for industry to go hand in hand.

In all these countries the centre piece of these institutional changes was the land reform; its significance, everywhere based on the principle of 'land to the tiller', was dual:[39] 1) it distributed productive property (and not simply means of consumption) to the majority; and 2) it created a substantial internal market in mass consumption commodities; the former acted as a stimulus for industrial products. South Korea, according to World Bank sources, has a more equitable income distribution than have most Third World countries, in fact comparable to that in the United States. The same sources also argue that, particularly in its initial expansion phase, 'domestic demand has been much more significant than export expansion as a source of manufacturing demand in South Korea'.[40] The emancipation of the peasantry, in other words, created a large peasant market both for industries producing agricultural tools and for those producing mass consumption goods.

Closely tied to the land reform was an active state whose economic policies had a dual orientation: to protect the internal market for domestic manufactures, and to direct local capital into investments necessary from the point of view of long-term economic development. The *Financial Times* comment on South Korea is revealing:

> One of the free world's most tightly supervised economies, with the Government initiating almost every major investment by the private sector and wielding enough power to ensure that companies which make such investments also make a profit.[41]

Whether in South Korea or in Taiwan, liberalization was not the first act in a developmental process cast along neo-classical lines; rather, liberalization was contingent on both the creation of a market for mass consumption and the building-up of the competitive strength of local producers.[42] Liberalization did not create competitiveness; rather, competitive strength was built up within the protective environs of an expanding home market and created the precondition for liberalization.

It is this issue of institutional changes, of social transformation, that the IMF and the World Bank – even the associated UN agencies that repeatedly talk of 'Adjustment with a Human Face' – have all side-stepped with neither explanation nor ceremony. And this issue must be central to any attempt to devise a medium-term alternative to the IMF's perspective.

Transformational (institutional) issues

There are, at present, two different and opposite conceptions of African economies to be found in mainstream social science. Though both are equally one-sided and misleading, each has become the theoretical basis of programmatic initiatives from outside the continent.

The first is the theoretical edifice of the IMF, best summed up in academic theory in the writings of Robert Bates, which proceed on the assumption that the economy in question – 'the patient' – is a fully-developed commodity economy, wherein the only link between economic agents is the market.

The opposite point of view has been best articulated – because it has been the most exaggerated – by Göran Hyden. His assumption, though never explicitly articulated, is that there exist no internal markets in Africa south of the Sahara; that exchange between peasants is based entirely on non-economic clan and family relations. Africa, according to Hyden, is stuck in 'the economy of affection'; the market, from this point of view, has still to be created. This is not the place to critique Hyden; suffice it to outline his point of view in relation to that of the IMF.

Once juxtaposed the two points of view highlight what is partial about each. It becomes clear that the IMF view ignores the fact that the involvement of African peasants in market relations is only partial, that the market will have to be substantially created before it can be 'freed'. In the Africa of peasant agriculture (as opposed to the Africa of capitalist agriculture) the market itself is a partial construct. The IMF's is an ahistorical point of view which has forgotten that the market, in Africa as in Europe, has never existed as a god-given entity, but has had to be created through social struggles. This was especially the case with the market for mass consumption commodities. Markets for mass consumption goods in Europe began roughly around the time the Atlantic slave trade began in Africa; previously, the only markets in Europe were for luxury goods for privileged minorities, as is the case in most of Africa today.

That the market is historically created, and that this is a problem of transition and transformation, finds no place in the IMF's analysis, and only marginal space in the World Bank's analysis, for the only 'structural rigidities' – structural impediments to the operation of a free market – understood by the World Bank are technical ones; in short, problems of economic infrastructure. The World Bank remains as impervious to social rigidities as does the IMF.

From the point of view of capitalist development, there is a key distinction between economic policy in countries with market economies and in countries in which markets are only partially developed. In the latter countries, unlike in the former, economic policy must have a transformational orientation. It has to be part of an overall strategy of capital accumulation and market-creation, and not locked into a short-run stabilization perspective of an accountant intent on balancing the books. The central questions must be of production and accumulation on the one hand, and market-creation on the other, not simply of 'freeing' existing markets.

To express this in the language of neo-classical economics: under present circumstances, supply is relatively elastic in only a tiny sector of the economy.[43] Rigidities, which constrain the response of supply to changes in price, include both the prior allocation of a substantial proportion of peasants' labour and the consumption needs of this peasantry, which limit the availability of land for market crops.

To return to our concrete discussion: from the point of view of production and demand-creation, what are the key social rigidities in contemporary Uganda? Put differently, what are the key social obstacles to increased production and the creation of a mass maket oriented to satisfying popular needs in today's Uganda?

To discuss this is to underline the limitations of the market from two points of view: that of accumulation and that of consumption. To begin with the question of production and accumulation: besides the generally acknowledged fact that peasants cultivate their own food – the so-called subsistence economy – the IMF view also ignores the fact that much of the peasants' sweat is pumped out of them by means of non- or semi-market methods that require the direct threat of force: forced appropriation of land, forced cultivation of crops (at one time or another, either as a compulsory export crop or as a compulsory famine food reserve), their forced sale (to state-created bodies, whether co-operatives or parastatals, but agencies that lack any meaningful degree of popular accountability), forced contributions (whether as a development levy for the state, or a membership fee for the single party, or a contribution to a host or visiting party or state functionary), and finally forced labour (justified not as labour for the state but as community labour for the upkeep of community roads, or a community school, or a community dispensary, and so on).

Force has been an integral part of peasant production in Africa, throughout the colonial period, and since.[44] Three institutions have been central to the operation of this process.[45]

The first is the system of chiefship which was reorganized during the colonial period to represent the state power in the countryside, as a power both fused (in all its instances, administrative, legislative, judicial) and personalized (in the form of the chief). The chief used his power, more or less depending on the circumstances, but always unchecked by any institutional counterbalance, to extort extra-legal exactions from peasants. As the power of the chief became militarized or was allied to that of military officers, the weight of these extra-legal exactions on the peasantry increased. In other words, with the militarization of political power, from the Obote I through the Amin to the Obote II regimes, the weight of extra-economic coercion in the exploitation of the peasantry continued to grow.

The second institution central to the process of extra-economic coercion of the peasantry has been the land system. Here too, there has been a process of historical development. As our earlier survey shows, it was really with the Amin decree of 1975 that the peasantry lost control over the land, even in the communal areas where clans had previously the right to allocate land parcels for use. Since then, insecurity of land tenure has been rife, particularly where land is fertile, well-serviced and has a high market value.

A word of explanation is necessary here. The land question in Uganda takes on a variety of forms. Its principal form is not that of land scarcity, but of insecurity of tenure. This is the case in the most productive areas, particularly in the crescent of land around Lake Victoria. There, the existence of landlordism has created a duality of rights: on the one hand, usufruct rights in the hands of peasants who continue to pay extortionate amounts as entry money to landlords or to existing tenants; on the other, property titles in the hands of landlords who play no part in the process of production on the land. The system creates a disincentive for peasants to invest their surplus in the land since they have no security of tenure, and for landlords to permit such a development since any permanent improvement by peasants will enhance their claim over the land. Peasant surpluses thus flow out of agriculture into transport and trade.

Finally, there is the institution of the co-operative, whose origin lies in the very struggle of peasants against middlemen exploiters. But, as our brief survey has indicated, without the organizational strength to control and hold co-operative officials accountable, peasants first lost control of co-operatives and their resources to these officials, and later to the state power itself, which instituted a series of legislative Acts to bring co-operatives under close state control. Today, the situation has reached the point where the co-operative – once meant to free peasants from the clutches of the middleman exploiter – has itself taken on that role, to the extent that it can 'embezzle' even the whole of the peasant's entitlement for the sale of an export crop.

Since the National Resistance Army/National Resistance Movement (NRA/ NRM) came to power, it has introduced measures that undercut one of these institutions: the introduction of Resistance Committees (RCs). The thrust of this reform edge has been directed against the fused and absolute power of chiefs, whose power to legislate bye-laws and to try cases has been transferred to Resistance Committees. The chiefs have, in fact, been reduced to the stature of a modern civil servant, with administrative powers only. But without a continuing and a protracted reform wave, encompassing land tenure and co-operative policies, this partial reform must necessarily remain unstable. Unless consolidated by further and comprehensive reform, RCs are bound to be subverted from within by the very forces that resist further reform.

The second prerequisite for economic development in an economy like that of Uganda is the creation of markets for mass consumption. For, even at the level of markets, Uganda is very different from the fully market societies of Europe, from which has sprung the IMF's theory. The market in Uganda is tiny, confined to the demands of a small élitist minority. The vast majority of the people – peasants – do not figure as agents of consumption in the market. Unlike the working class in Europe, whose consumption constitutes a real demand and a significant market for the capitalists, and a fall in whose income would gravely concern not only themselves but also the capitalists whose market their consumption demand constitutes; in Uganda, on the contrary, the vast majority of peasants, as consumers, are both marginal and insignificant. For capitalists in Uganda, peasants are simply a source of export crops, a factor of production; they do not count as a factor in consumption markets. This is the reality that has to be changed. It is the peasant (and the worker) who must be made sovereign in the market before the market can be declared sovereign in the economy and allowed to guide priorities. And finally, none of these changes will come without deliberate and decisive state action. For the real question about the role of the state is not its extent but its nature, not the size of state intervention but its direction. This much should be clear from an examination both of Uganda's experience and that of countries that have recently embarked on a successful course of industrialization. It was a combination of the stick and the carrot wielded by the colonial, and later the post-colonial, state that lured the immigrant bourgeoisie from trading and processing investments to manufacturing. And it was once again state action on the wage front that simultaneously created a stable working class and a regular market for these industries.

My point is simple: the terms of the debate as cast by the IMF – state vs. market – fail to capture the need of the hour in contemporary Uganda. That need is neither for statization, nor for privatization, but for democratization.

Conclusion: contradiction between politics and economics

There are today contradictory trends in society backed up by contradictory forces. On the one hand, there is the perspective of those who benefited from the dictatorships of the past two decades: the *mafutamingi*. Having enriched themselves through the violence and the disorder of the Amin and Obote II periods, they identify dictatorship with no other than the person of Amin or Obote, so that in the name of peace and security they may stabilize the institutions either created or consolidated throughout those periods. On the other hand, there is the perspective of democratization, of those who understand that dictatorship arose and became stabilized on the bedrock of such institutions as: the absolute chiefships, the statized co-operative movement; and by the removal of security of land tenure from the peasantry. As dictatorship consolidated it increased the element of force, of extra-economic coercion, in the process of accumulation.

In the late 1980s, some democratic reforms have been implemented to counter this tendency. Central amongst these has been the introduction of RCs, and alongside this the redefinition of the chiefship from an absolute to an administrative post.[46] Understandably, these reforms have brought to centre-stage the question of further reform, both of land laws and statized co-operatives. Events in 1988–89 show growing conflict between the RC movement and those who have come to control co-operatives and to grab land.

What else can be the meaning of reports of peasants in Mubende cutting heels of land surveyors, whose presence was an early warning signal that land-grabbers were about to follow? Of peasants in Iganga, who once crushed the peasant army of Alice Lakwena on its way to the Nile, but who have now been mercilessly evicted by a landgrabber in the person of a ministerial niece? Or the meaning of RC officials in Mbale putting into gaol co-operative officials who had appropriated the proceeds of peasant crop sales for personal gain?

These events are warning signals that need to be heeded. The IMF programme seeks to transfer resources from the popular classes to the *mafutamingi* stratum; its effect is to shrink local markets and direct entrepreneurs to seek dynamism from foreign markets. Such a programme represents an obstacle on the road to the continued democratization of Ugandan society; as such, it is bound to come into conflict with the majority. The current clash between RCs and land and co-operative grabbers will either intensify, or the RCs will be subverted from within to become 'the new chiefs'. In that situation, further continuation of the IMF programme will no longer be a tactical concession, but amount to a strategic defeat for those who stand for democratization.

In a situation where insecurity of land tenure discourages a peasant from investing the bulk of his/her surplus into agriculture, it is absurd to think that a change of relative prices will procure success. In a situation where peasant producers of export crops are robbed of their entire proceeds by unscrupulous co-operative officials, any talk of by how much these proceeds should be increased is no more than an exercise in mental arithmetic. In such a situation, to hand over the power to determine how social savings should be utilized to the beneficiaries of land speculation and co-operative embezzlement, united with those who reaped the harvest during the Amin and Obote II years, is an act bound to invite the wrath of those with the slightest commitment to a new and a democratic order.

It is not for nothing [writes Ake Sawyerr, the Vice Chancellor of the University of Legon, Ghana] that representatives of Western capital stress the importance of 'strong government' and praise the 'political will' and the 'courage' of those regimes able to hold the austerity line. Can they be referring to regimes strong because they reflect and represent the collective will of a conscious and committed people? . . . or are they, instead, referring to strength deriving otherwise than from the support of the mass of the people, backing the 'political will' of a minority to impose and maintain austerity programmes which the majority of the people would be unlikely to accept, were they given a say in the matter.[47]

From the outset, the IMF programme was presented and defended as a tactical concession, not a strategic orientation. That concession made sense in the existing context, because this context included both an international situation relatively hostile to the new government, and an internal state of affairs in which the NRM lacked either the organization or the perspective to go it alone in economic or political affairs. Attempts during 1986–87 to look for alternatives, both in resources and perspective, failed: the IDRC Report was too closely oriented to the short-run and failed to provide any coherent direction; overtures to Arab and Islamic organizations had small returns.

That experience should be the basis for drawing certain lessons. At the minimum, we should learn to anticipate crises and prepare for them publicly. It is the thesis of this chapter that continued implementation of further phases in the IMF programme, especially an open OGL with social savings in the hands of the *mafutamingi* – combined with a failure to democratize co-operatives and guarantee security of tenure to peasants – is bound to result in a crisis. It is hoped that this chapter will contribute to a discussion of the possible alternatives to the IMF whose programme for privatization clearly excludes any meaningful conception of democratization. For that reason, it is important to democratize the discussion on economic policy. Only through an expanded and public dialogue can Uganda hope to formulate an economic programme that will help sustain and consolidate a political programme for comprehensive democratization.

Notes and References

1. See the Uganda Government's Report to the Consultative Group (organized by the World Bank) which stresses structural constraints, 'among the most serious [being] infrastructure and technical expertise.' 28 May 1987, p. 8.

2. See, for example, A. I. MacBean, 1981, p. 76.

3. *Trade and Development*, 1986, p. 11.

4. Submission, 1986, para 29.

5. *The Economist*, 13 February 1988.

6. The best presentation of this position in recent years is by Akilagpa Sawyerr, 1988.

7. *Background to the Budget*, 1982–83.

8. Ibid., 1988–89, p. 11.

9. This is in no way an attempt to defend the actual types of expenditure in the budget – that is, in that miniscule portion of the budget after payment for oil, defence and debt servicing – but really an endeavour to direct the discussion to what I consider to be the principal issue.

10. The World Bank and the UNDP, 1989, p. 24.

11. That is my calculation from figures presented in the Budget, 1988–89. The Uganda Government, 1987a (p. 9), gave an even lower figure for 'the ratio of tax revenue to GDP – 3.5 per cent'.

12. Judith Brister, 1988, p. 18.

13. Uganda Government, 1987a, p. 6.

14. Treasury Circular No. ES 41/3, 22 August 1988.

15. Interview with Minister of Finance, 'The New Vision', 26 January 1989, p. 6.

16. *NOTU News*, 1989, p. 14.

17. Uganda Government, 1988.

18. *NOTU News*, op. cit.

19. In the literature are a few instances where, unlike the case of Uganda, demand management by the IMF has followed a period of real increase in demand and popular consumption. Thus, Charles Harvey argues that since demand cuts followed sustained increases in output, real wages and imports the duration and cost of austerity were low; Harvey, 1985, pp. 47–51.

20. Thus, the government's Policy Framework Paper stated: 'Consistent with the inflation objectives and the credit demands of the private sector, over the next three years the government plans to reduce substantially its net indebtedness to the domestic banking system. To this end, the government is committed to restrain the overall fiscal deficit on a commitment basis to 4.5 per cent of GDP in 1987/88 and to reduce it subsequently to 3.3 per cent of GDP by 1989/90.' Uganda Government, 1987a, p. 9.

21. Samir Amin's summing up: 'History proves that inequality encourages more parasitic consumption than saving, and that the highest rates of collective saving are obtained in the less inegalitarian societies' – is worth noting. Samir Amin, 1988, p. 167.

22. From the IMF's view point the infrastructure is meant to service the export–import trade, not the internal market – the agricultural, not the industrial sector – its function being that of export lanes leading to the sea, and not criss-crossing thoroughfares integrating different parts of the local economy.

23. Compare, for example, the deposit rate for long-term savings against lending rate for commercial loans: 28 per cent against 40 per cent in December 1986; 19 per cent against 22–25 per cent in July 1988. See, Background to the Budget 1988–89, Table 16, p. A20.

24. Uganda Economic Study Team, 1986, p. 46.

25. *Forward*, Vol. 7, Nos. 2 and 3, October, Kampala, Uganda, p. 7.

26. Uganda Government, 1987b, pp. 5, 6, 11: see also Uganda Government, 1987a.

27. The analysis that follows is based on empirical information collected by First Year political science students at Makerere University; it is my pleasure to record my debt to them.

28. In a survey of the industrial structure in Tanzania, Sam Wangwe argues convincingly that much of its problems are due to 'poor designing of projects and inappropriate technical choices detailed by sources of finance, not by the overvalued exchange rate'. See, Sam Wangwe, 1987, p. 159.

29. In his budget speech of 1987, 7 April, President Museveni remarked, 'A business class must decide whether it is historically relevant or not. A business class can be historically relevant or irrelevant – if it is assisting the economy to grow it is relevant, it is necessary. If it is a parasite, then it is an obstacle. So we must define what sort of businessmen we are. Are we enhancing the economic health of the country or are we parasites who only deplete the economic resources of the country' (pp. 5–6). My point is that the logic of the IMF 'conditionalities' is to give the 'parasitic' *mafutamingi* stratum control over the utilization of social savings!

30. Figures for industrial power sold by UEB (in m. kwh.) were: 1980: 84.7; 1981: 73.8; 1982: 99.2; 1983: 85.7; 1984: 73.8; 1985: 75.8; 1986: 40.8; 1987: 39.0. See,

Background to the Budget, 1988–89, Table 38, p. A43; Table 40, p. A45.

31. See *Forward*, op. cit. p. 8; Uganda Government, 1987b p. 11; and 1987a, p. 16.

32. Kenneth Hermelle, 1988, p. 24.

33. John Loxley, 'IMF, World Bank and sub-Saharan Africa,' in Kjell Havnevik, 1987, p. 53.

34. Just Faaland, (1987) in Kjell Havnevik, p. 123.

35. E. Maganya and O. Othman, 1988, p. 12.

36. For a discussion of the two issues, see M. Mamdani, 1976 chapters 2 and 4.

37. Vali Jamal and John Weeks, (1988) pp. 286–7.

38. Jennifer Sharpley, Stephen R. Lewis, 1988. Table 3, p. 18.

39. See, Clive Hamilton, 1984, pp. 38–9.

40. See Martin Fransman, 1984, p. 52; Richard Luedde-Neurath, 1980, p. 48.

41. Quoted in Leude-Neurath, 1980, p. 48; see also Stephen Haggard and Chung-In Moon, in J. R. Ruggie, 1983, pp. 185–7.

42. Hubert Schmitz, 1984; see also Charles A. Barone, 1983; R. Luedde-Neurath, 1984, p. 20; and Robert Wade, 1984.

43. Arun Gosh, 1988.

44. Interestingly, the World Bank's publications agree that, to the extent agricultural production has grown in Africa, it has been the result of more land being brought under cultivation by the application of more labour, not the result of increased productivity of labour. 'Most of the expansion in the 60s and 70s came about by area expansion. In relation to the rest of the world, Africa has fallen back very significantly in terms of productivity,' writes Rolf Gusten (1984, p. 55) of the East Africa Projects Department of the World Bank.

45. M. Mamdani, 1987, pp. 191–225.

46. Elsewhere (Mamdani 1988) I have discussed at some length the ambiguities and the struggle surrounding the role and definition of RCs in our society. See, 'NRA/NRM: Two Years,' Progressive Publishers, Kampala, 1988; also published as 'Uganda in Transition: Two Years of the NRA/NRM,' Third World Quarterly Review.

47. A. Sawyerr, op. cit., p. 32.

Bibliography

Amin, Samir (1988) 'A Note on the Concept of Delinking'. *Development and South–South Cooperation*, Vol. 1, No. 1.

Barone, C. A. (1983) 'Dependence, Marxist Theory and Salvaging the Idea of Capitalism in South Korea'. *Review of Radical Political Economy*, Vol. XV, No. 1.

Brister, J. (1988) 'The Cooking Pots are Broken'. *African Recovery*, Vol. 2.

Faaland, J. (1987) in Kjell J. Havnevik (ed.)

Fransman, M. (1984) 'Explaining the Success of Asian NICs: Incentives and Technology'. Sussex *IDS Bulletin*, Vol. 15, No. 2.

Gosh, A. (1988) 'Supply Side Economics: Is India Ready for the Recipe?' *Economic and Political Weekly*, 25 June.

Gusten, R. (1984) 'African Agriculture: Which Way Out of the Crisis?' *Rural Africana*, 19–20.

Haggard, S. and Chung-In Moon (1983) in J. R. Ruggie.

Hamilton, C. (1984) 'Class, State and Industrialisation in South Korea'. Sussex, *IDS Bulletin*, Vol. 15, No. 2.

Harvey, C. (1985) 'Successful Adjustment in Botswana', Sussex, *IDS Bulletin*, July.

Havnevik, Kjell J. (ed.) (1987) *The IMF and the World Bank in Africa. Conditionality, Impact and Alternatives*. Uppsala, Scandinavian Institute of African Studies.

Hermelle, K. (1988) Country Report on Mozambique, presented to SIDA, October.

Jamal, Vali and John Weeks (1988) 'The Vanishing Rural–Urban Gap in Sub-Saharan Africa,' *International Labour Review*, Vol. 127, No. 3.

Leudde-Neurath, R. (1980) 'Export Orientation in South Korea'. Sussex, *IDS Bulletin*, Vol. 12, No. 1.

—— (1984) 'State Intervention and DFI in South Korea'. Sussex, *IDS Bulletin*, Vol. 15, No. 2.

MacBean, A. I. (1981) 'Do Outward Policies Really Work?' Sussex, *IDS Bulletin*, Vol. 13, No. 1.

Maganya, E. and O. Othman (1988) 'The Debt Problem in the Context of the Third World'. University of Dar es Salaam, IDS.

Mamdani, M. (1976) *Politics and Class Formation in Uganda*. London, Heinemann.

—— (1987) 'Extreme but not Exceptional: Towards an Analysis of the Agrarian Question in Uganda'. *Journal of Peasant Studies*, Vol. 14, No. 2.

—— (1988) 'NRA/NRM: Two Years', Kampala, Progressive Publishers. Also published as 'Uganda in Transition'. *Third World Quarterly Review*.

NOTU News (1989) Letter to Prime Minister, Vol. 1, No. 1.

Ruggie, J. R. (1983) *The Antimonies of Interdependence: National Welfare and the International Division of Labour*. New York, Columbia University Press.

Sawyerr, A. (1988) 'The Politics of Adjustment Policy'. Khartoum, ECA/ICHD/88/29, 5–8 March.

Schmitz, H. (1984) 'Industrial Strategies in LDCs: Some Lessons of Historical Experience'. *Journal of Development Studies*, Vol. 21, No. 1.

Sharpley, J. and S. R. Lewis (1988) 'Kenya's Industrialisation, 1964–84'. Sussex, IDS Discussion Paper 242.

Uganda Government (1987a) Policy Framework Paper for 1987/88–1989/90. Presented to the Paris Conference, 8 May.

—— (1987b) Report to Consultative Group, 28 May.

—— (1988) Ministry of Finance, Circular No. IT/3/01/D, 6 June.

Wade, R. (1984) 'Dirigisme Taiwan-Style', Sussex, *IDS Bulletin*, Vol. 15, No. 2.

Wangwe, Sam (1987) 'Impact of the IMF/World Bank Philosophy in Tanzania' in Kjell J. Havnevik.

World Bank and UNDP (1989) Africa's Adjustment in the 1980s.

11. Mozambique: Economic Management and Adjustment Policies

Marc Wuyts

Introduction

This chapter explores the policy choices and constraints in managing adjustment policies in Mozambique – a country confronted by a deep economic crisis and ravaged by a war of aggression and of economic destabilization waged by the South African regime. The Economy Recovery Programme (ERP) – initiated in 1987 by the Mozambican authorities after negotiations with the IMF and the World Bank – provided an economic policy framework for adjustment policies to be implemented over the period 1987–89.

Economic reforms aim to restructure the patterns of accumulation and distribution within an economy, and consequently, such reforms affect the structure of its population's livelihoods. In this sense, macro-economic reforms can never be looked upon as merely a set of *neutral* policy measures aimed at achieving greater efficiency and economy in the allocation and use of resources. The *content* of economic reforms invariably matters in shaping the process of economic and social development as well as the balance of political forces. Macro-economic management sets the scene within which these developments take place. The question of the policy debate that informs such management, of the convergence and conflict of different interests that propel it, and of effective control over and the capacity for state action, are therefore key issues in the analysis of economic reforms. It is with these issues that this chapter is mainly concerned in looking at the experience of adjustment policies in Mozambique.

Hence, the primary concern here is not to provide account of the ERP experience up to date or to measure economic impact or social consequences; in any case, data are extremely scarce and often of doubtful quality. Whenever necessary, references will be given to the few analyses available on these matters.[1] Rather, it is the crucial issue of economic management in the context of adjustment policies that will be addressed. In doing so, it should be noted that the Mozambicans are of course in no way responsible for the interpretations of policy documents and/or arguments presented in this chapter.

The ERP provides an economic policy framework for macro-economic management which reflects a complex platform of different interests. At one level it is the outcome of an *internal* need for economic reforms: that is, the need to reverse the decline in production and to tackle the question of economic rehabilitation in a context of war. At another level it reflects the demand for 'adjustment' from international creditors at a point where the external payments gap reached crisis proportions and creditworthiness had collapsed. IMF and World Bank conditionality played and continues to play an important role in the design and management of adjustment policies.

Both views on adjustment do not necessarily coincide, and indeed there is considerable scope for sharp divergences of view on the content of adjustment policies. But neither is it merely a question of a simple opposition between two adversaries in negotiations, each with a relatively homogeneous policy stance.

The IMF/World Bank view on adjustment is well-known and widely debated and need not be elaborated here. Suffice to stress one point which is of interest to the arguments developed in this chapter. The IMF and the World Bank tend to present their policy stance on adjustment as a matter of technical economic necessity: cost and efficiency rather than effectiveness (content) are being highlighted and debated as the crux of the problem. Consequently, adjustment policies are located within the domain of technical economic expertise and hence, planning, decision making, resource allocation and the evaluation of performance must come to be seen in management terms. This conception of adjustment as a set of neutral policies for greater efficiency is instrumental in creating a domain where technical expertise can come to dominate political debate.[2,3]

The question of the internal need for economic reforms requires further clarification. In fact, conservative economists in the West tend to see economic reforms that involve the recognition or development of the market as evidence of the inherent superiority of 'market forces', whatever the context in which they are set. The question of developing viable socialist planning methods that recognize the market where it exists, and aim to intervene to influence such markets and to incorporate them within broader strategic objectives, is therefore put aside. Such planning methods are, however, essential in poor socialist countries with extensive peasant farming sectors, for all such Third World countries contain markets that must be recognized and acted upon, not ignored.[4]

In the case of Mozambique the pressure for economic reforms gathered momentum as the Frelimo Party prepared for its Fourth Congress (held in April 1983). The rapid escalation of the war brought home the need for organizing a war economy. But also, and importantly, the war *accentuated* some real weaknesses and vulnerabilities inherent in the system of central planning and of bureaucratic state finance operative from 1977 onwards (when the Third Congress laid down the strategy of socialist development). The question of economic reforms became a major point on the political agenda as a result of these developing contradictions. In the following pages the issue of the internal demand for economic reforms as a background to as well as a prelude to the ERP, will be briefly analysed.

Subsequently three major issues concerning the question of economic management in the context of ERP will be discussed. These issues highlight the need to evaluate 'adjustment' policies in a broader framework of economic management that reflects specific interest and which needs to respond to the concrete political and economic imperatives.

First I shall address the question as to the relation between the economy and defence and its implications for adjustment policies. Adjustment in a context of war must come to terms with the necessity to organize for a war economy, both with respect to the character of adjustment policies as well as to the rate at which recovery can take place. This issue, it will be argued, is not properly recognized in IMF or World Bank reports although the Mozambican authorities clearly see it as a prime concern.

The question of public provisioning and of sustaining/rehabilitating livelihoods in a context of adjustment policies in an environment of war is next considered. This raises not only the issue of preserving the socialist character of needs provisioning, but also the question of the timing and the scope of state intervention in dealing with the adverse effects of the war.

Finally, the question as to what extent the ERP and its dependence on foreign funding engender an effective erosion of the state's capacity to manage the economy in general, and the public sector in particular, will be dealt with. This entails not merely the restrictions imposed on national economic management by IMF/World Bank conditionality and a bewildering maze of micro-restrictions on the use of foreign aid funds by different agencies – governmental or non-governmental alike. It also involves the pressure to shift control over public expenditures away from the general state administration towards donor-funded and donor-controlled selective interventions.

Economic reforms: an internal necessity

The year 1983 – in which Frelimo's Fourth Congress was held – marked a critical watershed in the post-independence development of Mozambique; not only because the Fourth Congress was to make an assessment of the experience to pursue a socialist strategy since 1977 – the year in which the Third Congress laid down the task of developing a socialist society.[5] The period 1977–81 had witnessed radical changes in the organization of the economy in an attempt to construct a centrally planned economy rooted (principally, but not exclusively) in the dominance of the state sector within production and exchange.[6] This took place against the background of modest growth rates, which heralded a marked recovery from the initial post-independence crisis years of 1975–76.[7] From 1981 onwards, however, war combined with drought adversely affected production and people's livelihoods, leading to widespread deprivation and famine along with the enormous costs in terms of human suffering and material loss resulting from the brutality with which the MNR waged its war.[8]

Hence, the Fourth Congress would need to come to terms as well with the question of coping with a severe economic crisis and of organizing for a war economy. Linked to this, there was a growing realization that the problem was not simply that of falling production levels and widespread collapses in livelihoods as a result of imperialist aggression. There was as well a growing awareness that the event of war coupled with drought had brought to the fore some real weaknesses inherent in the system of economic management developed since 1977. This became the central focus of the debate on economic policy shortly before and during the Fourth Congress. Two points are of specific interest in this respect.

First, there was a growing concern that the effective capacity of the state to control the use of the economic surplus and to direct overall economic development had become progressively undermined by uncontrolled patterns of private accumulation within parallel market circuits, which in turn eroded the cohesiveness of state action itself. Hence, while in principle the state, through its central planning, exerted an all-powerful control over the economy, in practice this control tended to become largely illusory. Furthermore, there was also some recognition of the facts that: large-scale monetary imbalances were occurring within economic exchanges between the state and the wider economy; there was rampant inflation in the parallel markets; and rapid depreciation of the *metical* (the Mozambican currency) to the point where it provoked a widespread retreat into barter or towards the use of foreign currency, were in part the result of the character of planning itself. More specifically, large-scale public sector deficits financed through money creation were seen as a major element that destabilized the exchange between the state sector and the wider economy.[9] Consequently, there was a strong demand to impose financial discipline on the state sector so as to revalorize the *metical* and to restore normal exchange relations between the state sector and the wider economy.[10]

Secondly, and closely related to the first point, there was a strong pressure to shift back resource allocation in favour of the peasantry and also of private enterprise in order to compensate for the crowding-out effect resulting from the earlier planning emphasis on state sector expansion. Hence the demand to restore a proper balance in resource allocation across the different sectors of the economy (state sector, private enterprise, household production and co-operatives). This demand was also seen to be more in line with the directives for socialist development as formulated by the Third Congress in 1977.[11]

The central issue concerning the context of economic reforms therefore concentrated on the question of *how* to shift state resources towards the support of the wider economy so as to achieve a more balanced development in the context of a managed economy.

This question is of great importance in context of economic reforms in a socialist transition. Any attempt towards the partial decentralization of the patterns and location of accumulation outside the state sector inevitably poses the question of in whose hands, and within what form of organization of the social relations of production, accumulation and, hence, development will occur.[12] The reaffirmation of the importance of the directives of the Third Congress was indeed most relevant in this respect. The Third Congress documents had stressed that a strategy of socialist development had to come to terms with the inherited uneven development of colonial capitalism and, particularly, with the predominance of the peasantry as producers and as suppliers of labour power. Given this fact, as well as the limited managerial capabilities available within the emerging state enterprise sector, the need to mobilize productive forces in the economy would require the support of household production as well as leaving space for private enterprise. Hence, the need to maintain a proper balance between the state sector and the wider economy was recognized as necessary in order to guarantee the social reproduction of the different sectors in overall development. But the Third Congress documents also stressed the simultaneous need for transforming production relations in this process, both within and outside the realm of the state sector. Socialist development was to be based on central planning and the construction of a strong state sector on the one hand, and, on the other, also entailed the mobilization of local initiative in institutions of a socialist character (co operatives and communal villages) located outside the realm of the state sector, but supported by it. Hence, the question of the balancing intersectoral resource flows between the state sector and the wider economy was located in a conception of reproduction with transformation.[13]

The question, therefore, was not merely that of maintaining a proper balance in the intersectoral resource flows between invariant sectors so as to guarantee their social reproduction (possibly expanding at different rates of growth), but also that of transforming the character of production along a broad front – both within and outside the state sector – in the process. The Fourth Congress put this question partly back on the agenda in an attempt to compensate for the overemphasis on state sector development witnessed over the period 1977–83; and this, against a background of economic crisis provoked by war and drought.

The immediate concern was to recuperate production and finance the war. The overriding priority was correctly seen to be that of increasing production on all fronts. The question of how the character of planning and its management of market mechanisms influence the direction of production responses in the economy was, however, left rather vague.

A prominent view of the time – which in part, informed the direction of subsequent internal economic reforms – undoubtedly called for a retreat from planning through partial deregulation, allowing the momentum inherent in parallel markets more room for manoeuvre. In short, this view sought to effect a shift in resources from the state sector towards the wider economy by imposing greater financial discipline on the state budget and on state enterprises to avoid the negative consequences of the crowding-out effect and, by relying principally on market forces, to reallocate resources thus set free within the economy at large. Hence, the concentration of resources on the state sector combined with excessive reliance on state regulation of trade were seen to be the major impediments to increasing production. Enforcing greater efficiency on the state sector and allowing market forces greater room for manoeuvre were identified as the twin components of economic reforms to deal with the crisis.[14]

To achieve economy, efficiency and effectiveness in the public sector was undoubtedly of great importance. From 1977 onwards the system of economic management was characterized by its emphasis on state-centred accumulation. That is, economic policy mainly concentrated on an expansion of the state sector through the mobilization of domestic as well as foreign resources. Central planners were much less concerned with achieving economy in the use of such resources. Three characteristic features underscored this particular planning practice.

Firstly, to a large extent the main emphasis in planning fell on investment planning. That is, the main concern was with the expansion of fixed capital formation in the state sector.[15] The state budget was the principal instrument to distribute investment finance and the material resources for investment – which largely had to be imported – to all sectors of the economy. Material investment planning therefore became a major method by which the state intended to play the economy as a whole, and to develop the balance between the different sectors. In fact, government investment constituted virtually all the recorded investment in the economy in the late 1970s and early 1980s.[16] The effects of this investment pattern, as the Fourth Congress was to note in 1983, were particularly dramatic in agriculture. Ninety per cent of agricultural investment in the period 1977–83 went to the state sector, two per cent to the co-operatives, and virtually none to small-scale 'family' farming. And, within the state sector itself, investment in agriculture and in industry was concentrated on what were known a 'big projects' rather than smaller scale activities.[17]

Secondly, production planning was done by means of material balances. Hence, the production of goods and of services within the state sector was co-ordinated and regulated through volume planning: the principal concern of state enterprises and of public sector provisioning of social services was with production targets. Volume planning as distinct from cash planning puts the emphasis on meeting targets in the production of goods or the delivery of services, but it also provides less of an incentive to control costs and improve efficiency.[18] It concentrates on mobilizing resources to meet imperative planning targets, rather than on achieving economy in the use of such resources. Volume planning leaves the planning system highly vulnerable to unexpected increases in the cost of production due to price increases or to over-optimistic assumptions concerning planning norms on input use.

Thirdly, and linked with the second point, budget constraint within the state sector was essentially *soft*.[19] The corresponding financial system was characterized by what is often referred to as bureaucratic state finance – a system in which all surpluses of state enterprises are centralized in the budget and all losses financed through the budget (planned subsidies) or through credit creation by the state bank (unplanned losses). Money, therefore, is essentially passive with respect to financing production and investment in the state-centred accumulation might become self-defeating in its own terms, that design or by default – inevitably spill over into the wider economy.[20]

The central problem concerning these monetary imbalances is not, however, merely a question of monetary policy. It is not sufficient to strive for greater financial discipline within the state sector through introducing the need for cash planning along with volume planning, so as to achieve greater economy and efficiency as well as effectiveness in public sector management. Such measures are indeed important, but need to be placed within a broader context of planning intersectoral resource flows within the economy in a perspective of socialist construction, based on reproduction with transformation. The latter point was left more vaguely in the economic debate around the Fourth Congress.

The prior practice of state-centred accumulation *de facto* implied that the question of financing socialist development boiled down to rallying resources from the wider economy behind the accelerated development of the state sector. The central planning issue in this case appears to be to find mechanisms through which the greatest marketed surplus can be obtained from the peasant economy at the least expense to the state sector. The basic logic inherent in this policy is one that propels the state sector to organize its interventions in the wider economy by building on the best in terms of generating this marketed surplus, and hence, the tendency will be to accentuate existing patterns of differentiation among the peasantry and to favour the better endowed regions. This is the logical outcome of a policy which – by design or default – centres around increasing the quantitative net-intersectoral resource flows between the state sector and the peasant sector at the expense of the latter.[21]

Policy-makers in Mozambique became increasingly aware that this policy of state-centred accumulation might become self-defeating in its own terms, that is, in rallying resources behind the expansion of the state sector. The fact that the state economy appeared to 'lose its grip' over the wider economy was brought home very vividly through the decline in the official marketing of cash crops; the rampant inflation in parallel markets, and the development of speculative commercial capital that gained strength in the economy. But the extent to which state-centred accumulation effectively implied accentuating social differentiation in the countryside, and the mechanisms through which this came about, was much less debated or understood.

The fact that private trade occupied an important mediating role in the exchange between the state sector and the peasantry, and that this position allowed them to alter the terms of trade within the parallel exchange with the peasantry, as well as to concentrate this exchange on the richer peasantry and within the better endowed agricultural zones (notwithstanding formal state rationing of available supplies across different regions) became a powerful mechanism in propelling differentiation among the peasantry in the midst of an acute goods famine. Private commercial farmers and the better-off peasantry managed to survive and maintain, or even expand, their productive capacity. A large sector of the peasantry, however, saw their productive capacity severely eroded for lack of any meaningful support through market relations and state assistance. Private trade, rather than production, benefited most. The state, in contrast, lost control over markets and became itself dependent on the parallel circuits to secure the supply of food.[22]

The strong pressures at the Fourth Congress to shift resource allocation back in favour of the peasantry and of private enterprise reflected an objective necessity to confront the contradictions produced by state-centred accumulation.

But the momentum inherent in these uncontrolled patterns of private accumulation in the parallel circuits was itself an important element behind a demand for deregulation. Indeed, if such a shift in resource allocation were principally effected through market forces, the private farmers and the richer peasantry would be in a much better position to respond favourably to market signals, and hence, would be better able to consolidate and to build on the advantage already obtained. In contrast, the poorer peasantry would have less to gain from improved producer prices and from increased access to production inputs through the market, since they lacked financial resources and, furthermore, their production base was run down through neglect of state support or destroyed by the war. So, to integrate these sections of the peasantry within an exchange with the state sector would require a combination of proper market signals and a shift in resources from the state sector, through peasant associations aimed at rehabilitating their productive base and stabilizing their livelihoods. This would require a different type of planning, which involves managing exchange relations and explicit state support to local producer organizations.[23]

Hence, while the Fourth Congress stressed the importance of shifting resource allocation to meet the needs of the peasantry at large as well as of private farmers, the specific mechanisms through which this was to be done were left extremely vague. More specifically, whether economic reforms would require a partial retreat from planning so as to allow production to recover under the impulse of market forces, or whether planning itself needed to be conceptualized differently, including its role in terms of managing market relations, was also left vague. In part, the overriding priority to increasing production on all fronts set aside the concern with the character of the development of production relations through which it was to be achieved. Consequently, the macro-economic context in which such shift in resources was to be effected was not fully mapped out. Clearly, this also reflected the fact that this pattern of private accumulation within the parallel markets had become a powerful social force to be reckoned with.

The Fourth Congress, therefore, defined a new terrain within which policies of economic reforms needed to be constructed. Various, and often conflicting, social forces rallied behind the demand for shifting resources out of the state sector towards the wider economy. The need to re-establish exchange relations was not itself in question. The critical issue concerned the location of accumulation outside the state sector. In this respect the Congress documents remained ambiguous, leaving room for various interpretations as to what constitutes a policy of aiding small-scale production and of allowing private enterprise more room for manoeuvre. For some, therefore, the immediate policy necessity consisted of a tactical retreat from socialist transformation, by allowing production to recover under the impulse of private enterprise within the unofficial economy. The paramount importance of recuperating production in the depth of economic crisis gave this view a powerful position within economic policy discussions. Opposed to this, however, was also the recognition that the imperatives of the war and of preserving the socialist character of development required the continued intervention of the state within the economy.[24]

Both these themes have been evident in economic policy debates and initiatives since 1983. With the initiation of the Economic Recovery Programme, World Bank and IMF conditionalities came to play a prominent role in this policy debate.

Defence and economy

The relation between the economy and defence is of central importance for a country at war. This is not merely a question as to how to restrain and ration consumption so as to release resources to finance the war effort (a point to which I shall return in the next section). It also concerns production, and particularly, peasant production. In Mozambique, there has been much public discussion on this issue. In presenting the ERP, the Prime Minister argued that: 'No war is won just by soldiers on the battlefield, without production. Every country at war finds ways of combining war with production. We cannot separate one from another.'[25] Hence, economic reforms needed to address directly the issue of defence.

As shown in the previous section, the experience with state-centred planning had left the majority of the peasantry economically very vulnerable. Subject to the uncontrolled patterns of private accumulation inherent in the parallel economy, social and regional differentiation had become accentuated in a context of economic crisis and goods famine. The war brought home the need to re-establish the alliance with the peasantry. To enlist and consolidate the support of the peasantry within the war effort; to obtain marketed surpluses of export crops and of food, to support peasants' livelihoods and survival through the supply of essential consumer goods and services as well as of basic tools, implements and agricultural inputs, required that the state sector showed itself capable of re-establishing an effective exchange with the peasantry in the context of a managed economy.

This involved a move towards a model of market intervention, in association with deregulation and decentralization of some economic decisions towards the regional level.[26] On the one hand, this implied financial measures to ensure greater financial discipline within the state sector and to stabilize and revalorize the currency. It involved price reforms and associated market liberalization along with the devaluation of the *metical*. But, it also involved a move towards more decentralized planning and greater use of the state sector in support of small-scale production and trade. Furthermore it implied the growing recognition of the importance of channelling state resources to rehabilitate the productive base of the peasantry.

In fact:

An estimated 5.9 million Mozambicans – about one million families in rural and urban areas – are currently facing food shortages because of drought and terrorist activities. Of these, 3.3 million are severely affected, including 1.1 million displaced inside the country. In addition, about 2.6 million people are affected by food shortages in the commercial networks. A further 700,000 people are displaced in neighbouring countries.[27]

The enormous scale of the destabilization caused by the war has led the Mozambican authorities to formulate an Emergency Programme in order to provide a structural response to the social and economic consequences of the war. Indeed, it is argued that:

> the traditional prescriptions for relief aid are alone insufficient to break out of the emergency situation. The emergency in Mozambique presents unique features: chronic countrywide destabilisation from external forces, large sections of the population displaced, and constant shifting of the areas of natural disasters and aggression. The problems are structural, not transitory.[28]

Hence, the need to manage the underlying crisis simultaneously with short-term relief interventions, as well as with a more sustained programme to ensure the social and economic rehabilitation of livelihoods, to reconstruct the physical infrastructure destroyed by the South African backed MNR and to reintegrate displaced people into communities, as well as to assist them to prevent further disruption. Furthermore, the Mozambican authorities assert that 'emergency activities moving in such directions will improve and facilitate integration with the ERP'.[29]

In Mozambique, therefore, there is a government operational strategy emerging that seeks to combine the Economic Recovery Programme, the Emergency Programme and development activities (mainly defined as new investments in economic infrastructure) into a comprehensive strategy. This involves a concept of partial liberalization as a means to an end, as well as a more structural approach towards conceptualizing the use of state intervention and support *vis-à-vis* the wide economy. The essence of this comprehensive strategy is to cope with the relation of defence and economy in a context of acute crisis.

The economic crisis has, however, also produced a situation in which the country became heavily dependent on foreign grants and loans to finance its most essential imports. The question of IMF/World Bank conditionalities, as well as of various pressures of different donor organizations (governmental or non-governmental alike), is of central importance in assessing the management context in Mozambique. A salient feature, which characterizes most of the Western donor agencies, is the way in which they refuse, or fail, to address the relation between defence and production.

The World Bank's view on the ERP puts the emphasis squarely on liberalization and privatization. These will 'establish the conditions for more rapid and more efficient economic growth in the medium and longer term when the security situation and other exogenous constraints have eased.'[30] The interesting feature of this statement is the view of the 'security' situation as an *exogenous* constraint. Clearly, what is meant here is not that it is externally generated as a result of South African aggression, but rather, that it concerns an exogenous shock which slows down the rate at which adjustment can take place. The question of organizing the economy for the war is clearly not contained in this view. It is indeed remarkable that the World Bank's prescriptions for Mozambique follow the same standard package of policy measures as those prescribed for such countries as Tanzania or Ghana, notwithstanding the fact that Mozambique is confronted by a devastating war of aggression.

The World Bank repeatedly stresses the importance of shifting resource allocation in favour of rural producers – in particular of private farmers and the peasantry. This is to be done principally by getting prices right and by relying on market mechanisms. Moreover, it advocates further privatization of state farm land as well as of equipment.[31] Undoubtedly, most state economic relations with small-scale producers must by definition be done through the market and, hence, the re-establishment of exchange relations in a context of a stable currency is an important element of any economic strategy which aims to shift resources towards the peasantry. But two further conditions are needed here as well.

Firstly:

> A planning capacity has to be developed to manage local markets flexibly, further improving market intervention, coordinating state policy towards local markets and managing deregulation in favour of local producers.[32]

This requires a considerable degree of decentralization of planning within the state sector itself and the greater use of state economic power to intervene in markets so as to ensure that resource allocation favours production rather than trade, and family agriculture at large rather than private commercial farmers and a few better-off peasants.

Secondly, there is the central issue of mobilizing locally-based initiative and organizational capacities to enable a broadly-based recovery programme in production and to enlist the support of the peasantry in the war effort. This points at the role of peasants' associations and co-operatives in managing resource use at the local level. Mackintosh argued that:

> The Mozambican government has reduced its level of commitment to cooperatives as a method of transforming production, and resources and assistance have been going rather to private farmers. However, just as private farmers can benefit from an organized relation to the state, in terms of exchanges of produce for services and investment goods, so cooperatives and producers' associations can do the same. Cooperatives can also appropriate some of the benefits from both political pressure and trading activity which are at present going to large private operators. There therefore appears to be a very good economic case, in wartime conditions where markets are bound to be thin, for putting state resources into building

up organisations of small producers, to operate on their own behalf and assist the distribution of resources. The success of the urban consumer cooperatives provides an example of this potential.[33]

Both these elements – the need for active state planning which is responsive to the needs of rural producers at large and the importance of locally-based initiative and organizational capacity to manage resource use – are largely absent in World Bank reports. Deregulation is projected as an end in itself and state production is seen mostly as crowding-out private initiative. The fact that a policy which aims to rehabilitate and support rural production on a broad front will need to combine the mobilization of locally-based initiative and organizational capability (and not just the private initiative of some), with active state support, is therefore not considered in any depth. This question is, however, undoubtedly of central importance – both economically and politically – in order to articulate the relation between defence and the economy. The policy debate in Mozambique on the necessary interlinkage of the Economic Recovery Programme and the Emergency Programme clearly manifests the importance of this concern.

The substantial involvement of various donor agencies – multilateral, governmental and non-governmental – in providing funds and material resources for the Emergency Programme does not necessarily imply their better understanding of the relations of economy and defence. In fact, in many cases, the war is virtually equated with a 'natural disaster' – be it man-made – and hence necessitating relief aid. The question of emergency aid, however, is often delinked from any wider structural approach to economic rehabilitation, and, not uncommonly, rigidly separated from it. Hanlon argues this very forcefully as follows:

> The Mozambique 'emergency' is unusual because it is not a natural disaster where it is only necessary to provide food and tents until the flood waters recede and people can rebuild. Instead, Mozambique faces a permanent structural emergency in which South Africa uses state terrorism to try to destroy Mozambique's economic base. This means continued destruction and continued refugee flows, and it means massive rebuilding. Thus Mozambique has tried to link 'emergency' assistance to rebuilding. Donors have proved unable to cope. For example, many donors are paying for a massive airlift of food, seeds, and clothing to dislocated people in district towns; in some cases the airlift is needed because of security problems, while in others roads are damaged (or mined, or bridges are destroyed). Mozambique has asked for road building equipment, which would be cheaper than an airlift in some areas, but donors prefer to pay extra for the airlift because an airlift is 'emergency' and road building is 'development'. In some areas, the airlift is needed because Renamo terrorists attack food lorries. Mozambique has asked for 'protection vehicles' – armor plated lorries to carry troops to guard the food envoys, which would cost less than an airlift. Most donors say no, because this is 'non-lethal military assistance' and not emergency.[34]

In a similar vein, donor agencies involved in relief often prefer importing clothing, blankets, tools, and so on, rather than aiding local industry to produce them and buying from local firms.[35]

In summary, while inside Mozambique a policy debate has developed since 1983 concerning the need to develop responsive economic policies to cope with the relation of defence and the economy in a context of a deep economic crisis and the collapse of livelihoods, the donor community has done little to support such a process. Rather, its activities have tended to deflect policies away from this critical issue and to fragment the cohesiveness of government action – a point which will be dealt with in the last section.

Adjustment and basic needs

The Mozambican government is faced with pressures and choices, not only in economic management, but also in its social policies. Economic reforms in a context of a war undoubtedly pose sharp questions as to their social implications. This was and is definitely the case in the context of the ERP which has brought about sharp rises in the cost of living as well as cuts in public expenditures on health and education.[36]

The issue of preserving basic consumption levels while releasing resources for the war effort is a central priority for a country at war. In quite a different context and in a different time, Keynes – in his 1940 pamphlet *How to Pay for the War* – showed brilliantly how the resources to finance Britain's war effort were to be released without excessive social hardship by a combination of compulsory savings, a wage freeze, price controls, subsidized basic rations and family allowances.[37] This requires a strongly managed economy which seeks to preserve basic needs while squeezing luxury consumption to release resources. This also involves a comprehensive rationing system to secure basic consumption levels across the population at large.

In fact, the early planning experience in Mozambique was based on a principle not dissimilar from Keynes' basic ideas, although in a different context and for a different purpose. Socio-economic planning aimed to release resources to finance rapid economic development while securing basic needs. Hence, the supply of consumer goods, which fell short of demand at official prices, was rationed according to a quota system (relative to population size) across districts, while in Maputo a more comprehensive rationing system was set up from 1980 onwards. The provision of social services witnessed radical changes. For example, in health care, resources for investment and service provision were shifted in relative, and at some points, in absolute terms, from large to small and from centre to periphery: from central city hospitals towards the provinces; from complex medical interventions to simpler procedures; from doctor's work to that of para-medical staff, and from curative to preventive care.[38] Furthermore, to extend the reach of basic-needs provisioning across the population, social policy sought to combine central planning and state provisioning with a system of partially self-financed self-provisioning at community level. Consumer co-operatives, rather than state shops, proved to be more effective in developing organizational capabilities to ration goods among their members. Similarly, in health care, village health workers – financed by the local community – provided the lowest tier in a national health service. Local labour was mobilized to build a school, a clinic or a meeting hut. These developments – which were not devoid of problems – did amount to the partial decentralization of the management of basic-needs provisioning, including public goods, outside the realm of, but supported by the state sector, and involving the participation of local communities. There was, however, undoubtedly a problem with this, resulting from the non-correspondence between a social policy which aimed to decentralize needs-provisioning towards local communities on the one hand, and an economic policy which effectively centralized resources on state sector expansion, on the other.[39]

The war has brought about savage destruction by the MNR terrorists of health posts, schools, shops and other social infrastructure. This, combined with the massive displacement of people and the destruction of their livelihoods, has led to a situation of widespread famine and deprivation. The dimension of needs-provisioning in the context of economic reforms coupled with emergency interventions is therefore of prime importance. This requires an approach which integrates distribution with production in managing economic reforms. This process proves to be very contradictory and subject to considerable pressures from the donor community.

The IMF and World Bank exert considerable pressure to restructure needs-provisioning in the context of a two-tier economy.[40] The upper tier – propelled by liberalization, price reforms and the imposition of greater financial discipline – concerns needs-provisioning constrained by the ability to pay. Effective demand – that is, demand backed by income – determines access to consumer goods and services in this case. The lower tier consists of 'safety nets' aimed to protect vulnerable groups in the process of adjustment. Such interventions consist of special programmes of targeted needs-provisioning for the destitute. The philosophy behind this approach is quite distinct from the concept of a generalized system of needs-provisioning based on the intensity of need rather than on the ability to pay – a concept which underscored social planning in Mozambique. This approach is also quite different from Keynes' prescriptions as to how to finance a war while preserving basic needs. The latter view also puts the emphasis on generalized forms of rationing rather than on safety nets.

In fact, the logic of the IMF/World Bank position is based on two assumptions: 1) that the structural adjustment programme effectively establishes the conditions for efficient economic growth in the medium and longer term, and that the benefits of such growth will spread across the population at large; and 2) that in the short-run the adjustment policies may adversely affect certain vulnerable groups as a result of the process of restructuring. More particularly, a policy which aims to get prices right and, through this, shift resource allocation in favour of rural development, may initially hit hard on the poorer strata within urban centres, as well as on workers laid off in the pursuit of efficiency. Hence the need for temporary safety nets to smooth the period of transition. Stated differently, the upper-tier structures the path towards efficient resource allocation in the medium/longer run, while the lower-tier concerns short-term interventions to ease the process of restructuring. The latter is supposed to phase itself out as the benefits of growth trickle down over time. This – in short – appears to me to be the basic philosophy on adjustment and its social implications underlying World Bank action.

Leaving aside the questionable character of these assumptions in general, when applied to Mozambique they completely ignore the most central issue: namely, that the country is at war. This is plainly clear from the following statement by the IMF concerning the ERP:

> [The] economy's response to even these strong policy initiatives will probably not be sufficient to yield a sustainable growth and balance of payments outcome in the programme period (1987–1990). Nevertheless, the reform and adjustment measures provide a framework for more effective utilization of both domestic and external resources in support of structural and institutional changes which, *once the security situation improves*, can lead the economy to sustainable growth.[41] [My emphasis.]

The point is, that the economy itself needs to be organized to support defence so as to improve the 'security situation'. This is the central issue of economic policy in Mozambique today, and it requires a policy package that interlinks defence, production and needs-provisioning.

In the previous section, I argued that the rehabilitation of production, and particularly of rural production, cannot merely rely on improving price signals and on channelling resources to rural producers through market forces alone. It is necessary to re-establish the exchange with the peasantry through market mechanisms, but this needs to be done within a context of a strongly managed economy in which state economic power is effectively used to direct resource allocation towards a broad-based programme of rehabilitation. Economic rehabilitation, development and emergency activities need to interlock within a macro-management context. Needs-provisioning plays an important part in this context. Donor pressures towards establishing a two-tier economy effectively separate relief (emergency) activities from economic rehabilitation and development, rather than integrating them.

A case in point is food aid. Donor agencies often employ the distinction between regular (structural) food aid and emergency or relief aid. Mozambique relies on both for most of its (marketed) food supply. The former is channelled through the normal distribution network (including the rationing/quota system) and sold at a price determined by the counter value of the imports (even if it concerns grants). Successive devaluation brought about a rapid rise in food prices to the point at which many urban consumers can no longer afford to buy their rations.[42] The growing incidence of malnutrition puts pressure on relief aid through various selective programmes of supplementary feeding, which often target certain members of a family while excluding others. Donor actions in health care follow the same track. There are strong pressures to switch towards selective programmes of health care, such as those for immunization, essential drugs, diarrhoeal disease control and so on, each with their own separate funding and their own imposed structures.[43]

The basic issue is that the war necessitates the rehabilitation of livelihoods on a broad scale. This involves tackling both the production side and the needs-provisioning aspect at the same time. The notion of a two-tier economy implies a concept of so-called vulnerable groups which need temporary relief until such time that economic growth trickles down to them. Such a notion provides little guidance when the basic task is to reconstruct livelihoods destroyed in a war. Relief needs to be an integral element of such reconstruction, which also tackles the rehabilitation of production at the same time.

Donor 'assistance' and public sector management

Managing economic reforms in socialist development in conditions of a war of aggression requires coherent and cohesive state planning and action. The basic issue is not a retreat from planning, but a different approach. The components of such an approach are: more decentralized, and popularly-based planning and control of accumulation; close interlinking of rehabilitation, emergency and development activities with respect to production and needs-provisioning; and an emphasis on intervention in the markets as a tool of planning.[44]

Mozambique's dependence on foreign aid and debt relief to finance its essential imports as well as its public expenditures implies that donor agencies' preferences exert considerable pressures on state planning. IMF and World Bank conditionalities as well as multiple micro-restrictions on the use of donor funds can influence the content of economic and social policies, as shown in previous sections. But donor actions can also seriously impair the capacity for state action in terms of its organizational ability to manage public expenditures in particular, and the public sector at large.

One aspect of this problem that may appear trivial, but is far from it, is:

> ... the assault of the donor agencies on the professional resources that Mozambique can muster at the crucial central planning and policy level. Clearly no agency is prepared to make funds available without having a say in how these are to be used. Up to a point that is reasonable. But a few moments thought should make it clear that there is a world of difference between establishing a policy and executing it with in-house funds, and having to resell it to a plethora of different agencies with different philosophies, methods and constraints. Time wasted by officials at central level is in fact one of the scarcer resources.[45]

This problem, already apparent before the ERP, has amplified and assumed a new dimension since the ERP has been initiated. This new dimension concerns the issue of the brain-drain of more professional cadres out of the public sector.

The ERP *de facto* implied the imposition of cash limits on public sector borrowing, and hence, on public sector expenditures on salaries and wages. The steep devaluations of the *metical* and the price inflation of consumer goods rapidly eroded public sector incomes. This has led to a brain-drain from the public sector, the extent of which is little documented. This flow of professionals out of the public sector did not, however, involve a move towards private sector employment. In fact, the market for professional skills, technical or administrative, is relatively limited in the private sector. It concerns mainly bigger private enterprises which normally had sufficient cadres (in the specific circumstances of Mozambique) and whose incomes were also subject to the steep rise in the cost of living in a way similar to public sector employees. The real brain-drain takes place out of both public and private sector employment towards employment with donor agencies. Salaries in the latter sector are often set in dollars and therefore remain insulated against exchange rate devaluations.

Professionals move towards donor agencies' employment not only because of better income prospects, but also because they are so much better equipped in terms of transport, documentation, typewriters, computers, and so on. It is indeed an educational experience for any visitor to Mozambique to see the sharp contrast between a Ministry of Health, where not uncommonly even paper and pencils are scarce, and the offices of UNICEF with its modern typewriters and computers, documentation centre and transport facilities.

The growing market for employment of local professionals by donor agencies reveals an important trend. There is a marked tendency for donor agencies to refrain from supporting the general public administration and developing its managerial capabilities. Instead, donor agencies favour selective support to specific programmes often requiring their own institutional set-up and management. And, not uncommonly, this management is shifted under donor control. For example, in health care, the emphasis did not merely shift from supporting a general health service towards selective interventions, but it also implied a shift away from the Ministry of Health towards UNICEF in terms of management. Hanlon comments on this tendency as follows:

If and when the donors leave, who will train teachers, build roads, run health posts, provide agricultural extension, and so on? In other words, who will help rural development? Who will support the peasants? The answer, of course, is the government, and the Mozambican government has shown a very high commitment to providing services and assistance to those who need it most. But the effect of donor practices is to reduce the capacity of Mozambique's government to help those in need. Already weak government and private structures are bypassed, undercut, and overloaded so that they cannot cope. In other words, donors are making Mozambique dependent on aid.[46]

Non-governmental organizations – of which there are more than a hundred working in Mozambique – often amplify this tendency.

> Most try to have independent programmes working directly with 'the people' or 'the poorest of the poor'. Many distrust all governments, and make it a matter of honour not to work with governments. A few are openly hostile to the government; some are simply dismissive; both groups refuse to give resources to government and try to bypass government structures. They may help a few individual peasants (and feel better by doing so), but they reduce the ability of the government to help a larger number. When the project has all the cars and the district does not, it will be the project staff, not government people, who are able to visit the villages.[47]

Some NGOs – in contrast – realize that expressed needs in Mozambique often prove closer to the people than what NGOs try to do, and therefore they tend to support government action, rather than bypass it.

In summary, although most foreign aid in theory concerns the financing of public expenditures, in practice donor actions often severely erode the cohesiveness and capability for public sector management by the Mozambican authorities. This by itself is a serious impediment to the capacity of Mozambican authorities to manage their economic reforms in a context of war, apart from the fact of donor pressures on the content of such reforms.

Notes and references

1. Apart from official documents by the Mozambican authorities, the World Bank or the IMF, few sources are available which discuss the ERP. Two useful references are Hermele (1988) and Marshall (1988). An excellent background article is to be found in Mackintosh (1986).

2. This issue of shifting emphasis from the political to the 'neutral' technical economic is put forward eloquently by Hopwood (1984) in assessing the role of changing conceptions on public sector accounting in response to the changing views on the role of the state in the 1980s.

3. See also Harris, 1986, pp. 84–8, for a discussion on the IMF's ideological position of political neutrality and technical expertise in the light of its systemic role of constructing a free market economy based on multilateral economic relations.

4. Mackintosh and Wuyts, 1988, p. 136.

5. Background documents for both congresses are: Third Congress, Frelimo, 1977a; 1977b; Fourth Congress, Frelimo, 1983a; 1983b.

6. Wuyts, 1985, and 1989, ch. 3. For a discussion of the inherited economic structures, see Wuyts, 1989, ch. 1.

7. Wuyts, 1989, ch. 3, appendix.

8. Mackintosh, 1986, pp. 558–62; Hanlon, 1984; 1986; Green, et al., 1987; CENE/DPCCN, 1988, pp. 5–8.

9. For a discussion of the question of state planning and parallel markets see Mackintosh, 1986, pp. 568–9; Mackintosh and Wuyts, 1988, pp. 151–5; and Wuyts, 1989, ch. 6.

10. Machungo, 1987.

11. Frelimo, 1977a and 1977b.

12. Mackintosh and Wuyts, 1988, p. 137.

13. Wuyts, 1989, ch. 3.

14. This summary is based on my field notes from research on money, rural economy, and parallel markets undertaken by the Centre of African Studies (Eduardo Mondlane University, Maputo) in Maputo and in Marracuene district in 1983. See also ibid. ch. 6.

15. Mackintosh and Wuyts, 1988, pp. 141–6.

16. Ibid., p. 143.

17. Ibid., pp. 144–5.

18. For an interesting discussion on volume versus cash planning see Likierman, 1984, pp. 148–52. See also FitzGerald, 1988, pp. 52–5 for a similar discussion in the context of socialist planning.

19. Kornai, 1979, pp. 806–8.

20. Wuyts, 1989, ch. 5.

21. Ibid., ch. 6. See also, Saith, 1985 pp. 31–9.

22. Mackintosh and Wuyts, 1988, pp. 151–5; Wuyts, 1989, ch. 6.

23. Mackintosh 1986, pp. 577–9.

24. Mackintosh and Wuyts, 1988, p. 156.

25. Quoted in *Noticias* (Maputo daily newspaper) 16 February 1987.

26. For a more extensive discussion, see Mackintosh and Wuyts, 1988. A similar analysis in the case of Nicaragua can be found in Kaimowitz, 1988.

27. CENE, 1988, p. 5.

28. Ibid., p. 7.

29. Ibid., p. 8.

30. World Bank, 1987, p. 4.

31. Interviews with World Bank mission, November 1987.

32. Mackintosh, 1986, p. 578.

33. Ibid., pp. 577–8.

34. Hanlon, 1988.

35. Ibid.

36. Hermele, 1988, pp. 17–21; Marshall, 1988.

37. Seers, 1976, p. 205.

38. See, for example, Walt, 1983; Walt and Wield, 1983.

39. Mackintosh and Wuyts, 1988.

40. For a discussion of this in the case of health case, see Cliff, et al., 1986.

41. IMF, 1988, quoted in Hermele, 1988, p. 18.

42. Hermele, 1988, pp. 19–20; Marshall, 1988.

43. Cliff, et al., 1986, p. 18.

44. Mackintosh and Wuyts, 1988.

45. Cliff, et al., 1986, pp. 13–14.

46. Hanlon, 1988.

47. Ibid.

Bibliography

Cairncross, A. and M. Pur (eds) (1976) *Employment, Income Distribution and Development* Strategy, London, Macmillan.

CENE/DPCCN (1988) (National Executive Commission of the Emergency/Department of the Prevention and Combat of Natural Disasters) *Rising to the Challenge: Dealing with the Emergency in Mozambique – an Inside View*. Maputo, (April).

Cliff, J., N. Kanji, M. Muller, (1986) 'Mozambique Health Holding the Line', in *Review of African Political Economy*, 36, pp. 7–23.

FitzGerald, E. V. K. (1988), 'State Accumulation and Market Equilibria: an Application of Kalecki-Kornai Analysis to Planned Economics in the Third World', pp. 50–74 in FitzGerald, E. V. K. and Wuyts, M. 1988.

—— and M. Wuyts (1988), *Markets within Planning: Socialist Economic Management in the Third World*, London, Frank Cass.

Frelimo (1977a) *O Partido e as Classes Trabalhadores Mocambicanas no Edificacao da Democracia Popular*. Maputo, Third Congress Documents.

—— (1977b) *Directivas Economicas e Sociais*. Maputo, Third Congress Documents.

—— (1983a) *Relatorio do Comite Central ao IV Congresso*. Maputo, Fourth Congress Documents.

—— (1983b) *Directivas Economicas e Sociais*. Maputo, Fourth Congress Documents.

Green, H., D. Asrat, M. Mauras, and R. Morgan (1987) 'Children in Southern Africa', in UNICEF (1987) *Children on the Front Line*. New York/Geneva, pp. 9–36.

Hanlon, J. (1984) *Mozambique: The Revolution under Fire*. London, Zed Books.

—— (1988) 'NGO's and other Aid Agencies in Mozambique', background notes to ECASAAMA (European Conference against South African Aggression in Mozambique and Angola), Bonn, December 8–10.

Harris, L. (1986) 'Conceptions of the IMF's role in Africa', in Lawrence, P. (ed.) 1986, pp. 83–95.

Hermele, K. (1988) *Country Report: Mozambique*. Stockholm, SIDA, Planning Secretariat.

Hopwood, A. (1984) 'Accounting and the Pursuit of Efficiency', pp. 167–87, in Hopwood, A. and C. Tomkins (eds) 1984.

—— and C. Tomkins (eds) (1984) *Issues in Public Sector Accounting*. London, Philip Allan.

Kaimowitz, D. (1988) 'Nicaragua's Experience with Agricultural Planning: From State-Centered Accumulation to the Strategic Alliance with the Peasantry', in FitzGerald, E. V. K., and M. Wuyts 1988, pp. 115–35.

Keynes, J. M. (1940) *How to Pay for the War*. London, Macmillan.

Kornai, J. (1979) 'Resource Constrained versus Demand Constrained Systems', pp. 801–19, in *Econometrica*, 47(4).

Lawrence, P. (ed.) (1986) *World Recession and the Food Crisis in Africa*. London, James Currey.

Likierman, A. (1984) 'Planning and Control: Developments in Central Government', pp. 147–64, in Hopwood, A., and C. Tomkins (eds) 1984.

Machungo, M. (1987) 'The Economic Recovery Programme'. Extract from the presentation by the Prime Minister to the People's Assembly, Supplement to *Mozambique News*, No. 127. Maputo, AIM.

Mackintosh, M. (1986) 'Economic Policy Context and Adjustment Options in Mozambique', in *Development and Change*, Vol. 17, pp. 557–81.

—— and M. Wuyts (1988) 'Accumulation Social Services and Socialist Transition in the Third World: Reflections on Decentralised Planning based on the Mozambican Experience', in FitzGerald, E. V. K., and M. Wuyts (eds) 1988, pp. 136–79.

Marshall, J. (1988) *Structural Adjustment in Mozambique – The Human Dimension*. Paper prepared for the Canadian International Development Agency, mimeo.

Saith, A. (1985) 'Primitive Accumulation, Agrarian Reform and Socialist Transitions: an Argument', in *Journal of Development Studies*, Vol. 22, No. 1, pp. 1–48.

Seers, D. (1976) 'The Political Economy of National Accounting', in Cairncross, A. and M. Pur (eds) 1976, pp. 193–209.

Walt, G. (1983) 'The Evolution of Health Policy', in Walt, G., and A. Melamed (eds) 1983a.

—— and A. Melamed (eds) (1983) *Mozambique: Towards a People's Health Service*. London, Zed Press.

—— and D. Wield (1983) *Health Policies in Mozambique*. Milton Keynes, Open University, Third World Studies course material.

World Bank (1987) 'Economic Policy Framework, 1987–1989'. Mimeo (May).

Wuyts, M. (1985) 'Money, Planning and Rural Transformation in Mozambique', in *Journal of Development Studies*, Vol. 22, No. 1, pp. 180–207.

—— (1989) *Money and Planning for Socialist Transition: The Mozambican Experience*. London, Gower Publishing.

12. Nicaragua: Economic Crisis and Transition on the Periphery*

E. V. K. FitzGerald

Introduction

The central OECD economies that form the motor of the global market system appear to be emerging at last from a lengthy phase of adjustment after the end of the post-war boom, which involves new technologies and labour processes, redistribution of income and transfer of market power between countries and regions. This restructuring involves severe macro-economic disequilibria and differentiation in living standards as the new accumulation model emerges, even if it cannot be described as a 'crisis' in the classical sense[1] of a breakdown in social organization. The 'Second World' is simultaneously undergoing systemic transformation of a different kind, as planned economies emerge from the protracted stage of extensive and forced industrialization of essentially agrarian societies, into a more complex phase of industrial maturity and enterprise reorganization.

For those economies on the periphery of the world market, these changes generate – through variations in prices, market demand, technological supply, interest rates and so on – real shocks, which bring about a condition of financial instability and social tension frequently referred to as an 'economic crisis' in the Third World.[2] Nonetheless, no clear model of accumulation seems to be emerging from this experience of externally inspired 'structural adjustment'. This problem is particularly acute where there already exist internal systemic factors leading to stagnation or breakdown in economic organization.

Societies with subordinate market economies, which are attempting some sort of non-capitalist transformation to overcome just these systemic problems, constitute a special case among developing countries. They are frequently exposed not only to external market shocks but also to deliberate attempts to destabilize their economies by foreign powers. In these cases weathering the storm goes beyond structural adjustment to involve the defence of sovereignty itself.

In the following pages I discuss the main systemic characteristics of Third World transition economies, which render them more or less vulnerable to exogenous shock. These include both inherited social structures and those that

* I would like to thank my former students at the *Escuela Nacional de Formación de Cuadros* for stimulating debates on this topic over the years; and Edwin Valdes for help with the Tables.

appear to arise from the transition process itself on the one hand; and the forms of economic organization and international relationships that are set up, on the other. Of particular interest is the extent to which economic organization has been modified in order to respond to exogenously generated crisis, and the way in which this in turn aids or hinders the process of transition itself.

Subsequently, within the case of the Nicaraguan economy since 1979, the issues defined above are examined. Economic planning and policy in relation to external shock is then discussed in two periods: that of 'reconstruction' (1979–83) when external market shock and planned domestic transformation were predominant themes; and that of 'survival' (1984–88) when the creation of economic crisis as part of US insurgency strategy and the response of different groups in Nicaraguan society dominated. The following section looks at the problem of economic policy formation under crisis conditions and the survival strategies of different social groups.

By way of a conclusion, I briefly outline the current litigation between Nicaragua and the USA before the International Court of Justice at The Hague as to compensation for economic damage consequent upon US attempts to destabilize the Sandinista government. The judgement has important implications for the legal rights of small nations to preserve their sovereignty in the world economy.

This chapter itself does not attempt to come to any definite conclusions nor is it supposed to be a complete account of the Nicaraguan economic experience.[3] The contents should be seen as part of a longer-term collaborative search for a systemic interpretation of economic and social transformation in those countries of the Third World attempting to construct socialism.[4] If any conclusion is to be drawn, it might be to the effect that in the first stage of transition small economies should plan for survival rather than development.

Impact of and response to exogenous shock in the transitional economy

The economic problems facing an agrarian society in the early stages of industrialization are both complex and contentious; all the more so when it is engaged in the transition to a non-capitalist model of development.[5] I assume that such a transition arises from the systemic breakdown of the previous social formation and that two strategic state goals are the restructuring of production and distribution in order to achieve popular aspirations of basic-needs provision and equity on the one hand, and the desire for 'national liberation' in the sense of a less subordinate geopolitical position on the other. The widespread adoption in recent years of 'mixed economy' models of articulation between state and civil society in Third World socialism indicates a significant departure from traditionally orthodox socialist principles and practice in an attempt to come terms with the realities of heterogeneous forms of production and the complexities of socialized economic management.[6] I shall argue that these three factors largely determine capacity to respond to external shock.

Such an economy could be said[7] to be 'in crisis' when:

(a) sufficient exports cannot be generated in the medium term to pay for basic imports (raw materials spares and replacement equipment) for exports and basic needs, and to service existing debt (net of capital flight); in other words, where aid/loans are required for purposes other than investment;

(b) supplies of basic needs (food, health, transportation, education, housing, and so on) and their distribution at levels accepted as adequate for that society cannot be maintained (and raised with population growth); leading to social and political conflict over resource allocation;

(c) the state cannot rectify this condition rapidly because of the social conflict over how adjustment should be made, or because it lacks the resources (through 'fiscal crisis') to do so; leading to a lack of 'relative autonomy' necessary for the required degree of intervention.

This definition begs as many questions as it answers; but the failure to reach these targets seems to be what is meant in popular discourse by 'economic crisis'[8] and is clearly distinguished in practice from poverty or underdevelopment as such.

The 'agrarian question' in the transition to socialism is far from settled, of course,[9] but it is hardly contestable that there is a considerable risk of losing marketable production capacity – at least in the first few years of the transition. It is for this reason that in many cases an initial stage of 'mixed economy' is adopted in order to reduce the initial production shock and thus risk of economic crisis. Similarly, the nationalization of natural resource-based foreign firms, whatever the benefits may be in the long run, is bound to have immediately negative effects on production – particularly export capacity and the exporting channels as well as those for technically specific supplies, such as spare parts. The impact of ownership changes on industry and modern services does not appear to be so great, if only because the labour process is more closely constrained technologically, even though the emigration of technicians may become a serious problem if new cadres cannot be trained rapidly enough. Given that these activities are likely to rely on the foreign exchange generated by the primary sector, however, production losses in this latter will have serious multiplier effects upon the former.

The shift in the balance of domestic political power implied by social revolution implies rising expectations with respect to the standard of living of the majority of the population. In rural areas this may be met to some extent by self-provisioning (that is, increased household productivity) as a consequence of agrarian reform, but in urban areas and primary sector enterprises, the pressure upon the state to satisfy basic-needs requirements in terms of nutrition, housing, transport, utilities, education and health will be very strong. To the extent that these are met by central state expenditure, then this will probably lead to a permanent budgetary commitment and increased reliance on foreign exchange (or aid) to provide these services. Both will increase the vulnerability of the economy to external shock, and imply socially difficult welfare reductions and inflationary budget deficits if export purchasing power declines.

A model of basic-needs provision based on popular mobilization[10] – that is, the organization of local communities – reduces the foreign exchange commitment (by adopting a more 'appropriate technology' for primary services, construction materials and so on) and mobilizes surplus labour to replace the budgetary outlay. This model, a priori, is less vulnerable to external shock. Nonetheless, it should be borne in mind that the establishment of these 'primary' citizen entitlements inevitably generates socially effective demand for secondary provision of hospitals, high schools, electrification and so on – all of which do inevitably have considerable foreign exchange content. Despite this there is a real sense in which the new 'Department Two' of the economy can become both decentralized and import-substituting in order to make basic-needs provision relatively autonomous and thus less vulnerable to external shock.

The nationalization of foreign trade, banking and key production facilities logically leads to the state becoming responsible for investment decisions as well; if only because the residual business sector is unlikely to invest on any scale and the new co-operatives and small producers are as yet in no position to do so. The long-term need to industrialize the economy in order to tackle the three strategic goals defined above (structural transformation, basic-needs provision and reduced dependency) combines with the group interest of the 'state managers' in modernization as such; which generates an almost unstoppable drive towards higher state investment known as 'accumulation bias'.[11] This over-investment generates a tension with basic-needs provision – both in the concept of central versus local provisioning and in the allocation of resources – which eventually leads to forms of macro-economic 'crowding out'[12] in the form of budgetary strain and labour shortages.

Lastly, but not least importantly, large new investment projects (as opposed to adaptation of existing facilities or small enterprise expansion) tend to take a long time to come on stream and have a high import commitment in the form of spare parts and so on, both of which increase external vulnerability in the short- and medium-term – whatever the benefits in the long run. Without going to the extreme of denying the necessity for such state industrial accumulation[13] experience indicates the need to rectify the balance between state investment and civil consumption so that if foreign exchange availability declines suddenly, all the strain is not taken by basic-needs provision. It is also necessary to ensure adequate macro- and micro-economic (fiscal and pricing) measures to provide adequate domestic finance for investment so that reductions in foreign funds do not lead to unmanageable budget deficits.

It can easily be shown that in a planned economy under conditions of external market uncertainty there are advantages to be gained from reducing the rate of fixed investment so as to provide both more resources for repair and maintenance, and retain a degree of flexibility in consumption levels – in other words, keep a certain 'reserve' in hand to cope with external fluctuations.[14] By the same token, uncertainty implies that benefits can be derived from planning for a higher level of exports as opposed to consumption – that is, bias towards what is effectively the 'Department One' of such economies. This is because in the event of 'overshooting' foreign exchange reserves can be converted into (imported) consumption goods, while in the opposite case, home goods cannot be easily exported.

The economy in transition is subject to the transmission effects of world macro-economic disequilibrium upon the Third World as a whole, expressed in terms of commodity prices, interest rates, debt negotiations and market restrictions. To the extent that reliance on the international capitalist system is reduced, it might be expected that the impact of these external shocks will in fact be lessened. Central control of the balance of payments should reduce the scope for capital flight (both direct and indirect through transfer pricing and so on) and permit scarce foreign exchange to be reallocated towards national priorities, even though such central control may reduce flexibility in areas such as non-traditional export initiatives. But the extent to which adjustment is reached at the enterprise level in response to the plan will depend upon the combination of administrative measures with domestic price shifts (for example, rational changes in the real exchange rate) affecting profitability in such a way as to move production decisions in the desired direction. The failure to plan relative prices (and more generally, to transform 'relations of exchange' in line with relations of production) probably accounts for much of the rigidity of transitional economies.

The common experience has been of a shift in trade – and more significantly aid – relationships towards the CMEA countries. This opens up both new possibilities and new problems. On the positive side, commodity prices are more stable, being negotiated within long-term commercial agreements, and can contain a premium over world (that is, capitalist) market prices. Public investment projects receive capital aid including the transfer of appropriate technology; and emphasis is placed on the skilling of labour and the provision of adequate repair facilities. All this should permit both better planning of trade and a greater capacity for resistance to world economic fluctuations.

On the negative side, however, the (often sudden) shift in trading partners can cause serious dislocations. It is only reasonable to expect a decline in international commercial bank lending (but trade credit can be secured against export commodity futures) although the continuation of official bilateral aid will depend upon political factors.[15] The most obvious is the change in technology which may not only render vintage equipment virtually useless, but also be inappropriate to the local agricultural systems of regional export markets. The organizational characteristics of the CMEA, based on an integrated industrial network, central planning and a high degree of self-sufficiency, are such as to make the fluctuating requirements and production of Third World socialist economies difficult to accommodate.[16]

To the extent that current reforms in the Soviet Union and Eastern Europe involve a more market-oriented and entrepreneurial approach, this inflexibility will probably be reduced in future; but by the same token, there is an increased tendency to apply 'world' prices[17] and maximize hard currency returns on items such as spare parts. In consequence, it is probably most realistic to regard the world market as a single entity transmitting shocks from 'North' to 'South'; with long-term credit and aid being available on basically political criteria from both East and West.

Unfortunately, the transition to non-capitalist development has usually been accompanied by overt and covert attempts by world powers to destabilize the economy so as to detain this process. Current national security doctrine suggests[18] that such economic destabilization will undermine support for the proto-socialist regime at minimum diplomatic cost. Logistical support for counter-revolutionary insurgency is preferred to direct military intervention; the depredations of the insurgents destroy infrastructure and dislocate rural production of food and export commodities; aiming to reduce peasant support for the new regime rather than force military surrender as such. Obviously, this external shock is extremely serious for the transitional economy, as it both reduces supply and increases the need to commit resources (labour, food, foreign exchange and management skills) to the defence effort.

In parallel, a range of economic sanctions is usually applied in the form of pressure on multilateral financial institutions and bilateral aid partners, trade embargoes and the rupture of transport networks. These tend to exacerbate the effect of external shock, and are explicitly designed to provoke economic crisis.

This sort of external economic pressure can generate new potential for response. On the one hand, consumption expectations can be restrained or postponed by the appeal to the defence of the revolution, while labour productivity can be raised by much the same exhortations – which can be remarkably effective as long as the external threat is manifest under wartime conditions. On the other, quasi-military organization of the state administration provides an opportunity for effective central planning; while the territorial organization of defence (for example, peasant militias and co-operative settlements) can form the basis – as it has since Roman times – for subsequent agrarian modernization. But none of this can compensate for the fact that where a superpower deliberately sets out to generate an economic crisis in a small and poor nation, it is unlikely to be wholly ineffective.

In sum, the form in which these transitional economies receive external shocks is distinct from that experienced by their non-transitional neighbours; and the capacity to respond is also different – with their own strengths and weaknesses. The extent to which such response is successful depends not only on the flexible design of planning systems – based on a small but efficient central administration combined with decentralized production and provisioning – but also on the strength of civil society itself. It is in this context that the current 'mixed economy' reforms should be seen. They appear to be a response to both domestic systemic problems *and* external shock: it is probably neither useful nor feasible to attempt to distinguish between the two.

Economic policy in Nicaragua: from reconstruction to survival

Immediately on taking power in July 1979 – and in fact for some months previously[19] – the National Reconstruction Government worked out the central logic of the economic programme that was intended to reactivate the economy after two years of civil war, and lay the basis for a subsequent transition to socialism: the economic programmes for 1980 (entitled 'Economic Reactivation for the Benefit of the People') and 1981 ('Efficiency and Austerity') contain the central arguments of a mass of more detailed and strategic thinking.[20] I have written elsewhere[21] at some length on the vicissitudes of the Nicaraguan economy since 1979: here space permits only a discussion of those aspects of economic policy and planning relevant to the subject in hand.

The design of economic policy from the start had taken into account the problem of economic vulnerability: in part because Central America and the Third World in general were clearly going through economic crises, and in part because hostile action from the US was a strong possibility. The 1980 Plan had three main policy lines.[22] First, to reactivate production, giving priority to basic-needs satisfaction so as to achieve a redistribution of income from the supply side. The mobilization of the population services such as health and education would, moreover, make these basic needs less reliant upon imports, and thus upon fluctuations in the balance of payments. Second, to maintain strict control over the macro-economic balances, both by controls over budgetary and credit expenditures (accompanied by fiscal reform and banking control over producers) and regulation of wages and prices. This was not only intended to maintain the monetary incomes of producers (and thus production incentives) but also to insulate the real incomes of the poor from external shock. Third, a mixed economy (see Table 12.1) was to be maintained in order to reduce the production loss from too rapid a transformation of the relations of production; socialization of the economy after the original sequestration of the Somoza properties to proceed by the more rapid expansion of the state and co-operative sectors through investment.

As to the external sector, the deterioration in the commodity terms of trade for exports such as sugar, coffee, bananas and meat, which make up the bulk of Nicaragua's foreign exchange earnings were anticipated; as was the difficulty of access to US markets. It was planned, therefore, to diversify export and import markets as much as possible – particularly with Latin America and Europe – and to avoid replacing dependence upon one great power with another. The inherited public debt (at US$1,600 millions) was already comparable in size to the GDP and it was clearly impossible to meet immediate servicing requirements, especially with the commercial banks. It was decided therefore to recognize most of this debt (to avoid a costly break with Western markets) but to negotiate a five-year grace period with interest charges above the serviceable capacity to be capitalized.[23] As projected exports for the reactivation period of 1980–82 would cover only two-thirds of essential imports, considerable reliance on fresh concessionary aid would be necessary in the medium-term, although the long-term prospect for the balance of payments was considered by all observers – including the World Bank[24] – to be excellent, given Nicaragua's natural resource base and industrial position within the Central American Common Market.

Reactivation proceeded quite well through 1982, although less rapidly than had been expected. Most of the distributive goals were met, the mixed economy seemed to keep business afloat and the rate of inflation was tolerable.[25] Although the trade gap did not seem to be narrowing, this was largely due to the terms of trade effect which accounted for 56 per cent of the trade gap in 1983, and sufficient aid was available on generous terms to maintain essential imports. Trade had also been diversified. By 1983, however, just as the consequences of the US-supported *contra* incursions began to be seriously felt on production and expenditure, serious strains were beginning to become apparent in the economic model itself.

Significantly, these problems were closely related to those features of the 'reactivation model' that had been designed to ensure stability. First, the emphasis on basic-needs provision, as a means of real income redistribution, had the effect of reducing the role of wages as a means of mobilizing labour for production (particularly harvests) and raising productivity. What is more, the success of local provision of health, education, housing and food distribution created a massive popular demand for secondary support (for example, high schools, hospitals, utilities and transport) which in turn forced up the budget commitment. Second, the commitment to guaranteed prices (and profit margins) reduced the incentive for production efficiency and effectively obliged the government to subsidize exporters through a multiple exchange rate system; while the collectively negotiated production targets forced the banks to extend credit on demand rather than according to ability to repay. In consequence, the macro-economic instruments of fiscal and financial balance became passive, and instability became systemic.

Third, and probably most seriously of all, the 'dual' concept upon which the mixed economy model was based came into question. Not because of the relationship with capitalists; but rather because of the role of small producers. In the agrarian sector, above all,[26] the peasantry had become marginalized from the large state investment programme in the modern sector, had not received land (as the large state units were felt to be potentially efficient while the rural bourgeoisie was inviolate), and state marketing boards were acquiring harvests without an adequate supply of rural producer inputs or consumer goods. Food supply to the towns began to decline and, more alarmingly still, peasant support for the government (and by implication, resistance to the *contra*) began to diminish. Meanwhile, the rhythm of public investment in the state enterprise sector – principally export crops, irrigated food-grains, energy and transport – increased. While necessary for long-run industrialization, this model of accumulation accentuated the dualism of the economy because although two-thirds of production is in the modern sector (Table 12.1), two-thirds of employment lies outside it (Table 12.2). Moreover, this investment was seriously underfunded which exacerbated the financial disequilibrium (Table 12.4) and increased indebtedness and debt.[27]

Just as a start had been made on the necessary shifts in the model – including a distributive land reform, reunification of the exchange rate and strengthening of banking controls, recovery of the real wage and a scaling down of state accumulation plans – the extent and scale of the US effort to destabilize the economy escalated. The economy suddenly shifted from a phase of social reconstruction to one of military survival.

It is difficult to calculate the effect of war on a small, poor and open economy, but in the case of Nicaragua considerable analytical effort has gone into making as reliable an estimate as possible.[28] As Table 12.3 indicates, serious damage was caused by *contra* activities in the main export zones (fishing, coffee, mining and forestry in particular) and to food production (basic grains and livestock) in mountain zones, as well as to transport facilities, health posts and so on. Indeed, the objective of these activities was to undermine production and social services. The ECLA estimates that in the 1984–87 period on average the annual losses had a foreign exchange equivalence of 65 per cent of exports. Without such war damage or the embargo, the current account deficit in 1987, for instance, would have been 18 per cent of imports rather than the 62 per cent out-turn.

This impact was exacerbated by the imposition of a trade embargo by the USA in 1985, and effective pressure on the IDB and the IBRD to block loans at the board level, despite their prior approval at the technical level. Over the period, estimated losses from the embargo averaged US$102 millions a year, about 39 per cent of exports in 1987. The total value of disbursements held up was of the order of US$200 millions, equivalent to about one-half of the total public investment programme for that period.

For an economy with a severe foreign exchange constraint, a dollar of such resources lost had a multiplier (or rather 'divider') effect on the rest of the economy. Using the ILPES model of the Nicaraguan economy[29] to simulate the effect of restoring the lost income indicates a multiplier of the order of 2.2, and an average GDP loss due to the war and the embargo of 37 per cent in 1987 and 26 per cent for the period 1980–87 as a whole. In terms of growth, the IBRD forecast (in 1981) indicated that the economy should have expanded at about 7.8 per cent per annum between 1980 and 1985 and 6.8 per cent between 1985 and 1990; rather than the out-turn of 1.9 per cent and decline, respectively. These are, of course, only approximate estimates, but they underline the extreme vulnerability of an economy where traditionally about half of material production has been for export.

Military expenditure rose in order to finance the war effort, for although arms and ammunition were provided by socialist allies, local resources made up the bulk of counter-insurgency costs. Defence expenditure rose to nearly half the total budget and a quarter of GDP; forcing civil expenditure down in real terms and becoming the main cause of the inflationary budget deficit – for most of it was financed by printing money.[30]

Finally, the mass diversion of manpower for the defence effort had a severe disarticulating effect on the economy. Roughly a quarter of able-bodied males were mobilized in one way or another; affecting both factories and farms. What is more, nearly half the mountain peasant population were relocated or simply fled, disrupting the whole rural economy. Finally, the best technicians and administrators, doctors and engineers, were drafted into the army, leaving the civil sector without human resources.

Official government response was principally non-economic, of course: counter-insurgency campaigns, diplomatic offensives and political mobilization. On the economic front, the reduction of exports to a level below half of minimum imports prevented a recovery of trade balance while the war continued and meant that continued reliance on foreign aid was the only viable strategy for survival, rather than being used for essentially developmental purposes. Aid was available for much the same reasons: to enable Nicaragua to survive US pressure (although the donors' motives for doing this were varied) and thus credits as well as donations were granted for essentially political reasons. As Table 12.5 demonstrates, the level of (non-military) aid actually fell somewhat, but its origin changed markedly as the socialist share rose from 31 to 67 per cent.

The use of aid also changed, moving away from new projects towards production inputs and spare parts. The consequent accumulation of debt was serious: rising from US$4 billion in 1983 to over US$6 billion in 1987. In the second period, debt service was sharply reduced from an average of US$152 millions a year in 1980–83 (34 per cent of exports) to US$51 millions in 1984–87 (14 per cent of exports) by simple inability to pay and the implicit consent of the creditors, with only one notable exception. In fact the commercial banks, after the original grace period ran out in 1984, permitted effective default on an annual basis – although it should be borne in mind that despite early fulfilment of service obligations, the banks did not extend new loans to Nicaragua. The exception was the World Bank, which, under pressure from the White House, refused to reschedule loans and indeed had not approved any new projects since 1981.

Domestic macro-economic adjustment was also considerable in the aggregate, as Table 12.4 indicates. The external gap was reduced from 13 to 10 per cent of GDP and the domestic savings rate raised; however, this was not sufficient to retain stability and in fact disguises a worsening intersectoral imbalance. The state sector savings deficit (mainly the current government deficit) rose from five to eight per cent of GDP under pressure from defence expenditure, while despite repeated attempts to reduce public investment[31] the state investment rate remained rather high; attributed by the authorities to project lags and the difficulty of getting aid donors to switch from capital aid to repairs, maintenance and replacement.[32]

The inevitable consequence of such a combination of declining external finance and an increased state sector resource deficit, as in other poor LDCs during the present world economic crisis,[33] was to force up the resource balance of the non-state sector. Needless to say, these did not represent voluntary savings, but rather forced reductions in household consumption due to inflation affecting not only real wages but also the cash balances of small producers.[34] The effect of the enormous effort to maintain minimum supply levels of basic consumer goods to the productive workforce, and progressively tighter import controls, meant that this consumption effect was more intense in urban than in rural areas, and upon the middle class than the poor.

Nonetheless, the effect of this inflationary pressure arising from using forced savings to pay for the war and for continued state investment was not only to depress consumption levels, but to *disarticulate* the market economy.[35] The combination of high retail inflation and attempts to control wholesale prices inevitably led to parallel markets and thus the diversion of goods away from official channels: in the case of Nicaragua, away from the network of state wholesalers and private sub-contracted retailers which had been built up before 1984 as a means of reducing speculation. Labour markets became distorted as workers left the formal sector with its controlled wages for the informal sector; and it was no longer possible to maintain financial controls over state enterprises or even recuperate bank loans in real terms.

Official response to this disarticulation took two somewhat contradictory directions. On the one hand, the direction of land reform was changed radically[36] away from the dualist model of concentration on large state farms, towards the redistribution of land to the peasantry in a co-operative framework and the redefinition of the role of state farms in support of all producers in the area or branch. In the secondary and tertiary sectors, co-operatives were also encouraged[37] and the trend towards state monopolies reversed. These reforms were intended to reduce bureaucratic inefficiency and incorporate the informal sector into organized production. Unfortunately, resource constraints prevented these new and popular forms of organization receiving the necessary technical, capital and input support that they needed to initiate a new form of accumulation. On the other hand, price controls were gradually lifted, the exchange rate unified and adjusted to domestic inflation, wages systems converted from flat to piece rates, and state enterprises given more financial independence from ministries, in an attempt to raise productivity and reduce the budget deficits. This relatively orthodox approach to macro-economic stabilization had the effect of undermining economic planning and encouraging enterprises to misuse market power and hoard foreign exchange.

In the end, government response was to meet the external shock of 'low intensity conflict' by military and diplomatic means; production and organization were not reorganized as a 'war economy' in terms of nationalization or rationing, while the resources for defence were extracted indirectly through inflation.

The Nicaraguan response to economic crisis

In this section I shall attempt to look at this experience in a different way, by discussing the 'political economy' of policy formation in Nicaragua during this difficult period on the one hand and the response of different social groups on the other. It is necessarily speculative, but this is inevitable with such a difficult topic, which is not adequately covered by political or social theory, let alone analytical economics.

In the case of Nicaragua, economic policy was undoubtedly 'over-determined', particularly in the crisis period from 1983 onwards, by non-economic aspects of national defence which in turn inevitably generated macro-economic imbalance. This concept of 'over-determination'[38] should be distinguished from the situation – unfortunately common in Latin America – of a state lacking the relative autonomy necessary to make consistent economic policy decisions due to social group pressures in the economic sphere itself (for example, on wages, exchange rates, subsidies, or welfare), which imply ex-ante demand levels incompatible with ex-post equilibrium and must be balanced by inflation[39] or, by implication, external debt.

In the case of crisis response in Nicaragua four strategic policy areas can be distinguished: military defence; international relations; domestic politics; and economic management itself. My argument is that decisions taken in the first three prevented balance in the fourth. The achievement of macro-economic balance would have implied unattainable demand cuts because of the extent of the war damage discussed above, and the shift of all available resources to production for exports and basic needs – as is usual in other war economies.

Military defences implied enormous budget allocations, which distorted aggregate demand, and mobilization of labour, which undermined supply, in the mountains and a permanent anti-invasion force on the coastal plain. International relations implied continued service on the commercial bank debt (with little or no prospect of new loans, given the pressure from Washington) to maintain relations with Europe, and possibly a less controlled form of economic organization than would be normal in other countries under wartime constraints, even though these costs were to a great extent counter-balanced by increased socialist aid.

Domestic political considerations implied an attempt to maintain the consumption levels of the main social classes – workers, peasants, artisans and capitalists – in order to maintain political pluralist and a multi-class alliance against external aggression. This implied both the maintenance of the social base of the revolution through provision of basic needs (particularly health, education, public transport and subsidized food) under the post-1979 citizen entitlements, and the improvement of peasant incomes through food prices and rural infrastructure on the one hand, and the guarantee of profit rates and ample credit to firms in agriculture and industry, on the other. Under the circumstances, it is hardly surprising that the macro-economic balances showed large and alarming deficits, and that increased indebtedness and domestic inflation resulted. It was obvious to all concerned that macro-economic instability was undermining political consensus, making the defence effort more difficult, and reducing effective state control over the economy.

Many critics – while praising the Sandinista dexterity in military, diplomatic and political areas – have pointed out[40] that less inflation would have strengthened political support among the 'popular classes', and thus that the subordination of sound economic policy to political objectives eventually had a negative effect in terms of just those objectives. These critics do not fully explain why the deficits occurred, except to allude to 'policy errors' or to imply an 'excessive statism'. The former is either tautologically true as an ex-post description of events or demonstrably false ex-ante as a description of government intentions, as an inspection of official declarations ranging from the 1981 to the 1987 Economic Programme makes clear. The latter was undoubtedly a problem in itself, as we have seen above, but inflationary budget deficits are not an inevitable consequence of state expansion as such – as the example of Cuba makes clear – but rather of the inability to centralize a sufficient portion of the economic surplus.

This critical approach seems to miss the point. Undoubtedly if the government had been able to maintian consumption levels between 1984 and 1988, it would have been more popular among the poor and the middle classes. But to achieve significant improvement in macro-economic balances (which would have required a real demand reduction of the order of ten per cent of GDP ex-ante) would have required the sacrifice of one of the three major strategic objectives. The political cost of debt and inflation, while high, was lower than (say) the sacrifice of links to Europe or of complete rationing and the militarization of society.[41] Once the military threat appeared to have receded with the disarticulation of the *contras* and the end of their US logistical support in 1988, the balance of priorities between the four strategic policy areas could be reassessed and new economic policy criteria be established. The 1989 budget includes sharp reductions in military expenditure and manpower as well as the gradual elimination of monetized deficit finance; although external aid financing remains highly problematic.

It could be argued that more should have been done in the 1979–83 period to prepare for survival[42] under the wartime conditions that were bound to materialize, particularly after the election of Reagan in late 1980 – even after discounting the benefits of hindsight. At the time there were good reasons to believe that the only two feasible scenarios were outright US invasion or the spread of insurrection throughout Central America, if not both. Under these circumstances the main tasks were to consolidate the social basis of the revolution (for example, political mobilization around basic needs provision), construct an international solidarity network and build up the armed forces while maintaining the mixed economy to sustain production, and taking advantage of as much foreign aid that was on offer. In these terms, this could be seen as a rational response to anticipated external shock. The fact that US strategy would turn out to be confined to 'low intensity conflict'[43] was not foreseen by anyone in 1979.

Nonetheless, it was clear by 1983 that the model of economic organization established in 1979 for the reconstruction period contained serious weaknesses, and that the 'mixed economy' required redefinition. In particular, the balance of state accumulation, the relationship with the peasantry, export orientation, pricing policy, basic-needs entitlements, urbanization and labour organization all required a new structure.[44] These redefinitions were gradually implemented after the 1984 elections, starting with the second redistributive stage of land reform. Although this was also derived from defence considerations, it underlined the fact that a more stable and broadly-based economy would provide a better basis for national defence in the sense of being less vulnerable to external shock.

The question then arises of why the adjustment took so long. In part it was a result of the policy over-determination discussed above. But it was also due to social conflict about the direction of adjustment. Some examples should make this clear. The export incentives introduced in 1985 created considerable resistance among trade unions, who were being asked to support wage constraints at the same time. The attempt to reduce food subsidies to the whole urban population and replace them by supplies to wage workers alone met with widespread resistance among the informal urban sector. The plans to sharply reduce public investment by cancelling large projects and shifting resources to small producers met with determined resistance from technocrats and enterprise managers. What is more, these conflicts were reproduced within the government apparatus (for example, between the spending ministries on the one hand and the ministry of finance and the central bank on the other) and even within the FSLN itself (for example, between political secretaries representing the 'territorial interest' in food subsidies and rationed distribution, and the trade union leaders, respresenting the interest of production workers in commissariats) thus making rapid policy shifts all the more difficult.

As the government moved slowly on the redefinition of economic strategy, social groups began to work out their own 'survival strategies' in response to economic crisis, which in turn served to redefine the scope for state policy. The bureaucracy itself, needless to say, adopted survival mechanisms too. As is normal in such cases, each ministry or enterprise attempted to build up its 'own' resources, in terms of both non-budgetary income (enterprises for example) and foreign exchange (by establishing preferential links with aid donors), as well as retaining skilled personnel by providing non-wage incentives such as cars and housing. This gradual process helped some worthy institutions to survive external shock (for instance, the Ministry of Culture) but in other cases made rationalization extremely difficult, despite repeated attempts at *compactación* from 1987 onwards. Socially, the bureaucracy was also strengthened by the move towards decentralization of government to the regions after 1982, which was specifically designed to increase local participation and reduce the military vulnerability of Managua, but which also created a local 'proto-class' of enterprise managers, military personnel and state administrators who to a great extent occupied the vacuum left by the previous regime at the territorial level.

Nonetheless, the *funcionarios* are the section of the middle class most 'concientized' by the experience of war, having taken part in military and productive mobilizations and become accustomed to a new and more participative form of decision-making. This was not essentially a *political* issue as such[45] but rather a social phenomenon in that young administrators felt entitled and able to discuss all administrative matters quite freely. Reforms were thus difficult to implement without a broad consensus through the relevant bureaucracy.

Meanwhile, the components of civil society were steadily establishing survival mechanisms independent of the state. Firstly, because the capacity of the state to underwrite their economic survival was progressively weakened by the low intensity war (which was the object of the exercise, after all); and secondly, because in the aftermath of revolution itself the social 'space' was filled up from below by new or previously repressed groups. In the case of urban popular groups, this had both positive and negative aspects. Production workers showed a surprising ingenuity in repairing decrepit plant by 'innovating' spare parts, and in substituting for imported raw materials; but in order to meet family needs were forced to engage in second shifts as artisans and often to leave the formal sector altogether.

The urban informal sector swelled as the parallel market in scarce price-controlled commodities grew, enlarged by migration from war zones, and encouraged by the collapse of organized private commerce and the opportunities for auto-construction in city areas previously reserved for the rich. In fact, the urban poor came to rely more than before on extended family networks including not only formal and informal employment, but also small-scale production and close links to rural areas;[46] in practice, this not only invalidated any dualist concept of a segmented labour market, but made wage and even rationing policies largely ineffective. The formal sector (private as well as state enterprise) soon began to suffer from serious labour shortages and increasing employee turnover. This reallocation of their labour power, rather than strikes, was the effective response of the urban poor to the progressive deterioration of the real wage and the need for family survival.

Popular response to economic crisis in rural areas also involved the 'retreat into the family'. On the one hand, war and revolution as well as economic crisis intensified the pressure by landless peasantry for access to their own farms, albeit in the form of co-operatives. Direct land invasions were infrequent[47] but passive support for the *contra* was not unrelated to this pressure. Once land had been distributed and marketing channels been de-regulated, the social demand for inputs was manifested in the establishment by the main small farmers organization (UNAG) of its own chain of rural stores financed by European aid funds. These phenomena contrast markedly with the pre-1984 period, when the pressure had been upon the state to provide roads, electricity and so on. Rural workers were at some advantage over their urban fellows, because earnings were more directly related to productivity and they gained access to family plots – and in some cases collective ones as well. Technological response (in repairs, substitution of imports, and so on) was also highly creative. Seasonal labour, particularly for coffee and cotton, was extremely tight; although this was due more to low real wages than peasantization as such.

The role of family in crisis-response implies an important gender dimension.[48] Quite apart from the women's movement itself and government gender policy[49] the experience of war and economic crisis has changed the role of women in a double sense. First, by their taking the places of mobilized or dead partners in production and social organization, which mainly affected rural areas. Second, by giving a greater role to family networks – generally effectively headed by women – in household reproduction, which mainly affected urban areas. It remains to be seen whether this is a permanent effect which will continue after the war when men are demobilized and food supplies improve. The local organization of basic needs provision on the one hand and experience gained in production on the other, should effect a structural transformation. In terms of generational change, the participation of women at all levels of education is considerably greater than that of men, in the universities particularly, which will have a long-term impact. In the armed forces themselves, their absence from combat (a point of much criticism at the time) has implied a predominant role in skilled occupations such as communications, intelligence and administration, which in peacetime will further reinforce this educational differentiation.

The political strength of the FSLN has consisted in its capacity to incorporate these survival strategies – particularly at the local level – rather than resist them. For instance, the experience of Miskito relocation led to administrative autonomy for the Atlantic Coast and less reliance on Managua.[50] Its weakness has been the failure to adjust the state itself – and central economic planning – to these mutations in civil society. As in the case of reforms elsewhere in the socialist world, it is not just a question of substituting the market for the plan, but rather of devising new forms of social organization of the economy itself.[51] Indeed, the new forms of popular organization since 1979 themselves created effective forms of response to crisis. Local organization made primary health care (especially sanitation, inoculation, malaria control and infant care), adult education and self-help housing a reality. Co-operatives grouped small farmers and artisans and strengthened them collectively through joint credit, technical assistance and marketing facilities. The experience of local militias strengthened civil defence, which reduced the worst consequences of natural disasters such as Hurricane Gilbert.

The response of private enterprise as such to economic crisis should be distinguished from that of the families of managers and professionals. Business reaction in Nicaragua was very moderate; in any case as Table 12.1 indicates, little more that 29 per cent of production was in the hands of capitalists, due to the monopoly position of the Somoza group (in state hands since 1979) and the extent of the small-scale sector. It seems that the concept of a 'mixed economy' was viable in political terms at least,[52] and in fact, political opposition to the FSLN was not based on economic interest as such, while armed opposition was peasant-based and largely orchestrated from abroad. After an initial period of capital flight, which had been initiated in 1978, capitalists settled down to maintain production – although not to invest. Given the uncertainty about future prospects, this was quite explicable in strictly economic terms of rational expectations; there has been little or no private investment in Central America in the 1980s.

The response of agribusiness firms was more or less to maintain production (except cotton, which was declining throughout Central America due to poor world prices) and to insist upon official prices (that is, a dual exchange rate) that would secure profits as a mark-up on costs, although the lack of investment meant a gradual deterioration in yields.[53] This gradual crumbling was accentuated by the second stage of agrarian reform, which unlike the previous 'dual' model[54] did not guarantee a place for large enterprise. Even though it actually increased the size of the non-state agrarian area, it did so at the expense of large farms in both the public and private sectors. Industrial firms, which were highly dependent upon the state for imported inputs and markets, maintained production levels and received profits guaranteed by mark-up prices; multinational companies behaved similarly to domestic firms.[55] It would appear that the experience of Cuba and Chile had been studied by both sides, although the lessons drawn by each side may well be rather different. The government saw the advantages of retaining the administrative talents of private producers in a period of extreme economic difficulty, and felt no real political threat from them in the long-run. Business saw no immediate economic or political gain from withdrawal, and a long-term benefit from still being in place should the US eventually intervene.

The position of professional and administrative families was rather different: as a social group they were probably the hardest hit by economic crisis. Not only did their real incomes decline, but they had little means of reproducing their 'family assets' in terms of both household durables (car, freezer, and so on) and human capital (university abroad, and so on), while the ideological values of their children were under threat from the draft and women's liberation.[56] Their reaction was an accelerating rate of emigration to Central America and the USA, at a level greater than the production of new young professionals, who in any case could not make up for the experience of their predecessors.[57]

The reactions of the various social groups to economic crisis were thus extremely varied, and does as much to explain 'from below' the difficulty of coherent economic policy-making as over-determination 'from above'.

Concluding remarks: legal recourse or domestic adjustment?

The current debate on the obligation of states under international law to repay sovereign debt on schedule[58] has some bearing upon the question of economic shock transmitted through markets. Whether such world market destabilization can be properly considered unintentional is perhaps a matter of viewpoint. The aim of metropolitan macro-policy is to stabilize the domestic economy and encourage accumulation there, without regard to the world economy – coordination being within the OECD at best.[59] Nonetheless, failure to avoid repercussions on the periphery is hardly a matter of ignorance; perhaps the nearest legal equivalent would be negligence. Indeed the Lomé 'stabex' system explicitly recognizes such a metropolitan responsibility.

Even though the 'right to development' has been established in international law through UN declarations[60] there is, of course, no effective system of implementation through, say, the UN General Assembly. The system of international commercial law is, however, gradually gaining substance due to the internationalization of business itself. Litigation is resolved through an informal yet real system of 'arbitration tribunals' centred on The Hague, where by common consent a growing body of precedent and general treaty obligations are observed. To the extent that international companies cannot rely on the law of any one country (or the capacity of any power to enforce their interests on the rest of the world) they have a growing interest in the observance by these same powers of the principles of international law. In this context it may be of some interest to note that the 1985 US trade embargo on Nicaragua did not include prohibitions on subsidiaries of US companies trading with Nicaragua – apparently due to opposition in Washington by these companies – in marked contrast to the case of Cuba two decades previously.

Meanwhile poor countries must continue to adjust domestically to external shock, relying on the absorptive capacity of their social formations and the vagaries of financial geopolitics. The discussion in this chapter on the impact of and response to such shocks in transitional economies, and the analysis of the Nicaraguan case in particular, does little more than illustrate the complexity of the subject. Some tentative operational conclusions of some possible relevance to other countries in similar circumstances might be as follows:

a) economic planning should be based on the conditions for survival rather than development as the latter may undermine the former if overly ambitious programmes of capital investment or import-intensive technologies are adopted, increasing vulnerability to external shock;

b) export capacity and skills in foreign trade should be strengthened and managed as a national priority, ensuring that the relevant 'sub-systems' are efficient at border prices and that the labour force is as productive as possible, so as to gain flexibility in the face of changing world market conditions;

c) the basic-needs sectors should be protected and decentralized, output being based on citizen entitlement and the principle of self-provisioning, with state support in the form of inputs and secondary services, so as to maximize national self-sufficiency and thus minimize vulnerability to external shock;

d) the financial system (banks and the budget) should be a central part of the planning structure, ensuring macro-economic equilibrium by tight control of all expenditure once basic-needs targets are satisfied, controlling enterprise profitability, and maintaining balanced relationships between the state and small producers;

e) international networks should be used not just for diplomatic and aid purposes, but also in order to gain policy-relevant knowledge of the external environment.

A general conclusion might be that response capacity depends as much upon the economic organization and autonomy of civil society as upon the state itself; and that the strength of planning is a function of its capacity to articulate these potentials.

In 1984, as military intervention was building up towards its height, the Nicaraguan government introduced a case against the USA before the International Court of Justice at The Hague.[61] Despite objections from Washington,[62] the Court ruled the case as admissible, and gave judgement against the USA in 1986 on four main counts: mining of ports and attacks on harbour installations; logistical support for the *contras* in their destruction of life and property; violation of treaties by imposing a trade embargo; and intervention in the internal affairs of a sovereign state.[63] The Court is about to decide upon the appropriate financial damages to be awarded, deriving from the Nicaraguan claim submitted in 1988.[64]

The Court ruled that the direct attacks and the support of the *contra* were in breach of the principles of international law; and that the US had breached its 1956 treaty obligations by imposing the 1985 trade embargo. The GATT came to similar conclusions in respect to its own regulations. These legal definitions are important additions to the sovereign rights of small nations, all the more so because the previous initiative to legislate for the 'Rights and Duties of States' in the 1970s gained so little acceptance among the great powers.

Apart from constituting a notable legal victory as part of the response to external shock, the implications of this case for international law as a whole are therefore considerable. On the one hand, this judgement establishes a vital precedent for the rights of small nations to choose their own model of socio-political and economic development; and on the other, for the concept of compensation for the 'developmental loss' implied by what might be called 'deliberate external shock'. The legal concept of *lucrum cessans* (income foregone) is central to this judgement, for compensation is due not only for the assets of one state destroyed by another, but for the additional enterprise profits lost consequent upon such damage. The Nicaraguan compensation claim[65] includes the secondary GDP reduction consequent upon the foreign exchange losses caused by military destruction, as an extended sense of *lucrum cessans* to measure 'developmental loss'. The acceptance of this interpretation could transform the legal redress of small nations against deliberate external shock. Meanwhile, survival planning for the transition is a matter of sovereignty before development.

Notes and References

1. There is a long tradition in historical theory which treats economic crisis in the more general sense of crucial 'breakpoints' where the organizational system of the society cannot be reproduced (sustained from one period to the next) because the requirements for the technical functioning of the economy are no longer met by its current administrative forms (property relations) and that therefore some change in the social formation takes place – a theory associated with Marx but not uncommon

among other historical theorists of the period. The idea of crisis has been seen in more modern times as having an important political and ideological dimension; particularly that of the breakdown of hegemony in the work of Gramsci. These two approaches are synthesized by Habermas in his analysis of the failure of the state (or ruling class) to maintain the necessarily contradictory balance between accumulation and hegemony. Little serious work has been done to adapt these concepts – essentially developed for Western Europe – to the Third World context; but an excellent research agenda is set out by Evans et al (1985).

2. Crisis theory relates mainly to *internal* contradictions and forces for change, rather than external ones. The 'dependency' literature stresses external domination, but does not clearly specify shock. On the contrary, the vision of a subordinate economy which is permanently dysfunctional in terms of both accumulation and distribution implies that world market shocks can result in delinking and promote peripheral industrialization. The historiographical basis for this claim, however, has now been heavily qualified by recent research (for example, Thorp, 1984).

3. See the bibliography below, particularly FitzGerald (1985a, 1988b, 1989).

4. Research has only recently begun to take form on this topic, sponsored by the SSRC in the USA (see Fagen, 1986), with work at the IDS (White et al, 1983) and the ISS (Saith, 1985, and FitzGerald and Wuyts, 1988). The country listings vary from one author to another, but usually contain about 20 countries. The UNRISD itself is planning to take up this theme in its research agenda.

5. This is the central theme of Fagen (1986).

6. See FitzGerald and Wuyts (1988) for case studies.

7. This is my interpretation of the policy approach of Latin American structuralism (Rodríguez, 1980), strengthened by the theoretical framework of Kalecki (1976, 1985) and the technical analysis of authors such as Taylor (1983).

8. The Nicaraguan authorities have repeatedly and explicitly insisted (for example Wheelock, 1985) that their economy is *not* in crisis in this sense. Under wartime conditions crisis-like phenomena may well occur in aggravated form; Bukharin (1979) called this 'contracted reproduction' – in order to contrast it with Marx's expanded reproduction, that is, accumulation) without it being reasonable to call this a 'crisis' because it does not necessarily require social change to resolve the problem – but rather cessation of hostilities. For instance, Britain in the early 1940s could not be said to be in 'economic crisis' in the same way that it was ten years earlier or that Mexico was in the 1980s.

9. Saith (1985) contains case studies and an excellent taxanomic introduction by the editor. The process of transforming asset ownership and the organization of production and distribution will inevitably affect productivity. For instance, a redistributive land reform programme, while increasing capacity for the economic survival of individual peasant families by permitting self-provisioning, does also tend to reduce productivity in the commercialized export sector and food delivery to the towns, at least in the short-run, with serious consequences in terms of the definition of economic crisis discussed above. The conversion of large private estates into state farms (or subordinate co-operatives) may preserve production capacity, but adequate labour supplies may no longer be available (at least at a wage rate compatible with world prices) if seasonal workers have other income opportunities or new off-farm welfare entitlements. Management skills may well be lost in both production and marketing, leading to even greater long-term productivity losses than the distributive model. Finally, the nationalization of traditional – albeit exploitative – food marketing channels may well grant greater

state control over strategic commodities but frequently leads to the disarticulation of the peasantry from urban markets.

10. This argument is worked out somewhat more formally in FitzGerald (1985b).

11. Nuti (1981) is apparently the originator of this phrase, although he attributes the idea to Kalecki.

12. This argument is developed in FitzGerald (1988a) by combining the Kaleckian analysis of distribution and accumulation in developing countries with that of Kornai on the pressure of state accumulation on non-state sectors in socialist economies.

13. Saith (1985) calls this 'the hijacking of socialism by industrialization' but this seems to miss the point.

14. FitzGerald (1985b) explains this in more detail.

15. Stallings (1986) contains five case studies of the external financing problems of peripheral transition.

16. Cassen (1985) has the best contemporary survey of the issues and practice; although the situation is clearly changing rapidly under the combined influence of *perestroika* and *detente*.

17. Bogalomov (1983), a key Gorbachev adviser, is unusually frank on this topic.

18. Shafer (1988) and Gaddis (1982) show how 'low intensity war' and 'containment' emerged as part of the reassessment of US national security doctrine after Vietnam.

19. See the preface to Miplan (1980). I was then acting as senior economic advisor to the Government of Nicaragua, on loan from the Netherlands Ministry of Foreign Affairs.

20. See Ruccio (1986) for a survey of Sandinista planning efforts. The first two plans were published (Miplan 1980, 1981) and widely debated; the annual plans for subsequent years and the perspective plan were confidential – the official reason being war conditions – but the plan for 1987 (SPP, 1987) was published, and public debate renewed.

21. See in particular FitzGerald (1989).

22. That is, the 'sectoral balance' ideas of Kalecki rather than Keynesian demand management or the radical dualism of Preobrazhensky.

23. Weinert (1981) was a participant in these negotiations.

24. World Bank (1981) is unambiguous in this respect: the criticisms were comparatively minor and mainly concerned with improving the efficiency of public enterprise administration.

25. FitzGerald (1989). Taking the increase in the current account deficit between 1983 and 1987 respectively to be the 'trade gap', the table below shows the division between war losses (see Table 12.3), embargo costs (Government of Nicaragua, 1988) and the 'terms of trade loss'. This last is the difference between trade at current and 1978 dollar prices. The residual 'other' can be seen as attributable to policy errors etc: as can be seen, it is relatively small as an explanatory factor.

US$ *millions*	1983	1987
Terms of trade	237	72
War losses	132	224
Embargo costs	–	109
Other factors	53	89
Trade Gap	422	494
Exports fob	429	281
Imports cif	819	744

26. FitzGerald (1985a), Kaimowitz (1988). Utting (1987) reports preliminary results of a major study of policy formation on food security in Nicaragua.

27. FitzGerald (1989), Irvin (1983).

28. See FitzGerald (1986b) for methodology.

29. The ILPES model is reproduced in full, as are the original data in Government of Nicaragua (1988).

30. FitzGerald (1989) gives both sources and method. The original data base is a monthly reporting system by local authorities to the Presidency, using a computerized system set up with the assistance of the UN.

31. SPP (1987), Irvin and Croes (1988).

32. A notable exception to this rule was Dutch support for the health sector, which was switched to repair workshops and spare parts for all hospitals, whatever the original technology or donor.

33. The theoretical basis for the analytical framework of the 'accumulation balance' is given in FitzGerald and Vos (1989, Chapter 1).

34. FitzGerald and Vos (1989, Chapter 3) presents a general analytical model of this process.

35. See SPP (1987).

36. Kaimowitz (1988).

37. FitzGerald and Chamorro (1987).

38. Equivalent to the mathematical concept of a set of related functions with more equations than endogenous variables, which will therefore not have a determinate solution except by coincidence.

39. Rowthorn (1980).

40. See Corraggio (1986) and Vilas (1986) on Nicaragua: and Griffith-Jones (1981) more generally for transition economies.

41. FitzGerald (1987) gives the data; for a perceptive discussion of the Nicaraguan class structure, see Nuñez (1987).

42. In fact, the two-year 'honeymoon' before the first serious military attacks in late 1981 (the mining of the ports by the CIA, on which see ICJ (1986) for evidence) was well used in order to build up the militias and popular organizations, and excessive austerity at the outset – that is, the full implementation of the stabilization measures contained in the 1981 plan (Miplan, 1981) – might have hindered that process of regime consolidation by exacerbating domestic conflict.

43. Whether it was always intended to be so, or whether it was the result of stalemate once the *contra* were shown to have little internal political potential and the costs of invasion became clear, is a matter for considerable debate. I would incline to the latter view although most US experts incline to the former. In passing, it is worth recording that what was termed 'low intensity war' in Washington looked rather different from Managua.

44. Most of the papers in Spalding (1986) reflect this debate.

45. Indeed, in this sense the FSLN retains internally many of its military origins, inevitably reinforced by the war itself, although in national politics it is evidently able and willing to work in a pluralistic parliamentary framework.

46. Marchetti (1988) reports fields studies of the way in which urban families survive national economic crisis, as well as their (negative) perceptions of government economic policy combined with support for policy towards the war, social transformation and so on. This work also underlines the difficulty of characterizing a family as 'proletarian' (or otherwise) when it includes a mother in petty commerce, a father in a factory, a couple of sons in the army, a daughter

working as a secretary, an aunt in the USA and an uncle producing shoes.

47. Except in areas of high population pressure on the land (which are rare in Nicaragua) such as Masaya, where land invasions did take place in 1985.

48. Molyneux (1986) is particularly cogent on the distinction between the strategic and practical interests of women.

49. Which tended to be in some conflict over tactics, although not strategy, due to the official position that under war conditions gender issues should be subordinated to national defence.

50. Smith (1988).

51. FitzGerald and Chamorro (1987).

52. For a discussion of this proposition and some alternative views see FitzGerald (1988b).

53. Baumeister and Neira (1986).

54. Kaimowitz (1988).

55. Austin and Ickis (1986) reports on a survey of multinational affiliates in Nicaragua.

56. Many petty bourgeois wives seem to have felt far more threatened than their husbands by the Revolution. In many cases, an engineer (say) would actually feel more fulfilled by the opportunity to put his professional ideas into practice and even a farmer remained a person of standing; his wife, meanwhile, missed the charms of the local social circuit, had nowhere to shop, and worst of all – was answered back by the maid!

57. The avoidance of this haemorrhage had been one of the most important pieces of economic advice from Dr Castro on his first visit to Nicaragua in 1980.

58. The industrial countries in recent years (see, for example, *US Foreign Sovereignty Immunity Act, 1976*) come to hold that legal sovereign immunity for the acts of states (*actos jure imperii*) does not cover the commercial acts of states (*actos jure gestionis*). In other words, enterprises have the privilege of being able to make claims against states in the courts of third countries so as to enforce fulfilment of commercial obligations. In civil (national) law it is generally accepted that the terms of repayment for debts contracted when both parties expect certain future conditions affecting repayment ability to obtain can be declared invalid if those conditions change radically. Further, if it can be shown that contract fulfilment would cause undue hardship then much the same considerations apply. Both these legal principles of commercial law would seem to be relevant to a claim by countries suffering external shock for the right to ameliorate the impact by reducing debt service payments by reference to not only hardship to their populations but also to national security.

59. See FitzGerald et al (1989) for a discussion of this problem and that of Third World debt in the context of the world accumulation balances.

60. UN (1974, 1986) and Flory (1984).

61. One of the founding UN institutions, the Court itself is the only remnant of the League of Nations. States subscribed separately by treaty to the authority of the ICJ, except under specified circumstances.

62. As to the US justification that Nicaragua was intervening in Central America (a claim which the Court did not accept as proven) it was judged that even had this been true: (a) the complaint should have first been brought to the Court (or the UN) by the neighbouring countries, which had not happened; (b) the US would have to demonstrate a tangible threat to its own national security, which it had not done;

and (c) that the response should be commensurate with the damage claimed – while it was clearly far in excess.

63. ICJ (1986).

64. Which will presumably form part of an eventual settlement with the Bush administration; so as to avoid Nicaragua enforcing payment of the claim through the courts of signatory countries, as it would have the right to do and the USA in fact did over the Teheran embassy affair.

65. The Memorial (Government of Nicaragua, 1988) was prepared by distinguished international lawyers holding chairs at Harvard, Oxford and Paris – with the fascinated assistance of the present author. See FitzGerald (1986b) on the methodology for the economic damage estimates, which benefited from the technical support of the ECLAC. For an interesting parallel in Southern Africa, see Green et al (1987), who estimated a loss to the front-line states of the order of 10 per cent of GDP per annum.

Bibliography

Austin, J. E. and J. C. Ickis (1986) 'Managing After the Revolutionaries Have Won' *Harvard Business Review*, May–June.

Baumeister, E. and O. Neira (1986) 'The Making of the Mixed Economy: Class Struggle and State Policy in the Nicaraguan Transition' in Fagen 1986.

Bogolomov, O. (1983) *Socialist Countries in the International Division of Labour*. Moscow, Progress Publishers.

Bukharin, N. (1979) *The Politics and Economics of the Transition Period*. London, Routledge and Kegan Paul.

Cassen, R. H. (ed.) (1985) *Soviet Interests in the Third World*. London, Sage, for RIIA.

Corraggio, J. L. (1986) *Economics and Politics in the Transition to Socialism: Reflections on the Nicaraguan Experience* in Fagen 1986.

Evans P. B. et al (1985) *Bringing the State Back In*. Cambridge, Cambridge University Press.

Fagen, R. R. et al (1986) *Transition and Development: Problems of Third World Socialism*. New York, Monthly Review Press.

FitzGerald, E. V. K. (1985a) 'Agrarian Reform as a Model of Accumulation: the Case of Nicaragua since 1979' in Saith 1985.

—— (1985b) 'The Problem of Balance in the Peripheral Socialist Economy: a Conceptual Note'. *World Development*, Vol. 13, No. 1.

—— (1986a) 'Notes on the Analysis of the Small Underdeveloped Economy' in Fagen et al 1986.

—— (1986b) 'An Evaluation of the Economic Costs of US Aggression against Nicaragua' in Spalding 1986.

—— (1987) 'Notas sobre la fuerza de trabajo y la estructura de clases en Nicaragua'. *Revista Nicaragüense de Ciencias Sociales*, Vol. 2, No. 2.

—— (1988a) 'State Accumulation and Market Equilibria: An application of Kalecki–Kornai Analysis to Planned Economies in the Third World' in FitzGerald and Wuyts 1988.

—— (1988b) 'State and Economy in Nicaragua'. *IDS Bulletin*, Vol. 19, No. 3.

—— (1989) 'Problems in Financing a Revolution: Accumulation, Defence and Income Distribution in Nicaragua 1979–86' in FitzGerald and Vos 1989.

—— and A. Chamorro (1987) 'Las cooperativas en el proyecto de transición en Nicaragua'. *Encuentro*, No. 30.

—— and R. Vos (1989) *Financing Economic Development: a Structuralist Approach to Monetary Policy*. London, Gower Publishing.

—— and M. Wuyts (1988) *Markets within Planning: Socialist Economic Management in the Third World*, London, Frank Cass.

——, K. Jansen and R. Vos (1989) 'Structural Asymmetry, Adjustment and the Debt Crisis', *Working Paper in Money, Finance and Development*, No. 28, The Hague, ISS.

Flory, M. (ed.) (1984) *La formation des normes en droit international du développement*. Paris, Presses Universitaires de France.

Gaddis, J. L. (1982) *Strategies of Containment: a Critical Appraisal of Postwar National Security Policy*. New York, Oxford University Press.

Government of Nicaragua (1988) *Memorial on Compensation in the Case of Nicaragua v. USA*. The Hague, International Court of Justice.

Green, R. H. et al (1987) *Children on the Front Line: the Impact of Apartheid, Destabilization and Warfare on Children in Southern and South Africa*. New York and Geneva, UNICEF.

Griffith-Jones, S. (1981) *The Role of Finance in the Transition to Socialism*. London, Pinter.

ICJ (1986) *Nicaragua vs USA: Judgement of the International Court of Justice*. The Hague, International Court of Justice.

IHCA (1987) 'Slow Motion Towards the Survival Economy'. *Envio*, Vol. 5, No. 63.

Irvin, G. W. (1983) 'Nicaragua: Establishing the State as the Centre of Accumulation'. *Cambridge Journal of Economics*, Vol. 7, No. 7.

—— and E. Croes (1988) 'Nicaragua: the Accumulation Trap'. *IDS Bulletin*, Vol. 19, No. 3.

Kaimowitz, D. (1988) 'Nicaragua's Experience with Agricultural Planning: from State-Centred Accumulation to the Strategic Alliance with the Peasantry' in FitzGerald and Wuyts 1988.

Kalecki, M. (1976) *Essays on Developing Economies*. Cambridge, Cambridge University Press.

—— (1985) *Selected Essays in Economic Planning*. Cambridge, Cambridge University Press.

Marchetti, Peter (1988) 'Las medidas de julio: un paquete sin pueblo', *Envío*, Vol. 7, No. 85.

Miplan (1980) *Programa de reactivación económica en beneficio del pueblo ('Plan 80')*. Managua, Ministerio de Planificación.

—— (1981) *Programa económico 1981: austeridad y eficiencia*. Managua, Ministerio de Planificación.

Molyneux, M. (1986) *Mobilization without Emancipation? Women's Interests, State and Revolution* in Fagen 1986.

Nuñez, O. (1987) *Transición y lucha de clases en Nicaragua 1979–86*. Mexico City, Siglo XXI.

Nuti, D. M. (1981) 'The Contradictions of Socialist Economies'. *Socialist Register*, London, Merlin Press.

Pizarro, R. (1987) 'The New Economic Policy: a Necessary Adjustment' in Spalding 1986.

Rodríguez, O. (1980) *La teoría del subdesarrollo de la Cepal.* Mexico City, Siglo XXI.

Rowthorn, B. (1980) *Capitalism, Conflict and Inflation: Essays in Political Economy.* Atlantic Highlands, Humanities Press.

Ruccio, D. F. (1986) 'The State and Planning in Nicaragua' in Spalding 1986.

Saith, A. (ed.) (1985) *The Agrarian Question in Socialist Transition.* London, Frank Cass.

Shafer, D. M. (1988) *Deadly Paradigms: the Failure of US Counterinsurgency Policy.* Princeton NJ, Princeton University Press.

Smith, H. (1988) 'Race and Class in Revolutionary Nicaragua: Autonomy and the Atlantic Coast'. *IDS Bulletin*, Vol. 19, No. 3.

Spalding, R. (ed.) (1986) *The Political Economy of Revolutionary Nicaragua.* New York, Allen and Unwin.

SPP (1987) *Programa Económico 1987.* Managua, Secretaría de Planificación y Presupuesto.

Stallings, B. (1986) 'External Finance and the Transition to Socialism in Small Peripheral Societies' in Fagen 1986.

Taylor, L. (1983) *Structuralist Macroeconomics.* New York, Basic Books.

Thorp, R. (ed.) (1984) *Latin America in the 1930s: the Role of the Periphery in World Crisis.* London, Macmillan.

Tirado, V. (1986) *Nicaragua: una nueva democracia en el tercer mundo.* Managua, Editorial Vanguardia.

United Nations (1974) *Declaration on the Establishment of a New International Economic Order* (A/RES/3201/S.VI). New York, UN General Assembly.

—— (1986) *Declaration of the Right to Development.* New York, UN General Assembly.

Utting, P. (1987) 'Domestic Supply and Food Shortages' in Spalding 1986.

Vilas, C. M. (1986) 'Troubles Everywhere: an Economic Perspective on the Revolution' in Spalding 1986.

Weinert, R. (1981) 'Nicaragua's Debt Renegotiation'. *Cambridge Journal of Economics*, Vol. 5, No. 2.

Wheelock, J. (1985) *Entre la crisis y la agresión: la reforma agraria sandinista.* Managua, Editorial Nueva Nicaragua.

White W. et al (1983) *Revolutionary Socialist Development in the Third World.* Lexington, University of Kentucky Press.

World Bank (1981) *Nicaragua: the Challenge of Development.* Washington DC, IBRD.

Statistical Appendix

Table 12.1
Nicaragua: Ownership Structure of Production, 1983 (per cent contribution to GDP, by form of production)

Form/Sector	State	Capitalist	Small Producers	Total
Agro exports	28	42	30	100
Domestic consumption	19	15	66	100
Cattle	20	12	68	100
Industry	28	49	23	100
Other material production	90	5	5	100
Government	100	0	0	100
Commerce and services	38	12	50	100
Total	40	29	31	100

Source: Baumeister and Neira (1986) p. 188.

Table 12.2
Nicaragua: National Workforce by Class, 1984 (thousands)

	State Sector	Private Sector Formal	Informal	Sub-Total	Total EAP
Bourgeoisie	—	22	—	22	22
Artisans and Peasants	—	—	258	258	258
Employees	91	41	—	41	132
Workers	102	91	—	91	193
Sub/Semi-proletarians	18	95	292	387	405
Total Classes	211	249	550	799	1010

Source: FitzGerald (1987) p. 40.

Table 12.3
Nicaragua: War Damage and Defence Expenditure 1980–87 (US$ millions)

	1980	1981	1982	1983	1984	1985	1986	1987
WAR DAMAGE*:								
Material Destruction	1	4	11	59	28	18	14	37
Production Losses	1	3	21	107	190	145	230	281
to exports	1	3	7	75	132	130	205	224
to dom. consump.	—	—	15	32	57	14	25	57
Total Damage	2	8	32	165	217	164	244	318
(Damage/Exports)	—	1%	7%	35%	50%	49%	90%	71%
DEFENCE EXPENDITURE**								
Budgetary Allocation	130	159	182	278	310	384	401	465
(Allocation/GDP)	6%	7%	8%	12%	14%	18%	19%	21%

Source: *extracted from ECLAC (1988) *Notas para el estudio de America Latina y El Caribe, 1987:Nicaragua* (Mexico City); Table 25, p. 63. The footnote reads "This total does not include about US$600 millions which, according to preliminary estimations, were caused by the trade embargo and the external credit restrictions". In the original table, a sectoral breakdown is also given, which reveals that between 1980–87, agriculture suffered 43% of total damage, forestry 28% and construction 19%.

**Calculated from ECLAC (1988) Tables 3 and 23; and ECLAC *Surveys* for previous years. Data refers to the Central Government budget allocation, at 1980 prices, converted to US dollars at the 1980 exchange rate.

Table 12.4
Nicaragua: Sectoral Accumulation Balances, 1976–86
(% of GDP, annual average)

		1976–78	*1981–83*	*1984–86*
State Sector:	Investment	8.5	16.6	16.7
	Savings	2.6	−4.5	−8.3
	External Finance	3.3	13.4	9.7
	Resource Balance	−2.6	−7.7	−15.3
Non-State Sector:	Investment	10.7	5.0	3.4
	Savings	15.7	12.7	18.7
	External Finance	−2.4	—	—
	Resource Balance	2.6	7.7	15.3
National Economy:	Investment	19.2	21.6	20.1
	Savings	18.3	8.2	10.4
	External Finance	0.9	13.4	9.7
	Resource Balance*	—	—	—

Source: FitzGerald (1986b) Table 8.2.
*By definition the overall resource balance is zero for the national economy, as external finance is already included.

Annual levels of consumption (billion córdobas *at 1980 prices*)		*1976–78*	*1981–83*	*1984–86*
State sector:	Defence	0.3	0.9	3.3
	Civil	2.3	5.0	6.1
	Sub-total	2.6	5.9	9.4
Non-state sector:	Essential	10.2	10.2	9.1
	Non-essential	10.3	3.0	2.0
	Sub-total	20.5	13.2	11.1
Total Domestic Consumption		23.1	19.1	20.5

Source: SPP (1987), updated from SPP worksheets.

Table 12.5
Nicaragua: Structure of Medium- and Long-Term Concessionary Loans, Credits and Donations* (US$ millions)

	1981–1983	%	1984–1986	%
Western Europe, Canada, & EEC				
Credits and Loans	185.6		189.7	
Donations	69.4		112.2	
NGO Aid	109.0		109.0	
Subtotal	364.0	18.6	410.9	23.2
Multilateral				
Credits and Loans	245.9		—	
Donations	22.7		30.1	
Subtotal	268.6	13.7	30.1	1.7
Socialist				
Credits and Loans	529.1		1003.6	
Donations	72.2		184.6	
Subtotal	601.3	30.7	1188.2	67.2
Others				
Credits and Loans	694.3		121.0	
Donations	18.0		7.7	
NGO Aid	11.0		11.0	
Sub-total	723.3	37.0	139.7	7.9
TOTALS				
CREDITS AND LOANS	1654.9		1314.3	
DONATIONS	182.3		334.6	
NGO AID	120.0		120.0	
Grand Total	1957.2	100.0	1768.9	100.0

Sources: Ministerio de Cooperación Externa; TNI (1987).
E.V.K. FitzGerald & R. Vos, (1988). "Problems in Financing a Revolution: Accumulation Defence and Income Distribution in Nicaragua 1979–86", *Financing Economic Development: A Structuralist Approach to Monetary Policy*.

*Includes multilateral, bilateral and NGO sources.

Notes on Contributors

Edward J. Amadeo is Assistant Professor in the Department of Economics at the Pontificia Universidade Católica in Rio de Janeiro. He received his Ph.D. in Economics from Harvard University, and has published numerous articles in major Brazilian economic journals as well as a book on Keynes's principle of effective demand. He has acted as a consultant for WIDER and the United Nations University.

Yusuf Bangura is a Research Fellow at the United Nations Research Institute for Social Development (UNRISD). He was formerly a lecturer in political science at Ahmadu Bello University, Zaria, Nigeria and a visiting research fellow at Stockholm University and the AKUT GROUPPEN, University of Uppsala. He was educated at the London School of Economics and Political Science, and has published widely on the socio-political contexts of the African crisis and on the effects of adjustment policies on Nigerian workers.

Björn Beckman is Associate Professor in the Department of Political Science at Stockholm University. He taught for many years in the Department of Political Science, Ahmadu Bello University, Zaria, Nigeria, and has published books on cocoa politics in Ghana and on wheat and underdevelopment in Nigeria. He was educated at the Universities of Stockholm and Uppsala.

José Márcio Camargo is Associate Professor in the Department of Economics at the PontificiaUniversidade Católica in Rio de Janeiro. He obtained a doctorate in Economics from M.I.T in 1977, and has written most recently on monetary reform policies in Brazil.

E. V. K. FitzGerald is Research Director and Professor of Development Economics at the Institute of Social Studies, The Hague. He has acted as an advisor to the governments of Peru, Mexico, and Nicaragua, and as a consultant to several international agencies. He is the editor of the *Journal of Development Studies*, and the author of books on Peru, Mexico, public investment and development finance. He received his Ph.D. in Economics from Cambridge University in 1973.

Dharam Ghai is Director of the United Nations Research Institute for Social Development (UNRISD). He worked previously for the ILO and was Director of the Institute for Development Studies, University of Nairobi. He was educated at the Universities of Oxford and Yale, and has written several books and numerous articles on a wide range of development problems, especially on employment, poverty, and agrarian problems.

Blanca Heredia teaches at the Colegio de México. She was previously a Research Fellow at the Center for the Social Sciences at Columbia University. She received her Ph.D. in Political Science from Columbia University, and has written on economic liberalization, the private sector, and the regime change in Mexico.

Cynthia Hewitt de Alcántara is Project Leader, Food Security, at the United Nations Research Institute for Social Development. Before joining UNRISD, she was associated with the Centro de Estudios Sociológicos at El Colegio de México. She studied at Vassar, Columbia and the University of Leiden, obtaining a doctorate in development sociology in 1982. Her research has centred on issues of rural modernization, technological transfer, peasant organization and urban food systems.

Mahmood Mamdani is Associate Professor of Political Science at Makerere University in Kampala. He obtained a doctorate in Government from Harvard University in 1974, and has written extensively on many Third World issues, most recently on politics and class formation in Uganda.

Thandika Mkandawire is Executive Secretary of the Council for the Development of Economic and Social Research in Africa (CODESRIA) in Dakar. He has been a consultant to several international agencies. He did his graduate work at the University of Stockholm, and has written extensively on African development problems.

Richard Sandbrook is Professor in the Department of Political Science at the University of Toronto. He received his D.Phil. in Comparative Politics from the University of Sussex in 1971. He has written books and articles on the politics of economic stagnation and basic needs in Africa.

Jorge Schvarzer is Director of the Centro de Investigaciones Sociales sobre el Estado y la Administración (CISEA) in Buenos Aires. He has previously worked for the United Nations Development Programme (UNDP). He was educated at the Facultad de Ingeniería in Buenos Aires, and has researched and written extensively on economic matters in Latin America.

Clive Thomas is Director of the Institute of Development Studies, University of Guyana. He has taught at the Consortium Graduate School of Social Sciences, University of the West Indies, and has acted as a consultant to several international agencies. He received his Ph.D. in Economics from the London School of Economics in 1964, and is the author of several books and numerous professional articles on development and trade issues, especially in the Caribbean.

Marc Wuyts is Senior Lecturer in Economics and Econometrics at the Institute of Social Studies, The Hague. He received his Ph.D in Economics from the Open University, Milton Keynes, England in 1986. His areas of research and publication include money, finance, and development, planning and Third World socialism, and Mozambique.

Index

UNRISD

The United Nations Research Institute for Social Development (UNRISD) was established to promote in-depth research into the social dimensions of pressing problems and issues of contemporary relevance affecting development. Its work is inspired by the conviction that, for effective development to be formulated, an understanding of the social and political context is crucial, as is an accurate assessment of how such policies affect different social groups.

The Institute attempts to complement the work done by other United Nations agencies and its current research themes include the social impact of the economic crisis and adjustment policies; environment, sustainable development and social change; ethnic conflict and development; refugees, returnees and local society; the socio-economic and political consequences of the international trade in illicit drugs; and social participation and the social impact of changes in the ownership of the means of production.

ISER

The Institute of Social and Economic Research (ISER), established in 1948, is the research arm of the Faculty of Social Science, University of the West Indies. It has branches on all three campuses of the University and focuses on development issues in the Caribbean and the Third World. ISER publishes a quarterly journal, *Social and Economic Studies*, and a wide range of monographs and working papers.

The Institute collaborates with several governmental and non-governmental agencies throughout the Caribbean.

Zed Books Ltd

is a publisher whose international and Third World lists span:

- **Women's Studies**
- **Development**
- **Environment**
- **Current Affairs**
- **International Relations**
- **Children's Studies**
- **Labour Studies**
- **Cultural Studies**
- **Human Rights**
- **Indigenous Peoples**
- **Health**

We also specialize in Area Studies where we have extensive lists in African Studies, Asian Studies, Caribbean and Latin American Studies, Middle East Studies, and Pacific Studies.

For further information about books available from Zed Books, please write to: Catalogue Enquiries, Zed Books Ltd, 57 Caledonian Road, London N1 9BU. Our books are available from distributors in many countries (for full details, see our catalogues), including:

In the USA
Humanities Press International, Inc., 165 First Avenue,
Atlantic Highlands, New Jersey 07716.
Tel: (201) 872 1441;
Fax: (201) 872 0717.

In Canada
DEC, 229 College Street, Toronto, Ontario M5T 1R4.
Tel: (416) 971 7051.

In Australia
Wild and Woolley Ltd, 16 Darghan Street, Glebe, NSW 2037.

In India
Bibliomania, C-236 Defence Colony, New Delhi 110 024.

In Southern Africa
David Philip Publisher (Pty) Ltd, PO Box 408, Claremont 7735,
South Africa.